"Home run! Gary Comer has rediscovered and masterly communicates the missing elements in today's evangelistic approaches. This book has helped me improve my own friendships with unbelievers. I am encouraging others in our ministry to read this indispensable and excellent book to shape and empower them to help those who are not yet followers of Christ discover the greatness and wonder of his salvation."

—DAVID MILLS,
Senior Pastor, Faith Community Church

"There are lots of books about faith, about sharing faith, and about coming to faith. This one is about living your faith in such a way that people want faith, too. This is one about helping others find faith as a real part of their lives. . . . In a postmodern era, we can't be stuck with the old tools of modernity. Now, thanks to *Soul Whisperer*, we don't have to be."

—MATT HANNAN,
Senior Pastor, New Heights Church

"I am truly excited over the impact Gary's book can have on the body of Christ in its effort to make disciples of all nations. I see thousands of God's people benefiting from a serious reading, study, and application of *Soul Whisperer*. After all, the book is largely based on and named for the ultimate soul whisperer, Jesus Christ. One cannot miss increased effectiveness in sharing one's faith than by implementing both the teachings and example of the Savior. Comer has nailed it for us!"

—G. TED MARTINEZ,
Professor, Talbot Seminary

Soul Whisperer

Soul Whisperer

Why the Church Must Change the Way It Views Evangelism

GARY S. COMER

RESOURCE *Publications* · Eugene, Oregon

SOUL WHISPERER
Why the Church Must Change the Way It Views Evangelism

Resource Publications
An Imprint of Wipf and Stock Publishers
199 W. 8th Ave., Suite 3
Eugene, OR 97401

www.wipfandstock.com

ISBN 13: 978-1-62032-183-6

Manufactured in the U.S.A.

This book is fittingly dedicated to the Lord Jesus Christ,
the original soul whisperer.

"Students are not above their teacher, nor servants, above their master. It is enough for students to be like their teacher, and servants like their master."

Contents

Foreword

Anyone who has been paying attention during the last half-century has observed significant changes taking place. Every aspect of society—social, educational, technological, and spiritual—has undergone major adjustments. Church ministry is no exception. Whether it is worship music, leadership, or outreach, what used to work in church ministry no longer seems to be as fruitful.

While Christ's Great Commission continues to be the driving motive for discipleship, the ways that evangelism are accomplished today are quite different than just a few years ago. For years Christians were taught various evangelistic approaches for sharing the gospel of salvation. Training was offered using the Four Spiritual Laws, Steps to Peace with God, the Roman Road, Fran Evangelism, Evangelism Explosion, and Contagious Christianity, to name just a few of the more well-known plans. While all of these methods, formulas, and strategies were effective for a time, each has become less fruitful as modernity has been replaced by post-modern thinking.

The truth is most of us who were trained in past forms of outreach have become ever more frustrated as we have seen fewer and fewer people coming to Christ and his Church in the last decade. As the world has become more pluralistic and less friendly to Christianity, our old methods no longer appear to be producing disciples, or even getting a hearing for the gospel message. We are experts at telling the good news of salvation, but people do not seem as willing to listen to our words.

Fortunately, some people are beginning to get a handle on how to reach people for Christ in our postmodern age. My good friend, Gary Comer, is just such a person. To my knowledge, few people have wrestled with the challenge of reaching people for Christ in our pluralistic society as deeply. And, as he concludes, "It's not about telling; it's about helping people to hear." It is about being influencers rather than tellers. It is about whispering into people's souls so that they respond to the gospel message and live it out in their lives.

Soul Whisperer will teach you how to prepare the non-believer's heart to receive and live the gospel of salvation. It will show you how to *draw* people to Christ, rather than simply *telling* them about Christ. Wow! Drawing people to Christ. Helping people to hear. Preparing souls to receive and live the gospel message. That's what I want to do. If that is what you wish to do, then read and reread *Soul Whisperer*. It will stretch your spiritual thinking about evangelism . . . and . . . reshape the way you speak, so that Jesus can whisper through you into the hearts of others.

—Gary L. McIntosh, PhD
Temecula, CA, June 2012

Preface

Though undetectable from his cool, confident demeanor, wealthy business tycoon, Saito, has an insurmountable problem. A rising competitor will soon sink his Tokyo Empire. Like a man trapped in a darkened room with no doors, he searches elusively for a way out. Dom Cobb, too, thinks his life is slipping away. He recalls a memory of his two small children playing outside their home; yet tragically, he cannot go back. Blacklisted from re-entering his country, he is on the run. What might possibly bring these two falling stars together? It could only be something of unusual promise.

Cobb, you see, specializes in a rather cunning sort of corporate espionage. His niche is extracting valuable data embedded in dreams. By meddling so frequently in others' dream-states, he spins a top-like totem as a way to test his own reality. Not only has this trade got him in trouble but also a disturbing image from his exploits haunts him.

They say it is darkest before the dawn. Desperation, by a strange twist of fate, leads ordinary people to sometimes think extraordinary thoughts. Forced outside limits, Saito's ingenuity rises to a new level! So just as Cobb makes off to hiding, Saito's helicopter intercepts, where en route he divulges an outlandish proposition. He wants Cobb, not to extract, but to plant an idea—with the potential to dismantle his competitor's company. Seeing no other solution, Saito aims to reshape the whole sequence of events. If Cobb is willing to stretch his skills for this purpose, Saito assures he can pull strings to get him home with his kids.

When Cobb exits the copter, Saito makes a riveting appeal: "Do you want to take a leap of faith or become an old man filled with regret—waiting to die alone?" Cobb must now choose exile or attempt "inception." Unbeknownst to Saito, implanting an idea is something he grasps, having done it before. The new assignment is far more sophisticated, however.

Cobb's task is to enable an inheriting son to hear the dying words of his father in a profoundly different way. To achieve this objective, the son will have to go three layers deep: a dream within a dream within a dream.

Exploring feasibility, Cobb engages Eames, who enlightens: "No it's perfectly possible, it's just bloody difficult. Listen, if you are going to perform inception, you need imagination."

Cobb responds, "Have you done it?"

Discretely Eames relays, "We tried it—we got the idea in place but it didn't take."

Trying to understand Cobb follows, "You didn't plant it deep enough?"

"It's not just about depth," he responds. "You need the simplest version of the idea in order for it to grow naturally in the subject's mind—it's a very subtle art."

Later in a conversation with Saito, Cobb explains, "You ask me for inception. I hope you understand the gravity of that request. The seed that we plant in this man's mind will grow into an idea—this idea will come to define him—it may come to change everything about him."

* * *

The realization of Christopher Nolan's award-winning film (starring Leonardo DiCaprio as Cobb, and Ken Watanabe as Saito), took nine years to achieve. For viewers trying to keep abreast of all that was occurring at each dream level, and who took their own "kicks" back to reality, it was some ride! My reaction was to appreciate the biblical parallels. In fact, what is surprising about the film *Inception* is to notice how Jesus used this exact terminology.

It was our Lord who talked of implanting. He taught how the "seed" or word often would not "take" if the conditions for receptivity were not there (Mark 4:14–19). He touted its fruit-bearing potency when it did (20), and how development transpired in stages to eventually become something fully formed (28). He declared the smallest seed could produce a massive tree (30–32). Alluding to its eternal significance, Christ described the joy of a great harvest! (Matt 13:39). Before there was any mention of the church, or the inspiration for Nolan's movie, these were the teachings of Jesus.

As I meditated on the movie's theme, passionate stirrings simmered. First, is it possible a new idea with a skill set could have a potent affect in shaping the church and the lives of its members? Have you ever assessed your Christian life and wondered if you were missing something? Do you, like me, have a nagging sense that there's more to our current version of Christianity? Does not Jesus still have much greater works for you to achieve? Could it be possible that a change of thinking might break down the door, so to speak, to a radically altered projection of your life and faith? Sound crazy? Farfetched? Maybe—maybe not! Thematic to this blockbuster is the probability of things hoped for. I dream of a movement from God not yet realized: one that flows through all of his people, not just pastors—one that penetrates this world in a far more transformative way—and one that is thrillingly eternal in significance! I bet somewhere within your heart recesses you long for this, too. I bet you want a bigger part. I know I do.

In addition, I thought this secular film gave more credence to the power of an idea than many Christians believe they have as carriers of the gospel. This observation becomes strikingly clear when you study current church mission efforts, and see shocking statistics. Unlike Jesus's teachings, the average Christian, impotently, reaches few. This stark contrast conjured a series of questions. Have we failed to appreciate the full efficacy of God's seed entrusted to each of us as Christ-followers? The attention given by Cobb's team to get a life-altering idea to "take" and naturally "form"—fascinated me. Why is little said or written about the non-believer's faith formation? When it comes to spiritual influence, aren't we rather unimaginative? Though we do not ever want to make a response to Christ more difficult than necessary, why do we treat the planting of the gospel so simplistically? Can we only reach those who think like us? Do we not realize, like this movie, that design elements exist in the mission realm, too? If all of that seems a little hard to wrap your mind around, ironically you are beginning the journey of discovering something new and transformational!

Upon further reflection, I found myself pondering: Are church members willing to step up to an increasingly difficult challenge of helping spiritual "inception" occur? Personally, most of us know someone who is not yet in the faith. In this moment, numerous unbelieving friends likely invaded your mind immediately. Can you picture their faces? If you are a possessor of the true gospel, you know that everything is at stake—their whole present experience as well as their eternal state—and, of course, you want to reach them—don't you?! Perhaps you are a church leader trying to help entire groups or communities influence their spheres. You could be an outreach mover and shaker; or an advocate of God's justice amongst the forgotten and disadvantaged, and you believe the gospel is critical to completing that holistic picture. Or you might be a missionary aiming to impact whole countries. Maybe you are seeking to have influence where the Lord has planted you in the marketplace or your neighborhood. Together, we are all seed-carriers, and share solidarity in our desire to expand Christ's kingdom.

Allow me to implant an idea by asking a pointed question: Why bother reading this book on spiritual influence when you can just go tell people about Jesus? What an amazing number it would be if we tallied all the times you and I have said or heard: "Go tell the gospel." Certainly these are well-intentioned words. Yet it makes an assumption that "telling" is what is necessary. If they just hear it. If I merely tell my friend, neighbor, classmate, work associate, or contact—that will do it? Right?

You may not have thought this through or voiced it aloud, but don't we all know intuitively that "telling" the gospel's content is not the sole answer? The challenge we face with reaching most today is not in the "telling" but the "taking." You do not need a new formula for telling, but rather need to comprehend the criteria for God's seed to truly "take" in your friend's life—so it can bear fruit. Doing that successfully is something radically different than merely telling; it is, to the contrary, a very sensitive, structured, and skillful art. *Soul Whisperer* teaches this art. From cover-to-cover you will learn influence skills for implantation, faith formation, and missional living. It is about your role in partnering with God to shape a person's mind and heart so they could believe and follow.

I write as a seasoned practitioner of evangelistic mission with people from all walks of life. We will get to the nitty-gritty of being effective in the harvest fields around you, near and far. I cannot guarantee your loved ones will come into the faith, but you can bring the seed to them in a way that has the greatest chance of yielding eternal results. With God's drawing power there will be miracles. I write from my passion to unleash the power of the gospel to set captives free and bring them home!

My favorite scene from *Inception* is the closer. As if emerging from a long, drugged sleep with nightmarish events, Dom Cobb wakes at the end of his flight. A seat away, the son awakens with a revised impression of his father's wishes; he needs to be "his own man" and "not follow his father's footsteps." Also awakening in the first class seats is Saito and the rest of Cobb's team. As the brain fog slowly lifts, team members glance perceptibly at one another knowing they cannot converse. With only the intimate connection of the eyes they savor the pleasure of a profound accomplishment—"We did it!" They had achieved the planting of an inspirational idea that would alter the course of a man's life, a family fortune, and a world industry. Inception is exciting stuff!

Two millennia beyond the cross and the birth of the church, no more thrilling assignment exists than to extend the gospel of Jesus to a hungry and hurting world! We are given the grand opportunity to lead people into a journey with God that will alter their lives—their families—their world—and their eternity. This is our calling. Yet a question hangs before us: Are we going to remain stuck in the same stale, simplistic thinking of how to communicate the Good News or are we ready to take a leap of faith into a divinely ordained challenge to try something different for potentially greater results? For those wavering—may you spin your own totem and grasp reality on what is, and what truly matters. For all takers—your pathway lies ahead!

Acknowledgments

I am deeply grateful to all the visionaries who have gone before me to stimulate thinking and stir the missional spirit. *Soul Whisperer* is a bold attempt to further that conversation.

I want to first acknowledge my beautiful wife Robin and two boys: Matt & Nate, my parents Andy and Adoree, for their faith in my journey, and all my many friends and supporters who have believed in me.

Not every book written gets a hearing. I have to thank my Publisher with its Editors at Wipf and Stock, who took a risk in backing an innovative work like this one. To my team at Sandals Church I will always be indebted. So many of the stories come out from our ministry together; as I like to say, "not mine, but our stories." In that same vein, I have gained so much from my work with the Southwest Church Planting team! I extend specials thanks to Directors Bill Malick and Dave Reynolds for their Great Commission vision.

As to the writing itself, I must give ample credit to my friend Bob Brown who was willing to read, edit and interact at the early and later stages. Also, Don Toshach for rising beautifully to the occasion of copy-editing plus!

I would be remiss to not acknowledge my closest travelling companions who have been there through thick and thin: Eric Oleson, Pat Roman, Don Betsworth, Andrew Boganwright, Randy Chase, Don Roseberry, and Rod Merritt.

Finally, several ministry colleagues have proved pivotal: Pastor Matt Brown for his gracious spirit and authentic inspiration, and Dr. Gary Mc-Intosh, for believing in this book, and that I could be an author one day! Also, I must note personal mentors Matt Hannan and David Mills who have invested in me.

1

Soul Whisperer

When one has finished building one's house, one suddenly realizes that in the process one has learned something that one really needed to know in the worst way before one began.

—Friedrich Nietzsche

I am not one to throw around the word "prophetic" gratuitously. Rarely do I ever use it. If I do, it is a high compliment. I greatly value the person who can speak with corrective clarity to a current course, or offer predictive words of our future. Oddly then, recently I found myself stumbling upon a prophetic utterance from an unlikely conduit—a woman from long ago. Impoverished by our standards. Thirsty. Known to be immoral. Could prophetic words really come from such a source? Having perused this text innumerable times, like a laser guided missile, a simple phrase jumped out in a new way, locked on, and would not let me go! The line referred only to a routine matter. Yet I found it inferring something highly relevant. Perhaps you recall in John 4 the Samaritan woman's words to Jesus. She is baffled by his predicament of being at a well but lacking necessary equipment. If you paid me to synthesize where church influence and world culture have collided in the twenty-first century, I could not say it better than her, "You have nothing to draw with and the well is deep" (John 4:11).

Within this chapter, you will make your own assessment on whether her words nail it for our time—even two thousand years later! You may not be able to tell at first. Yet if you are willing to test and observe honestly, I believe you will come to the place of seeing what I see. If you do, it may just change your whole way of thinking on what it will take to reach a post-Christian world. I hope for nothing less.

What is intriguing was how her statement managed to be both true and false at the same time. As to drawing water it was entirely true. But in the larger spiritual sense, ironically, what she said could not have been more false. No one knew how to draw the heart like Jesus! The Samaritan woman would soon comprehend his deep, deft touch, which would transform her world. This same kind of influence ability is desperately needed in Christians today. At the threshold of a global culture, never has there been a time when we needed to look so closely at Jesus—than now.

In history's greatest epoch a man walked the earth with the capacity to draw souls. Our New Testament is jam-packed with accounts of Jesus's soul whispering. Though many have written of these encounters, few have focused on what made his manner so out-of-the-box. Have you ever asked why he spoke as he did? We are going to see what gave his words pin-pointed power. Has God's voice ever come to you, as with the Samaritan woman, in a way that had your name on it? His signature voice directed to your signature life! Was that not a powerful experience? How Jesus handled people is a lost art that I believe we can dig out and recapture in a way that will revolutionize our reach. Put on your miner's hardhat and switch on the light!

Several driving principles surface from a study of Jesus in terms of how he related to and reached those in his midst. Consider his interactions with two polar opposite people in chapters 3 and 4 of John: a high-standing, moralistic Pharisee pursing the basic need of spiritual understanding, and a common, unreputable Samaritan woman pursuing the basic need of water. Notice the disparateness. Each of these individuals had different starting points: ethnicities, religious backgrounds, viewpoints and lifestyles. How odd if Jesus had given them the same message. How dishonoring it would have been to their personhoods! Of course he did not! The fact is Jesus did not make the same presentation to anyone. His exchanges with people were unique and dynamic. He practiced the most foundational principle of evangelism: *We start where people are.* It is only when we understand their starting point that we can actually begin the evangelistic process (which is helping them through the necessary progressions to faith).

For the Pharisee, his starting point was his high religious standing. Jesus knew who came secretly in the night. Nicodemus belonged to Israel's elite elders. What did someone like him need to hear? Simply, he needed to start over in a radically new way. All the works of his religious devotion meant nothing! Nicodemus sensed it, and he sought out Jesus for answers. Spiritual life came through God's Spirit. For the Samaritan woman, the starting point was her deep needs, symbolized by the well she had journeyed to that day. Her inner thirst was never satisfied, not by water, nor by men. She needed to realize Jesus could meet the perpetual yearnings of her heart. He was the "man" who could provide "living water." Can you see the powerful soul whispering abilities of Jesus? In these very personal encounters, we observe this book's three permeating principles:

- Start where they are

- Read what they need

- Know where to take them

Both Nicodemus and the Samaritan woman heard the voice of God. Literally. They received divine words that penetrated their souls. Those kinds of words do not return void. The Pharisee left deeply troubled and enlightened in the most important of ways. The Samaritan woman left with a heart bursting to tell a whole town! When you learn the soul whispering skills of Jesus, you, too, will have conversations where people will hear God's voice. Your words. God's voice. How incredibly awesome is that?

What you have likely picked up so far is that I am proposing a change of course with our gospel messaging. How can an ancient water-seeking woman's words shed light on a necessary shift?

DEVELOPING A NEW MQ

Imagine having an IQ that is so high that you would never anticipate meeting another person . . . *like you!* Imagine, however, being that brilliant and then having an opportunity to meet with a master mathematician, but not even knowing to mention that you are exceptionally gifted at math.[1] Imagine having world-class ideas percolating in your head everyday, yet without any sort of guiding direction. Imagine possessing a mind

---

1. Gladwell, *Outliers*, 114–115.

equally comparable to Einstein's,[2] but at life's midpoint, not being helped to achieve anything tangible with it. This is the story of Chris Langan, as told by Malcolm Gladwell, in his book, *Outliers*.

Gladwell contrasts Langan's journey to another man named Robert Oppenheimer. Also brilliant, Oppenheimer conspired to poison his tutor while in college.[3] Being found out, he somehow pulled off an appeal to his academic supervisor, coming across so impressively that therapy became the extent of his punishment. Years later, despite the known background, he landed one of this century's most prestigious jobs (the Manhattan Project). Get this. All it took was hearing Oppenhiemer talk in a single informal interview.[4] The comparison between the two men is stunning. The one guilty of attempted murder is given a once-in-a-lifetime opportunity; the other equally brilliant man, Langan, remains in obscurity. The question Gladwell asks in his book is, "Why?"

Developed with detail in *Outliers*, the distinction between these men relates to knowledge. Both were intellectually endowed. Yet Oppenheimer had learned how to speak to his superiors. As the author puts it, "that's not because he was smarter than Chris Langan. It's because he possessed the kind of savvy that allowed him to get what he wanted from the world."[5] Here is how Gladwell describes this type of knowledge:

> The particular skill that allows you to talk your way out of a murder rap, or convince your professor to move you from the morning to the afternoon section is what Psychologist Robert Sternberg calls practical intelligence. To Sternberg, practical intelligence includes things like: Knowing what to say to whom. Knowing when to say it. Knowing how to say it for maximum affect . . . It is knowledge that helps you to read situations correctly and get what you want. Critically, it is a kind of intelligence separate from the sort of analytical ability measured by IQ . . . IQ is a measure to some degree of innate ability. But social savvy is knowledge. It is a set of skills that has to be learned. It has to come from somewhere.[6]

In telling the stories of success, or lack thereof, Gladwell makes a compelling case for the importance of acquired "know how." Bereft of those skills,

2. Gladwell, *Outliers*, 78.

3. Gladwell, *Outliers*, 110–113.

4. Gladwell, *Outliers*, 112–113.

5. Gladwell, *Outliers*, 114.

6. Gladwell, *Outliers*, 115–116.

the voice of a genius like Chris Langan could not be released to the world. He needed a different kind of ability altogether. If only he had learned how to navigate life. If only he had received practical help from others around him. But he did not. And according to the premise of *Outliers*, no one makes it alone.[7]

A *New York Times* Staff writer, Gladwell has become a prolific author due to exceptional analysis. Those of us privileged enough to have read his array of books have gained from his craft of explaining the world we live in, and even more importantly, aspects of our lives. Though this sociological study is not espousing anything particularly religious, does not his conclusion stir up something provocative for Christians to consider?

Simply stated, intellectual prowess is not what we lack. Sure, we could be smarter! It would be great to have more C.S. Lewis-like intellectuals in our families, associates and fellowships. Though I would agree with many pastors that believers could know more and be better equipped with information about the Bible and their faith, the fact is most believers know the Christian gospel, but influence few with it. Faint mission statistics loudly testify to this fact. This suggests a different kind of knowledge is missing. To this we should ask, "How significant is that vacuum?" In my admittedly biased view, the answer to this question trumps even a stellar analysis on success, like *Outliers*. This is because the church lacks practical intelligence (PI) of the most critical kind. We lack PI in the area of mission. God has intended the evangelistic "making new disciples" mission to be the central hub of all activity—the vital heartbeat of his movement. It is what he left us commissioned to do (Matt 28:18–20). In recent years a rising awareness of mission primacy has begun. Allow me, with greater specificity, to sharpen my point by clarifying that we are deficient in the know-how-agility of "spiritual influence." This is precisely what Jesus possessed! It is what made him so dynamically effective with every individual he encountered.

To gain a better feel for our current state, consider a sampling of recent conversations with church leaders. Sitting down with a pastor of a 600-person church, I soon learned that his church collected transfers from other churches, but they were not reaching anyone outside the faith. As we discussed his scenario, he confessed, "We do ministry, but we don't know how to do mission." From another case study, an executive assistant astutely observed, "Our people struggle to have basic spiritual conversations with non-believers." When visiting with outreach leaders at a Southern California megachurch, Anthony, one of the top guns, pleaded,

---

7. Gladwell, *Outliers*, 126–132.

"If you could broaden our understanding of proclamational evangelism, that would really help." An executive pastor of a 3,000-member church I interviewed balked at the idea of members being "intentional" in sharing the gospel, fearing they would scare people off. In a consultation sought out by an evangelism pastor of a large established church and one of their recently sent-out church planters, both testified to having miniscule evangelistic success. Similarly, an associate pastor admitted to not being able to name anyone the church had reached over the past two years (with the exception of the children's ministry). Adding even more fuel to an already stokin' fire, my personal observations from scores of training classes indicate that Christians are ill-equipped and grossly unprepared for their gospel-messaging role. Across the board, when it comes to disseminating our faith, we don't seem comfortable, and perceived or real discomfort leads to a lot of people in mute mode.

So herein lies the common struggle of the whole church. In other words, using Gladwell's term, this lack of knowledge is no outlier. To some degree, the vacuum exists everywhere and with everyone. It affects churches and individuals in significant ways. When it comes to interfacing with non-believers, we regularly wrestle with how to relate, what to say, and when to say it. There are times when our well-intentioned messaging will be counterproductive. I have had to coach some in church event contexts to hush. I am reticent to say that these words have come from my mouth, "Just don't share the gospel!" It sounds heretical—doesn't it?—especially from an evangelist! But it's not! We have to learn not only how to engage in spiritually related dialogue, but also when to do it, and in the right relational context for impactful effect. These are the things to be learned when we expand the evangelistic conversation to being about influence. This is practical intelligence.

Some will undoubtedly argue that they know all that is required for pointing others to Christ. Clearly, many are knowledgeable. I would counter by saying, "No, not all. You don't know *all* of what you need to reach many kinds of people." Neither do I. Most Christians know very little. This is a problem—one that is growing exponentially in a pluralistic time of worldview multiplicity. Can you see what is happening? An already apparent knowledge gap in the church is only widening. The evangelistic task has become more difficult due to the increasingly distant, disparate starting points of the people we are trying to reach. Sound challenging? It is. The Samaritan woman spoke prophetically about the well being deep. With heart dispositions and world-perspectives that begin farther away, simple, static presentations of the gospel no longer suffice. As the ancient woman so aptly observed, you will have to get the right tools to draw from the depths.

If you are a Christian, then you have a Great Commission calling to reach people outside the church. The fact that God chooses to use us for such a great cause is wonderful! It is a divinely appointed privilege to be cherished and taken seriously. So allow me to ask you to reflect. How schooled are you in that redemptive action? How much have you gleaned about inspiring others toward God? This is critically important for your spiritual life, and for that of others too! The level of your development in this area will directly influence the spiritual journeys of those around you. Does that get your attention? Is it time to increase your mission's quotient? Got MQ?

ARE YOU AN INFLUENCER?

In my opinion, Gladwell's distinction between the two types of knowledge is a spot on way to see what's amiss. The general church does not possess the kind of practical intelligence that works in the real world. In an attempt to make further diagnosis, it seems to me that there is a specific reason for the gapping hole: We are weak at mission because we are not trained as "influencers." There it is: my million-dollar idea right upfront! This is evidenced by the way we view and practice evangelistic discourse. For many decades the church has trained its people to be "tellers" or "presenters," not influencers. Almost every book, conference, and tool is built on the notion derived from this modern paradigm. The comparison between the two concepts (presenting and spiritual influence) is direly needed. In today's climate, you can know how to present the gospel, but if you don't learn the subtleties of influence, you won't even make it to the table with many non-believers. You'll be shut down or tuned out before within a sentence of speaking. You won't get a chance to be heard!

Spiritual influence has a broader scope than just gospel presentation. It has everything to do with who you are because influence is rooted to your personhood. It is a deeper conversation about our lives, and also about the people we are reaching. Soul whisperers. That's who you and I are intended to be. Moving beyond "telling" the gospel to deep heart-level influence. Developing the soul whispering practice of Jesus in a way that most people have never seen. Jesus was an influencer, not a teller.

As demonstrated by his varied interactions, Jesus personally customized words to each individual—and you can learn it, too. You may be saying, "Wait a minute here. He is the Lord. Omniscient-all-knowing ability belongs to him alone! He can have these kinds of conversations and insights, but that's not me—I could never do that." Oh, but you can! Keep reading. You will soon know how to do these exact things. You can actually draw people's souls. You must learn to start where they are, not where you are. You must be able to read people's hearts and needs. And yes, you will have to know where to lead them if you are to reach them for Christ.

You can acquire the soul whispering abilities of Jesus, but it will require humbling yourself and becoming a student of the gospel and human nature. There is a lot to take in. I once sat in a room, floored after hearing seventy-one-year-old author Eddie Gibbs declare how he was on the biggest learning curve of his life. Seventy-one and still growing! When it comes to the gospel and mission there is so much we do not know. If you are willing to invest some time, God will teach you, and spur you to be increasingly fruitful for his kingdom.

Your ability to influence happens by mastering how to draw in dialogue, understanding pathways to faith, acquiring specific skills, and your holistic engagement. Let me speak for all the pastors in the land—we need you! Wherever God has planted you, whether a local church, campus ministry, missional group, church plant, missionary or compassion outreach, a neighbor, a workplace, or in your community, influencers are in short supply and greatly needed. In a pivotal time of church history, today's church must rise to the challenge of becoming an effective, influencing missional movement—once again!

GETTING OUT THERE

Many churches are taking strides in the right directions. Some are beginning mission-minded groups that seek to engage their neighborhoods and communities. The goal is to get out there—create the place and space to walk amongst unreached people. Praise God for this vision! Other churches champion outreach ministries focused on service. With some good movement happening, big questions remain. How do we interconnect with non-believers in the culture? This question applies to those willing to join our groups, and the great many who are not yet there. Not just how do we relate, which can be challenging for Christians, but how do we have influence for Christ? How do we connect in a way that feels natural for us and is also effective in shaping people's hearts spiritually? It's not as easy as some think.

I would compare the scenario to my first rock-climbing experience. After getting roped and carabineered up, with chalked hands I made a novice attempt at "goin' vertical." My friend, playing coach, yelled at me, "Grab that handle!" I looked all around on the rock face thinking to myself, "Where is it?" He pointed to a little bump. To his seasoned eyes it was clearly the way upward—but I couldn't see it. This is what we have in today's churches. Teachers exhorting their people to get out there and share the gospel, and members sighing, "Where's the handle?" When I hear a leader charge his people to take Christ to others, I wonder what is going through the minds of the congregation. Do they have any idea on how to go about that super-important-very-difficult-endeavor in an effective way? Might as well climb a vertical rock face!

Training at a church, an elder pulled me aside and said, "You have revolutionized the way I view evangelism." A pastor told me, "The skills you are teaching should go national." An older man sought me out after my talk and wanted to get me on the radio. Being a no-namer, I laughed! But I got what was happening. The reason behind the response is the vacuum of insightful training on influence. Being church long-timers, they had learned only to tell, but never to draw. When suddenly handed actual drawing utensils (skills), people get excited about mission! I love to see Christians impassioned by having the tools they need to impact this world. This is very different than being told you should do something without adequate training. Is anyone frustrated out there in Churchland? Vision without tools accomplishes nil.

When you learn to draw it makes for a different kind of experience for the non-believer, too. The woman, who had travelled a good distance to a well, after encountering Jesus, leaves her water jar (John 4:17). Imagine that. John notes this slight coloring detail; but it's a big point isn't it? Suddenly, the necessity of her trip seemed so trivial that she scurried back, still parched, to share the news with her people! Who gives a rip about H2O, when you just got offered "living water?" Applying Jesus's skills is exciting stuff for all involved. How do you not just tell the story, but also help to draw for real effect? As you will see, all of these skills are related to who you need to become in Christian character. You will discover experientially that you cannot apply them without your own transformation. Hold on! I hope you are ready to grow!

IT'S TIME FOR A NEW PARADIGM

A staff member at a highly evangelistic church once expressed, "If the gospel is presented properly, it will bear fruit." Although that puts an awful lot of pressure on the presenter (better get your words just right!), it sounded (sort of) correct, I surmised at that time. We do need to share the story with others clearly so they understand and can respond. For the record, and to set some at ease, I care very much about doing this at the appropriate time and leading people to make salvation decisions. Then why did the comment bother me so much afterwards? It's the emphasis that's off.

The church has historically put great stock on people "hearing" the good news. It is not hard to see why the "telling" paradigm is pervasive. On the surface, tremendous biblical support exists for the basic idea of getting the word out. I agree with Paul when he states that faith comes from hearing (Rom 10:14). But are we guilty of being so literal—that we have lost sight of the heavenly aim? Jesus frequently said, "He who has ears to hear let him hear" (Mark 4:9). Certainly, he meant a deeper hearing, one that registered in the heart. I believe Jesus would agree with this statement: *It's not about telling; it's about helping people to hear.* In other words, God doesn't want the telling act; he wants the discipling aim! We can mistakenly think of evangelism as "presenting" when God's goal is the heart formation for discipleship. Like the North Star to the navigators of old, this should be our guiding target. I don't merely want my friends to hear the gospel—I want them to respond and live it. If that is to happen, it will involve a preparation process, not just a proclamation. Of course, we do need to get the message to the world; but not just so they hear it one time. We are not the police writing tickets to satisfy a quota; the goal is to make disciples.

Contemplate the significance of what I am saying through a hypothetical scenario. Granted, this is a very simplified example, nothing like reaching a neighbor who could be: indifferent to spiritual things, skeptical of Christian claims, coming from another faith, spiritually confused or wounded, pleasure-seeking, accusing of God, or politically distanced from Christianity. You will learn to draw these and more. But let's begin with a simpler picture. What if you had a son who was not a Christian, and you had to choose one of two people to exclusively communicate the gospel. Your decision would be determined by interview. The first person tells you they would jump right in and explain away; there is no reason to hold anything back. They aim to explain the gospel with the utmost clarity. They would illustrate and use verses. What your son needs, they tell you, is the Word. The goal would be to lead your child to respond to Christ right away. "You wouldn't want anything to happen to them, would you?" It all sounded good—you guess. The result will be your child coming to faith that night. With the task completed they will report back and then go on their way.

The second interviewee thinks differently, however. They want to talk to your son and get acquainted first. They feel it is important to spend time discerning your child's level of openness, understanding and receptivity to spiritual things. Having a desire to bring your child along gradually, they would seek to meet numerous times. Ideally, the result of this hangin' out is that conversations grow more natural and meaningful. Their hope would be that at a certain point several real questions would arise: ones your child would not feel comfortable and safe asking initially. As they progress together a deeper conversation would develop. Based on experience, the second interviewee explains that it is not uncommon to uncover a heart barrier. Your son may very well discern that following Christ means something; it will change his life. He may take a momentary step back as he begins to wrestle with the notion of becoming a Christian. Only when it has become evident that these seeds of faith have taken root and proper course, will the second person lead your child to respond to Christ and his cross. In the days following, they intend to show back up, warmly received by your son at that time, to go hand in hand with him to church.

So which person would you choose? And which truly did the will of God? I realize many would say both did; but I mean who accomplished what God wanted? If this was real life, and you had a crystal ball to look into the future at each scenario's projection, I wonder if you would see with even more clarity the wisdom of the second? I hope you intuit some of that now. Let me add that if you tried to do the first person's approach with the more difficult to reach people that I had described above, you will get nowhere. But if you took the second person's approach and infused skills, you could potentially, by God's grace, reach them all!

GREATER RESULTS AWAIT!

I'm offering you a new way to do evangelism. By reframing it as spiritual influence, I hope to help Christians take a million steps forward into God's super-exciting movement! In my view, the reframed emphasis could not come sooner. There are four major geographic regions where the Christian church is not growing. The first two— Japan and Europe are givens.

Since there is some underground movement in the Middle East, let's add Australia third. Gazing at the globe for one more, guess whose next on the list? North America. How could that be? We are mired in an outdated, ineffective way of thinking that is not sufficient to bring the people of today from where they are into the faith. Due to the current gospel mode's image problem, Christians enmasse have checked out on evangelism altogether. I've sat personally in these circles and mourned the reaction. Paining over this has birthed in me a new dream.

What if we could replace the negative perception with a new paradigm that is not only more sensitive, but also more effective? Just think of what that could do! The missional potential of the church is far from realized. We are, in many ways, a sleeping giant. To awaken, however, we must radically change our whole approach. Have you heard the definition for insanity: "Doing the same things and expecting different results." We can't afford to do the same things anymore. With a rapidly expanding world population of currently 7 billion people, 4.5 billion of whom being unbelievers, there is far too much at stake! *Soul Whisperer* teaches Christians how to partner with God in the proper preparation of the non-believer's heart.

I confess to being a reluctant convert to this new thinking. Through my many ministry years (I am super old in my late forties!), I have engaged consistently in gospel-sharing. It is my gift to interact naturally with people I just met, and to explain biblical content. Yet I don't approach people with that mentality anymore. I guess you'd say I gave it up. "My name is Gary—I'm a recovering teller." I stopped believing it would achieve the ultimate goal. I shifted my thinking: From telling to influencing. Let me be quick to say, I am a total believer in the verbal part of the process. Instead of a rote presentation, you will learn principles to guide your words. And I should add, using the California vernacular, these skills shred!

Jesus said, "My sheep hear my voice." Do you hear his voice? What is he whispering to you right now? Does he not want you to follow him in his mission? He goes on to say, "I have other sheep that are not of this sheep pen. I must bring them also. They too will listen to my voice . . . " (John 10:16). This means that if we are to reach anyone there will be a moment when they actually hear the divine call. How amazing is it to think that God's voice can resonate through your words! This is not a mystic moment, mind you, but one that is simultaneously sensitive to the honed frequency of a unique human being and an intimately personal, soul-seeking God. Jesus whispers today. He wants to shape you to speak words for him.

His words, being living and active penetrate to the soul. If evangelism is to be recovered, it must be redeemed from the "presenting" shallows to venture into the "drawing" depths. It is the heart that hears and responds. We must learn to draw like Jesus.

Discussion and Engagement

1. Take a moment to share about specific friends, family, neighbors, or work associates who are outside the faith. Describe in as much detail as possible what you think their starting position is.

2. How does discerning the starting point inform you on where you might begin with initial conversations?

3. The author states that you can read people and know where to take them in a spiritual journey. Do you believe you can learn these skills patterned by Jesus? Why or why not? Hopefully

2

Soul to Soul

You don't have a soul. You are a soul. You have a body.

—C.S. LEWIS

I always love when someone turns me onto a good movie that I haven't seen—so here is my offering to you. *The Snow Walker*. Inspired from the writings of Farley Mowat,[1] it is the adapted story of a self-absorbed American cargo pilot who reluctantly picks up a very sick Eskimo woman and attempts to get her to a hospital. Enroute the aircraft encounters difficulties and crashes into the frozen tundra of the Alaskan plains. A survival story ensues, where the young Eskimo woman teaches him not only to survive—but how to live. By the time of her death, this selfish man is transformed. He had taken on more than her skills. Walking alone through blizzard conditions, the final scene fittingly shows him being embraced by an Eskimo community; he had become one of them.

How does God transform us to be like him? This is a great question for a Christian, since the very term "Christian" means "little Christ's." Christianity is first and foremost a follower's faith. A disciple becomes like his Master. Even though God has gifted teachers within the church, our ultimate discipleship is to Christ himself. Thus, we are to be like him.

---

1. Mowat, *The Snow Walker*, 121–131.

Have we taken time to discernibly appreciate what he was like? Or have we made him an image version of us, sort of like the artist's Anglo version of Jesus? The Bible does not withhold authentic data on its main star as we look afresh at the Gospel accounts of Matthew, Mark, Luke and John.

In the Samaritan woman's story that we previously touched on, the reason Jesus is going solo is that his fellow travelers are off on a 7-Eleven run! Famished, they are desperate for a meal. Returning with the goods, the disciples assume their Master must be hungry too and try to get him to eat. Instead of receiving their offering, Jesus sees how instead they have served him up a teachable moment. What nourished and sustained him was not something from a menu: "My food . . . is to do the will of him who sent me and to finish his work" (John 4:34). From those empty-stomached words of Jesus we see just how deep the mission of God goes! It begs the question, "Is God's mission our food?" Is it the nourishing sustenance— the true food—of our lives? Are we anything like Jesus in this way? Apparently, the disciples were not even close. Jesus tells them that he had food "they knew nothing about" (32). He was not preaching to the choir; they didn't have the same kind of mission resolve. A gap was evident with the lowly understudy disciples, but what of the posh religious elite?

When Jesus first called Matthew, he remained at his new disciple's home to hang with the notorious tax collector crowd. Ticked over this perception, the highly devout Pharisees called into question his associations with "bad company." Jesus's response exposed a similar divide. He directed his pious observers, "But go and learn what this means: 'I desire mercy, not sacrifice'" (Matt 9:13). Have you ever meditated on this verse, which Jesus referenced in two separate instances? (See also Matt 12:7). He refers to sacrifice because that is what the Pharisees valued. They measured their lives according to religious devotion. By tapping a text pulled from the story of Hosea, a man called to love an adulterous wife, Jesus declared something that is truly stunning to this day. God's primary aim is not religious duty, but for his mercy to touch the world. He could not have said it more plainly then when he embellished, "For I have not come to call the righteous but sinners" (Matt 9:13). This is the heart of God! It is why we have stories of a seeking shepherd and a compassionate father, reaching to the one lost sheep or wayward son. Like the disciples, the Pharisees didn't possess the same heart. They couldn't fathom why this rabbi spent so much time with these moral losers. They measured spirituality along an entirely different line.

Before we get too prideful in pointing fingers, we need to be brutally honest. This may be painful, but what about you and I? What possesses us? Is it God's mission? How do we measure our spiritual lives? Do these passages affirm or challenge you? Okay, I'll go first. I'll admit to being challenged. I don't look much better than these groups. I watch the *Food Network* religiously—I'm way into food! Compared to me, the disciples look like spiritual giants; they only want to fill their stomachs, I want to tantalize mine. In comparison to the Pharisees, I routinely find myself falling short on dishing out God's mercy. Like them, I am often content to hang with my Christian friends and glory in God's gifts. I, too, fail to see how he most desires his grace to go outward. It is shocking to consider that his mercy-reach through me is the measure of my spiritual life! Yeah, I'm challenged when I look at Jesus—way so!

Chances are likely that you, too, see the gap. You may also recognize that you need much more of him. It makes me think that perhaps we throw around the term "Christ-like" too flippantly. Have we reduced it to a handful of disciplines and missed his heart? His brand definitely appeals to us, but in soul-to-soul comparison, we do not align very closely. Would we describe ourselves as Michael Jordan-like if we didn't play and love basketball with a passion? Without Jesus's mission practices demonstrated in our lives, are we not doing the same thing? Perhaps we need a new kind of discipling altogether—one that mirrors his very soul.

Growing into his ways, however, is never automatic. We all know the church gig. You go to a service. Sing to God. Hear the message. Come home. Survive another week and then do it all over again! What is disturbing is how it is entirely possible to go through this routine while your life is still devoid of looking anything more like Jesus. His approach, life rhythms, posture with people, choice of friends, kinds of conversations, hang-outs, and actions all remain radically different than ours. In today's Christianity, it is easy to become institutionalized. This is when you morph into a byproduct of Christian culture that's not from Jesus. Duped, we miss his adventure. Before you know it life can pass you by without having touched anyone outside the church. Like a person restlessly searching for their calling, this bothers me. You too? If your church only wants you to come sit, listen and serve, then you might encourage them that there's more to experience in Christ. Declare to yourself and those who would listen that your food is to accomplish "God's unfinished business;" and that you are about "mercy" not sacrifice. If your leaders are worth their salt, the stirring in your soul will thrill them!

If not, look elsewhere for those who share this desire.

caring for people

THE GREAT STEP BACK

The lack of sufficient influence training is the biggest factor hindering the church movement. The good news is that the study and implementation of Christ's mission methodology and skill-set has the potential to create enormous change. Yet before we dive farther into his manner of reaching the hard-to-reach, we must acknowledge a significant complementary piece. What will it matter if we learn his skills but do not have his inner compass? It is his loving zeal for lost people that moves him to action. Make no bones about it, if we do not have his driving focus, the fruit, or lack thereof, will show.

I have trained scores in missional living and many have acquired insight on Jesus's ways. Yet months and even years later, I have observed how some have not influenced anyone, nor made any real investment to do so. They continued to embrace a spirituality that was all about 'them.' Attending endless Bible studies, church services, and seminars may have yielded more learned followers, but not more effective ones making a difference in people's lives. It was as if the greater story of what God wanted to do in this world, modeled by Christ in their Bibles, never got through. Jesus came to this earth to lay his life down for the lost. Are we not called to do likewise? I believe we can reach so many more than we are now, but it will take Christians who intrinsically love like Jesus. How do we, as his followers, embody his heart? Do we need our own frozen-tundra journey to become something 'other' than what we are right now?

So how now do we get Jesus's compassion for those around us?

THE PRACTICE OF "ALIGNMENT PRAYER"

Prayer

Have you ever noticed how we only pray about things that matter to us? Not surprisingly with Jesus, his heart for mission pulsates with prayer. Vertical dependence with the Father is vital, even for him. Mission is, after all, heaven's activity. Looking at his disciples, Jesus guided them to pray missionally, "Ask the Lord of the harvest, therefore, to send out workers into his harvest field" (Matt 9:37). Naturally, we view this verse as a general request for more workers. Yet it is highly likely that Jesus targeted the words specifically to his inner circle. Recall, they were the ones in Samaria with earthly appetites, who questioned his association with the woman, and prejudicially dismissed her ethnic group. In that paralleling passage Jesus directly challenged his guys, "I tell you, open your eyes and look at the fields! They are ripe for harvest (John 4:35)."

Like them, we can hear his words and quickly jump ahead for God to raise-up others, while failing to look within. So right now, in this moment, we are not going to pray for anyone but ourselves. Who amongst us is Christ's equal? Rightly, then, we will benefit from coming before Jesus to confess that we see this disparity. We are not as much like him, as he would want. He loves us and accepts us, but he also knows that our real fulfillment is in being intimately connected with him and being an integral part of his kingdom business. This admission draws us to humbly ask for divine enablement. As we do so, it will cultivate desire. Seeking God for his work to be done in us is critical in every ministry. We should know that God would use prayers to transform our lives, and expand his reach in the process.

Which of these sentiments is right for you? Here's one of my favorites: "Do in Me what you need to do, so you can do through Me what you want to do." There's a classic for your whole life. If gutsy, you might try this one on for size: "Smash this selfish stone-like heart of mine!" If you just raised your hand, I want to shake it for being so honest and brave! How about, "Sear my soul with your deep love for the lost?" Or another, "Make me a servant to carry the cross for those who will one day pick up their own." Brother or sister, similar to Solomon's desire for wisdom, when we ask these kinds of things in earnest, God answers those prayers—and will hold you to your commitment! According to Jesus's own words, we will not have to beat the door down at midnight. He promised, "If you then, though you are evil, know how to give good gifts to your children, how much more will your Father in heaven give the Holy Spirit to those who ask him!" (Luke 11:13). Please note that God's good gift is himself. Is there a greater gift than his personal presence with its transforming power? Is this not our first step? Should we not ask the Lord to remake us in order to fulfill his work? Maybe then, and only then, will we marry heart to skills and see the wonders of God displayed.

As we journey forward, like Jesus, we will have to fight to stay on course. Having begun my diet, my wife booted me out of the house for eating from the cookie jar. I tried to redeem myself by going for a run, "I will show her how devoted I am!" Pounding the pavement around my regular coffee stop, what shows up on the sidewalk—a marshmallow! I was trying to recall how long tasty food could be on the ground and still be safe to eat. Was it five seconds or five minutes? Not knowing, I decided to leave it there and keep going but it left me thinking of life's distractions and how timely, targeted, and tempting they can be. We live in a world of options where even good things get us sidetracked. Christian, you have to make life-priority determinations. If you don't, you will be drawn to lesser things, and fail to achieve the greater things. The Proverbs wisely warn, "Above all else, guard your heart for everything you do flows from it" (4:23). Living for God's mission is a life commitment. It will take heart cultivation to keep running down the path, and not have the first opportunistic morsel pull you away. I sense the Spirit asking each of us, "Are you willing to ask God boldly to make you someone big in his mission picture?"

THE PRACTICE OF "ENVISIONED WINE"

This practice is about seeing people differently and being in tune with what to say at the right time that draws a person in. To illustrate, that, for instance, take John's Gospel. It is absolutely unique in his selection of subject matter, the way he orders the material, his focus on Christ's divinity, and the appeal to the philosophic-minded of his day. His adaptive choice of the word "logos" for the second person of the Godhead connected a word commonly used by three philosophic schools (Middle-Platonism, Stoicism and Philo's writings) to Christian theology.[2] Of the four Gospels, I would also say that John is most distinctive for literary artistry. This is why God selects him to write Revelation, for he needed an artist to depict future events. In his Gospel, the "Beloved Disciple" uses metaphorical contrasts like "light" and "darkness," and symbols. He alone showcased the seven symbolic "I am" statements of Jesus (bread of life, the gate, good shepherd, light of the world, etc). Being the artist of the bunch, it is fascinating to notice layering in his writing. When I use the word "layering," I intend to convey that there are, at times, tiered levels of meaning. If you are not astute in observation, you might easily miss something right before your eyes.

Will seminary scholars want to curb the creative breadth I am attributing to this biblical author? Perhaps. But don't you agree that our Bible is amazing, and that its big picture themes are discoverable even beyond the literal words? If contemporary writers can layer a script for impact, could not the infinitely creative God breathe these kinds of strokes through his

2. Green, *Evangelism in the Early Church*, 120.

imaginative human agent? I think so. Honestly, I believe the Scriptures have tiers in many other places, too! When we gain this higher perspective, it opens our eyes to the way Jesus viewed people. His "envisioning pattern" must become part of our modus operandi.

One such tiered case is the story of the miracle at Cana. On the surface it is a relatively simple first showing of Jesus's divine power. By turning water into wine he provides an initial glimpse of who he is, which marked the beginning of his public ministry. But is there more to it than that? Of the four Gospel writers only John includes this story. We can imagine why that was so. In light of everything else Jesus did—was it really that important? Water turned to wine—a slick parlor trick to impress guests at a wedding? Whoop-de-do. It's possible, only John saw the greater imagery behind Jesus's bartending. Look at the miracle from a higher viewpoint. Jesus has the servants fill stone earthen jars with water. Then he tells them to draw from those pots. The author repeats the verb "draw" twice in the narrative. What is drawn? Vintage wine. Taking a moment to smell its fragrance, swill in his mouth and swallow, the headwaiter is blown away by its grade. To him, the owner has un-customarily waited till late in the party to dig into his finest reserve!

So, at one level the miracle makes a public debut of Christ's power, but at another, does it not picture something else? This seemingly insignificant first act displayed symbolically what Jesus's entire ministry would be! He came to draw rich, fully fermentable faith out of human vessels. He would be the one to transform people on the inside to become their potent best. What is the response to this miracle? Not only does John describe the filling and drawing of wine from the pots, but as a result, it draws the disciple's faith (John 2:11). Like the vintage wine shared that night, fresh faith filled his disciples with qualitative joy!

If this greater theme lies within the water-to-wine story, then Jesus's ministry should unfold in suit. This is where your study of Scripture will lead to far richer treasures. Because I believe you will see that this first miracle portrays his ministry life perfectly. In fact, recognizing his "faith drawing orientation" will explain dozens of puzzling passages. It tells us why he acted in very specific, even bizarre ways with people.

Why did Jesus use his spittle to pack blind men's eyes with river mud? (John 9:6–11). What was the point? Was the saliva-dirt chemical reaction necessary as an agent for the miracle? Of course not! For a blind person, though, feeling the mudpack, and then being sent on an anticipatory errand to go wash it off in the pool, created a faith-activating experience.

Why did he compare a Canaanite woman to a scrounging dog? (Matt 15:26). Does that not seem unbecoming of our Lord? Yet his somewhat derogatory reference evoked from her a faith proclamation that he praised. She now sits honored amongst all people in the heavenly realm. Why did he circle back to first find and then talk with a blind man who did not yet know his healer? (John 5:14). Why bother? The man could see. Obviously, Jesus had something much more transformative in mind. Why did he stop in the midst of a huge crowd and ask, "Who touched me?" (Mark 5:24–29). This moment, which miffed his disciples and caused a human traffic jam, also drew a woman to come forth, fall on her knees, and make profession. Why did he reach over and put his human hands on the decaying limbs of a leper? (Luke 5:13). The common denominator to his many varied interactions is his artful way of drawing faith. If you follow the Gospel's stories to their outcomes you will see how his actions and words align consistently with this theme. He is the Master! We will learn from his high precision skills.

Growing in his drawing ways begins with adopting his eyesight. Observe two distinctions. *First, Jesus's eyes exhibit a profound value of lost people.* Even in a crowd he sees specific persons. He stops and engages individuals along his way demonstrating how each matters. Do we do this? Jesus sees the ones others have marginalized. Who are they in your sphere: A reclusive neighbor, the loner classmate, the market clerk, the forgotten friend, or a street-corner migrant worker? At times he sees whole unreached groups, like when he pans the Samaritans coming out of the village and declares, "Look on the fields, that they are white for harvest" (John 4:35 NASB). By connecting agricultural imagery to the Samaritan garment color, Jesus called his disciples to see this ethnic group with a new set of "mission eyes." This, too, must happen with us. Somewhere, hopefully early in our spiritual journey, we stop looking past lost people and start seeing them everywhere. Maybe you are already doing this. If not, make it your assignment today. Go and watch those on the outside. Mission-minded people have moments when they see non-believers and say, "Now here's something worthy of my one and only life."

Second, Jesus's eyes reveal a profound vision for lost people. As we see with the first miracle at Cana, Jesus had the ability to look past water and see wine. We must take on this same lens. Just as a compelling vision is essential to grow churches so too we must have it to grow people. We should be the first to believe they will believe! To do that, like him, we will have to become visionaries of divine transformation. When drawing others to faith, we share his mindset, a belief that God holds the key to their greatest potential; which is nothing less than their vintage best life. This perspective is absolutely critical. If we do not first have his eyes, we will not lead them to higher ground.

Having a greater vision for your friend's life is a theologically packed foresight. Only theists have such an exalted view of human beings. This "imago Dei" (image of God) doctrine remains under attack. Alan Bloom in his classic book, *The Closing of the American Mind*, describes when it began. Up through the Middle Ages, it was commonplace to refer to human beings as souls. When people died at sea, the record contained the verbiage: "thirty souls lost at sea," consistent to the S.O.S. cry: "Save Our Souls." Enlightenment thinkers of the eighteenth century, however, did not like the clear connotation of divine nature and immortality conjured by the word 'soul.' Thus, they sought to strip 'soul' from the vernacular by replacing it with the word 'self.'[3] This shift has reverberated forward, relegating humanity to a lesser position, removed from the divine calling.

Soul whispering, then, in its purest form, is all about transitioning others back from self to soul. Like Jesus, our role is to deal with people at this restorative level. It is about reclaiming the divinely endowed position, the fullness of their humanity. What an honor God has bestowed upon us to serve him in this way. So let me ask you whose side you are on. In other words, when you look at non-believers, do you see water or wine?

THE PRACTICE OF "DIVINE DANCING"

Something else happens in the ministry-launching miracle at Cana. Again, it's a big picture concept. Jesus has waited on the Father's lead to begin his mission. Because of this, tension exists in the dialogue between Mary's desires to meet a practical party need and the start of Jesus's public ministry. Ironically, Mary's strange, rather presumptuous demand for more wine happened to coincide with the Father's timing. Jesus's response, "My hour has not yet come," revealed to Mary that her request did not force the divine hand (John 2:1–4). In fact, Jesus would not have proceeded without the Father's leading (even if he was good earthly son). Yet providentially, her words fit into God's masterful timing. The hour, or time, for Jesus's ministry launch had arrived. The Father would now be glad to fully showcase it.

3. Bloom, *The Closing of the American Mind*, 173.

If we are to become God's influencers then we must be highly attuned to the Spirit's leading. Like Jesus, we do not rush ahead of the Father. This is a critical point that needs to be made in the beginning of our journey together. Countless numbers of my own conversational mistakes have taught me this lesson the hard way. Being patience-deprived, I have had to learn "not to press." When I have overstepped his bounds in zeal or ego, God has had to remind me that this is his show, not mine. Recall Jesus's words, "And I, when I am lifted up will draw all people to myself" (John 12:32). Who does the drawing? At times, you must wait patiently on the Lord to work. Let me say it in a slightly different way: Evangelistic influence is an art. There is a right time for everything, and a wrong time too. In the chapters ahead, you will learn particular influence skills. *When* you use those skills, however, is subject to God's lead. I am not suggesting being passive, but we never barge into conversations or use tools haphazardly. We learn to be sensitive to people and God at the same time. You will have to pick your spots for meaningful Spirit-led conversations. Your role, like a dancer, is to follow his lead.

As you grow in sensitivity to God's directing, you will also discover that God will not disappoint. His inner voice to your surrendered heart will be spot-on for your friend! The Spirit will guide you in conversations. Sometimes he will lead you forward, and other times shut you up to merely listen and affirm the other's journey! As his human servant, you are his paintbrush for influence, and he knows both the types and timing of the strokes needed. This Holy Spirit- governed engagement through you captures the sacramental nature of evangelism.[4] You will sense the Holy Spirit in profound ways. When this happens, it is personally thrilling, as you experience God using you! The concept of following his lead in a divine dance begs a spiritual question, "Are you close enough to God in your walk to follow his moves?"

THE PRACTICE OF "HOLISTIC ENGAGEMENT"

→ spiritual growth

With Jesus, the most fully developed spiritual person is also the most missional. Unlike what we typically see in the church, there is no division between these camps. Why do we have some doing mission and others not? Are we not all supposed to be like Christ? By 'missional,' I refer to how Jesus lived for the mission of his Father; he was sent for a purpose bigger and greater than any of his personal needs. From Latin, Biblical scholars

---

4. Dorsett and Root, *The Sacrament of Evangelism*, 16.

Soul Whisperer = still small voice God to you you to another

call this 'missio Dei' —the mission of God. He handed off or transferred this exact calling to his followers, "As the Father has sent me, I am sending you" (John 20:21). Obviously, Jesus's missionality did not happen in a vacuum, but flowed deeply out of his being, which was fully tuned to the Father. If we are to take on his soul whispering ways, we need his spiritual rootedness.

Yet a debate rages on how to raise the mission value. Do we need spiritual formation first in order to become missional? In slightly different terms, "Is spiritual renewal the fueling fire of evangelistic fervor?" Some believe it is. They claim if we focus on our own growth then the heart for the lost will naturally arise. History affords us several "renewal movement" examples, where the idea was to get so close to God that it would literally propel the church outward. Interestingly, the studies of these experiments indicated the expected response did not occur.[5] Analysis pinpointed that once personal growth became the goal, people never felt spiritually whole enough. Like a revolving circle, the inward focus cycled back to one's own perceived need. Can we not observe what happens when people in a relationship or organization demand attention for themselves? Psychologists routinely give self-obsessed clients the task of doing acts of kindness and charity for others. They know that when a person looks outwardly, they begin the journey to health. In the church, we can get obsessed with our own growth, not realizing the answer is looking outside of ourselves.

In this way, mission is a bit like marriage. Before getting married I appraised the divorce rate saying, "I can't believe 50 percent don't make it." After a year of wedded bliss-less-ness, I recanted by saying, "I can't believe 50 percent do!" Marriage is tough. It takes two committed people to deal with their individual and collective baggage and make it work. I eventually learned to view marriage as God's gift—to force me into love. To that end (or is it a beginning?), I am grateful, because I am often selfish. Like a marital commitment that requires people to selflessly give, pursuing others on God's mission pulls us upward in love. This, too, is God's perfect design. He wants to forge you into being something other!

What, then, is the formula for developing the missional heart? Certainly it is spiritually based, involving deep connection to the Father. It is also deeply experiential; you will have to cherish God's grace to desire it for others. Yet the idea of spiritual formation coming out of mission, not preceding it, is what the Bible pictures. Some things only form from seeing and doing. We must get our feet wet. Jesus enlisted the disciples into

5. Snyder, *The Problem of Wine Skins*, 17.

[handwritten margin note: filling your self spiritual deeper than not satisfied go back to try again but never moving on to reach another outside of yourself.]

mission at his initial calling (Luke 5:1–11). "Leave the nets, boys, time to become fishers of men." Though our spiritual nurture does have a place in the equation, when we look at the book of Acts, there was no maturity standard. On the contrary, all those in faith had the ability to spread the message. It happened spontaneously, organically, and proactively through training with teachers like Paul and Barnabas (Acts 11:25–26). When they got out there—they and the church grew! The adage says, "There's the classroom, and then there's the laboratory." You can only learn so much in a church pew. At a certain point, you must "go to grow." Experiential engagement becomes your teacher. I have written all this to say that if you do not engage with those outside the faith—your spirituality will be truncated. It is worth repeating: *Spiritual formation comes out of mission.* This presents one of the great leadership challenges of our time. The church must shift from a dominant teaching paradigm to practical training and engagement that extends God's reach.

With this same spirit, why don't you change the way you read this book? What normally happens when you pick up a page-turner? You dive in and read a section hoping it ministers and taught you something. Well, go ahead and do the same, but this time stop at the end of each chapter and ask God for the courage to act. Seek him to teach you in practice what you are learning in the pages. God will show up when you step out. Guaranteed. It's a time-tested truth. Do not think even for a second that he doesn't know the processing happening in your mind and heart. He is the God of mission, and the giver of divinely appointed opportunities. As you engage relationally with non-believers, he will develop you. He is already going before you preparing the way! I have taught these concepts to untold numbers of people through the years, and every time God does something miraculous. This book is not just about your learning—it's about God touching someone through *you!* This is a big deal. If you wait until the end to begin—you will have missed the ride. At the close of each chapter there are questions to encourage engagement steps for that day or week. Don't be afraid to apply them. Vincent Van Gogh said, "If you hear a voice within you saying you cannot paint, go ahead and paint and that voice within you will be silenced." Aspects of confidence, training and breakthrough, come from doing. read-apply-engage

NOT JUST WORDS!

When we study the missional nature of Christ, it immediately challenges false notions. Some mistakenly think evangelism is merely about presenting. They fail to see the holistic influence dynamics that Christ modeled. Reducing mission to words misses the greater picture. It's never just about your words; it's about the loving environment you create with people. Thus, you must grow in qualities to be an influencer. When you embody the character of Christ's missionality, you deliver a message within that relational context. It's about who you are, not just what you say. Each chapter in the first section is crucial because you will learn skills related to Christ's character. Prepare to be stretched. Just as marriage purposes to force spouses out of themselves and into love, so missional engagement pushes us to grow.

Your influence capacity will depend upon the willingness to surrender yourself spiritually, and to allow Jesus to mold you as his disciple. You will have to become intensely committed to his practices. By taking the outlined steps you will be drawn into manifesting his virtues. It is the only way. This is no shortcut. By learning the skills of Jesus, you will become more like Jesus. *how? without study*

NOT JUST LIFE! *Living v Speaking*

Christ's holistic influence also challenges the idea that all we need to do is live the spiritual life. A saying working its way through our churches comes from Saint Francis of Assisi. I have heard it voiced prolifically as a kind of mantra—something Christians live by. You may have heard it yourself. He said, "Preach the gospel always; when necessary use words." With a bit of saintly wit, he communicated the truth that our lives are meant to exhibit faith. Sadly though, I fear it is now disheveling the notion that living our Christian lives is all we need to do. This belief is false, and was not the intention of St. Francis. We need words! There is power in words used wisely. People won't "get it" if we don't learn how to verbalize our faith.

Have you seen the movie *Avatar*? Director James Cameron opened our eyes to his vision of a new world. When my family went to the theatre, we entered a beautiful bioluminescent landscape with cool-looking creatures, blue-skinned people, and floating Sky Mountains. We saw integrated connection links between people and the natural world, including horse-like creatures and large predatorial dragon-hawks (banshees). Without the visual we would have missed the wonders of Pandora!

In a contrasting twist, the way people's minds open to faith is primarily verbal, not visual. Now that might sound a little strange at first. I fully realize that unbelievers sometimes see distinctions in Christians. Clearly they do, when new believers manifest sudden transformation. Yet because secular people categorize religious types, and cannot discern spiritual things, it is mainly through "words" that they learn about faith. Hear me on this important point.

Being an assistant coach to my son's baseball team connects me to people in the community. One evening while our boys took their swings at the batting cages, I was having a casual conversation with Robert. We had talked a few times previously, and were now at ease with each other. He brought up international travel saying they had been to England and France. I told him of my trips to Asia, Italy and Africa. It interested him that I had gone to Africa, so I shared reflections on Kenya saying, "One quarter of Nairobi's population live in the slums. I have this lasting memory of driving through a stop-point, and seeing moms with their kids selling bottles of strawberry milk at ten o' clock at night. Life is hard there." I mentioned being involved with churches, and how one of my big impressions of the Kenyan people was how their worship helped them to transcend life's hardships. I said, "They showed up to church to be lifted above it all." He then replied, "Religion is supposed to do that for people."

So I asked him if he had a church background. He said he and his wife grew up Catholic, but left the church long ago. I knew then that he was not a believer. I continued, "You can experience faith in a way that can sustain and nurture your life; this is what God wants for you." He turned toward me with a surprised look and said, "My wife would never think that faith could be something nurturing!" (Funny how he put this on his wife.) I affirmed, "It can be this way for you and her, but there are some steps you must take to get there." Before departing he shook my hand with a warm smile, and I knew the interaction had connected. A week later, in the middle of our doubleheader, I mentioned that we had a meaningful conversation and asked if he would like to get together for coffee to talk more. He said he would!

The fact is there is nothing visually distinct about me. Besides my P90X highly cut physique (kidding), I am just an aging balding dad with a son playing baseball; but when I opened my mouth regarding faith, Robert's thoughts of God expanded in major ways! Contrary to what you will hear, what we say is often more potent than how we live. Please understand I am not advocating licentiousness, or that how we live doesn't matter. Obviously, we can ruin our witness. If we are rude, insensitive, judgmental, arrogant, gossipy, uncaring, ungracious, not honest about ourselves, hateful or racist, and then try to share the love of Christ—it probably will not work. What I am saying is people will not be reached unless we can talk about the tremendous meaning of faith; just watching our lives alone will not do it. But if we learn to use words to dialogue descriptively we can open up people's minds to what they would never see on their own. We are the painters of a whole new world!

Is this not what Jesus did with the woman at the well? She is carrying out the routine task of fetching water when Jesus engages her in a conversation about "a spring of water welling up" within her (John 4:14). With those few choice words her mind is transported to an entirely new picture of what life could be. Behold the power of words! Notice, if Jesus had said nothing, she would not have realized who it was who graced her presence, and what he could offer. Evidently, verbal influence is stamped within the design of God, being critical to human beings connecting and determining meaning. The late Paul Hiebert, in his book *Transforming Worldviews*, observes the potency of verbal influence saying, "All cultures use both sight and sound, but in most, sound is the dominant sensory experience. Spoken words are more immediate, relational, and intimate . . . "[6] It is fascinating to consider that throughout church history, oral tradition has often been our primary teacher. The Apostle Paul recognized this simple truth when he appealed, "And how can they believe in the one of whom they have not heard?" (Rom 10:14). Our words are the gateway to faith.

Both heart character and verbal skills are necessary. We must journey into a discipleship with Christ that is holistic in nature. I hope you are ready to go and grow!

* * *

The next step on our journey is to read the current culture we live in. The cultural assessment chapter, *Signs of the Times,* will tee us up and position us for greater influence. We need to understand our time and discern where influence resides. May God open our eyes!

---

6. Hiebert, *Transforming Worldviews,* 15.

DISCUSSION AND ENGAGEMENT

1. When you consider the mission focus of Jesus, in what ways can you see a mission gap with your own life? Explain.

2. What do you think about the idea of spiritual formation flowing out of mission? Is that a new concept for you? Describe how you can see this to be true.

3. How do you feel about the challenge of growing into a deeper discipleship with Christ? Is that scary, especially when it deals with evangelistic mission?

   IS
   study

4. Do you agree with the author that words are necessary for people to "get" the Christian faith? Talk for a moment about your own story of coming to Christ. What did you hear?

Use your words!

3

Signs of the Times

You know how to interpret the appearance of the earth and the sky.
How is it that you don't know how to interpret this present time?

—Jesus (Luke 12:56)

It was like having a private viewing with the master himself. Alone in the room, I found myself puzzling over how a painting's canvas could look so much like a photograph. This was the question dancing in my head as I gazed at Leonardo da Vinci's "The Annunciation" in the Uffizi Museum in Florence, Italy. This famous fourteenth-century Renaissance portrayal belongs to the classical period, and standing before it, I tried to guess how da Vinci did it; photographs are image copies; paintings are done with a brush. Could I see his actual brushstrokes? Deep in contemplation, I moved in close and then even closer getting my eyes a mere inch from the canvas when . . . Rrr Rrr Rrr . . . the sudden shock of an alarm! The Italian security guard was over immediately as it dawned on me that I was the perpetrator. "Don't get too close," he said. Euphemistic words for "Back off man, don't breathe on our masterpiece!"

It is now obvious that I am no expert in browsing galleries and appraising paintings, but I must confess to having developed an eye for art's genres. What fascinates me most is the undercurrent of thinking driving artistic periods of time. Art often reflects cultural thought. This could not have been more dramatically illustrated than when my wife and I viewed art in the medieval city of Sienna, which featured gruesome body dismemberment storyboards. We were witnessing cold-blooded murder! Turning to my wife I said with a hint of sarcasm, "What a romantic time we're having in Italy." I suppose there's a reason why they call it the Dark Ages.

Though I would have loved to be a painter, I am rather a personal evangelist who likens faith sharing to a relational art form. With this in mind, I want to pose a somewhat "off the wall" question. If evangelism had a likeness to art—then what "genre" would resonate today? In other words, in our postmodern time what art style best matches the cultural shift that has occurred? I am sure this is not the usual question being discussed at your dinner table. I believe the answer is actually quite telling about the nature of spiritual influence. It was Jesus who alluded to interpreting the present time. That is what I aim to do in this chapter—make an assessment on where influence resides—in the spirit of defining more sharply the inroads for impact. Before we learn to read individuals, let's first read the culture that is shaping them. This is not an intellectual exercise, but a way to determine how to navigate the turbulent waters and avoid the icebergs. Though certain sections will focus on reaching people of various worldviews, we must first contextualize the time period that all inhabit.

It is not hard to take a quick amateur's survey of art's notable master-painters. Most can easily recognize the classic Renaissance period of Michelangelo and friends with its dominant biblical imagery and accentuated oversized human features. Then we had the period of the Romanticists who were not romantics, but rather reactors to the rationalistic Enlightenment. They used art to reveal intuition, imagination, and feeling. Rejecting the more dramatic, emotive depictions of the Romanticists,[1] the Realists tried to show the common man with his everyday issues. These painters stopped embellishing their subjects and started capturing them—exactly. Following the Realists, you had Impressionists like Monet, who purposefully blurred lines of distinction and used lighter colors in ways never seen before.[2] This eventually led to new kinds of interpretive works from the likes of Post-Impressionist Vincent Van Gogh, and opened a crack in the door for the modern art scene. Artistic connoisseurs have their particular tastes, yet seeing what inspired art provides additional color commentary (pun intended).

---

1. Janson, *History of Art*, 565.
2. House, *Monet in the 20th Century*, 2.

So what artistic style best informs present-day evangelism? Do you have it? To me, the answer is clear as day: It is Realism. If we compare an art movement to evangelism—the style that best suits today is to capture the realistic view of life and faith. This is what the Realists tried to do. In my opinion, embracing this idea will do the most for the spread of the gospel. If correct, the gospel movement would benefit from non-believers seeing our faith in its stark naked reality. The Realist painters passionately sought to express their subjects through that which is perceivable, and did all they could to negate subjective Romanticism or any elements distorting how something truly exists.[3] Just as Realism was a reaction to the fallaciousness of Romanticism,[4] postmodernism is a reaction to the idealistic notions of modernism. This is a significant parallel that should not be missed! With a new kind of grit, Realist art begged us to see the world around us. Even the choice of subjects provoked criticism because no one before had given artistic esteem to common peasants—Realism was radical in its day.[5]

Is this not the spirit of God moving in the hearts of the church? God is opening our eyes to people, needs, influences and systems. Have you ever taken a prayer walk into the world of non-believers—through your neighborhood, school, community, and city? Ever thought that looking with new discerning, non-discriminating eyes may be just the thing that God uses to change this world? Ever think that the time has come to size up the heart disposition of your non-believing neighbor or work associate? Ever consider that getting a true read on what is happening inside your teenager is long overdue? Ever get a gut feeling that trying to act super exemplary with non-believers might not be what they need? This was the cry of the Realists. They were sick and tired of all the fake fluff— they wanted people to notice what was really there.

Another fascinating distinctive of Realism is the use of darkness. Because darkness permeates life they sought to portray this in their paintings.[6] You can always pick out the Realists by the darker themes and backgrounds surrounding their subjects. When critic Théophile Gautier compared Realist painter Edouard Manet's Christ with J.R.H. Lazenger's, he said, "If Lazenger's Christ is too pale, too clean, too scrubbed, Manet's on the other hand, seems never to have known soap and water. The livid

3. New World Encyclopedia, "Realism," lines 1–9.
4. New World Encyclopedia, "Realism," line 1.
5. Finocchio, "Nineteenth-Century French Realism" lines 4–11.
6. Wong, "Manet's The Dead Christ With Angels," lines 1–6.

aspect of death is mixed with soil halftones, with dirty, black shadows which Resurrection will never wash clean."[7]

For us, to work within a relational context of seeing and valuing people, we must become adept at sharing an accurate picture of faith— what Christ means to us and what he could mean to someone else. This requires having insight to life and faith. It also involves going to the darker, authentic places of YOUR story . . . I realize how vulnerable that sounds; closing in on what is real in our lives sets off our own fear alarms! We don't have to bare our souls to save souls—do we? But that is precisely where we will need to lean if evangelism is to regain penetrative potency.

POSTMODERNISM AND THE CHURCH

To further our read on current culture, let's be clear on terms. It is customary to compartmentalize older "Moderns" from younger "Postmoderns." Allow me to point out that albeit, at the time of publication, anyone above the mid-forties could be classified as modern—everyone swims in a postmodern sea. In other words, you cannot avoid interfacing with a newer mindset. No one today thinks in the pure modern ways of the past. That day is over. The term "Modern-Postmoderns" is a more accurate depiction of our current societal state. It recognizes the pervasive influence of culture. Consider how the same media sources and current events have affect on all. Have you considered that in the next decade, anyone fifty and under will have grown up within postmodern values? I have consulted pastors still holding to modern thinking and who do not understand the change. No wonder their churches are in trouble; they have failed to read the signs of the times.

I mentioned earlier that art reflects cultural thought. At the turn of the century in 1999–2000 when people were wigging out over the potential threat of Y2K, the first *Big Brother* and *Survivor* episodes hit our television screens. Now shows with the reality angle have virtually taken over, garnering a notable 17 percent of the viewing market.[8] According to *Reality TV World*, by April 2012 976 reality-show-seasons had aired.[9] Daniel Petrie Jr., president of the Writers Guild of America-West said, "We look at reality TV, which is billed as unscripted, and we know it is scripted."[10] But

7. Hamilton, *Manet & His Critics*, 57.

8. Booth, "Reality is Only an Illusion, Writers Say," lines 31–34.

9. Reality TV World, Shows Listing.

10. Booth, "Reality is Only an Illusion, Writers Say," lines 10–11.

even though people are cognizant that these shows are manipulated and sculpted for the viewing audience, they still watch. Producers are smart. They understand postmodern viewers are apt to entertain media connecting in some way to actual experience. Just as the Realist painters rejected what did not represent everyday life, people today like bona fide stories because they can either relate to them or it gives them a sense of escape or superiority.

With mission, this overarching value displays in how non-believers smell out phoniness from Christians. Since we have sins too, they often think of us or even call us "fakers" and "hypocrites" to our faces. Notice it's not because we sin, but that we pretend not to. Sadly, the notion that we have to be above them is misguided. Postmoderns are not attracted to the idyllic with its "trying to look better than you really are" pretentiousness. Although strains of relativism (there are no ultimate truths to bank on) and tolerance (all culturally derived beliefs are equal) are trademarks of postmodern thought, relational authenticity is the critical factor for influence. In my experiences of working at a distinctively postmodern church, I can tell you that most are not hardcore bent on destroying truth, and will embrace the absolute claims of Christ if reached by authentic Christians. But, I suppose, there is the catch: What is an "authentic" Christian?

Many champion the notion of an exceptionally devoted life—a shining example; sort of like a new shinny penny. Is that what comes to your mind by the use of the word "authentic?" And is that what you think is necessary to reach people today? Do you have to be perfect and untarnished to be an instrument of God? If you have heard murmurs that God couldn't use you unless you are fully righteous, I have a sound byte for you to consider: "God hits home runs with crooked sticks!" In the Bible, he used an immoral woman to save a whole town! (John 4:27–31). God uses imperfect people all the time; we even have a name for them: Pastors! Look at me as living testimony. I am amazed how much God has used my life when I'm often a mess. Don't buy the lie of Satan, and perhaps some overly saved Christians, to keep you out of the game. If you are waiting to be fully maturated—you will never feel worthy. You don't need to have it perfectly together—who does anyways?

Don't get me wrong. I know the pursuit of righteousness is precious to God, essential to vitality, and a worthy biblical goal. You and I both need it! "Seek first his kingdom and his righteousness" is my life verse (Matt 6:33). Yet we must assess the degree of attainability and how much it currently influences culture. A comparative look into history can hone our assessment. In his classic book, *Evangelism in the Early Church*, Michael Green claims the moral quality of the early church attracted people who saw in Christianity a life not found elsewhere. He argues that virtuous living was key to legitimizing a new religion and applies this as a universal principle.[11] What his book does not address, however, is how postmodernism has altered the contemporary scene. So let me spice up the conversation by making a couple potentially controversial distinctions.

It is a mistake to assume that the influence formula for the biblical first century is the same as today. Doing so is not comparing apples to apples. The pre-Christian climate of the early church is entirely different than our post-Christian climate (other than a return to a very different form of pluralism[12]). It is not just that the gospel was at that time "breaking news." Nor is it the politicized Christian image damage that has accumulated over the years/decades/centuries. We must recognize that the cultural progression beyond modernity has interjected new values in ways unprecedented. This has led to a historic seismic-level shift, which has affected the epicenter of where influence resides. I am all for virtuous living, but am wary of how much it is emphasized for effective witness; as if our messaging is directly tied to sanctification levels. In striking contrast to the biblical period, we will find our raw humility, the honest confession of our sins and struggles, will gain as much credibility for the gospel now—as virtue did in the earlier time. This is such a radical change, that if not embraced, our influence potential dissipates (and usually by forcing us out the door!).

What I am saying here is counterintuitive to modern thought. Now twenty-two years into postmodernism (using Oden's Berlin Wall fall as an historic marker[13]), people still say, "If you live the spiritual life then others will *see* Jesus and come to know him." First, we have to ask if that is true? Are people drawn merely by our virtue? From my observations, it is increasingly rare. Still, some think if we can only get the church to be righteously perfect enough then we will reach our culture. I challenge this. It is a modern romanticized concept. Have we come to terms with the fact that even if we upped the ante and coerced every churched person to get it together to appear like superstars of righteousness—that that perception is not winning people. Today we have a plethora of "righteous churches" filled with supposed "righteous beacons" that are not reaching anyone.

11. Green, *Evangelism In the Early Church*, 183–85, 274–75.

12. Hirsch, *The Forgotten Ways*, 62.

13. Oden, "*The Death of Modernity and Postmodern Evangelical Spirituality*," 45.

Solid stats back this. According to the recent research by David T. Olson of two hundred thousand churches surveyed, 69 percent were either plateaued or declining.[14] This sobering snapshot looks even worse when you consider that it sits within a population expansion. As my wife says, "Our churches are nice, just not very effective."

Additionally, does not moralistic idealism set us on a slippery slope? Christians, even at their best, remain sinners. As the wise adage says: "The church is a school or hospital, not a museum for saints."[15] We have to be careful that Christian moralism (where the focus is on external behavior) does not hijack grace. This issue affects the church in many ways. I recently talked with a twenty-seven-year-old woman who described that when she shared her sin-struggles at church, they shut her down from talking. It was just not acceptable. Are you surprised to hear that she left in search of a "grace culture?" Her story is sadly commonplace. What have we done, if we have not helped people fall in love with Jesus and his grace? This inside issue also bleeds profusely into mission.

Unlike Jesus's type of sinner-supping love, Christian moralism drives a wedge between the very people God wants to reach. It creates an attitudinal divide. When the 2010 Lausanne Evangelism Conference convened, guess which issue topped the docket? Leighton Ford spoke these preparatory words: "When *so many* regard Christians as intolerant and arrogant, it could be a worthwhile advance if Cape Town 2010 emerged a church proclaiming and practicing a generous evangelism reflecting the generosity of the Lord Jesus."[16] Without humble recognition of our own sin and need we lack his gracious posture. We might not realize how subtly we distance ourselves (from "those" people). A Christian group gathers at a prison for a ministry day. Looking into their eyes, the mobilization leader refocuses, "Let's just remember that we are all prisoners." Only after recalibrating were they prepared to cross the grounds of a prison to do redemption work.

From an apologetic perspective, if we marry our message to spiritual superiority—will we not ultimately lose the point? Skewed or not, do not unbelievers readily know Christian failures: crusades, inquisition, southern racism, and public sins? If they looked hard enough at you and your church members, will they not see deficiencies? When righteous sanctification becomes the trump card for influence, we have only played into the

---

14. Olson, *The American Church in Crisis*, 132.

15. Shoemaker, *How to Become a Christian*, 88–89.

16. Ford, "A 21st Century Reformation," lines 24–27.

Devil's hand, as he will cunningly exploit our "romanticized" fallaciousness. Many are not impressed with the crosses hanging on our necks, and nor should they be, since we are all on a journey. God graciously takes people from where they are, muck and mire, and moves us all forward in a long gradual progression. As Christians we fail God all the time, but he still loves us. This "grace picture" is what makes Christianity unique over all other faiths, and impressive![17] It must remain our abiding message, posturing us to reach any and all.

To be fair, let's humbly acknowledge that the present behavior gap between Christians and non-believers is not always distinguishable. This does not mean there is no difference. It does mean we live amid temptations and share the same sin condition. Some data, like an equal divorce rate between Christians and non-Christians cannot be swept under the rug (The Barna Group had 33 percent for non-Christians; 32 percent for Christians).[18] Other studies reveal the "us-them" grand difference is not grand. Hugh Halter and Matt Smay in *The Tangible Kingdom*, tell of a survey given to both believers and non-believers which indicated both groups struggled in these same areas:

- Marriage
- Parenting
- Doubting God
- Trying to be a better person
- Pornography
- Materialism
- Forgiving people who have sinned against them
- Divorce
- Sexual problems within marriage
- Loneliness
- Substance abuse
- Alcohol
- Marijuana use
- Panic attacks

[Handwritten margin notes: problem is not to change our tactics, but to change our own behavior. bottom line change my relationship with Jesus. Teach spiritual purity first]

17. Keller, *The Reason For God*, 172–73.

18. The Barna Group, "New Marriage and Divorce Statistics Released," lines 27–29.

- Relating with children
- Anger issues[19]

The list suggests the church should be filled with messy sinful people to go with the righteous sinful people (a little humor there). Like the Realism painters, you may want to take a survey at your church to see what actually exists (if only members can feel safe enough to be honest—make it anonymous).

I recently witnessed the frontman of a popular Christian rock band apologetically explain that some believers were having marital struggles. Though his heart was right in doing this, I cringed at the aura of cover up that would be immediately felt by unbelievers present. What is wrong that he had to tip-toe into that? Why in Christian circles are we so afraid to admit our fallen reality? Does this omission not come across as disingenuous? Why do we feel like giving a scrubbed "romanticized" version of Christianity, when we live in a postmodern culture which values straight up honesty, transparency and truth? As you will see, what you communicate about yourself and the realities of your faith will touch every relationship and majorly affect your influence ability. Not only are non-believers looking for what is honestly real in you, they also are looking for God to intercede in their life-experience. In other words, they are drawn by how spirituality intersects at the darker nitty-gritty levels.

THE RAP ON GENERIC INFLUENCE

Playing devil's advocate, let us analyze what it would take to draw people through what I term "generic influence." Now don't get all hot in misinterpretation; I am talking about general, not personal, influence. Christian influence could happen wide-scale—if people perceived the culture as evil and lacking, and then observed how Christians are different, and how that benefits them. I believe that was the situation of the first-century Roman Empire that the author Michael Green describes. In that time, Christians demonstrated a higher level of morality over pagan practices, and a surprising sacrificial love for the common citizen.[20] The people of that time perceived both as benefits. By their service (ministering to the dying during two major epidemics), the early Christians actually improved life

---

19. Halter and Smay, *The Tangible Kingdom*, 166.
20. Green, *Evangelism In the Early Church*, 274–75.

conditions in the Roman world. This won citizens into the faith; we could say that righteous virtue won the day.[21]

Our current situation diverges, however, in that the culture is still evil and lacking, but people do not always see it as such, and our difference is not always noticed, and not generally perceived as helping them. Of course, this highlights where we need love and skills to interject. Granted, there are exceptions in certain environments where Christians stand out, such as compassion efforts to sin-saturated subcultures. Likewise, every once in awhile someone without any relational connection will show up at a church door desperately looking for hope. From the culture's view the candle in the window still exists—though it flickers faintly.

The formula for the culture to be drawn by righteous virtue alone is not there. Again, I am not saying we can't influence by how we personally live and love, but the impact from seeing our generic Christian lives is greatly diminished. For years, I have used a *Highway Video* piece called *Awe and Reverence* in training classes. Though it is now a bit dated (love that layered hair), it is an emotive piece that stirs the heart and conversation. The interviewer, Richard Greenwood, asks people at a mall what they think about Christians. In one section, he asks five sequentially, "Do you have any friends who are Christians?" Then following, "Do they seem different than non-Christians?" An Asian man sincerely states, "I can't tell *any difference.*" Another gal says she sees nothing different in her Christian friends but her "Jehovah Witness friend is more . . . polite." Three more state they notice nothing.[22] After the video I would ask what the class thought. People always say it made them sad. Sad they were outside Christ; sad they couldn't see Christ, or anything for that matter, in us. I don't think the *Highway Video* people set out for this capture; they just asked a question and it surfaced.

If we do not assess our rather anemic general influence, we can make a critical error of overestimating what others see when they may not see anything at all. Gulp! An overinflated influence ego kills mission. If we think that all we have to do is "show up" and "shut up"—we have failed to read our times. Unlike periods of the past, cultural conditions cloud the generic draw. With a skeptical, highly legalistic, media-saturated world it is hard to foresee this changing. If my assessment rings true, then we must face it. We are like a playoff basketball team that loses in a best-of-seven series and resolves, "We've got to make adjustments—our season is on the

21. Stark, *The Rise of Christianity*, 73–94.

22. Highway Video, "Awe & Reverence."

line." Christians, our influence is on the line—our friends are on the line—our culture is on the line. If they don't see it by merely watching, then how will they realize the significance of our faith? How do we get through?

INFLUENCE DIALING

Are you ready to dial in? What is not occurring generically can play out differently along intimate relational lines. Spiritual influence has moved from the general to the particular. People are more apt to be impacted by someone who gets close and personal with them; the time of missionality is upon us! This is because it is up-close that people can see what is real. Today, that is where spiritual influence lies—not the church institution as much as the church in a person. I am not saying the church gathered is not crucial, because the worship or group context often touches those who attend and is one of God's divinely ordained channels of impact and inclusion. Nor am I saying that proclamational preaching is not vital. Yet influence today resides in relationships. Research tells us people journeying into church and forward in faith do so on the elbow of a trusted friend.[23] The power of influence has shifted to the streets—hand-to-hand, face-to-face contact gives us the best chance. Isolated Christians influence no one. The church must become mission-focused since relationships form the lens to what Paul called "the mystery of Christ" (Col 4:3).

The question is how do we get near enough that they might peer in, look close and then closer, to eventually see the brushstrokes of our Master? As I moved mere inches from Leonardo's masterpiece, influence resides in close, because that is where people see authentic strokes: Real need. Real hope. Real lack. Real love. Real darkness. Real light. Proximity enables others to glimpse within humans something of God. You might ask yourself if non-believers are close enough to you that they could possibly see an authenticating faith? Take a moment to look at a simple equation:

Relational Closeness + Real Pictures = Influence

Under the shadow of the postmodern shift, if we are to have influence we must become effective at living and articulating a realistic faith by providing windows to see it "just as it is." We can allow non-believers to peer in by describing faith's meaning, and also by sharing our true lives. I call these two windows: *Description* and *Disclosure*. By the way, neither skill is

23. The Vision New England Study, lines 18–20; Stanley and Young, *Can We Do That?*, 1.

a strong suit in the church. Perhaps it tells us why the statistics are disturbing when it comes to true blue unbelievers making the journey to Jesus. In this assessment, I introduced the equation and its windows, which will be developed along practical lines in the next five chapters. Think with me as we build a foundation for greater influence.

So far we are gaining a cultural read. The next chapters, then, develop the character-related skills of Jesus within this framework. Amazingly, Jesus's manner of engagement fits perfectly for our postmodern pluralistic time. Each aspect of the influence formula will be essential to the results you and I seek. No one wants to spin wheels—we're aiming for spot on impact from our efforts! Having only scratched the surface, we must go deeper. As God works his brushstrokes into your life, he wants to display a real picture of faith to others. Relational closeness and the two windows of *Description* and *Disclosure* can showcase God's strokes. Both character and skills will be required. Let us now journey forward in developing how to do it.

DISCUSSION AND ENGAGEMENT

1. This chapter offers a read on our current postmodern climate. Did you agree or disagree with the author's assessment? In what ways?

2. What do you think people see from observing Christians in general? What about your life? Have you ever had someone become a Christian because they were impressed or moved merely by the way you behave?

3. Though this chapter only introduces the concepts of the two windows, can you see how it would help people if they saw our faith in its stark naked reality?

4. In your opinion, how would a Realism view of faith's meaning help people today?

PART I

Pattern:
Developing Spiritual Influence

4

The Signature

We need not wonder how God feels, because in Jesus,
God gave us a face.

—Philip Yancey

Stories carry content in meaningful and memorable ways. This might explain why we have so much narrative in Scripture. In essence, the Bible is a love story between God and mankind. The leading character, Jesus, is also famous for story telling. As the Psalms foretold, he would be a man of parables (78:1–2). Some of the most enriching, compelling and provocative tales the world has ever heard arrived from his mouth (although in our current age of biblical illiteracy many do not even know that!). Yet Jesus was so much more than an orator. He was not only a story-teller—he was a story creator. If we are to assimilate his skills, we will have to learn his ways of story creating, too.

Usually we remember biblical stories by words, but commonly with Jesus; they are weaved through a combination of words and action. By encountering people multi-dimensionally, Jesus takes influence into personal experience. We will see how much fuller his thinking is than ours. In this section, I will attempt to capture how Jesus wants to pry open our mental scopes to view evangelistic mission through a wider lens.

Corporate motivational speaker, Doug Stevenson, lists seven different story types that can be tapped into effectively:

Vignettes—A brief descriptive incident or scene.

Crucible—A severe test.

Imbroglio—An embarrassing moment.

Minerva—An ancient tale.

Credibility—Someone else's story.

Pattern—Multiple stories sharing a common theme.

Instructional—Back and forth from story to lesson.[1]

He identifies that three: crucible, imbroglio and pattern—can work as a "signature" story, one you can be known for, and even famous.[2] Don't we all have some embarrassing moments we do not want to be known for? I do! Stevenson singles out these three as particularly potent stories because you easily recall the details that make it come alive. One of these fitting the signature motif is "pattern." He describes this kind of story as having a repetitive structure, which builds suspense and anticipation. Usually, it is marked by a specific gesture, or phrase that becomes noticeable by the audience when it occurs and then reoccurs. He says, "It is a sophisticated technique which the best professional speakers use."[3] Not surprisingly, the disciples had this type of illuminating moment while observing Jesus.

Along the seaside villages of Galilee, in a dramatic fashion, they saw a "signature pattern" emerge when he performed two identically sequenced healings (Mark chapters 7 and 8). Imagine if you had a front-row side seat, the privilege of watching the Lord in action, and were responsible to portray not only what he did, but also how he did it—, for the whole world to see. If so, you'd be living in the shoes of the Gospel writers. The details contained in these texts were not lost on them, and must not be lost on us either. Should we not be doubly observant when the Scriptures reveal a signature move or course of action through repetition? Like Kareem's skyhook, Lebron's throwback slam, or Dirk's one-foot fall away, a signature move is something that consistently succeeds. We are going to discover a pattern that will work for our influence. Let's examine the biblical accounts back to back.

1. Stevenson, *Doug Stevenson's Story Theater Method*, 88.

2. Stevenson, *Doug Stevenson's Story Theater Method*, 89.

3. Stevenson, *Doug Stevenson's Story Theater Method*, 88.

> There some people brought to him a man who was deaf and could hardly talk, and they begged him to place his hand on the man. After he took him aside, away from the crowd, Jesus put his fingers into the man's ears. Then he spit and touched the man's tongue. He looked up to heaven and with a deep sigh said to him, "Ephphatha!" Mark 7:32–34.

Jesus did more than just touch

> They came to Bethsaida, and some people brought a blind man and begged Jesus to touch him. He took the blind man by the hand and led him outside the village. When he had spit on the man's eyes and put his hands on him, Jesus asked, "Do you see anything?" Mark 8:22–23.

These encounters bring to mind my junior high days when our class sought to simulate the disability experience. In an attempt to understand blindness, each student pledged to wear darkened goggles for a whole week. To get around at school a designated classmate played the seeing-eye guide. Next we rode around for a week in wheel chairs. It was a great idea, which had tremendous potential, if we didn't cheat. But that was a big "if." I cheated. Thinking back, it is safe to say, everyone did. The fact is that non-disabled people can't really know what it's like to be blind, mute, deaf, or crippled because the able-to see-, talk-, hear- or walk reality is always within reach. But that was not how it was with these disabled men. The reality of hearing and talking, or seeing was never within reach—not until this moment with Jesus. Suddenly, they are with a person who could change everything! Yet their ability to discern this was not automatic, nor were they properly prepared for all that Jesus intended to do.

WHAT'S IN A HEALING?

To appreciate what unfolds, please note that in all of Scripture we do not ever see a limitation to God's omnipotent healing power. We know from the story of the Roman centurion and the healing of his servant that Jesus's power was not tied to anything other than the Father's will (Matt 8:5–13). The centurion discerned what his Jewish followers had not: all that Jesus had to do was "say the word." He did not have to touch the individual, be present, or even be in the general vicinity. So why does Jesus not heal everyone from a distance? Why all these "steps" in the healing process? And why do we need to observe this pattern twice: once with the deaf and mute man, and then again with the blind man?

All the repeated detail is meant to create an imprint. In his soul whispering ways, Jesus is modeling spiritual influence for us. Let's unpack the sequence. Consider the deaf mute. Jesus takes the man "away from the crowd." He does this to create a meaningful moment. This was not going to occur in the middle of the chaotic mass. Therefore, he took the man out to a remote place. In the parallel passage with the blind man the witnesses document how Jesus takes him "by the hand" all the way "outside the village." Let us stop to reflect on our interactions with non-believers. Do we create personally intimate moments? Or are we always just talking on the surface level or in a group? Jesus gets them away where he can have a concentrated time that would have impact.

Separated and alone with the deaf mute, Jesus then puts his fingers in the man's ears. This physical gesture showed understanding to this man's plight. How much do we know of our friend's personal challenges? Have we gotten to that level? How many probing questions have we asked? Do you have a clue on what is really going on? Is it time to get that Realism-view of what has shaped your friend's disposition toward spiritual things? Jesus "got it" with this guy. The question is, "Do we?"

He then spits in his hand, and puts the saliva on the man's tongue. Gross! Literally swapping spit—it's like they kissed. Do you get how intimate this moment has become? Again, what about our connecting? Are we able to go to the more personal, even sensitive, places in the evangelistic journey with someone with whom we have enough relationship? Or are we just making a presentation—throwing truth their way with a take-it-or-leave-it attitude—don't really care to know you, no getting together, no phone call or text, no significant heart-relating. In stark contrast, this man is getting special treatment from Jesus according to his unique predicament. How do you feel when someone gives you special treatment? I know what it's like for me. It touches me deeply. "Wow! Someone really cares!" Mark, perhaps along with his co-writing influence Peter, picks up each one of these very personal actions of Christ and seems to be saying, "People, this is how it's done!"

From observing what has happened thus far, notice the experiential aspects. It is visceral. Physical touches. Earwax. Wet spit. Do we not need to think more of the sensory dimension with non-believers? What are they feeling in their time with you, and if applicable, the church ministry? There are many ways to bring them into the affections of faith. Do they sense your love? Are they experiencing inside your Christian community something markedly Christian? This, my friends, is not assumed. Many come and leave unaffected.

Another experiential angle to reaching people is to get them moving into service. Monique brought her non-believing neighbors along in her fight against human trafficking. By participating in the awareness-raising "freeze," campaign, the neighbors felt God's compassion. In the context of their helping she had conversations with them about faith. We need to think of what our friends are experiencing, not just our message.

After touching the deaf man's tongue, Jesus looks up to heaven. Though the deaf man could not hear, he could see how Jesus looked upward. Think of how this gesture lifted the man's mind spiritually. In this case, the gesture created expectation from God. Do we follow suit in enabling people to make the connection with how the God of heaven can help? Learning to connect people's needs with God's resources is directly related to sharing the gospel. This is a big one. The upcoming chapter "The Gospel Key" is devoted to giving you the skills on how to do this precisely! Rest assured, there's much more to come on this point.

Then Jesus sighs. Why does Mark include that detail? This human expression clearly reveals empathy. Jesus took the man's condition to heart. John Calvin noted: "this man's sorrows were his sorrows."[4] Let's stop for a moment to size up empathy. Some of us are more naturally endowed to be empathetic, while others, like me at times, can be downright cold-hearted! Though I have a feeler personality, I admit to not having much empathy sometimes. I have to slow down and work at it. I will always remember watching the movie *Titanic* in the theatre with my wife. During the freezing ice-cubed sinking scene with the two main characters adrift, holding onto life by a thread, I began commenting on the movie's special effects, "Look at how blue Leonardo is?" Turning toward her, I see she's sobbing. Later I realized, "She wasn't just watching Kate Winslet—she was Kate Winslet!" Here I am analyzing the movie, while she's in it! You get what I mean? Can you truly step into the shoes of the person before you? Do you listen with empathy to your friend's life situation, or feel a kindred spirit to their sin condition? When was the last time you spent time with a nonbeliever and afterwards shed a tear over their lostness? This is a profound experience—if we could only get there.

Last in the sequence of steps, Jesus shouts, "Ephphatha!" Certainly the person would have picked up his passionate intensity with this one-word exclamation. Obviously, he wanted something big to happen in this

4. Calvin, *Commentary on a Harmony of the Evangelists*, 93.

man's life! In Aramaic the word means, "be opened." If a mouth reader, then these would be the last words he read; or if healed instantaneously, the first ones he heard!

DIAGNOSING A SIGNATURE

So why all of these—count them, six,—steps? Could not Jesus have been more efficient? Six? Three would have been easier. Let's look closer. First, Jesus is not only performing a healing but something of far greater significance—the heart formation for faith. He didn't merely see physical limitations needing restoration; he saw water that needed to become wine. These back-to-back passages model a process of Jesus drawing people through his personal engagement into faith. If by chance you are still on the fence with this premise, take a look at what happens next with the blind man's partial recovery: "He looked up and said, "'I see people; they look like trees walking around.'" Once more Jesus put his hands on the man's eyes. Then his eyes were opened, his sight was restored, and he saw everything clearly" (Mark 8:24–25).

The first healing left the man blurry. Is that not strange? Why did this happen? Did Jesus need to heal in a progression by a second laying-on of hands? Are we to think God's omnipotence required a two-step process? More bluntly, was it too much at one time for the Creator, or did God have some kind of temporary glitch? A God-glitch? Or a divine dropped call? How do we answer these absurd- sounding questions? If you know the God of Scripture, you are now screaming an emphatic "No!" Our great God is not impotent in any way. Therefore, the only logical and reasonable reply is that Jesus did the miracle progressively to help the man's faith. In this case, Jesus actually ratchets down his power, leaving the healing momentarily uncompleted. Fascinating.

Is this not a picture of the non-believer's journey? Do we not also have to make adjustments out of sensitivity to an individual's intake ability? Have you ever found yourself with a non-believer, and thought saying, "Maybe I need to take this in steps, and break it down into bite-sized chunks?" Ever stop to think that maybe you need to invite him or her somewhere with you, or to hang with your group, before the next big conversation? By harnessing the incremental building power of process, Jesus deems the second laying-on of hands is when his full sight will be restored. What an accurate portrayal of the way it works. Starting in spiritual darkness, non-believers begin to see in a new way, but then must progress further to obtain true clarity, and we are right beside them playing a significant "hands-on" role.

Let me ask you: Does this pattern look anything like your evangelistic engagements? One of the most important questions regarding spiritual influence is not related to what you say, but rather how you walk alongside. Are you taking the actions to draw your friends into a projection towards belief? This is what we must learn. You can start moving in this direction by asking key questions:

- What would it look like to walk "hand in hand" together?
- What actions could take you to more intimate, meaningful levels?
- What experience can you lead them into that could be impactful?
- What kind of follow up conversations would benefit your friend's journey?
- What feeling could you invoke to connect with faith?
- What picture might you paint to give perspective on faith's meaning?
- What pinpointed challenge do they need to hear from you?
- What is the next step in their progression towards God?

Notice the holistic nature of these faith-formation questions. Jesus took into consideration the full view of each person's humanity: Mind. Feelings. Experiences. Responses. Relationships. Conversations.

It is a pivotal moment when we stop looking at mission along "telling" lines, and start engaging with the fuller faith formation process. One is impotent, shallow, and weak; the other a process experience that is deep, personally intimate, far more meaningful, and effective. If we are to have a chance at forming faith then, like Jesus showed us, we must draw close to a non-believer. Often this is something we initiate; others times God thrusts it upon us.

DIVINELY APPOINTED RELATIONSHIPS

"Can you please follow-up with a guy?" This is how I met Chris, a thirty-year-old not yet two years in the faith. Within a minute's time on the phone, I liked how personable, humble and clear he was in his thinking. After introductions he proceeded to tell the account of how he had become linked to a man with a scary story, both past and present. His friend Michael intimidated people by his look, words, demeanor and associations. The tattoos on his neck said: "Pure" on one side; "Evil" on the other. He was known as a Satanist—, angry at heart, filthy in appearance, racist toward people groups, and misogynistic toward women. Strangely, Chris met Michael in his apartment complex because Chris's girlfriend lived across from him. Other neighbors told Chris "not to make him mad" and "to just to be nice." Heeding their advice, but remaining intentional, Chris made efforts to connect relationally when they crossed paths, always being careful not to set his scary neighbor off.

One day when Chris walked by his apartment, he overheard Michael cursing his name! Terrified, Chris thought he'd better call to see what was going on, and discovered the ranting was not directed at him, but the man living above his apartment. Providentially, as it played out, the phone call moved the relationship further. Chris and Michael began a friendship. They talked weekly. Sometimes the conversation would take Chris away from time with his fiancé. Michael's drunkenness and the hole punching in walls frightened him, but he hung in there. When Chris told his mom that he was meeting with a Satanist, she became frightened, too, but after praying, she relayed back, "God told me not to be afraid."

Chris eventually learned Michael's story. He claims a pastor had sexually abused him when he was seventeen. "This is what happened to me—God doesn't love me." There was a residue of shame, and an underlying sense of unworthiness. He thought others were better than him, and at age thirty-four, he was now stuck in his ways. Chris intuitively countered the false thinking on many fronts. One day in a conversation, he was able to tell Michael, "I love you." Chris shared his own dark issues and what God was doing in his life. Then he said, "It would be amazing to see what God can do in yours." In the midst of all the darkness, Chris said there would be pinholes of light. One day Michael said, "I wish to have the peace that you have."

As I listened to Chris, it impressed me how he handled himself. I encouraged him to keep boundaries and avoid being with Michael during times of drunkenness, and yet, to not be afraid. "Greater is He who is in you, than he who is in the world" (1 John 4:4 NASB). We should not back down from the fight for this man's soul. As vile as his actions could be, his worth is beyond measure—Jesus died for him. I sensed God had orchestrated this encounter, and that a miracle breakthrough would come. Our church aligned its intercessors, and I began a relationship with Chris to coach him toward bringing Michael into the faith. I told him, "Reaching him may become quite supernatural. We will seek divine intervention at the right point, but now you need to explore his thoughts of God, find out what is there, and begin building the undergirding formation for faith."

The most significant part of it all was how Chris incarnated Christ's reach to Michael. While others judged, Chris consistently represented Christ's love. This was key. Where Michael might not get the message in any other means—through Chris it came. Again, I was so heartened that he didn't shrink at the challenge. Though at times it scared him, he kept walking forward. A Christian friend, perhaps wanting to protect Chris, told him that maybe someone else could now take things over. I countered this strongly. I told Chris that God had authored their connecting and that should not be taken lightly. No one could just replace him! He needed to follow this through. Chris was already not heeding the bad advice of his security-driven friend because he, too, sensed God in it.

YOUR STORY BOARD

Obviously, most relationships with non-believers do not have this kind of courageous intensity, but often can be mutually enriching. Non-believers can be a blessing to you in so many ways! Undoubtedly, they will help you grow in Christ's love. But the point is this. Unlike Jesus's highly intimate signature pattern that we have examined, Christians too often fail to get positioned for influence. In our highly relational world, influence flows through relationships. If we do not enter the world of a non-believer, we will not achieve God's mission.

In my faith-sharing skills class, I ask all participants to draw close with a non-believer in a committed consistent way. It is incredible to see what happens as a result when this happens. Before a recent class began, I received an email from a gal saying she did not think she could make the first session and was trying to decide if she should come to my class or her small group. I replied:

> Hi Lauren! Missing the first week would be okay. I could catch you up—and there is repetition with certain themes. Let me ask you an important question—do you have a non-believing friend or family member in your life right now? This class will impact their journey not just yours.[5]

Afterwards I thought, perhaps my reply seemed manipulative. You are nodding your head—yeah! But God knows, I was not meaning to be. I

---

5. Author Email Re: to Lauren Short, February 15, 2011.

was trying to be sensitive to what God wanted to do through her. What if God had positioned her to reach a friend and she was now taking the off-ramp away from that endeavor? She wrote back, "Wow, okay, I need to think about this." When a Christian earnestly steps up to engage with a non-believer, it is a big deal. In the spiritual realm, it is a moment that causes all heaven and hell to take notice. Think about that! If a believer truly walks alongside a non-believing person in a close way, God commonly does miracles! He is looking for his servants to step up into the life of another. Jesus held hands, walked, connected, touched, spit, empathized, demonstrated, inspired, prayed, cried out, and even healed people—all to help faith formation. What about us? Are you willing to become a story creator?

What was great about Chris was that his commitment equaled the task—neither intense fear, a gorgeous girlfriend, nor a persuading friend, altered his course of meeting with this man. With this kind of commitment the miracle could follow.

I will always remember the day one of my non-believing friends stopped our conversation mid-stream and said appreciatively, "You have met with me for seven months." I absorbed the sentiment of his expression and responded, "I will meet another seven months if that is what it takes for you to believe." It took all that time to create a scene where he looked into my eyes and knew I loved him. Two months later my former atheist friend did what his wife and others thought would never happen—he became a Christian. What if I had quit? Maybe God would have done the work through another, but I would have missed out on the fulfillment of an incredible story!

What I have found time and time again is the reason we are reaching so few is that we fail relationally with non-believers. I surmise that one of the great regrets of the Christian life will be the divinely appointed relationships we did not pursue. Strangely, many will say they were just too busy. But maybe, like Lauren, you didn't realize how you needed to get positioned for the divine script to unfold. Christian brother or sister, it is our time, and it is not too late! In the chapters ahead, I will tell the rest of the story with Chris, but for now I hope you think of the amazing stories God wants to write through *you!* Stories that are: rich, vivid, deep, powerful and inspiring. Ones that look like they were pulled right out of our Bibles . . . ones that you color with action and words . . . and ones that will make the annals of redemptive history. If you are truly willing to dive in relationally with a non-believer, your life can look a whole lot like the signature of Jesus. God waits with pen in hand!

DISCUSSION AND ENGAGEMENT

1. As you observe the number of intimate gestures in the two healings, how do your relationships with non-believers compare?

2. How can you deepen the intimate relationship between yourself and a non-believing friend?

3. Which of the steps jumped out at you as a way to help faith formation in the life of someone outside the church?

4. Do you think we would reach more people outside the faith if Christians were truly willing to enter their worlds? Describe in your own words why this is important.

5. Are you willing to commit to getting "close" with a non-believer? If so, please identify them by name and pray for God to use you in his or her life.

5

Window of Disclosure

Honesty and transparency make you vulnerable.
Be honest and transparent anyway.

—MOTHER THERESA

Out of the box in every way, the musical *Wicked* takes a twisted view of the Oz story. With creative brilliance, it pulls back the curtain on the stories of Galinda, the Good Witch of the North, and her friend, Elphaba, who will become the Wicked Witch of the West. The storyline surprises audiences by how it gives an endearing view of this villainous character. Causing birthing room shock and awe, the green-skinned Elphaba grows up in the shadow of her more winsome counterpart. The lyric writer captures the raw tenderness of comparison in the song, "I'm Not That Girl." According to mirrored reflections, she knows she was not born for "the rose" or "the pearl." Her difference, she fears, will mean the love for which she so desperately longs will always go to another. In her mind, this is the way things are. Heaven knows it's true—at least from her perspective.

A meaningful conversation with Sandals' church staff focused on the younger crowd. In reaching people in their twenties we pay acute attention to trends. Conversations periodically leak prevailing thoughts of this young adult group. Seeing Christians as the moral bunch sounded fine at first, until we followed the rationale all the way through. Metaphorically speaking, some had concluded that they have, like Elphaba, "green skin laced with sin." One man could not fathom how God could help him with his daily struggles. For that reason, he could never see himself becoming a Christian. Statistics reveal a solid percentage of young men scope porn every week. Not surprising for this age group, other behavioral discrepancies abound. What is most troubling, however, is that they distance themselves from church because they surmise that we don't have the kind of problems they are hung up on. Our skin is winsomely pure while theirs is dark green. Accepting this as the way things are, they view church as a moralistic club of which they do not belong.

Wearing my church consultant hat during a stay in the Northwest, I met with an associate pastor to develop a missional plan. The senior pastor had emailed his staff addressing the lack of growth, which has existed for about six years. In his memo, he stated, "Their church service was definitely not the problem." In other words, the real issue stemmed from the body's failure to invite. With the associate being over outreach, I probed of his efforts and he relayed a story. At Easter he had invited his neighbors (they happened to be AA recovery people) to church. They came! The pastor had pumped up his message, "The Hope of Easter," guaranteeing it will be a great morning for guests. But after the service, his neighbors pulled him aside and told him point-blank, "There was no hope in that message."

Knowing the pastor's preaching proficiency, I went online and listened for myself. Unfortunately, I had to agree. Not that the message was poorly or dispassionately delivered. It clearly communicated the historical significance of the resurrection and appealed for a response (though there was little). What it lacked, however, was something so essential that these unchurched neighbors would not ever return. Let me capture it in one word: *Disclosure.* His message shared nothing that touched his own need. The result left the associate wondering if there was any use in getting new people to attend. In his eyes, the prevailing pulpit sunk the plan before it began.

As I observed the pastor's message development, I saw how he could easily revolutionize his whole ministry. All he really needed was to be— smashed! Not with alcohol, but with God's humbling hand. If his pride could find its rightful place, he could open up before his people and have an amazing ministry. Isn't there a verse about that somewhere? ("Clothe yourself with humility before others and God will exalt you (*and your ministry too!*" 1 Pet 5:5, italics are mine). If that morning, he had filtered the Scriptures vulnerably through his personal need for Christ's grace and power—his people, including this precious-to-God guest couple, would have embraced it. They would have left saying, "Lord, I need you, too!" Or atleast, "Thank you for bringing hope and giving me some of it!" Instead, some left declaring they would not darken that church's door again. Unintentionally, they got talked down to. Looking into the despairing eyes of this associate, I now had the task of helping a pastor see his ministry in a new light—the light of his darkness! I mentioned the scenario to a friend who said, "That's a difficult thing to do." Oh boy was she right. How do you tell someone of high position that they need to humble themselves, and that personal pride is hindering Jesus's ministry?

Would you be shocked to hear that this is not an isolated problem? Another pastor told me of his extended search for a position. When he departed a past ministry he thought a church would just "snatch him up." He searched and searched and yet no one would pull the trigger on him. I asked, "Have you ever shared that experience with your congregation?" "Ever delve into those feelings?" Sadly, he had not ventured to this vulnerable place. I responded, "Do you realize how many identify with the feelings of being unwanted?" Who hasn't had it touch their life in some way: a firing, not being selected for a team, a "let's just be friends" talk, being left outside the campus clique, or just wondering if what you offer is valued? Why would he not want to connect deeply?

Though I began to feel sorry for myself over my consulting challenge, I couldn't help but dream of all the circles he might reach if only he could find the courage to be human. I envisioned him vulnerably sharing his life each week, and by doing so, inviting increasing numbers into their community. His church could be the place of honesty, hope and grace that people would never want to leave! But this seemed beyond his comprehension of what pastoral ministry was about. He wanted to preach the Word. In truth, he loved pontificating. And yet dying all around him were people desperate for someone to identify with their journey. That's what the two neighbors wanted. They came for hope.

PLATFORM STORY

What if we could orchestrate an exercise with all the pastors in the land—and launch it live on the web for all to see. It would require gathering every top leader, men and women, for one awesome event in a great arena. Perhaps one in Texas where everything is super big! Once we got everyone to arrive we'd have a moment of truth and say,

"What we want to do is honor those whose lives truly meet the title of "Pastor." So, what we're going to do is have you walk and stand on one of two platforms. Over here to the right, we have a large platform with a white cross. Over here we have another platform. If you have submitted yourself to Jesus with total surrender, your public and private life are tightly aligned, and you have lived above reproach in all ways consistently for all your pastoral days, then come stand on the white cross platform—we want to honor you!"

Christians from the entire world are watching this moment. As the cameras zero in on the crowd they are looking for their pastor. As this moment ensues— massive Facebook entries clog the web. "There's my pastor!" "Where's Pastor Sue?" "Why did Pastor Neil just leave the building?" "Why isn't Pastor Kim going over?" "I see Pastor Jones up on the platform—what is he doing up there?" Then several thoughtful observers notice something very interesting. As some make the walk with great distinction—others known to be godly men and women do not. People watching are confused. What is going on? Why isn't so and so going over? Many onlookers cannot imagine there could be sin in their life. Is something happening here that we are not getting? More Facebook flurries.

Believe it or not, many pastors from all the spectrums would first laugh, and then mourn such a spectacle. Though the culture celebrates pastors for their leading righteousness, let me break a bit of news—your pastor has sin! Oh yes. Just ask their spouse! What is wrong with *us to* think that anyone should stand on that platform? Who, honestly, has lived a totally surrendered life, or even come close? There is only one human who did. Why would anyone make a walk like that as if the description given fit? If you think my illustration is not pertinent then consider that I am currently trying to help a guy who is, in all practicality, standing on that white cross platform every week before his congregation. My crazy job is getting him to step off from that perched place so his church would have a chance to grow. As a little side note, Jesus had words for the Pharisees because they loved the places of honor at gatherings; they were platform standers (Matt 23:6).

Before we get all puffed up in judging pastors, we need to realize they are not the only ones who need to step down from their pedestals. This vulnerable character practice is critical for your evangelistic influence and mine. Within the postmodern time, stepping down is stepping up!

THE DOWNWARD WAY OF JESUS

As Christ imitators, have we truly followed his example when he stepped down to enter humanity? The Apostle Paul details what it took for him to leave his heavenly glory, "although he existed in the form of God, did not regard equality with God a thing to be grasped, but emptied himself, taking the form of a bond-servant, being made in the likeness of men" (Phil 2:6–7 NASB). Technically, scholars describe this act by its Greek verb as the "kenosis"—the emptying of the independent use of his divine capabilities. In other words, Christ did not hold onto his highly exalted position, but willingly surrendered himself to become human, submitting himself to the Father's lead. If we are Christ-followers, do we not also need to empty ourselves of something? From his example, should not our precious pride make the list? More pointedly, how can we be full of ourselves when Jesus emptied himself?

Less technical, yet still deep theologically, we also refer to this stepping down as "the humiliation of Christ." Coming down was a humbling act. Other monotheistic religions reject Christianity because they are not willing to accept that God would need to do lesser, undignified, human things like use the restroom. Yes, God lowered himself in a big way. It wasn't like he was afraid to get his hands dirty either. Though he remained sinless, Jesus dove headfirst into the sin-saturated lives of human beings. He still does! In addition to making an atoning sacrifice, he identified with our weak condition, which gave us a humanized picture of God (John 1:14). Strangely, we face a similar choice. If we are not courageously willing to lower ourselves through deeper levels of disclosure—others may not gain a glimpse of the divine. With already spiritually blinded eyes, non-believers cannot see behind the curtain unless *we* pull it back and allow them to.

I am not sure if you see how crucial this is. Let me draw the curtain on what I see happening in the thoughts of non-believers. Recently I had a conversation with a young gal about her spiritual journey. Prototypical of so many, she said, "I would never have wanted to go to a church—I wouldn't want to be judged. But your pastor spoke at my college and he talked about his struggles, so I decided to visit your church." Kristy ended up coming into the faith. Likewise, forty-something Mary Anne remarked the reason she came was because the church talked transparently on real issues. She, too, is now a Christian. Non-believer James tells me he likes church because the pastor has sins, too. I see this dynamic at play all the time with the unbelieving crowd. Do you? If we extended the platform story out to include the non-believer's chat room reactions, like a political focus group rating performance, white cross standees would receive dismal marks. Even anger! Can you hear the whispers under their breath?

Hearing a small group leader had led someone to Christ, I celebrated her evangelistic gift. She replied, "I've had quite a journey." I sat pondering her words, since I knew she was not referencing a long ago testimony, but rather, her assorted missteps. Your ongoing testimony with its fresh messiness has tremendous appeal. Non-believers today want to see how God is helping you now—not what he did years ago when you were unsaved. No doubt about it, disclosure reveals the kind of honesty and humility that attracts them to Christ.

Just as this window remained foggy to my minister friend, it is not clear to all. A speaker quips, "I was a sick, self-possessed liar and thief, filled with murderous intentions all before I was—eight years old." People laughed. The joke's punchline is that some Christians cannot point to a change that makes for a dramatic testimony. They even feel gypped, like they don't have the kind of story that would intrigue others. With all due respect to these stellar citizens, I find myself asking, "Why not?" I don't have a pristine story, but if I did, this is what I would do *for the sake of the gospel*. I would tell non-believers what they don't know. At the right moment within a relationship I would say,

> "I hope you don't think I'm this perfect person—I want you to know it isn't true. I am a sinner at the core of my being. Every day I need Christ because my heart and mind are not where they should be. I fight a battle with self-centeredness. At times I am loveless. Without God's help—where would my life be?"

This powerful testimony any Christian can render—just think how God could use it! By disclosing a real picture of human deficiency, Christ's light can suddenly be seen. Of course, sharing like that takes genuine honesty and courage. This skill requires your character. You might need to take the lion's walk down the hall from the classic Oz story. Courage!

Researcher Brené Brown's twenty-minute TED Conference talk on vulnerability resonated into a viral hit. How many viewers went online to hear this academic talk vulnerably about vulnerability's power? 50,000? 500,000? Nope. 5,000,000! Let that number sink in![1] In her subsequent address, she stated, "Vulnerability is the most accurate measure of courage."[2]

1. Brown, "The Power of Vulnerability" speech, June 2010.
2. Brown, "Listening to Shame" speech, March 16, 2012.

Most of us, corroborating, know that it is never easy to admit before another human being that we are: weak, fragile or broken.

This type of disclosure also requires self-awareness. If you do not see that you need Christ everyday, you will not convince others of your faith's relevancy. Outside of articulating your need, you may never get to what they truly need to hear.

DIALING IN DISCLOSURE

This essential disclosure window enables you to discuss faith naturally. Nothing is more instinctual than talking about *us*. Christians commonly feel awkward interfacing about faith and the gospel. If you feel like this—you are not alone. Well then, why don't you lessen the burden by talking authentically about yourself, and have it open up discussion on spiritual matters? This you can do. Not only is it more fluid, you will find that non-believers will listen if you share vulnerably. Don't you listen when someone pulls back the curtain to disclose something personal?

When I meet with pastors to grow their churches, I will at times discuss the four "S's" of disclosure: *Sin. Struggle. Striving. Story.* Each creates a window to deepen spiritual leverage. If you are to reach anyone you must first identifiably connect. Non-believers all share in the same four human dynamics, and in this way, they are no different than us. Each of us has sin. Each of us has struggles that make life difficult. Each of us has striving—things we are going after but have not yet achieved. Each of us has a story—the obstacles that God places before us to draw our character. As you pursue relationships with non-believers overtime, meaningful disclosure can happen in each category. Let us touch on the dynamics.

As a relationship grows there will be times to openly disclose an area of sin. This has numerous impacting results. First, they see you are a person of integrity. You are honest about your life, and do not hypocritically present yourself as better than you are. This registers huge influence points with postmodern people! Second, it models humility. If your friend is to find faith, they will have to embrace the same posture. By confessing, you show the way. They, too, have sins to own up to. At your moment of disclosure, many non-believers will be thinking about their stuff!

As a personal example, one issue I share with non-believing men is my struggle with lust that traces all the way back to my adolescent years. Does it shock you that both Christian and non-Christian men deal with lust? 95 percent of the time, my disclosure is something they know all about—causing them to be more aware of their sin. But I have Christ forgiving, renewing, and working in me. He is my hope and strength. When I disclose this with guys, I share that, too. Another sin I commonly share is my emotional reactiveness. For most of my married years, I have worn my feelings on my sleeve and talked too freely with the person I most depend on—my lovely wife. It has not always been healthy. I will disclose this selfish pattern with non-believers. They typically look on empathetically. Often it draws out disclosure of some issue in their life. When conversations go to these deeper places, something very significant happens. Can you see it? The relational bond deepens.

One day Janice visited Libby's home. Surveying how well kept and decorated it appeared, Janice complimented her. Libby, not wanting to give a false impression, grabbed her by the arm, walked over to a large bedroom closet to reveal the mountain of mess she had hidden. Janice was so taken by this vulnerable gesture that it led to a friendship, which later led her to faith. True story! C.S. Lewis said, "Friendship is born at that moment when one person says to another: "What! You too? I thought I was the only one."[3] You confidingly disclose and they reciprocate; which builds the kind of relationship where influence can occur. At the close of *You Lost Me*, David Kinnaman writes, "If you want to reach this generation, and every generation to come, go first with your story and give everyone around you the gift of going second."[4]

People sometimes ask me, "How do you lead so many to Christ?" I tell them that evangelism is not merely about making a presentation—it's about understanding spiritual influence. I know how to go to deeper places in relationships, where at some point, people will listen. Because I look at evangelism through the lens of gaining influence, I get positioned to reach people. One of my rules of thumb is to make sure the unbeliever thinks they are better than I am. Not hard to do! I do this often conversationally, honoring the non-believer for their qualities, while simultaneously using my shortcomings to shape perspective. This breaks down the walls and allows me to speak into their life later without impeding offense.

Some say, as Christians, we shouldn't talk of sin. I disagree for multiple reasons. The most obvious being that without sin there is no need for a Savior! Many religions and worldviews do not even address sin as a problem. Christians, however, live every day before a holy God. If you give it thought, ignoring sin keeps everything shallow. When I first became

3. Lewis, *The Four Loves*, 247.
4. Kinnaman, *You Lost Me*, 214–215.

a Christian I did not realize the degree of my self-centeredness. But the farther I ventured into God's light, the more darkness I saw in myself. You always know Christian maturity by deeper awareness levels. If you are growing in your relationship with Christ, you should be able see the sin latching to your soul. This kind of insight far exceeds those outside the faith. Let me ask, can you identify your own junk? If you can, then that marks maturity. Even when we are living above those things through Christ, we still have vulnerabilities and capacities for sin—don't we? This, too, we can share. Leveraging your personal insight will help non-believers see their spiritual need. Through disclosure, they can glimpse Christ's grace and renewing power. By seeing that you have to yield your weaknesses to him everyday, you give them a true picture of the Christian life. It begins their discipleship.

Qualifying, we don't always need to be disclosing (that can appear overly needy or that we're dumping our burdens on people). Pick appropriate moments when it's right to put yourself out there. I confess to failing in authenticity at times. It's often hard to be transparent. In an evangelistic class, Alex revealed that he didn't know if he wanted to follow Christ. Feeling the need to dig down to the heart motivation for faith, I went further into my story. Trying to plant a seed, I wanted Alex to see the end line of his pursuits—that he wouldn't find from the world what he was searching for. So I shared of when I lost focus in my midlife and started looking around for something else that did not even exist. I spoke generally of a season of drift.

Then when we broke out into discussion groups, non-believer Nicole asked me point-blank, "You were a senior pastor. Can you tell me what happened?" I told her about getting in trouble some years back and losing a position, but also of God's grace in carrying me forward (I tell my story in chapter 8). It was raw. I could not have felt lower in that moment as it stirred up old feelings of shame. I sat sulking in a depressed state, wrestling if I had only offered a bad example. Yet something very different was going on in her mind. She had asked the question for herself. This came out when she said, "We all get lost sometimes—I have been lost my entire life." Looking into my eyes she then added, "I want to stay after today *to become a Christian.*" In my humiliation came joy! She wasn't looking down on me, but rather saw honesty and the grace of God she longed for. That night she committed to Jesus and has become a beautiful Christian woman.

Because of my pride, I still want to look good. I am trying to put Christ first. It's an ongoing battle. Do you think it was easy for King David to talk so openly of his sins in the Psalms? (Pss 25; 32; 40; 41; 51; 69; 103). Have you ever considered that for many the Psalms are their favorite Scriptures? Identifying so intensely with humanity, the psalmist ministers deeply. They illustrate why the disclosure principle is so potent.

Sometimes you disclose, not a sin issue, but a life struggle. This, too, can be vulnerable since we don't ever want to look weak. Paul modeled this beautifully by disclosing the crazy intense times he and others faced. He told us while in Asia they "despaired of life itself" (sounds close to suicidal; 2 Cor 1:8–9). Pastors, it's possible you could use this! What if you talked about Paul at the edge of life, and then authentically shared, "I have had suicidal thoughts, too." (With pastors this happens on Mondays!) Then unveil how you got through it! You just reached a segment of the culture. Guess what? Non-believers randomly showing up with those hidden thoughts are coming back next week! Other times Paul shares his emotional state: "fear and trembling" ministering in Corinth (1 Cor 2:3) and "distress, anguish, and grief" while writing from Macedonia (2 Cor 2:4).

Tragically, in some churches if a pastor shared an authentic emotion such as "fear," like Paul did, they could be chastised or even removed, being dubbed as "unspiritual." This should not be! Paul's pattern provides insight on how to disclose. Anytime we share what we felt, it will color life's picture, and make our experience relatable. The listener may not have gone through the same thing, but can identify feeling-wise. Because Paul openly disclosed his difficulties, we see the Christian life is not problem-free. We share in life's troubles just like everyone. If we are careful not to give simplistic spiritualized answers, non-believers can glimpse how we walk through life with the Lord.

Another angle is to disclose something we can't achieve. This exposes our limitations. Being a church plant, the Sandals congregation had met in a dozen different locations before getting its own building. When the timeline for leaving the rented facility and the move to their new place did not align, Pastor Matt Brown shared his anxiety. The fact the church did not have a place to meet was killing him. He had tried to put it at God's feet again and again, but he just couldn't give it over. He said, "I can teach others how, but I can't do it myself."[5] Does it surprise you to hear that this moment captivated a massive room? As he divulged you could hear a pin drop. A pastor at the top, with thousands under him, just admitted he was failing in faith, and utterly powerless to do anything about it. Did people leave disheartened? Not at all! People left with hearts broken wide

---

5. Brown, "Gospel of John" message on February 7, 2010.

open—crying out to God from the bottom of their insufficiency. Everyone related in some way. Non-believers experienced something so honest that they left determined to bring their friends. People still talk of that message a year later.

What have you tried but have not achieved? How about loving a hard to love person? Forgiving someone? Losing weight? Surrendering your materialistic dreams? Giving up a coveted habit? Getting over it? Filling the void of a personal need? Holding to God's Word? Growing God's church? Reaching a significant goal? Are you willing to expose your deep insufficiency and desperate need for grace? It will be powerful when you do.

As we disclose, we let people into the story of our lives. Story has everything to do with the obstacles before us. In 2 Corinthians 12:8, Paul talks about his "thorny" pain. It has become so great that he asks God to remove it not once, not twice, but three times. Can you feel the dramatic tension he is having with God? This is Paul disclosing his personal story. It's not your story or mine; the principle he teaches may apply to us, but this was his story. It was his "thorn in the flesh." We each have our own divinely written script. Story has everything to do with our dreams and their inherent conflicts. These are the things, like Paul's thorn, that come from God to deepen our dependence and spiritual character.

What have you had to deal with and overcome? If you are willing to disclose your story, it will open up all sorts of influence possibilities. In the upcoming chapter on the lines of spiritual dialogues, I will show how to develop a "story-line" conversation with a non-believing friend. There is also a whole chapter on how God wants to redeem our brokenness. But for now, I want you to see that your story is one of the ways to utilize the disclosure window.

The Apostle Paul's Disclosure Window		
SIN	*Sin-Nature Vulnerabilities*	Rom 7:14–25
STRUGGLE	*Life Difficulties*	2 Cor 1:8–9; 1 Cor 2:3; 2 Cor 2:4
STRIVING	*Limitations to Achieving*	1 Thess 2:17–18; 2 Cor 1:23–2:2
STORY	*Overcoming Obstacles*	2 Cor 12:6–10; 2 Cor 6:3–10

THE DISTORTION ISSUE

Let's readily admit that it feels risky to expose our weaknesses. Perhaps that's because we want to show ourselves as exemplary and falsely think our witness depends on it. We learned to tell our testimonies as if they were complete: This is how I was before Christ, and now I am like this. Ta da! As if it's done. But the reality of Christian growth is a progressive journey. If sanctification is a life-long course filled with ups and downs and divinely orchestrated events, then should that not also be our testimony? How amazing that God faithfully bears with us! Is that not part of the gospel? Also, if we do not disclose then we have made ourselves appear better than we are. Please realize that according to postmodern values, pretense is the greatest sin of all. Do you feel the tension of this spiritual Catch-22?

In 1 John 1, we see a grave consequence to denial. If we deny, we distort God's character; making him a liar (1 John 1:8). Most agree with this at the salvation level, but do not take it into their Christian experience, where denial of sin distorts the truth about us, and the gospel message. Two fatal perceptions arise. Non-believers either conclude, they cannot be perfect like us (being "green-skinned," they do not belong to our group), or we are not as perfect as we say we are (and they do not want to share in our hypocrisy, labeling us "fakers"). Not taking disclosure seriously can unintentionally distort our message in serious ways. In addition, if we do not courageously open up, relationships remain shallow. This creates a stinging blow to influence. Following the pattern of Jesus means getting close relationally to give faith formation a chance.

Kristina had come to church only one time before landing in our *Steps to Faith* class. As seven of us gathered, I knew she was the sole non-believer. Looking around at my veteran team, I thought I'd spice things up a bit, "Let's go around and share something that others don't know about you." In my mind this was just an icebreaking way to create conversation. Nathan shares that he plays guitar. His wife Ashley discloses that she is a health nut. Then, it was Kristina's turn. "My husband and I are drug addicts. He is now in a detention facility. But it is good. I had asked God to help us and he answered my prayer by taking my husband away. That is why I am here."

Now put yourself in the shoes of the person next in the circle. How would you follow that? What words would proceed from your lips? "I'm a Yankees fan." "I do cross-stitch." "I like Italian food." I watched the middle-aged man struggle with what to say. Then, he dug down, and said, "Alright, something you don't know about me is that I have a real problem with anger; I mean the wanting to 'take you out' kind. There are times when I just get livid with my wife and kids." Running into him later, I pulled him aside and said, "I am so proud of you! You could have played it safe, but instead stepped down for her. It was beautiful! She had taken a step toward church and you met her right where she was. I knew she felt accepted— like she belonged. You could see it on her face. Because of your courage, we became a family in just one meeting!"

His disclosure set in motion a domino effect within the group bringing out all sorts of revelations: Drug addiction. Witchcraft. Debauchery. More drug addiction. Each story telling her she was not alone. Three weeks later she shared some personal challenges and asked for my phone number. As we punched in each other's contact info, she knew we would be there for her. That day she came to Jesus.

THE POWER OF REAL PORTRAIT

It is unfortunate Christians have bought the notion of needing to have it all together before they are able to share Christ. The idea of looking good was not the way the church began. It is amazing to see how far we have drifted from divinely laid roots. Let's step back and consider the lives of the founding pastors. The first is Peter. As a man used greatly of God to lead the Jerusalem church and forward the gospel, Peter also had character flaws. Do you remember his statement to Jesus: "I will lay down my life for you" (John 13:37). He thinks he is this super-courageous, loyal guy. Not only is he delusional, Peter is out of control. He does crazy, violent things in the heat of the moment like in the garden when he decides to slice up the temple guard. Missing the man's head, he takes off an ear with his sword. Anger freak. Then, when pressed, he makes three blatant denials of the Lord he loves. A little servant girl's inquisitiveness lands the question that takes him down. Notice that Peter fell after walking with Jesus for three years—it was a post-conversion sin. Depression follows, as it always does when we fail. What does he do next? The camera shot takes us to the beach, now look at him—he's quit and gone back to fishing!

What is the real picture of Peter? He's a prideful, unstable, angry, disloyal coward and denier of Christ. Quitter. Can you relate in any way to him? Many of us do. His life with all its faults and failures looks amazingly similar to each of ours. Strangely, his story demonstrated God's amazing grace. In his book, *Jesus and the Eyewitnesses*, Richard Bauckham claims

Peter must have chosen to personally disclose the "denial" details.[6] How else would we have known? By humbly revealing his failure, he has ministered to us all. His choice made it possible to fathom what God's grace could be. If Peter failed terribly, and God restored him, then that means grace can cover my life as well! This is the leader of the whole movement—what an intriguing and unlikely picture of one of the most influential leaders the world has ever known. It begs the question, "What about our lives?" Do non-believers see the restoring grace of God when they look at us? Do they see our need for his grace today?

Traditionally, we have thought of God's light shining from good deeds. Yet with careful attention to Jesus's words there is an even bigger idea, "For whatever is hidden is meant to be disclosed, and whatever is concealed is meant to be brought out into the open" (Mark 4:22). It suggests the hidden mystery of Christ should be brought out into the light and displayed for all to see. From the very words of Jesus, I see the disclosure window. I am willing to use my darkness to backdrop his light, because in the end my story doesn't matter, but his does. Who really cares what others think about me? It's how they see him that's crucial!

On another line, disclosure showcases God's greater story. Consider that Peter's ministry should have closed with him going back to his old ways, living out his remaining days pulling in fish. Too bad he didn't measure up, some would have said. But his failure was not the end of the story with God, who is always bigger than our blow-its and far more gracious than we can imagine. In fact, Peter is at the place of throwing in the towel, and Jesus is ready for him to lead a world-changing movement. Such are the redeeming twists and turns of God! Just one more needed step to set that in motion. Jesus must get him back in the game. So just when Peter is once again finding his groove with fishing, Jesus shows up at the seashore (John 21:1–19).

"Hey Pete. What's happenin' man? Catch any big ones? I came to have a little chat—can you give me a sec to ask for your life? You see I am getting ready to begin my church, and need someone to be in the lead role. Guess what Pete, you are the guy—my one and only choice."

Still fighting his failure, Peter responds, "There is someone else more worthy—isn't there? One who is more qualified, who has lived a purer life and would represent you better?"

"Not so, Pete. You are the most qualified. I have prepared you for this. Everything that happened, all of your story with all of its missteps will be

---

6. Bauckham, *Jesus and the Eyewitnesses*, 178–79.

used according to my plan. And Pete, I don't work through prideful vessels, only humbled ones. Welcome to the ministry of my Spirit, bro. Now I need you to get ready to go fishing for men. And listen up, Petros, the catch is going to be great—so get ready to rock this world!"

If you have experienced the hand of God humbling you, stripping you back, breaking you down, exposing your limitations; then recognize his preparation. He must make his messengers portrayers of grace. If no real humility exists—chances are low others will see Jesus. If, however, you know your true need and are willing to disclose it—God can use you to reach into many lives. Like Peter, he will magnify a harvest one hundred fold through you.

Consider also Paul. The majority author of the New Testament, formerly Saul of Tarsus, described himself as "a blasphemer, persecutor, and a violent man" (1 Tim 1:13). Innocent blood stained his hands. Paul was like Javert, in Victor Hugo's masterpiece, *Les Miserables*—the chief inspector going after Christians, punishing them and voting for their deaths. When he stood in front of the Roman authorities, Paul tells his dark story (Acts 22:4–5). In 1 Timothy 1:16, Paul embellished his perspective, "I was shown mercy so that in me, the worst of sinners, Christ Jesus might display his immense patience . . . " How else would infinite grace shine forth if not displayed from the backdrops of his followers? With Peter and Paul, God's grace was incomprehensible.

Could God have used them so greatly without their disclosure? Is it by coincidence that the two prominent leaders of God's movement are known in this way? As the Apostle John wrote, "The light shines in the darkness" (John 1:5). I wonder whose darkness he wants to shine out of—now?

DISCUSSION AND ENGAGEMENT

1. What do you think of non-believers concluding they do not belong because we do not have sin? Are they right?

2. The author talked about Christians who present themselves as better than what is true. Why do you think the church struggles with self-exaltation?

3. Do you have a story of disclosing something real with a non-believer? If so, what was his or her reaction?

4. If you are reading the book with others, break into groups of two or three and practice disclosing in one of the four ways: —Sin, Struggle, Striving, or Story. —Remember to disclose in such a way that the listener can glimpse what Christ means to you.

5. How does it make you feel to consider that the two most prominent people in the New Testament were known for their sins?

6

The Gospel Key

Give me a lever long enough and I shall move the world.

—*ARCHIMEDES*

In the past three decades, the culture's awareness of autism has increased with the escalating number of affected children. The U.S. ratio is now one in eighty-eight kids.[1] On the high functioning side of this disorder is Asperger's Syndrome. These kids are often brilliant thinkers, but prototypically struggle verbally and socially. One pattern is the inability to pick up "social cues." Where other children naturally absorb social behavior, children diagnosed with Asperger's do not, and need specific instruction on what is appropriate in social settings.[2] This syndrome has touched many families and we are one of them. Having an Asperger's child emphasizes the value of reading people. From a family who's lived it, how important is reading others in relationships? It means so much—almost everything, in fact!

Today's NFL quarterbacks are not merely physical specimens with strong throwing arms, but play callers, game-plan executers, and pre-snap play adjusters. One of the most critical aspects of quarterbacking is the

1. Center for Disease Control and Prevention, *Prevalence of Autism Spectrum Disorders*, 7.

2. Attwood, *Asperger's Syndrome*, 15.

ability to read defenses. For the casual observer, one may not realize all that is done to help quarterbacks make a "read." Players are sent in motion to force defenses to adjust, which gives information to the quarterback. Defenses initially disguise their alignments, so quarterbacks run snap-counts deep into the play clock looking for clues from the final positioning. If a quarterback reads a defense correctly, he either knows where to attack and sends signals to teammates through verbal commands or physical gestures or audibles to a new play. Future Hall of Fame quarterback Peyton Manning does not have the best arm in his business, yet his ability to call the game has made him a football legend. How important is it for quarterbacks to read defenses—often it means the difference between winning or losing.

The recent Iraq wars and the fight against terrorism have given everyone an education of military operations and the importance of reconnaissance. In the field, the right information is the most valuable commodity to commanders, because if they have it, they can make good decisions. Without it, they are blind to what is coming at them. Today, we have million dollar unmanned drones and satellites, and there are plenty embedded human eyes on the ground, all to read and report what is happening. How important is good reconnaissance for a battle? It's often a life or death matter.

If the ability to get a "read" is critically important in almost every field, why would it not be necessary in the realm of spiritual influence? Reading people has become increasingly vital in our skeptical, multi-worldview age. You may have a neighbor who comes to your home chomping at the bit to learn Christian truths. If you see that kind of hunger, your role is to explain the purpose of God's intervention, and when the person is ready, lead him or her to faith. Increasingly, however, that scenario is not occurring. In the context of relating with outside-the-faith friends, we intuitively know if we tried to present the basic truths it would come across as forced, or maybe even worse, be completely ineffectual. Although we have something powerful to share, our words can end up landing like a big dud. The effort goes nowhere and we wonder why.

Part of what is wrong here is that we are "presenting" and not "reading." The well-intentioned presenting idea violates the first principle of evangelism, which is *starting where they are, not where we are.* "Reading" will enable you to see where a meaningful conversation could develop. How does one do this? Keep reading.

In Christian circles throughout the modern era, the presentation model has taught us to offer the same message to everyone. However, as stated previously, this approach was not the practice of Jesus, who customized his words based on each individual's need. Have we sufficiently seized this skill that permeated his ministry so distinctively? When we examine church history, uniformity was not the mode of the early disciples either. Even in its infancy, the Christian movement learned the gospel message did not resonate in the same way with all. To appreciate this dynamic, and learn a valuable new skill, let us go back and trace the initial flow.

FIRST CENTURY FLASHBACK

Eclipsing the per-acre per-head ratio for the modern city of Chicago by ninety-six, one hundred fifty thousand people pack two square miles of real estate. Single room flats built on top of each other house whole families. Splattered throughout the homes are a few official state buildings, baths, and many religious temples, including a prominent one dedicated to Jupiter. Though aqueducts channel fresh water, the ethnically diverse populace relies on stagnant cisterns, leading some to drink only what is boiled. Trash and debris fill the narrow streets adding to the reeking smells of emptied chamber pots. Signs of disease mark faces and bodies. Welcome to first century Antioch, the burgeoning Roman city, so strategic to Christianity's expansion.[3] In this crowded messy mix of races and religions belie the birth pangs of a movement. In the hearts of a few Christ followers, the desire for inception kindles; but how does a Jewish concept "take" in Gentile-minded soil?

To answer this question, we must first deduce the prevailing first-century psyche—their unique starting point. Similar to the magnetism of America, the Roman Empire began as a haven for outcasts, a land to make a new start. Being a gathering place from various regions, the empire became a religious free market environment. Temple systems arrived with their gods from many parts of the globe: Isis, the "Savior goddess" came from Egypt. Jupiter, Venus, and Apollo originated from Greece. Cybele, the mother goddess with her reborn companion Attis, stemmed from Phrygia (what is now Turkey). The secretive sun god Mithrael, whose origins remain mysterious, surfaced to become lord of the Roman armies. The cult of Bacchus had oriental Grecian roots tied to a particular priest.[4]

3. Stark, *The Rise of Christianity*, 149–56.

4. Stark, *Discovering God*, 125–55.

There were others too, and of course, the empire also had Jehovah, the God of Israel, who were well known in that era as a people with a distinctly monotheistic culture.

Each religious system provided teachings, gatherings, and rituals intended to bring blessings from the gods. With private funds the people built numerous temples as the new faiths arriving in Rome were exceedingly more vigorous in attracting loyal followers than the traditional temples. Stark writes, "The new faiths appealed directly to the individual rather than to the community, linking faith to the conscience. They satisfied the intellect by possessing written scriptures and by presenting a more virtuous portrait of the gods."[5]

It is inside this diverse and robust religious climate that the gospel is born. The initial messaging thrust focused narrowly on the Jews. As recorded in Acts, Jewish converts were doing all they could to convince their brethren that Jesus had fulfilled the prophecies and was indeed the Messiah. Literally thousands of Jews became Christians in response to the first messaging waves. But the gospel was not only for them. God had to show up in creative ways to break a prejudicial exclusivity. By pouring his Holy Spirit upon a Roman centurion's household coupled with Peter's non-kosher food vision, God opened eyes to a larger picture (Acts 10). He intended his gospel to penetrate all parts of the world. With the cross God had turned his mission strategy on its head; instead of drawing through one nation, he would now send it through all. This radically adjusted strategy naturally created a pragmatic problem.

A NEW MESSAGING CHALLENGE

The message "Jesus is the Messiah" worked for Jews of that day. It was a clear declaration of good news for a people looking expectantly. Yet it lacked meaning to non-Jews, who were not anything akin to their Jewish residents. Having a distinct Greco-Roman culture with its own religious systems, they thought differently. Besides a slight percentage of converting Greeks, the Jewish people weren't reaching the rank and file Roman, who did not have good feelings toward Jewish culture with its "circumcisional" expectations. Some Romans became "God-fearers" because they saw in the Jewish faith the true God, but held back from full conversion. Thus, an impetus for a distinct Gentile message pre-existed.[6]

5. Stark, *Discovering God*, 128.
6. Green, *Evangelism In the Early Church*, 115–16.

Opportunistically, then, in the neonatal phase of the church, Christians began contemplating a new "penetrative" message. It may have originated from the disciples who had traveled by sea all the way from Cyrene to Cypress; that would have been a conversation as big as the Mediterranean! (Acts 11:20). Perhaps it surfaced casually as believers reclined to dine together, or spilled out from backroom chatter. Although we do not know how, we do know that a message surfaced that would "take" in the Gentile world. The phrase "Jesus is Lord," referenced in the Romans 10:9 confession, became the cry of the new push. "Some of them, however, men from Cyprus and Cyrene, went to Antioch and began to speak to Greeks also telling them the good news about the *Lord Jesus*" (Acts 11:20). "Jesus is Lord" was a relatable, laser-focused message to the empire's highly religious culture. It took a crucified man and exalted him above the pantheon of gods! It meant many things: Jesus is Lord over the false lords, Lord over the demonic spirits, and Lord over sin. Several esteemed scholars including Michael Green, Charles Van Engen, and missional designer Alan Hirsch give special attention to this development.[7] The early Christians essentially rekeyed the gospel to open the Gentile door. Same truth, different packaging. The messaging shift worked with massive results! When the Gentile mission far surpassed that to the Jews, our New Testament takes on a sudden Gentile tone. The Apostle Paul in the book of Romans uses "adoption," a sole Gentile practice (Jews did not adopt because of the blood lineage value) to describe God's relationship with us![8] (Rom 8:22).

The history is intriguing—the implications even more so. The expansion showed how the gospel adapts. What we see happening at a macro scale between Jew and Gentile in the first century, can also occur on a micro scale with individuals and groups today. In other words, at the practical interfacing level, the gospel is adaptable to people's lives. This does not mean we are changing its core truths. That is what we must never do! I recognize the gospel is ultimately about the cross and resurrection (1 Cor 15:1–3). Yet the Scriptures reveal a preceding key to the cross. Just as the early Christians tailored the message for the Jews, and then distinctly for the Gentiles—you, too, can tailor it. In fact, "resonation" is one of the best ways to chart the gospel's movement. Let me amplify this thought.

We are accustomed to think of the gospel as salvation, however, look at the initial messages: "Jesus is the Messiah," and "Jesus is Lord." Neither

---

7. Green, *Evangelism In the Early Church*, 115–16; Van Engen, *God's Missionary People*, 92–94; Hirsh, *The Forgotten Ways*, 24–25.

8. Green, *Evangelism in the Early Church*, 117.

phrase is directly about the cross. Yet when a Jew accepted the declaration "Jesus is the Messiah," they would believe in what Christ had done on the cross for salvation. Similarly, when a Gentile accepted the message, "Jesus is Lord," they would trust in his sacrifice and be saved. Consider the following graphic, which illustrates the order it occurred. Observe how the relevant message went first, then the arrow points forward to the cross.

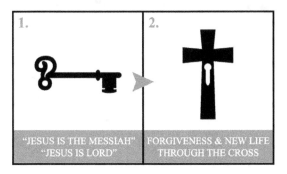

The structure illumines a way to focus spiritual dialogue; each person has a signature message resonant with him or her. It is how the gospel speaks to his/her particularized situation. When we begin sharing, *this is our starting point*. Relevancy goes first. Notice Jesus himself modeled this with the Samaritan woman, Nicodemus and many others. In his famous Luke 4:18–19 pronouncement regarding his gospel ministry, we see a whole list of keys:

> The Spirit of the Lord is on me,
> because he has anointed me
> to proclaim good news to the poor.
> He has sent me to proclaim freedom for the prisoners
> and recovery of sight for the blind,
> to set the oppressed free, to proclaim the year of the Lord's favor.

At his mission's outset, Jesus expressed the gospel by its benefits: Freedom, recovery, liberation and favor. We can easily observe from his interactions how he did not always talk of forgiveness. You would think, he, of all people, would be constantly telling others about their dire need for justification, and make his case for the cross with theologically developed concepts. Yet in his "out of the box" way, he does not do this. Rather, he relates along personal storylines, connecting dynamically within each group's unique cultural context. Although it is the cross that will bring about spiritual blessing, Jesus knew the conversation began elsewhere.

If you learn to utilize "the key," it will make it easier for you to engage in spiritual conversations. The "relevancy first" approach focuses on creating a meaningful glimpse of faith, enabling people to see what it could be for their lives. In a relationship context there is the right time to give attention to the cross—usually later. Now granted, if you just said the same thing to everyone it would be simpler, because you do not have to think about it, just say it. You will also find it ineffective. Let us remember the reason the seeding of the gospel is not simple is because it is so significant! Beginning where they are will enable you to reach more people. Your first step is not telling people "Jesus died for your sins," but rather, asking the question, "How could a relationship with Christ be meaningful to my friend?" How would *they* perceive it as "good news?" This honors them as individuals by recognizing their unique journey.

DISCONNECT WITH THE GOSPEL?

Getting a "reading" on a conversational starting point is necessary so the "good news" is able to get a hearing. As Christians, one fact we don't like to face is how our beloved salvation message is so easily brushed off. It might do us a lot of good to see how non-believers perceive our messaging. Unlike us, they cannot appreciate our eternal perspectives. Living in the present, they think of the issues before them; and most are not moved by our talk of a "personal relationship with God" either (unless they come out of a highly ritualized religious context where "personal" could be their key!) At the risk of sounding sacrilegious, have *you* ever experienced "disconnect" with the gospel? I'll confess that I have.

One day, two Christians from a local church came to my door. They proceeded to tell the forgiveness message to me. I am slightly reluctant to admit that although I love the Lord and his gospel with all my heart, at that moment, what they said was not relevant at all. I had pressing needs. If they had been able to listen to what I was going through, they may have been able to show how Christ could be the answer, and at that time, I would have listened to every word! But they were stuck on the one-idea-one-tune gospel. They failed to see it as the full symphony it is to the world. Can you see why Jesus began by uttering words that landed in the sweet spots of people's lives?

Observe how Jesus engages the Samaritan woman (at times I will refer to her as Samantha). He doesn't tell her what she needs; he draws according to her need. Jesus said, "If you knew the gift of God and who it was who asked you for a drink, you would have asked him and he would have given you living water" (John 4:10). The assumption from his words is that if she knew the benefit offered she would seek it. This is Jesus's use of a key. I prefer the "key" metaphor in concept (though "gift of God" is used here). A key opens something. It is a message that has the ability to lift the pin-tumblers inside a person's heart. When Samantha heard the words "living water," it resonated in and with her big-time. She wanted it!

This same spiritual-leverage is attainable for us. Since, however, we do not have Jesus's omniscient sight into human hearts, we have to dig out what came naturally or should we say supernaturally to him. But the clue is found in his words: "If you knew the gift of God . . . " Determining the uniquely personal "gift of God" will enable you to draw your friends. For Samantha, she had repeatedly journeyed for water, and sought fulfillment through many men, but still had an insatiable thirst. Knowing this, Jesus offered to quench the unmet desire of her soul! Nicodemus's key was different, but "living water" was hers.

In our highly individualized world, you must assess what precisely the gift of God is for your friend? Picture in your mind a non-believer. Maybe it's a neighbor, workmate, friend, or family member. Do you know what their key is? It will be something that draws their desire because, like Samantha, they will see its value. Usually, we don't know what it is at first. The challenge, then, is reading their life-situation to decipher a specific spiritual benefit. This dives us into hearts as we zero in on needs, drives and dreams.

READING THE KEY

Learning this practice is analogous to a childhood exercise. Growing up we all played a version of "connect the dots"—where following a numbered pattern with a pencil or crayon revealed a picture. If we aim to increase evangelistic effectiveness, we need to become adept at helping others connect the dots to spiritual meaning. Let us now sharpen this ability by attempting to read keys for several life scenarios. Are you ready?

What if your non-believing friend was a new mom? What is the "gospel key" to her? I asked this in a class and someone said, "Rest!" People laughed. I responded with David's words: "The Lord is my shepherd, He makes me lie down in green pastures." That was a good try. Moms do need rest—they are exhausted chasing around those tireless tykes or as my friend says "little terrorists." Though the key could possibly be deep rest, I question if that message is enough to draw most new moms toward faith. It might not be her "key." When I think of a new mother, I see the concern she has for her child. This is a propelling innate force. I recall the newspaper story of a Big Bear mom who got pinned by her overturned car that had rolled down a bank and landed in a stream. When the authorities arrived they found her dead with arms locked in place holding her child above the water. Stories of a mother's love can make you cry. What often happens is that birthing a child awakens a mom and sometimes a dad to spiritual realities; they begin to think of their child's spiritual standing. So the gospel message that resonates deeply with her is: "A relationship with Christ can give your child and family a spiritual foundation." This is her key. Don't kid yourself that it's not! (pun intended).

If she wants a spiritual foundation for her child she will embrace a relationship with Jesus. This is the signature message leading to her openness to Christ and his cross. Confirming this idea, a young single mom in the class, Lindsay, shared that this was her story! We cannot ignore the realities of people's lives. Understanding their different situations and needs is how we tailor the message relevantly. It is what the early church did to turn their world upside down.

What is the gospel key to someone out of work, worrying about the future? Have you ever met someone there? Is this you right now? As I write, I am out of work—it has been a year. Again, I asked this to a class when our county registered double-digit unemployment. I followed, "Would God provide for you even in the worst of economic times?" I could tell the question trolled the depths of their faith-level. To their credit most expressed conviction that God would. I added, "Your ability to help others come to faith is linked to your insight on everything Christ is to *you*." If they didn't believe God would provide even in the worst of times, they could miss seeing the gospel's appeal. They could easily fail to see that what the anxious person truly needed was—Jesus!

I told my group of leaders that being out of work myself, I was living this part of the gospel and could share it with integrity. I believe with all my heart in the incredible, provisional capacity of our infinite God. He would provide for my family even though the unemployment agency told me no one was going to hire me (they said I should go teach at a college). If the Lord connected me to a person facing anxiety issues, I could help them see how Christ would carry that burden and be their miraculous provider.

Now it helps if you have stories. I have a million. God has been amazing in this time of transition; his ability to provide blows my mind. One day I drove home from church on fumes. While nearly running out of gas with no money to stop and fill up, ironically, my heart overflowed with joy from seeing people come to faith in our core beliefs class! Though I saw the red gauge I eagerly wanted to get home and rejoice with my wife. Making it, the next day I tried to start my truck. I kept turning it over. Then it dawned on me—the night before I had run out of gas—precisely in my parking space. Having a full gas can in my garage, I stepped out of my truck and had a moment of worship as I reflected upon God's faithful provision through all these crazy months. I could have been calling from the roadside, but that didn't happen. I had not come up short—not even a drop! It created a picture of God's undeniable faithfulness.

During this out-of-work time, my family had been provided for, even blessed. Twice we had eaten out at P.F. Chang's China Bistro because of gift cards we had received from weird things like winning our neighborhood Halloween costume contest. God provided through a friend "sick" pirate costumes (I was a killer-looking Jack Sparrow; the make-up is crucial), and we won a $50 gift card! When you are gainfully employed these things go unnoticed, but when you are on the edge, they are clear signs of God's hand. Two days after our washer broke down, my sister-in-law called saying she had run into an old friend who was looking to donate her used but high-end washer and dryer. I could go on with a gazillion more!

So the key to the unemployed person relates to how God will provide through his infinite capacities. If they hear that message, then we can talk much more about what it means to follow Jesus. In this way, the key is a bridge to a greater conversation. Learning the concept for the first time, one person said, "I would never have thought to ask what a relationship with Christ would mean." As the idea sunk in, she began to think deeply about her perfectionistic friend. What is the gospel's message to her?

ANSWERING OBJECTIONS!

Some object to the 'key' idea, saying, we should not tailor the gospel to anyone. They argue that non-believers should only want to give God glory, and that is the only valid motivation to become a Christian. The statement sounds noble, but is it true? Is that even possible with pre-Christians? Is it biblical? Have we failed to recognize the number of times Jesus appealed to people's personal motivations? Take the woman at the well as an example. Is "living water" not a relevant appeal to her in that particular moment? Our "good news" gospel is all about God's offer. Hebrews tells us that anyone who comes to faith does so because they believe God is "a rewarder of those who seek him" (11:6).

And what about the Gospels themselves? Were they not adapted to appeal to their unique audiences? Matthew filling his pages with prophecy that would satisfy his Jewish brethren . . . Mark giving a straightforward, no-frills account to fit his simpler minded Roman readers . . . Luke reversing Christ's genealogy, going from Jesus all the way back to the first man Adam, in order to appeal to the Greek's fascination with the perfect human . . . John plugging in the popularly used philosophic term "logos" to connect with the intellectual schools of his day.[9] If we object to this idea of adapting, we might as well throw out the Gospels.

As selfless as some want us to be with our faith, we cannot remove self-interest from its fabric. John Piper makes a compelling case for this in his classic book *Desiring God*. Wanting to enjoy God for all he is, and all his benefits, is not wrong, it's right![10] Our problem in reaching others is not that they have spiritual self-interest; it's that they have no interest. It burns me up that our gospel is often shared in a way that is irrelevant. All that we have in Christ can't get a hearing. Is it because our faith is irrelevant, or is it because we are poor at helping people see just how relevant it is?

Now, it is true that Jesus challenges us to count the cost of following him. We have many accounts of his commitment calls (Luke 14:25–34). Eventually, we will get to the call of the cross. We are not soft-peddling anything by teaching people how to begin meaningful conversations. The Gospel writers confronted their audiences, too. This is why Matthew included Gentiles in his Jewish genealogy with a humbling notation to David's sin, and also why he highlights the Magi coming at the birth, as if to say, "Where were we? How come they got it—and we didn't?" There are moments when we must do this with people. Yet the first phase of evangelism is appraising personal appeal.

Therefore, the critical question is: "What aspect of a relationship with Christ is 'good news' to your friend or family member?" This means you have to get in close, listen to their hearts, observe needs and drives, and appreciate the fullness of the gospel. Christian friend, let me ask you an important question. Do you believe the Bible when it says that through Christ God has not sparred us any blessing? (Rom 8:32). Do you believe God can meet your every need? (Phil 4:19; Matt 6:33). Then how could Christ meet the needs of your friend? You will have to become a student

---

9. Green, *Evangelism In the Early Church*, 120.

10. Piper, *Desiring God*, 13–20.

of them first, and seek God for resonant insight. It often takes time and perseverance. This is the "gospel key."

Notice how this changes the way we think of evangelism. It begins with relationship and then ventures into discovery. We have to get in close to discern how the gospel will be heard by each individual. Often God has to enlighten us as we prayerfully ask, "God, what aspect of knowing you do they need to see?" "What would draw them toward wanting a relationship with you?" The Spirit of God already knows, so ask him.

PINPOINTED ACCURACY

One Sunday, a pastor did something atypical by giving his entire message inside a fenced cage. Can you picture this? It was visually captivating. At the end people came forward, Christians and non-Christians, many with tears in their eyes, who knew they were in bondage and wanted desperately to experience the freedom that comes only through Christ. They knew it was a "signature" message bearing their name. Do you believe God is so personal that he can bring a message that will hit people right where they are? I do. Jesus was just like that. He did not give the same message to anyone but measured carefully what each needed to hear.

After stumbling into the key during my time with a non-believer, I diagrammed it on my whiteboard, and then taught the concept in a training course for the first time. Two weeks beyond the class, trainee Janel told me she led her cousin to Christ utilizing the key. This is how it happened. Kayla, active in the military, prepared to ship off on her new assignment. As she disclosed anxieties on what awaited her, Janel saw how she lacked anything solid, unchanging, and anchoring. This insight led to a conversation about faith. Janel jumped in and described what it meant to know Christ; he was the steady, guiding, ever-present compass and companion she lacked. Kayla suddenly saw faith in a new light. Pursuing her interest, Janel then uncovered her cousin's "having to be perfect" view of Christianity. When she explained that the very reason we need Christ is because we're all flawed, Janel led Kayla into the faith. She now serves our country in an uncertain world on the solid Rock!

Sean is a Christian electrician. Tom is an atheist-agnostic electrician. Working side by side, Sean disclosed a number of personal issues. He and his wife had recently separated. By disclosing, Tom learned of Sean's beliefs as he is seeking God to help his marriage. Reciprocating, Tom shared some of his challenges as well. Listening intently, Sean noticed a theme.

Tom has major problems with stress. He especially noted when Tom said, "I feel like I carry the weight of the world on my shoulders." Being trained in this skill, Sean recognized a key. He then initiated conversation about Jesus's words, "Come to me, all who are weary and burdened, and I will give you rest" (Matt 11:28–30). This begins a dialogue. Not surprisingly, Tom responded engagingly. A week following, Sean discovered that Tom went to buy a Bible. Three weeks later, he began attending church! This story demonstrates how the skills work together. Sean utilized both the Disclosure and Description windows to influence his friend.

Twenty-one and in college, Susan questioned the $30k her parents spent for each of her first two years at the university. As the dialogue developed with her friend Meg, Susan appeared to be questioning the payoff of many pursuits: college, career, even boyfriends seem less than they were cracked up to be. She is finding that fulfillment is not easily found in life's offerings. Listening to her carefully, Meg begins to interpret what she is saying synthesizing it this way, "You cannot get away from the deeper dimension of who you are meant to be: a spiritually connected-to-God person." This, in Meg's view, is Susan's key. Meg is now waiting for the right conversational moment to reveal it.

From these real-life accounts, can you see what I mean by pinpointed? We can bring this more sharply into view by considering the definitions of two technical words. "Synchronic; syn=same." The word means: "at a given time not connected to preceding events." Its opposite is "Diachronic: dia=through." Diachronic refers to something "formed in the progression of time."[11] From my observations, most keys are diachronic. It is the person's journey through life that creates the responsive effect. Having walked in the issue a person's radar is highly attuned to an answer. Thus, you know you are nearing a key, when the message gets tightly defined. It's not a general message, but rather a very precise capsulation derived from their need. Therefore, it sings of relevancy! Have you ever shared the gospel with someone, and heard the reply, "That's good for you." What they really mean is that it's not relevant to them. We'll stop hearing that put-off so often, when we make the shift from static presentations to surgical prescriptions!

After a trip to the city's safehouse, mobilization leader Monique begins to mentally process the key message for those coming out of human trafficking scenarios. With no hinting guidance on my part, she zeroes in on the theme of "identity." From her many conversations with victims, she

---

11. Hiebert, *Transforming Worldviews*, 31–69.

believes this is the key message, due to the exploitation of their person-hood evidenced by guilt, shame, and distortion. We talked about specific things she and her team have heard them say. Like the guy who said he is "just taking up space," and the gal who still identifies herself by the "prostitution" label. She sees how what they have gone through has deeply affected self-perception. Thus, the penetrative message needs to focus on who they truly are inside God's purview. We even later developed a few lines that in the right time within the relationship development could be powerful. Needless to say, what occurred on our way back from serving that day was an enormously rich discussion empowering a leader in her unique mission. She now knew what training to offer her team!

Introducing the concept to church planters in Arizona, Pastor Gavin tells me, "Many of the young members of our church want to share Christ, but it's awkward for them to just bring up the cross. But this approach is far more natural, because it starts the conversation with where their friends live."[12] Though it is not as simple as a rote formula, we have found that even our new believers, when taught, are fully capable. During a two-month course, neophyte Laurie had written down six names of non-believing friends to pray for. At the end, she reported that on one day she had gospel conversations with four on her list! She said, "Each conversation fell into my lap. I did what you said, I listened to them first, and then I shared something about faith that related to what they said." Joyfully, she explained, "I had incredible talks with all four!" We saw the immediate fruit when one of her contacts joined us for our closing lunch. He is now journeying with us at church.

IMPACTFUL COMMUNICATION

Let us return to Jesus's encounter with Samantha to see the sequence from a communication perspective. Going beyond the expected protocol between man-woman, Jew-Samaritan relations, Jesus's direct request for a drink draws her interest. This is a faith formation action that we can apply by loving people in exceptional ways. Jesus, then, wanting to take it much farther does so with one dynamic sentence. Fully grasp his words: "If you knew the gift of God and who it is that asks you for a drink, you would of asked him and he would have given you living water." From this verse comes a three step drawing process:

---

12. *Southwest Church Planting Forum*, May 8, 2012.

1. Discover their key.
2. Describe their benefit.
3. Direct their response.

His sentence, when broken down, decrees all the communication elements. *If you knew. . .* Like Samantha, non-believers don't know the gift of God. Jesus understood that he would have to help her see what a relationship with him would mean. This applies to all our redemptive relationships as well. We are the ones who must assess the spiritual remedy to their life's pursuits, which will guide what we share.

Pointing to the significance of *who he is*, we distinguish his offering. She could get water from many places, but only Jesus offered "living water." In our communication, we focus on a spiritual benefit of knowing God. Just as Jesus described the benefit vividly through the term "living water," we, too, must create a descriptive picture. Not that it has to be a metaphor, but the idea is to describe what it would mean for them to have a relationship with Christ. When communicating, you paint a picture of a preferred life, a window to what they could have. As I wrote previously, we are the painters of a whole new world!

Finally, within this descriptive offer, Jesus extends an invitation for her to seek him for the gift: "*. . . you would of asked him and he would have given you living water.*" To do this, you simply answer the question of the person's coming to faith. If my friend became a Christian, I see this happening—_____ (fill in the blank). When you work this drawing process all the way to providing a compelling picture, you will be amazed at how God will use your words. Take a look at the whole process:

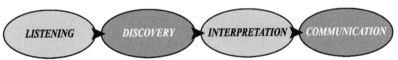

Having listened, discovered, and interpreted a specified message—you must share it. Sometimes this occurs in the natural interchange. Other times, when you suddenly and excitedly discover their key, you should take a page from Jesus's faith formation practices and pull them aside for a focused conversation. Like a poker player with a loaded hand, wait for the right moment when you have a chance to talk in an intimate way. Remember, evangelism is an art. There is the right time to speak with insight about what they could have. There is also a right time to keep quiet and listen. If you do this in the Spirit, with love and sensitivity, you will offer a vision they could not project themselves. By the way, sharing the signature message may begin a whole dialogue. Do not expect them to fully grasp it at first, though sometimes, it will amaze you at how they respond.

Consider additional examples of this interpretive communication. Of course, you will need to use your words, not mine. As you read these true to life appeals, I hope you sense how potent this moment can be. In fact, I have seen people come to faith through some of these very descriptions:

> • Anna (abandoned) . . . "When you become a Christian, you will experience how God will always be there for you—it will give you a deep sense of security knowing he will never leave you. Earthly relationships will fail us, but God never will. You can learn to depend on him as he walks with you into your future."

> • Les (broken) . . . "God is able to recover your failures. This is what God does. He takes all the pieces and works them together for good. If you follow him, you will be amazed to see how he can redeem your life."

Let's stop for a moment with Les. Are we overpromising? Not at all! Our great God is fully able to redeem people's broken lives! He will "work all things together for good" to those called to his name (Rom 8:28). Anyone despairing needs to hear this. Jesus is the answer for Les!

> • Johnny (addictions) . . . "You could experience God's power to overcome, get free, and live a new life. If you follow him, God can do that for you. He provides power to those willing to yield themselves to him. You could live an awesome life, with a spiritual high that's far better than any doped- up experience out there."

> • Jenny (self-esteem) . . . "God can help you come into a full realization of just how important and precious you are. He made you for a relationship with him. You are the highest of his creation but he wants you to know that in a profoundly personal way. If you decide to follow Christ you will experience forgiveness and the touch of his loving presence within you."

> • Alex (marital troubles) . . . "If you follow Christ you will discover what Christ can do for your marriage. He can begin delivering you from your selfishness that's at the root of all problems. The only way, though, is putting him first. When you do, he will heal your marriage by changing you from the inside out."

Notice this one's depth. Sometimes the key will go to these very honest, even confrontational places. Alex's marriage needs Jesus!

> • Frank (anxiety) . . . "Through a relationship with God you could replace the worry you feel right now with his peace. It all comes through having that trusting relationship with him. If you came to know Christ, you will be blown away by his ability to personally care and provide for you."

> • Jamie (hurting) . . . "The Lord is an amazing healer. He can come over and help you feel whole and healthy again. He wants to touch your heart. If you follow him he will do that. I hope that you give him a chance to be real to you."

Do not be afraid to delve into the area of healing. God will intervene when a person begins seeking him.

> • Samuel (intellectual search) . . . "I could see how your becoming a Christian would help you make sense of the world and provide answers you are searching for. It will give you solid standing. There is an aspect of knowledge that happens through faith. When you believe God will help you understand these things."

> • Jackson (success-driven) . . . "Your ambitions could be fulfilled in bigger ways than you could ever imagine. By serving Christ in his mission, you will discover a level of significance that is far greater than anything this world offers. Worldly success is temporary and empty; his reward lasts and fulfills."

Summarizing, the key enables you to initiate deep, meaningful conversations about faith with your friends. It begins relevant dialogues that can eventually lead to a fantastic discussion about the cross and committing one's whole life to Jesus.

Stepping back and looking from the big picture, people in the church are usually comfortable talking with non-believers about life issues. Some can talk on the core message of the cross. What we are not good at doing is having conversations that connect the two! Take a moment to ponder the grey area of this graph.

This is what "the gospel key" does well. It creates a way to picture faith's dynamic. Let me be quick to say, this skill takes practice. Reflect back on your spiritual journey. What was it that drew you? Think deeply about your friends outside the faith. Study them. What are their dire needs, desires, drives and dreams? Contemplate faith and its relevance. Sprinkled throughout this book are examples of how the key works in real life—see if you can locate any. Hint: There's one in the next two chapters!

God wants to use you. If you learn to practice this communication principle it will advance your spiritual influence significantly. Within each of your relationships with non-believers, you will find yourself whispering right into their souls!

DISCUSSION AND ENGAGEMENT

1. When you first began to read this chapter, did you view the gospel as a one-tune message or a symphony to the world?

2. Share in the group about what drew you into a relationship with Christ. Can you see in your own story the gospel key?

3. Take a moment to talk about the specific needs and life situation of a non-believing friend. Can you guess what the gospel key might be for them?

4. Apply this chapter by working the four-step process with one of your non-believing friends, or a developing relational contact.

7

Compassion Calls

Compassion is sometimes the fatal capacity for feeling what it is like to live inside somebody else's skin. It is the knowledge that there can never really be any peace and joy for me until there is peace and joy finally for you too.

—FREDERICK BUECHNER

You are in the throes of a meth addiction. Child Protective Services moves in to take custody of your children. Life is brutal! Fortunately, they allow two of your three children to remain with you as you go to a rehab home for sixty days. While there others invite you to a Monday morning book club. Reluctantly you straggle over there since there isn't much else going on. Sitting in the circle you learn the leader is from a church. She seems kind and you grow to like her. You also catch that on Sundays, she swings by to take the women to services. You decide to give it a try. The whole experience surprises as you truly enjoy it! But more than that you felt something different when you are there. You are not sure what it was, but wonder if it is God. You begin to talk about the Bible and spiritual questions. One day the pastor calls people forward and you feel particularly drawn. Finding a whole new power to beat your addiction, Christ begins to transform your life and bless your children in ways you can no longer count. Now everyday you walk with the Lord!

This story occurred in 2010. Tragically, it is not occurring enough.

Can you envision an eight-foot wall of whitewater rushing toward you? Growing up in Southern California I surfed steadily for a decade. On big days, every surfer has experienced what it's like to get caught inside the break. Big swells can be trouble, and for unseasoned surfers, dangerous, as wave after wave crash before you. Being caught inside, even for a few waves, is not where you want to be. The best surfers are in such good shape that they paddle hard and swim under the waves with their boards to get out quickly. Others, less skilled, get pummeled. Is this an apt metaphor of the contemporary church? Are we caught inside the break? For an institution called to Christ's mission, it is not the place to be. Perhaps, we are not in shape enough to engage our world.

Compassion-mobilization leaders want this to change. For them, a passion burns to take the church outside its walls to touch a hurting world. They espouse what is called a holistic gospel. It is a broad-scoped theology of the kingdom where God works through his people to reconcile the whole world to himself. Reconciliation includes: individuals, community life, systems, structures, and cultures. The gospel is not limited, as we have come to see it, to the good news of personal salvation—it includes establishing justice in the created order, and a reconciling of all things (Col 1:15–20).[1] Whereas the missional movement is a corrective, saying all are called to mission, the compassion movement is a corrective to a more holistic view of God's redemption. This is a giant leap from the "God has called us to fish—not clean the fishbowl" mentality. Much energy and creativity is focused to solving community problems. The movement has expanded the picture of what God has called the church to be and do.

Drawing inspiration from God's character, theology champions this vision as God's universal call to serve "the least, the last and the lost." One author notes that the Poverty and Justice Bible has nearly two thousand verses reflecting God's heart.[2] Consider the charge of Isaiah 1:17:

> learn to do right!
> Seek justice,
> encourage the oppressed,
> defend the cause of the fatherless,
> plead the case of the widow.

---

1. Stearns, *The Hole In Our Gospel*, 20; Corbett and Fikkert, *When Helping Hurts*, 33–34.

2. Stearns, *The Hole In Our Gospel*, 24.

MIRROR, MIRROR

For most, the compassion subject creates a mirroring-moment. Even with a feeler personality, I do not ooze warm-hearted "get into their skin" empathy. My wife tears, I glisten. Looking at Jesus, I only see the gap. His compassion spills over—while mine remains corked in the bottle! I have taken steps to become more engaged. Inspiring examples abound. Monique is passionately moved by the "human trafficking" issue. She feels called to intercede for these victimized people. I began partnering with her ministry team to these who have been coerced and bullied beyond their wills.

During my trips to Kenya with *Truth Ministries International*, our team visited a camp of recently displaced refugees. After eyeing the stark conditions, leader and a personal mentor David Mills pulled out his checkbook to purchase hundreds of mattresses. Later, he spoke of his own transformation, saying, "At a certain point in my travels, I began to do what I could."

Undoubtedly, compassion both builds and draws upon our character. On the way to school, my fifteen-year old son tells me he loves the song line, "Break my heart for what breaks yours." I reminded him of our time in Mexico where the teacher challenged us to live the song lyrics, or stop singing them. Do we really want our hearts broken over what breaks God's? God hears the cries of the poor and helpless. He desires justice in the land. If we were broken over what breaks him, it would revolutionize our lives!

From many personal observations, most Christians are not setting love records. In a new believer's *Basic Training* session, I once gave the assignment to show love to someone outside the church and then report back. In anticipation, I was excited to hear what occurred. I just knew God would take those small acts and do some heart-meltingly big things. So you can only imagine my reaction when I discovered that none of the twenty-three had followed through.

Trying to recover in front of them, I commented on how difficult it is to get outside our agendas. I made the point that it is very possible, as believers, to rarely show an exceptional love. Often we do little for those on the outside. But then, redeeming the day, one of the wives mentioned that her husband, James, who was in the class, had acted. Whew, we all clapped! He had fixed a car for a woman for free—and not only hers but also the car of her ex-husband. Can you believe that? I must quickly note, however, that from this large group, the one person who showed love that week happened to be a non-Christian. With this being a spiritually fired up class, the sequence seemed even more poignant. Just because we carry Jesus's name honorably, does not automatically mean we emulate his ways at times.

Love's compassionate outpouring is the calling of God, and has marked the Christian movement from its early roots. In his book, *The Rise of Christianity*, Rodney Stark posits one of the big sociological factors contributing to Christianity's rapid spread was how the Christians responded to major epidemics. Decimating a third of the empire's population, illness pushed the elite pagans and their priests from the city. Many Christians, in contrast, stayed to nurse the sick. Faith in eternal life superseded even the fear of dying. Returning pagans could not but ponder something profound in Christians. This, according to Stark's analysis, led to conversions en masse.[3] May we never forget the principle illustrated in our early history: Compassionate love opens hearts!

GLIMPSES OF THE MEGACHURCHES

Seeking fresh data, I studied the outreach efforts of ten megachurches: Crossroads, Center of Praise, The Grove, Harvest, New Heights Church, Mariners, Rancho Community, Rock Harbor, Sandals, and The Village Church. Not being partial, though I am on staff at a large church, I also coach church planters who are on the other side of the spectrum, but chose these ten megas merely to evaluate a broad range of community ministries. Some have said there is no evangelistic fruit to speak of within these kinds of outreach. Not so! Take a glimpse at a few noteworthy highlights hot off the grill:

From Sandals (Riverside, CA):

Martha has served in the foster care ministry for fourteen years. She provides emergency care to kids who come to live with her for one to six months. Because they are often in crisis she has moments when she tells them directly, "I know something that can help you" and often leads them to Christ. At night she prays for the children individually, touching their faces, creating an experiential moment. The kids tell the newer ones how she prays and touches their faces in this way (please note the faith formation technique!) Martha has led hundreds of children into the faith. She brings them to church, and tells them, "You may not be able to go to

---

3. Stark, *The Rise of Christianity*, 73–94.

church when you leave, but there will be a time when you can decide on your own."

Rachel serves at MFI, a rehabilitation recovery home for women. Each Monday morning she leads a book club. Within two years, seventy-five rehabbing women have come to the church and fifteen have made significant spiritual commitments.

From Rancho Community Church (Temecula, CA):

This church offers "free" counseling to anyone in the community. A professional oversees the ministry. Despite the suburban locale, the church is ministering to roughly twenty displaced homeless families each week. Rancho's goal is to give an ambitious 33 percent of their budget to needs outside the church.

From Crossroads (Corona, CA):

Living up to its early creed of being "A church anyone can come to," the disability ministry at Crossroads is exceptional. Imagine watching quadriplegics lifted into the waters of baptism! Crossroads is a lead partner with the Orange County Rescue Mission to build a new facility for homeless in its region.

From New Heights Church (Vancouver, WA):

New Heights Church has started their own medical clinic to provide services for the underinsured. One hundred eighty volunteers staff the facility. Pastor Matt Hannan says, "Our doctors do everything they were told not to do in medical school. We approach medicine holistically—learning about their spiritual story is an important part of their health."

From Center of Praise (Sacramento, CA):

Partnering with the Dream Center of Sacramento, church members form a receiving line to welcome the homeless each Saturday morning. Dr. Kim Stokes describes, "Everyone's heart is filled, as they clap, touch and connect with the people entering." As they minister, Kim says people often break down in tears. The team members only qualification is that they are "Spirit filled, and Spirit led." "You cannot transfer what is not in you," she adds. With this spiritual dynamic of the Lord's presence, tremendous ministry takes place and some do come to faith. They also have a specialized ministry to youth at the Juvenile Hall.

From Rock Harbor (Orange County, CA)

Two non-profits groups, Solidarity and Micah, have launched out of the church. Each group has relocated inside targeted areas within their county to live alongside as redemptive communities. Rock Harbor, like

Sandals, is in the process of transition, moving all groups in a mission-focused trajectory.

From The Village Church: (Flower Mound, TX)

Similar to many others, The Village Church utilizes recovery ministries to meet deep needs, and initiate salvations.

I visited or called, asked pointed questions of all these churches, and took copious notes. Then I put my mind to the challenge of today's church by answering, "How do missional groups and compassion ministries engage with evangelistic effectiveness?" What does that look like? Senior pastors commonly aim to establish a loving reputation, believing that this will ultimately draw people from the community. However, I wanted to take it further, by asking what would Jesus have us do? What should Christian compassion entail? With the research came a number of insights and a few surprises. As I analyzed, three interrelated areas became pertinent: (1) Biblical Model, (2) Structural Design, and (3) Holistic Engagement. Let's examine each.

CHRIST'S COMPASSION MODEL

From reflection on Jesus's life, in my view, this is a most telling passage:

> Jesus went through all the towns and villages, teaching in their synagogues, preaching the good news of the kingdom and healing every disease and sickness. When he saw the crowds, he had compassion on them, because they were harassed and helpless, like sheep without a shepherd. Then he said to his disciples, "The harvest is plentiful but the workers are few. Ask the Lord of the harvest, therefore to send out workers into his harvest field." Matt 9:35–37

Seeing the crowd stirs Christ's compassion. Note how he saw the full dimension of human need by describing both *life* and *spiritual* conditions. He refers to life condition need by two phrases: "diseased and sick," and "harassed and helpless." Yet Jesus also describes them as "sheep without a shepherd," clearly referencing the spiritual condition connected to knowing God, the true shepherd of their souls. The duality begs the question, "Does our compassion match his holistic vision?" This is the most important query that Christians everywhere must wrestle with. Substantial room for growth exists on both sides.

In recent history, the church has wrongly neglected physical and psychological life condition needs in favor of gospel presentation. As the title infers, *The Hole In Our Gospel* challenges the church to fulfill its greater mandate to the world. Richard Stearns, the president of *World Vision*, rebukes the church for not addressing the culture's causal elements and calls for "social revolution."[4] A starving person needs food and a job, and unjust systems must be challenged and changed. Correction occurs when we embrace a holistically styled compassion. Today, more churches are stepping to the tune of a broader love.

Yet as the pendulum swings, we have also erred by ineffectively addressing the spiritual. We should not think that by serving we have achieved even close to God's vision of redeeming lives. In other words, if we do not love people all the way into relationship with Jesus, they remain "sheep without a shepherd." Through my research, which included interviews and first-hand observations, I could not but help notice a settling-to-serve mindset. Using my art comparison to evangelism styles, the genre Impressionism with its low definition (LD) might capture it. Too often, we show compassionate love, but don't reach anyone. Lacking a holistic plan we only left them impressionistically fuzzy about the Christian faith. God's servants were better positioned but not properly prepared to bring clarity and wholeness to the inquiring soul. In the end, we gave bread, but not "the Bread of Life." They never got from us his infinite healing grace and power.

One nugget arising from my research deals with how the pre-mindset determined outcome. Let me explain. When the serving motivation of Christians was their spiritual formation, it truncated disciplemaking. In simpler words, if the people serving are doing it for their own growth in Christian expression, then it ends there. Few in those contexts got saved. If you think it over logically this makes perfect sense. These ministries were content to only give bread. The holistic vision of Jesus was not achieved.

In contrast, those who said evangelism was the top priority were more inclined to see full gospel impact. Though many of these churches still lacked an engagement model, the evangelistic intention added disciples. The bottom line became clear: If top leaders didn't champion the evangelism value, kingdom growth would not be seen. There were always exceptions where faithful Christians reached others despite direction. One megachurch leader with the spiritual formation focus and fifteen mobilization ministries admitted he couldn't tell you anyone they had reached

4. Stearns, *The Hole In Our Gospel*, 15–24.

evangelistically over the past year. He struggled with feeling like the compassion workers could just as well have served *The United Way.* This trend was true of others as well.

However, if the top leaders were truly holistic, then you saw glimpses of Christ's vision being realized. Most could affirm some evangelistic fruit. In the strongest mobilization efforts, the leaders even tracked salvations. When I asked, Laurie Beshore, of Mariners Church in Orange County, California, if she could tell me of people saved through their efforts, she gave me a number: 521—for that year! She said, "We never got any traction, until we started counting."[5] Tagging them as the flagship church of the bunch, Mariners adopted John Stott's phrase from the Lausanne Conference on Evangelism, "The Whole Church taking the Whole Gospel to the Whole World." With their leaders seeing salvations as an important measurement, the people followed it through.

DESIGNING FROM THE BOTTOM UP!

Despite forward progress, my big picture feel is that a slight step back from the missional movement has occurred. I checked my read on this with a high-level friend, and he agreed, absolutely. The initial buzz from the missional conversation has quelled. It is partly related to how churches want to see greater gospel results. Initially they thought it would just happen, but the promise didn't pan out so easily. We should not throw the baby out with the bathwater here; but we do need to create the context for influence to take root. This requires thinking as designers.

In my high school football days, our coach railed at us: "Go out there and hurl your bodies with reckless abandon!" He wanted us to forget our fears and become human projectiles. The attitude works with football and is not a bad beginning point for churches either. Just get out there! Forget about inviting or sharing, just release Christian love with full abandon. This alone could be big! I would never discount the impact that can occur when Christians love tangibly. If people are hungry, let's find ways to give bread. We may never know how God used us. I also acknowledge that there are contexts when we are called to love without the evangelism piece. Activism has a place in the church to confront injustice and create change. It should be noted that compassion workers would find fault with pastors who cannot commit to anything that will not immediately grow their church. They have a point—don't they? If we think every engagement has

5. Phone interview with Laurie Beshore, September 8, 2011.

to include an invitation to Sunday, we can fail to invest ourselves, missing what can only happen once we get extended.

Yet if we are to heed Christ's holistic vision, how do we integrate his wisdom? What if we took love's outward thrust and infused design? Churches commonly initiate service days to help, give something away, or bless people. The question lingers on whether people end up becoming followers from the day's activity? The answer is no, no, no, no, no and yes. Hit, miss, miss, miss, miss and miss. Sometimes a person is blessed and they might even show up at your church. Just getting out there in the community can gain attention. Though single act service is always better than doing nothing, the downside to this approach is the relationship angle. Typically, the one-time event does not offer nearly enough time and context for relational formation.

In contrast, what if instead you engaged people in your community consistently? This achieves something better than the "one-hit wonder" through providing an avenue for familiarity. When you show up regularly, people notice something qualitatively different. They figure out where you are from, get to know your name, and may even ask: "Why are you doing this?" In today's world, you may not fully connect how much consistency equates with love. With relationships there is an exceedingly higher chance for spiritual influence.

Denise volunteers weekly to "cut hair" at the women's rehab home. Suddenly, she is no stranger. In fact, Andrea, one of the residents, even knows when Denise is coming, so if she wanted to talk, she makes her way over. As relationships form, opportunities arise for further connecting. When Andrea comes with Denise to church, it naturally fosters spiritual conversations. These kinds of consistent service opportunities abound, but you do need to look for the angle. At the Crossings Church, members provide six-week English lessons, which affords a relational development context. Being aspiring English speakers, these bilinguals seek conversation, and gladly follow their new friends into church. Likewise, Danielle serves as a mentor for teenage foster kids, which naturally fosters relationship. Similarly, the county anti-human trafficking task force ministers to victims of sex or labor trades, where mentors begin as drivers. Providing transportation is the first step to building trust with people who have been coerced and exploited. Director Jennifer O'Farrell states, "Clients in the system see a difference when non-paid people help. That means you really care!"

Working a relational approach often requires imagination. Interacting with the *Guest Chef* kitchen ministry leader of Sandals, Eric said conversation with the homeless is limited. Most people from the church primarily serve food. Yet he also added that he talked with the facility director about helping with resumes. I seized on the idea! From a design perspective can you see how that would deepen their ministry? Helping someone put together a resume would provide a vehicle to get personally acquainted. Whenever relationships develop, influence can follow. Hearing about people's backgrounds and discussing dreams enables compassion ministers to disclose pieces of their own journey and deepen relational bonds. Can you see how a little imagination can make a big difference?

Oftentimes you will need to adjust schedules to increase relational opportunities. Many entering safe houses or rehab homes are on the clock. They will be there for a limited time, usually one to three months. Therefore, it is wise to up the ante through more frequent visits, as permitted. Weekly is much better than monthly. This adjustment will pay off toward gospel impact. Don't think that God won't honor the effort—he will!

Does this design not dispel the one-hit wonder? A critical question for churches, missional groups and compassion ministries is, "What can we do consistently?" The principle is not related to size. Even smaller churches or groups with lesser resources can find places to pursue ongoing service. Another good question to ask is, "What can my church do uniquely?" Although you can always partner with other churches or organizations, it is prudent for each church to periodically assess unaddressed needs. Neglected areas within your community create openings for pinpointed impact. Open your eyes! Make a drive through your neighborhoods, visit organizations and discover what no other church is doing.

THE HOLISTIC CHALLENGE

The evangelism piece in the compassion movement remains an issue. This is a crying shame because this church wing is well-positioned and postured for spiritual influence. Whereas the church has traditionally exalted itself above the culture, the value of dignifying "the least of these" empowers believers to ditch the arrogant baggage. Compassion leader, Nicole, disdains how the church is known most for its "judging." Countering ignorant attitudes through education, the compassion culture ministers from a place of understanding, and a spirit of humble brokenness. Consider a note received from a young modern-day Samantha:

> I am going through a major spiritual battle right now. I believe in God, but men and prostitution hold me back from fully giving my life. I'm a single mom, and I've gotten off the drugs and a real job but the devil just won't leave me alone. I just need prayer for good people to be sent my way, also that my daughter will grow up to be nothing like I've been. Also for protection.

A compassion team member comments, "I can see how that could so easily happen. You strip one time to make some desperately needed money and before you know it you are doing things you never imagined." The team at Sandals is connecting with these "industry gals" and walking alongside them into faith and the church. They feel loved in the grace environment of Sandals where the pastor and members talk openly about their sins. When one of the gals came forward and disclosed her marital issues, we quickly confessed that we all have struggles here, and she replied favorably, "I've noticed that you guys do that here." One thing is for sure. By getting involved in these ministries, you will fall in love with these non-believers. They are beautifully precious to God!

When the gracious posture is right, some might even receive our message. Who better than us to represent the gospel to people that Jesus loves, but our culture demeans: the sinners, beggars, needy, prostitutes, lepers and tax collectors of our time? Episcopal Priest Margaret Guenther in New York, points out that when Jesus surprises the Samaritan woman with knowledge of her sexual life, that "she does not feel found out or accused, but rather—for the first time—truly known." She goes on to say how his gracious candor liberates her to become the teacher and bearer of good news![6] In striking contrast to his way, some Christians will leave a church if the wrong people start showing up. You know the kind they don't want their kids hanging around. Seeing the church as a country club for the squeaky-clean, believers with this attitudinal warp know nothing of God's heart. But the compassion movement does!

Yet despite this rightly aligned posture, and the teaching of top mobilization leaders, the evangelism focus suffers. Some readers may be surprised to learn that evangelistic emphasis exists in notable compassion books: *Walking with the Poor, The Hole In Our Gospel, Honor, and When Helping Hurts.* Yet as the word from the streets trickles back people question, "Has the apple fallen too far from its tree?" Will the pendulum prompt a countering book, "The Hole In Our Compassion?" A seminary professor leaks concern, "Outreach is not about evangelism." In a 2010, *Outreach*

6. Guenther, *Holy Listening*, 50.

magazine article, Dan Kimball scribed *Why Justice Requires Evangelism*, where he affirms a non-reductionist form of the gospel as good and re-freshing yet observes: "But emerging generations are often solely learning the Gospel as an emphasis on justice. They actively participate in justice projects and stay aware of global happenings. However, I am concerned that they aren't learning about the importance of evangelism."[7] Appealing for a greater justice movement, he argues that without new disciples we will not be able to meet the proliferating cultural needs.[8] Kimball reminds his readers, "But we all do die. Everyone will face judgment, and there is but one Savior and one cross."[9]

Paul Johnson, in his book *Modern Times*, denotes how Einstein be-lieved in absolutes but the populace thought his theory depicted a relativ-istic world and missed his essential conviction.[10] Is this what is occurring? Are people embracing outreach, and leaving behind a key essential? For some, evangelism seems to be the link that gets lost. Part of the problem is the unattractive perception of the "telling paradigm" with its stereotypical abuses that feel intrusive and uncompassionate. Many Christians would not be opposed to evangelism per se, if they saw it in a highly relational, sensitive, soul whispering way.

One leader articulated, "Some are okay, but others are clearly not favorable towards evangelism and have distanced themselves from that camp." Although this could be said of the whole church, the evangelism image seems to run against the grain in this subculture. In *Compassion, Justice and the Christian Life*, the book opens with a story of the author teaching "neighboring" as the primary biblical mandate, and his insightful point is set in contrast to the narrow "evangelism" focus. The chapter and book by Robert Lupton are actually really good, but his story furthers a negative impression.[11] The stigma of the insensitive narrow-minded "save souls only" Christian hinders the conversation. Yet it shows rather starkly why we need to reshape evangelism holistically.

Besides this leery feel, why else does the evangelism piece get lost? What naturally occurs when you get out there in the field is that people's life condition needs are so big that it drowns the whole focus. You will experience this feeling when you encounter the enormity of need! I have

7. Kimball, "Why Justice Needs Evangelism," lines 19–23.

8. Kimball, "Why Justice Needs Evangelism," lines 61–65.

9. Kimball, "Why Justice Needs Evangelism," lines 28–29.

10. Johnson, *Modern Times*, 1–4.

11. Lupton, *Compassion, Justice, and the Christian Life*, 15–17.

Want to meet needs of people but not become the provider for people

become overwhelmed numerous times in my involvements in dark and desperate situations. But my first glimpse of this came from a somewhat lighter scenario many years back on the campus of Cal State Long Beach, when we began a ministry to international students. I befriended Makoto from Japan and took a trip into "Little Tokyo" in downtown LA, where he introduced me to eating eel! Then, there was Raj from India, who was more than brilliant, and used only one carefully folded paper napkin to my ten. There were also students from boats fleeing Cambodia with horror stories to make your skin crawl. As we began to meet deep needs, I recall being swept up in the joy of these international students. At a party, the connecting was so sweet that I honestly thought bringing Christ into the conversation would only screw it all up!

Then, our church hosted an international speaker, who met with campus leaders separately regarding our ministry to internationals. He proceeded to explain why we should not overextend hospitality. In his view, we could disrupt their spiritual search. I initially reacted, "What?" But as his words sank in, I began to appreciate a deeper wisdom. It raised a provocative question: Is it possible that in our compassion we can fail people spiritually? What a thoughtful query for anyone involved in outreach. Obviously, we want to love people in the name of Christ, yet do we have the wisdom to weigh the greater good? Do we realize that we are not meant to be the answer ourselves? We are so privileged to advocate for the disadvantaged, to represent Christ's love as his hands and feet, yet as idyllic as that beautiful language is, we can never replace him. They need Jesus.

Not in anyway trying do discourage loving acts, it's right to soundly inquire, "How much can *we* truly offer?" Did we touch them, but not in the profoundest way? Have we loved, but not led them toward God's? Did we help, but forgot the Helper—the Spirit who comes into a life to: seal, change, lead, prompt, illuminate, guide, love and empower. Do they not need God's resources? Of course, there is that salvation thing too: Past sins forgiven—a new start—life in God's grace—the hope of heaven. In their excellent book, *When Helping Hurts*, Corbett and Fikkert write of treating the symptoms without getting to poverty's core issues. They offer perspective on ministering wisely to the poor, which addresses the spiritual foundation with God that will affect everything else![12]

In my view, evangelism would benefit by being reframed within the compassion culture's language. First, we honor people at the highest level when we seek to know their faith journey. Expressing honor and dignity is

---

12. Corbett and Fikkert, *When Helping Hurts*, 54–55.

compassion distinctive. In that same spirit, evangelism profoundly honors and dignifies people by recognizing their cross-worthy price and potential, being made in God's image. Below I have attempted to reintegrate evangelism by teaching it within three dimensions of human poverty. By contextualizing the evangelism value within the compassion culture's language, perhaps we can re-engage those evangelistically marginal. Of course, I also sought to redefine evangelism by developing "the drawing paradigm of Jesus." Moving away from the telling motif, compassion workers can acquire a soul whispering style that is more relationally sensitive and effective.

HOLISTIC ENGAGEMENT MODEL

In his book, *Walking with the Poor*, Bryant Myers outlines four dimensions of poverty saying, "Due to the comprehensive nature of the fall, every human being is poor in the sense of not experiencing key relationships (God, self, others, creation) the way God intended,[13] ultimately connected to a broken relationship with God. When we engage in compassion ministries we are ministering to people with multi-dimensional need. In following Christ's vision, we must seek to minister in the deepest ways possible. For simplicity, let's keep our "Life Condition / Spiritual Condition" distinctions we learned from Jesus, but define three areas:

Poverty of Need	Life Condition	Relief/Rehabilitation
Poverty of Community	Life & Spiritual	Relationship
Poverty of Spirituality	Spiritual Condition	Regeneration

This breakdown addresses needs existing in every human being. In fact, it is helpful to look at each area vicariously by applying it to your unique situation. Ultimately, we are no different than the person on the street. First on the list, we all have a life condition where there is: poverty of need. It may not be for food, shelter or finances, but could be for guidance on a decision, support in parenting, space to function, or opportunity to excel. In compassion ministries we usually begin with one's life condition. With love, we aim to help people where they are, stepping in to provide relief at a basic level. Sometimes it means assistance, or working to bring justice in the systems and structures of a fallen world. This must be done in a way that actually helps.

---

13. Myers, *Walking With The Poor*, 87.

If you get involved in compassion, you must do so with wisdom. *When Helping Hurts* tells the story of the church that gave out Christmas gifts at the housing projects. After consecutive years, these servants wondered why they never saw any men at the doors. What they learned was that when the church people showed up with charitable gifts the men fled out the back. It shamed them! We can mean well but do harm. The Christians who participated, on the other hand, ended up developing even more judgmental baggage. They were harmed too. Corbett and Fickkert write, "If we treat only the symptoms or if we misdiagnose the underlying problem, we will not improve their situation, and we might actually make their lives worse."[14] There are times when even our love is not helping. If relief creates dependency, it can undermine the discipline needed for dignity and development. Yet often relief is the first step to a better future.

At the next need level each of us experiences poverty of community too, because as humans, we are made for relationships. Have you ever felt like a stranger in your own church? We know when a deficit exists for "community." Within Christian fellowship, we enjoy relationships marked by a deep common bond in Jesus. As you minister, be mindful that some may have never experienced Christian love, and connecting relationally can do wonders. Just make sure you love at a high level. Corbett challenges us to go beyond relief, "A better and far more costly solution would be for your church to develop a relationship with this person, a relationship that says, 'We are here to walk with you and to help you use your gifts and abilities to avoid being in this situation in the future.'"[15] In the movie *Million Dollar Baby*, the woman fighter, Academy Award winner Hillary Swank, vulnerably divulges to her trainer, "I've got no one but you Frankie." He had become family. We should offer nothing less.

Going even deeper than community relationship is the need for an ongoing relationship with God. Again, we all know the importance of this centering relationship, which is a fountain of blessing. The spiritual intimacy need is profound, and people will not ever be right outside it. Fawn Parish, in her book, *Honor*, writes, "We were made to honor God. We will never be fulfilled apart from knowing the nature and personality of God. We were created to explore him, to honor him and find him; we have no ability to fully be ourselves without fully knowing him."[16] So we could describe ministry at three distinct levels:

14. Corbett and Fikkert, *When Helping Hurts*, 54.
15. Corbett and Fikkert, *When Helping Hurts*, 55.
16. Parish, *Honor*, 39.

LEVEL 1: Poverty of Need · *We helped - served - loved.* ~~Food Pantry~~

LEVEL 2: Poverty of Community · *We helped - served - loved, but also ...*
Connected relationally.

LEVEL 3: Poverty of Spirituality · *We helped - served - loved,*
Connected relationally, but also ...
Led them to faith & discipleship.

At times we only get to level one; that alone may be an amazing work of extending Christ's love. Yet it should be our intention as much as possible to go to levels 2 and 3. That is because we know the Lord has so much more that he desires for their lives. As the church we are called to make disciples, leading people toward the fullness of God's life and mission. If you are currently involved in compassion efforts, take a moment to examine the level of your present ministries.

Author Bryant Myers has an insight from the book of Acts in seeing how gospel sharing is sometimes the second act. At the birth of the church, the outpouring of the Spirit was Act One, and Peter's message explaining what it meant was Act Two.[17] This is often the way it looks in mission. We start with love and eventually it moves to the greater question of life. Life is what Jesus offers. We are not the answer, but he is more than they could ever imagine!

START HERE ↓	*LIFE Condition* ▸	1st Act ▸	*LOVE*
MOVE TO	*Spiritual Condition* ▸	2nd Act ▸	*LIFE*

SERVE — LOVE — TO DISCIPLESHIP
THEM   THEM

In writing the mission design strategy and curriculum for Sandals community groups,[18] I wanted every group to do an ongoing project: A community garden, a beautifying venture, service to the city, a compassion outreach, a neighborhood improvement, meeting needs of families, raising benevolence funds. By design, every group would determine their project, set out the time to engage over an extended period, and invite their non-believing neighbors to participate alongside. We started first by looking at needs, loving our neighbors, befriending and partnering. Out

Ministry Mapping

17. Myers, *Walking With The Poor*, 209–10.
18. Comer, *Community Group Mission Guide*.

of relational investment, with a few barbeques thrown in, we'd get to know people through asking questions in hopes of getting a read on their starting points. From there the members would work together to assess specific spiritual benefits. The model adopted the "The Gospel Key" concept where we taught our people to listen and discern before speaking. We aimed to engage conversationally in the relevancy-first sweet spot. From there, we had our people invite them into the group, and progress in discovering and moving through belief barriers. The whole purpose was to walk them into faith and discipleship within a community context. Please examine carefully the model:

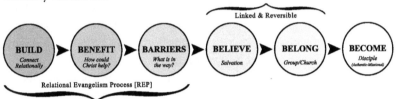

Compassion/Missional Group Evangelism Path

One observation is that it takes a whole lot of commitment and compassion to walk them into the faith. Serving is a lot easier than evangelism. But how thrilling to work together to touch your community holistically. We have an amazing calling in seeding the fullness of Christ! (John 10:10).

I love to build things. When my sons were young we built a castle. One day when mom was away, we taped a lighter to a plastic dragon, ran a string from the top balcony to the living room floor, connected him to the line with a paper clip, turned off the lights, and had him fly with fiery fury into the castle! Then our knights gallantly fought him flames and all (please don't tell). Here is a model with the potential to lead people out from the dragon's fiery flames! Let us not forget the spiritual battle. We are in a fight for people's souls, and God's restoration of a burned and broken world.

DISCUSSION AND ENGAGEMENT

All desire thru
no follow thru
1. When you see Christ's compassion on the crowds, how do you measure up? Is compassion a natural strength, or area of needed growth?

2. How much of your time is spent ministering to needs outside the church?

3. Discuss in your group the three levels of poverty. Can you personally identify with one of the three needs right now?

4. How can you or your group prepare to engage in holistic compassion?

5. Talk about the engagement model. Can you see how you can get out there and walk someone all the way into the faith? Have you ever done this?

8

Bridge of Brokenness

It is often difficult to believe that there is much to think, speak or write about other than brokenness.

—HENRI NOUWEN

Being a movie buff, anything that M. Night Shyamalan does—I'm there: *Signs, The Village, The Sixth Sense.* As soon as *The Lady in the Water* came out my wife and I scraped up the coin to secure two tickets to get an early look with other enthusiastic fans. But viewing the post-reaction, perhaps M. Night had pushed the envelope too far with this eerie, off-the-wall, fairy tale come true. The gathering that night seemed disillusioned. I loved it. It was an artistic stroke of movie-making brilliance in my view. In case you didn't see it, or could benefit from a bit of interpretation, here's what connected with me. It's a story about "Story"—a nymph from another world. The wolf-like Scrunt comes after her and despite attempts at protection she is torn up leaving long blood scratches on her legs, and dragged away for dead. Rallying to help, a conglomeration of apartment dwellers gather to decode a message. It reveals they must conduct a ceremony requiring the laying on of hands from seven sisters, special witnesses, and words from "the healer." This formula is her only chance.

At first, a woman identified by the nearness of a butterfly is thought to be the healer, but her earnest efforts fail. Then it becomes apparent that the healer may be "Mr. Heep," the apartment's maintenance man with the stuttering problem. We learn he had lost his family. A man had broken into his home when he was not there and killed them all. He lives with the great pain of the tragedy. If only he had been there. Though he hides it well, others know he walks everyday with the limp of his great loss. Now he is called upon to intercede for Story. One of the characters encourages him to let her feel his energy. He begins to pour out his pain over his family taken from him. As he does this, in step with a magical soundtrack—the lady is healed.

Why did the writer cast Mr. Heep as the healer? Did he observe this truth in life? Was it from his own experience that he learned healers rise from the ranks of the wounded? Sure we can see how God uses wounding to forge counselors, but what about evangelists? Is there any correlation for those who trigger spiritual healing through the Great Physician? Does God shape us to be his instruments of redemption?

I have my own raw, dark story of brokenness. Growing up a wild secular kid, God saved me in college and radically transformed my life. Within two years, a Long Beach church brought me on as a campus-college pastor before I eventually went on to plant two churches. By God's underserved grace and power I had a fairly steady spiritual walk for two decades. Yet when I headed into midlife the train came off the track. I lost my center spiritually, started to experiment with drinking, and while junked up one-day (in lust) I impulsively shoplifted. In some ways it was a total anomaly to my life; in other ways, it pictured me perfectly. By nature, I tend toward indulgent pleasure-seeking. When Christ is not at the center, look what happens. It's me!

Though I immediately went off to counseling, ashamed and afraid to disclose what I had done, I ended up losing my pastor position. At moments with my elders, we thought it might work out, but in the end it didn't. They decided it was best to move forward with their other leaders. When the church decision came down, my wife and I glanced at each other in a nod to God's sovereignty saying, "Our time here is done." It began for us the most interesting chapter of being: displaced, unemployed, un-hirable and newly broken. Clearly confused by it all, I wondered if I would ever do "pro" ministry again. Yet twelve months later my wife said reflectively, "This was the hardest and most amazing year of our lives." Let me share a slice of what occurred in the aftermath.

Though the sin was my fault, the ousting naturally left me feeling betrayed. After all, I had *started* the church! Anyone who has experienced a break-up knows that emotional intensity. Anger built within. One morning after boiling over, I realized if I was going to make it forward I needed to forgive. I made a phone call, owned my mess, and offered a branch to a beloved staff member. It was a beginning.

Months after leaving, while stewing over the failure and feeling discarded, I found myself giving thanks to the God who was still with me. I remember saying, "I am so glad I have you!" At the time, I routinely met with a skeptic gal at our church. I initially knew her from providing marital counseling. Her husband, abruptly, chose to separate. Suddenly we had parallel lives; both of us were trying to come to grips with feelings of loss and betrayal. Yet something distinguished the processing—can you see it? Having the Lord comforted me, while she was going through this alone. Though she had friends, she didn't have the God who was bigger than all the loss she was facing. She did not know the One who would lead her forward, and never abandon her, the God of goodness who would work things out for good despite the great blow.

So when we met, I felt led to explain at a deep level why I believed she needed a relationship with Jesus. With emotion I appealed descriptively— God would take care of her future and never leave her side. He would be the One she could always count on! The timely message cut through in a way I could not previously. A week later, having helped her over a wrong perception of faith, my skeptical friend gave herself to Christ. Trusting his sacrifice, she now has Jesus, and he has her. Afterward, I sat back contemplating what had transpired. In the trauma of my debacle, God took an insight from my brokenness and used it to lead her to faith. In the months and years ahead, this same scenario would play out with others. It is the array of those experiences that inspired this chapter. This is the one I never wanted to write!

Am I implying that God can only work through pain? Certainly not. People respond when they see the gospel as the good news that it is. However, in his divinely sovereign way, God does shape our lives for ministry and mission through difficulties and challenges. The reciprocating principle of 2 Corinthians 1:4 applies to evangelism as well. The text says that God our Father "comforts us in all our troubles, so that we can comfort those in any trouble with the comfort we ourselves receive from God." Have you ever dug into this passage? Paul is in distress. Intense pressure leads him to despair of life itself. He and his ministry team are so overburdened that only God could carry them through. Have you been there? Ever feel that kind of pressure or type of breaking that takes you to the end of yourself? Paul concludes that they went through all this to benefit the Corinthians (2 Cor 1:6); that receiving God's deliverance and comfort resulted in the comfort and salvation of the Corinthians. Not just comfort, mind you, but salvation! Note that the word "parakletis," which is used for comfort, literally means the divinely given ability of "standing beside a person." The idea is that we are empowered to do the Lord's work by what we have gone through.

In all my Christian years, I had never heard a message on how God shapes us to bring salvation; yet there it is in our Bibles. What it says is so true. God takes our brokenness, comforts us, and then redeems it for his redemptive plan. Have you grasped that God has a purpose for everything you have gone through? He even knows the people you will meet, and how your life experience will touch theirs. To reach others we must identify ourselves with them. This is what Christ did. He became one of us—being made in our image (Phil 2:7). The identification principle is powerful in ministry and especially evangelism. When your story crosses into the world of a non-believer, God has prepared you to bring his message in a very personal way. Your life becomes a bridge for the gospel. Do not underestimate the significance of how your story connects. Nor should you under-esteem the sensitivity that comes through pain.

GOD'S REDEEMING SLIGHT OF HAND

One night my wife and I sat down and watched *You've Got Mail!* Toward the end of the movie, Meg Ryan's character has her family bookstore closed by a ruthless competitor. Crushed, she says, "Everyone else is going on with their lives, but I feel like something died inside me that no one can do anything about." She reflects upon this painful change to her life, and says how she is writing a children's book. Knowing how much I had been writing, my wife looked at me sensing the connection. Later, I had a similar déjà vu experience when I read *Culture Making* by Andy Crouch, where he shares about the magazine he tried earnestly to rebuild, only to have the owners shut it down. He lay around for a year in a lonely state, but it was then he started to write his amazing book.[1] Unlike them, my sin led to my demise, and yet, we all felt deep loss, and a sense of failure. We felt like something in us had died. I too journeyed into a time of deep reflection writing extensively. Why do you find inspiration in these soul-searching moments? Could it be that in a bigger view, loss is about

1. Crouch, *Culture Making*, 259–60.

addition not subtraction? You would be amazed to see how much vision God has birthed through pain!

My wife Robin loves games and it seems she is always finding one for "her boys" to play. On this dinner night, she asked "Tell us your favorite movie, the character you liked most, and why?" My oldest son Matthew chooses *The Lord of the Rings*. Can you guess his character? The soon to be king Aragorn? Nope. The valiant Elf bowman Legolas? Nope. The leader-wizard Gandalf? He's too old! My son's choice is Faramir, the younger brother to the heralded Boromir, general of Gondor. Matthew notes how under-appreciated he is by his father. There is an underlying pain of rejection, a sense of not living up to expectations, from a father who looks down on him. (In case you are wondering, it is not a picture of our father-son relationship, but Matt is sensitive, and feels with this character). As you encounter Faramir yourself in the scenes, you can see pain but also qualitative depth. Pippin notices this before the great battle of Gondor, matching him with his brother, "I see his strength in you." Pain has made him sensitive. He sees others experiences. After a small skirmish where they cut down mercenaries, he talks about the life of his slain enemy: "His sense of duty was no less than yours. You wonder what his name is. Where he came from. If whether he was really evil at heart. What lies or threats led him on this march from his home, and would he rather not stay there in peace." How fascinating that my sixteen-year-old son would choose him as his favorite character.

Brother or sister in Christ, what do you walk with? Pain is not the worst companion. You might find it goes a long way in deepening empathy and developing you as a person. Do not despise God's master hand at shaping you for his work. Veteran counselor Dr. Dave Ferreira says, "God picks pain to minister his Spirit." In his many years as a helper, he has observed that people who have gone through pain have keen insights. Once they are healed (so perspective is not distorted), they can see things that others miss, and the Holy Spirit appears to work extraordinarily powerful through their brokenness. This kind of sensitivity is huge in evangelism. The soul whisperer can empathize with real life journeys. Your ability to relate to other's plights opens doors for the kingdom. I once sat with a woman who with tears in her eyes told me that because of her abortions and addictions she could not follow Christ. The shame over her life was like a force field pushing away the grace of God. I never would have seen how acute this experience was and how to appeal to her had I not journeyed through my own experience of shame, where I as a pastor, even wondered if I was forgiven.

There is a ministry equation that might not be as revolutionary as E=MC2, yet it is just as significant in the spiritual realm.

Identification + Insight = Impact

When you take true identification with others and add insight, you are positioned for influence. I have seen God use this alignment prolifically. Though I wish I could have avoided the sin and suffering that now colors my world, I find myself relating to so many more people, as if God had switched out my single lens for a kaleidoscope. I discovered that with the limp came a lens. God overwhelmed me with the sense of how he wanted to use it all. Every one of those broken lines in my new scope were at his disposal. I continued to run into people where aspects of my story connected with theirs. I knew what it was like to feel judged by the church. Rejection. Shame. Outcasted. Unemployed. Unwanted. Stuck. Sin-addicted. Angry. Shattered. The very struggle that had brought me down now drew me with others. Isn't that strange? Whenever this deeper sharing occurred influence seemed to follow right behind.

At first I fought it. I cursed it. Why God? Why did you allow this? It's ultimately your fault! I could never seem to shake the limp, even to this day. It's as if he branded my heart, searing it permanently like a soul tattoo. I reasoned with God, "I'm no Old Testament prophet here—stop messing with me! I'm just a nobody-recovering sinner–clearly you have made a mistake in not healing this wound entirely." One day an inner voice dawned, "I want you to know how they feel outside my church? Now you will never forget!"

In the time of processing my sudden sin-spoiled-life, there was one illustration that provided the greatest perspective. It is the work of counselor, Melinda Reinicke, who writes fairy tales about life issues. This particular story is called, "The Painting." It tells of a painter whose canvass is permanently marred by an evil dragon. His life dream for the painting is ruined, and as his anger burns over the loss he rips into the canvass even more. Without anyone else to turn to, he brings the canvas to the Great King:

> "What brings you here this long way?" asked the King with concern as he gripped the painter's shoulder in greeting. "This." The painter fumbled to uncover his wretched canvas. He had once dreamed of unveiling the painting under very different

circumstances. The King eyed the canvas and heaved a deep sigh. "The dragon certainly left his sordid marks. But, who did this?" He pointed to the slashes made by the painter. "I did, after I discovered the blotches. . ." the painter confessed with shame. The King pursed his lips and nodded without condemnation. "No doubt, you have come here hoping I can tell you how to remove the dragon's marks. But, the remedy is far more powerful than that and will gaul the dragon to his very core."

"Tell me what the remedy is!" exclaimed the painter with relish. "Come, let's walk," answered the King and they headed out of the encampment into a nearby meadow. "What do you see my friend?" "A grassy field. Hills and mountains in a distance," puzzled the painter. Then the King drew him to stand beneath a strong oak tree at the field's edge. "Now what do you see?" "The same as before, but through the low hanging boughs of this tree," answered the painter as leaves on the branches fluttered and danced before him in the breeze. When he grasped the King's version for the marred canvas, the painter's face filled with excitement. "It will take all of your artistic talent, and there will be times when you feel like giving up before it is complete," warned the King compassionately. "But promise me, friend, that you will not slash the painting again or abandon the project. If you give in to destruction, the dragon wins." The painter agreed with renewed determination.

It was admired by all who saw it, a painting of exquisite depth and beauty. Those who looked on it felt as though they stood in the very place. The peaceful lake, graceful hills, and regal mountains were not viewed from some distant point. They were seen through swaying branches speckled with dark fluttering leaves. When the dragon heard of it, he was incensed and still fumes over it to this day.[2]

Can God truly turn wreckage into masterpieces? Is it possible the God over us is that great? I especially loved Reinicke's attention to the painting. Did you notice the "dark fluttering leaves," and her lines: "exquisite depth and beauty" and "not viewed from some distant point." Her story offers a glimpse to the kind of influence God enables through brokenness. Something happens that takes us deeper in humility, transparency and understanding. It is there we can minister in ways that would be impossible without the scars.

2. Reinicke, *Parables For Personal Growth*, 57–60.

Where Satan seeks to demean and destroy, God redeems. One day conversing intimately, I reflected on God's hand on my life noting that Satan was second to God and would not win. My friend accentuated the point by adding, "Not even a close second." Isn't that encouraging? God is so much greater that he will ultimately get the final word! His purpose for you and I will prevail with his infinite ability to take marring blows and bring out good. If you have experienced your own version of brokenness, it might be the time to stop and ask, "Whose program are you aligned with?" Do you see God's redeeming artistry? If by chance you don't right now, believe me—you will. Every brushstroke in your life is carefully placed. He makes no mistakes.

BROADENING CONTACT POINTS

One day taking my usual "cut the stress" run, I came upon a sidewalk section with a New Testament ripped in shreds. Someone had torn out page after page, crumpling and throwing them to the ground. I did what I normally would not do—I stopped. I stood starring at the sight wondering what precipitated such an act. There was a story here. Did a Christian do this? Did they pray for a long time and when it went south said, "Screw this ask anything and it will be done crap?" Was it an unbeliever exploring the Bible, who decided the whole thing wasn't for them after all—having flirted with faith they ripped it before storming back out to the world? Did one's newfound faith lead their spouse into a rage against the book that is now disrupting their life? I didn't know. But I gathered there was a personal story behind that scene. I took a moment to pray—that God's grace would bring them around.

For anyone thinking the brokenness concept applies sparingly, you might want to think again. Although people are great at masking, most have pain. In a small group seven men share life maps. This exercise enables people to tell their stories. The different color post-it-notes laid out on 8 x 11 sheets offer a visual display of the good events (green), and those they would place in the bad category (yellow). As the stories unfolded, every one of these macho men had sins, disappointments, and wounds to disclose. If you live long enough it is likely that you yourself, something or someone will hurt you. Don't be fooled by all the smiling faces; in the quiet moments people are contemplating those crazy experiences—trying to make sense of it all.

On an altar call Sunday at Sandals, 216 people came forward in response to our pastor's call. I met them upfront and collected cards as our team ministered individually. Sending out follow-up details to ministry leaders, I observed the high rate of brokenness noted by the ministers: Marital issues, emotional abuse, all types of recovery needs, prostitution, depression, etc. Here's a mere sampling:

- I have been through rough times that had me almost kill myself, and I just can't let the anger and heartache go.

- I am addicted to heroin opiate and need a lot of prayers. Will go to rehab Mar 15 for thirty days.

- I know in my heart I am a bad person, but I ask forgiveness and I still continue my bad habits. I tell myself God loves me no-matter what. I don't know what to do with this feeling. Deep down I'm really depressed!

- I need to move forward in my life. It has been in a rut since my divorce. I have faith in my Lord Jesus Christ, but at the same time I feel alone.

- I ask that you pray that I may forgive myself of my past sins because I am unable to forgive myself. It has held me back.

A compassion leader, Brittany, in humble recognition of our sin condition voiced, "Don't we all have brokenness?" Though it is biblically correct to define our general condition as broken, there is a kind of brokenness that originates from God. As odd as it may sound, God initiates this experience. We see this in Peter and Paul's stories: The rooster and the thorn. Each story marked by the number three. There's a saying, "When God wants to do an impossible task, he takes an impossible person, and breaks him." Richard Bauckham argues compellingly that Peter's breaking was not to denigrate him, but rather to qualify him for his apostolic task.[3] Brokenness enables God's servants to do his work without usurping his glory. By giving the limp, we lean on his power, not our own. In being less we become more. Can you point to a moment when God showed you who you really are in this world? Downsized, he gives us a chance to become something bigger. This is a tremendous truth. When God redeems your life, even at its darkest dip, it will make you a worshipper!

Christian friend, what have you walked through? Do you realize that God wills to use it all? He wastes no wound. Are you willing to put your

---

3. Bauckham, *Jesus and the Eyewitnesses*, 180.

experiences at his feet for the gospel's sake? You will have to come to a place of saying, "Lord, I am willing to share my brokenness, if you can use it to help someone else know you." Many of you are doing this faithfully already and are reaping fruit for the kingdom! Do not think you have to identify with everything, but you do need sensitivity to draw close, share life, and get deep. If you can't be real, you may never see the deeper need in someone that only Christ can meet. People today benefit when someone can show the meaningfulness of knowing God. As a soul whisperer this is what you do.

I don't know if you have ever considered all the intersection points you have with non-believers. Let me suggest some possibilities and see if you could sign your name by any of these. My signature is on most. If you can, you could relate to many since these experiences fill the pages of their lives. NBA great Kevin Garnett said, "Most people have gone through something in the past that makes them who they are in the present." What have you gone though?

- Set backs
- Conflict
- Loss
- Legal issues
- Failures
- Marital struggles
- Singleness issues
- Anger
- Health challenges
- Unemployment
- Anxiety attacks
- Hurt and frustration
- Sin struggles
- Relationship breakdown
- Family issues
- Unforgiveness
- Addiction/Substance Issues
- Abuse in its various forms
- Shame
- Overwhelming burdens

- Rejection

When we see a list like that we naturally dismiss it as negative—a yellow post-it-note instead of the green, and yet God pulls each experience close to his breast and nurses it with divine purpose. We find ourselves echoing the words of Jesus when he explained the rationale for a blind man's condition, "but this happened so that the works of God might be displayed" (John 9:3). Brokenness enables us to speak other's experiential language. This dynamic is very powerful and often necessary. God broadens our reach by the identification with feelings. In other words, you might not have gone through the exact thing, but being able to relate feeling-wise enables you to share life and spiritual insight.

INSIGHT'S EDGE

When it comes to influence, insight on life's journey is what we need. I have always loved Psalm 40, and call it "The Testimony Psalm." In the early verses David admits to being in the mire. He testifies to how God has delivered him from the slimy pit, and set his feet firm (6–7). Now he has a powerful story to tell. He does not hide it. He knows God's fame is tied up in his life. This is true for you also! As you disclose people will see how Christ has helped and redeemed you in life's mire. Instead of the perfect, plastic Christianity image, they encounter the God who is involved deeply in real issues. When you have gone through something, believe me, others will listen.

Have you experienced insight's potent effects in your life? Attending a New Year's service, I stood up for one of the four responses to the pastor's message. It was the one about ongoing healing. My wife later asked me why I chose that one. As we dialogued, pent-up feelings over spilled! Introspecting with others about what occurred, I saw for the first time how unhealthy I had become (it was like I was able to step outside myself—weird!) I was waiting for something to happen to feel okay with my life. What would God say? "Did I not already redeem you? What are you waiting for?" Insight defrosted the window enabling me to see how my present experience linked detrimentally to my past and future: Hurt from the past—entitlement toward my future. Sick! It took an epiphany, to deliver me from the bonds! I repented and cut those moorings—I will not live another day like that! I wrote a blog, "Fear Not Your Dreams" because we can fully trust Jesus with whatever happens. Regardless of what the future holds, you and I will be okay. God will faithfully steward our lives according to his plan, and we can live each day knowing this. I thanked God for my friends and their insight.

When you offer true insight, your non-believing neighbor's ears will open as their interest is piqued. Try it. If married, talk openly about your marital issues and what you have learned. They will soak up your words. Don't be surprised when your step of disclosure draws forth a significant exchange, and perhaps a hidden need. Marriage is tough for all; who doesn't have struggles from time to time?

Can you relate in any way to this scene: "I had this dream of what my life would be," she throws the pot to the ground, shattering it. Tears cascading down her face, she picks up a piece, "This is my marriage." Looking into the eyes from the women's gathering, she picks up another broken piece, "This is a dear friendship." She picks up another, "This is my ministry situation right now." Putting the pieces in a box, she says, "All I can do is bring this to Jesus." This powerful teaching captured an incredible truth—God welcomes broken pieces! He takes broken pots and does extraordinary things. Broken lives become a beautiful mosaic, being touched by the Master's handiwork. One of the amazing restorative things that he does is prepare us for mission. True to form, this leader testified that God was clearly more dynamic in her ministry afterwards.

What insights has God given you? How are you using those for his glory? In addition to others, God has given me a ministry to those sunken by shame. I call them "letter wearers." Believe me when I tell you, the letters cover the alphabetical gamut: S—The boyfriend haunted by angrily spitting in his girlfriend's face. M—The woman crying in our class because her infidelities targeted married men. I—The man cuffed and taken away in front of his kids and onlooking neighbors because of his sordid indiscretion. V—The veteran waking at three each morning disturbed by the violent things he had done. Did you know that for both believers and unbelievers, that forgiveness is not their whole remedy? One man tells me, "I know I'm forgiven in my head, but I don't feel it in my heart." I gleaned how to help them only because I know what it's like to wear the letter. What special insight has God afforded you?

Recovery fits the equation perfectly. Out of brokenness comes deeply needed wisdom on how to springboard admission of defeat into victorious living. Not how to stop a compulsion, but how not to start. Brilliant! The same insight principle applies in so many areas. A middle-aged man comes to the men's gathering and sees younger guys in the throes of turmoil: marital breakdown, children's issues, job loss, etc. He looks at them and says, "I've been there." What does he have that they don't—wisdom to face life's realities. Why was he talking to me? He was offering his brokenness to minister. I paused to savor the beauty of his heart.

Needless to say, Jesus incarnates the concept, being the ultimate bridge of brokenness. From his broken body flows spiritual healing. We are all called to be like him—broken vessels bringing healing to a hurting world.

HOW GOD REDEEMS BROKEN DREAMS

How fitting that Jesus's first resurrection appearance occurred with two depressed, broken-dream disciples trying to comfort one another over their loss. Do you recall the story of the two on the Emmaus road? We all know what it's like to have thought we were on the verge of winning the championship, only to be taken out in the first round. This was the emotional aftermath the first Easter Sunday. When Jesus encounters them stealthily, he uncovers dashed hopes: "They crucified him; but we had hoped that he was the one who was going to redeem Israel" (Luke 24:20–21).

Their sentiment reminds me of a time golfing with a friend where we spent an afternoon crossing fairways to the roughs finding our balls together. Eric would swing, watch his ball fly off to some troubled spot, and then he'd say, "That wasn't exactly what I wanted." After he had repeated the line a couple times I started to crack up—what a great description of life! We have a vision of where it should go, then we take our swing, and find ourselves saying: *That wasn't exactly what I wanted.* The relationship didn't work out—it might have even ended bitterly—*that wasn't exactly what I wanted.* The house dream fell through—*that wasn't exactly what I wanted.* The little problem became much bigger than I thought it would—*that wasn't exactly what I wanted.* I never imagined making that mistake—*that wasn't exactly what I wanted.* We were hoping for the Messiah, and there he is on a Roman cross—*that wasn't exactly what we wanted.*

According to the Easter story, at this bewildering moment Jesus showed up. It's still true today! The message he gave those "roadies" two thousand years ago has enormous power. Let me spell it out and have it minister to you right now. Jesus wants to say this:

> You know that dream you had—the one that didn't quite work out? Well, I have an even bigger one for your life. In fact, it is so much bigger—that no matter what happens to your lesser dreams, if you are linked up with me, my dream will fill your life

with sustaining hope and vision. You may fail to see your dream
come true, but I will make sure my dream for you does!

Why did Jesus encounter those two? They had small thoughts of a political comeback for Israel, when God was going after the whole world! His
dream was for them to be right smack in the middle of it—key players in
a thrilling movement! Likewise, God wants to redeem broken dreams for
his redemptive plan. This same hope is what we bring to a hurting world.
No matter what you are going through, we know a God who is greater. He
is the author of redemption!

A woman discloses a bad choice that hurt everyone in her family,
and one day, she lay around knowing there was nothing she could do. She
walked outside into her backyard where, ironically, a lawn virus had killed
all the sod. But on that day, in the middle of this dead, poisoned turf, she
noticed a new patch of healthy green grass. She stared marveling—as if
God had spoken through a donkey. It was a clear message. "This is what I
do, my daughter! I redeem all things. I am the Master of bringing beauty
out of deadness. You will see this in your life." She opened up and shared
her story with her non-believing neighbor on how God's grace carried her
forward. In time, her neighbor came to faith, because she too wanted a
relationship with "that kind of God."

At the time of writing this chapter, I began meeting with a twenty-
six-year-old non-Christian man, married with three kids, and some really
rad award-winning arm tats. Within a few months, I learn his wife had
decided to leave him. He is suddenly living with a friend in an apartment.
I begin thinking of how to minister to him. When I first became a believer I dreamed of being the one with the stupendous life, using my shiny
example to point others to Jesus. But in this moment he is broken and
hurting, and all I can think of is drawing close to tell him my story—that
it would be something that offers hope without the shallow pat answer.
There is so much more I could say on this subject, but right now its time
for me to go and make that call . . .

DISCUSSION AND ENGAGEMENT

1. Take a few moments to think about some of your dreams and disappointments. How does God want to take your life and build his
   greater dream?

2. Have you experienced a time when your life experience crossed into the story of a non-believer? If so, share about this in your group.

3. How specifically can God use identification and insight from your life story with someone in your life right now?

PART II

Process:
Creating Lighted Journeys

9

Engaging in Mission

The Church of God does not have a mission in the world. The God of mission has a church in the world.

—Tom Dearborne

Many will not argue with the statement that J.R.R. Tolkien's *The Lord of the Rings* is the greatest movie ever made. Still, some don't get it. They have tried to watch, and cannot see why others would make such a grandiose conclusion. They know under Peter Jackson's direction that it's climaxing episode won Best Picture—yet is it not merely a story about some little guys trying to ditch a piece of hardware? Why all the hoopla?

What crowns this film a masterpiece is the theme of a greater story. Before mankind is made extinct by evil-overlords, the ring-ridding quest becomes the centerpiece of a cosmic battle, which will decide the destiny of all. Oddly, the whole world hinges on the actions of the unlikeliest of heroes—hobbits: Frodo Baggins, Samwise Gamgee, Peregrin Took and Meriadoc Brandybuck. Being so small, the other races of Middle Earth have overlooked them. As simple Shire folk, they grapple to comprehend their parts in the grander scheme of things. Yet the quest, which they choose to pursue, becomes the greatest adventure of all. At the end of the movie, when the four are together hoisting a few beers at the pub, they can barely fathom what they had done.

The idea that our lives serve a greater story is the brilliant insight of J.R.R. Tolkien. A Christian, he knew the epic battle raging for hearts and minds. He also knew how we strain to see our place. Most of us fail to appreciate how God's movement actually hinges *on us!* Incredibly, God has entrusted forward progress to his small and weak people. In doing so, he thrusts us into his greatest activity: the redemption of the world. One of our Adversary's biggest ploys is to get us to think our part is insignificant or unnecessary. Have you ever found yourself asking, "Is this all that God has for my life?" Ever feel like you don't make a difference, and your life does not affect anyone? Lies! Nothing could be further from the truth. Within the parameters of Christian calling, you have a role that can impact ever-extending networks of people. Each person has the potential to advance God's kingdom exponentially. It's often impossible to know what God might do through our efforts.

Two Intervarsity students connect with a young freshman. Inviting him to their dorm room, they get acquainted and share the gospel in a way he had not previously understood. Young Jay Pankratz becomes a Christian. Proceeding to disciple him, he later blossoms into a pastor. He follows God's lead from the Midwest out to California. One day looking around in a restaurant, this very white Kansas kid, notices how no one looks like him. In this moment, he begins to question why his church is not reaching other ethnic groups. Diving into God's Word he discovers the Greek word for "nation" is actually "ethnicities," which ignites a calling. Today, under Pankratz's shepherding, Sunrise Church of Rialto, California has grown from hundreds to over five thousand members equally divided (or should we say united!) between Anglos, African Americans and Latinos. Who would of thought this—from a little time given to the quirky dormie three doors down? It's hard to envision. We're like those hobbits being entrusted with the greatest assignment on earth.

True to Tolkien's epic tale our mission has all the dimensions of a great cosmic battle. We have to face fears, limitations, the need for perseverance that goes well beyond ourselves, and the literal attacking forces of darkness. Also, like the story, we must choose to engage. A choice lies before us on whether or not to go after a relationship with someone outside the faith. We can further the movement, or it can stop with us, too. Our role is not easy. Many are not signing up to follow Jesus. We don't always know what to say, or how to influence friends or loved ones; yet there is reason to hope—God is on our side! As we grasp the magnitude of the mission, we can take heart that the reason it is not simple is because it is so significant. People's eternal destinies are at stake!

FACING UP TO FEAR

With great challenges comes fear. Fraught with unforeseeable problems, the producers of the movie, *Jaws,* learned there's nothing easy about filming on the ocean. Throw in the fact that the main star—a three-ton, twenty-five-foot mechanical shark would not work—and you can see how their vision and the film's completion hung by a thread. Director Steven Spielberg had to figure out how to make a movie about a shark without having one. Forced to innovate, his team devised a special camera to film at the water's level, which gave the impression of something being there and looking on. The composer added what is now a famous soundtrack to create a sense of eerie presence without any sight of the creature. In a bizarre twist of Hollywood luck, the shark's absence, according to Spielberg, "made the movie."[1] Moviegoers were terrified by something that was not there. Such is the power of fear; imagined or not, it is real! We can tell people not to fear, or that there is no reason to fear, but that will not take it away. Most people have some levels of fear when it comes to talking about their faith. It is not as scary as public speaking, but some think *it's* close!

A faith-sharing course title grabbed my eye by promising to do it without fear. I laughed. Why are we doing that? Unfortunately, the alternative does not make for an appealing seminar title: "Share Your Faith with Fear." I suppose no one would come to that one. You might be comforted to know that the Bible is filled with people who encountered fear. Frightened by his sudden appearance, the "hiding out" disciples thought the resurrected Jesus was a ghost (Luke 24:36–37). Do you remember those scary flashlight stories growing up? When Jesus charged them to take the gospel to the world—there was fear. When the church encountered fatal persecution—there was so much fear that they scattered (Acts 7:59–8:1). When the apostles were thrown in jail—there was fear (Acts 5:18; 12:1–5). When Paul began preaching in Corinth—he describes how he experienced "great fear and trembling" (1 Cor 2:3). Fear is part of the mission equation just like it is in every significant endeavor. Can you imagine Frodo saying, "I'll take the ring to Mordor as long as you tell me there will be no fear?"

Like it or not, learning to do things with fear is one of life's most precious lessons. In sports, I tell my sons, "When you are nervous that just

1. Bouzereau, *The Making of Steven Spielberg's Jaws,* 1995.

means you are ready and your heart is in it. Just get those butterflies to fly in formation." If you are fearful about getting out there in mission, it's only because you see its importance. It means you are ready for God to take you to new levels of influence!

Since we know fear has paralyzing properties, consider two things that helped the disciples. The first was their perspective on the mission itself. Although they had so many reasons to cower, we know from history that they did not. Here's why: It's because their mission was greater. In the same way, the significance of what we are doing is so great, that fear can find its rightful place—in the backseat or trunk. On the day Peter and John were held-up and threatened, the early Christians prayed:

> Now, Lord, consider their threats and enable your servants to speak your word with great boldness. Stretch out your hand to heal and perform signs and wonders through the name of your holy servant Jesus. After they prayed, the place where they were meeting was shaken. And they were all filled with the Holy Spirit and spoke the word of God boldly (Acts 4:29–31).

Notice how despite the threats their mission focus remained. They knew something big was going down! This same impetus can drive us forward. I am sure there were dozens of times when those hobbits considered giving up the quest, but the mission was greater. Divine purpose enables us to dig deep and summon the courage to act. Let us not allow a little anxiety to prevent God from touching lives. In prayer you step up asking God to get those butterflies to fly in formation, so that you can do what God is calling you to do.

During a time of open sharing at the end of a new believer's class, a young somewhat shy mom named Lindsay talked of what happened when she named her sin-vulnerability for the first time. We all felt moved when she did this because her particular core sin happened to be "fear" and here she was sharing this in front of the entire class. It was not hard to see how it had plagued her life. But on the very night of naming it she said, "God began to help me overcome." A couple months after she sent this email:

> Recently, at church I had an amazing experience with a young woman sitting next to me in service. During worship she sat with her head down and when I looked at her I instantly heard the Lord tell me to tell her, that Jesus loves her and that everything she is going through will be okay. I was so afraid to tell her what was so obviously being played over and over in my head. I

fought it at first or was hearing the enemy telling me to leave her alone, but obeyed Jesus and spoke up. It was such a step for me. She thanked me and asked if I really heard that. I told her "Yes, I knew it sounded crazy and I have never done that before." She stood up with me the rest of worship looking more at peace.[2]

I cannot remember a mission's experience without the fear factor. In 2004, I made my first trip to Kenya. Invited onto a teaching team, I traveled with a group from a sister church. All the others had previously visited except myself and another teacher. At LAX we sat down for a pre-flight meal and I learned about Dubai. It turns out my traveling group had a terrifying experience at this stopover in the Middle East. Having lost their luggage, the authorities tried to hold them overnight. The impression was the Dubains had manipulated a scenario to get them to spend money. They were all reminiscing and buffing out the story, while I felt my anxiety level raise ten measures. It sounded so terrible! I wrote in my journal, "I have a funny feeling that other hostilities, or potential dangers are kept undisclosed. I am amazed at how little I know about this trip." Heading to the other side of the world I had no clue as to what the experience would be like. I tried to trust God, but had to admit, I would have loved more information.

There were a few other scary surprises like the time the Kenyan pastors asked me to give an off-the-cuff, open-air evangelistic message! One thing I did right was to go through the pre-travel steps with the Center for Disease Control (CDC). They set me up with ten pops of an anti-malaria drug called Malarone. The woman told me, "If you get bit by a malaria infested mosquito you will get malaria, but the drug will kill it inside you." I was a bit stunned by the idea of this—and half-heartedly thanked her for that detail. Later in the trip when we journeyed up to Nakuru, northwest of Nairobi, we spent the night at one of the Kenyan team member's homes. After the meal, our host John Njorge told me I would have to sleep in the mosquito netting, since there were plenty of mosquitoes, and then added, "These are the bad kind—they have malaria." That night, I got into my net, and tried to feel safe, but also knew I am a mosquito magnet. They are drawn to high metabolism, carbon dioxide people, and that is me to the T. I did sleep intermittently, and when I got up noticed three big bites on my body.

Then that morning on my way to preach at a rural Pentecostal church, I felt this sharp pain within. All sorts of fears raced through my mind as

2. Lindsay Ludwin email to author, March 8, 2010.

I contemplated thoughts of contracting malaria. As my imagination ran amuck, I had something going for me that helped to fight back fear, and do I dare admit, panic! That being—I was prepared for this. Everyday, I had taken my anti-malaria drug, and in a way the strange knowledge from the CDC nurse also helped me. Looking at the monstrous bites, I thought, if I am infected, then that sharp pain was probably the drug working. That morning I got up and delivered my passionate message on prayer. God has a great sense of humor! Of course, I never did get anything, and was glad I didn't freak. It would have robbed me of a great experience with that church.

We all know fear can rob us from our mission—if we let it. Although we may not be able to eliminate anxiety in evangelism entirely, we can see the other remedy: Preparation. In the book ironically named, *Can We Do That?* esteemed Pastor Andy Stanley notes "fear and ignorance are the two primary obstacles to personal evangelism."[3] He insightfully observes that the people are unequipped, and also that "fear and ignorance" go together. The reason people in churches are fearful of sharing faith is that the church has poorly prepared them for the task. The byproduct is fear. This dynamic is accentuated in our North American church culture because of all the baggage with scary, non-relational evangelism. Programmatic-telling approaches increase trepidation, because they push people into doing what is unnatural. However, when we provide a picture of what relational evangelism looks like, make it natural to who you are, take the pressure off having to answer questions from the tip of your tongues (you can always circle back and it's good to show humility), and teach you skills to be fruitful, then you can move past fear.

Perhaps, due to the limitation of the presentation model, a perspective exists that because the people cannot do the messaging—the role falls to the professionals. Some have quantified that only 5 percent can converse with others about faith.[4] I sympathize with the stark reality of these pastors strapped with our outdated evangelism mode, but I can't help but wonder if today's church is suffering from listlessly low expectations. A staggering 95 percent currently cannot converse? Is that healthy? Does not Jesus want his representatives to become much more? If members are not equipped to do messaging, we will never become the penetrative force needed in today's post-Christian climate. We must go outside "the joining circle." In other words, gospel impact needs to occur with those who are

3. Stanley and Young, *Can We Do That?*, 1.

4. Searcy and Henson, *Ignite*, 101.

not willing to gather with us—at least initially. That implies messaging ability from the people—preferably the kind that draws them.

At Sandals, one of our running jokes is that when you are talking with your unchurched friend, you can't stop in the middle and say, "I need to get my pastor!" This type of co-dependent thinking reflects the need for much greater empowerment. One of the strengths of the early church was its mobilization. When Philip engaged the Ethiopian eunuch in his chariot, he was ready for the communication task. Yet today there is a reticent dullness in Christians from lack of good training that links to mission experiences. While recruiting a team to follow-up unbelievers, a gal emailed me: "Am I qualified?" My reply, "Yes, you learn from doing!" She stepped up and had amazing conversations. Here she is thinking she can't do this—when we desperately needed her to do the work of influence for the kingdom! The more she practices, the more she is able.

During a training course, Fernando comes alongside a non-believing workmate offering spiritual input when there is opportunity. His friend shows interest, but one day apparently stepping back, declares, "I want you to know that I believe in evolution." Fernando responds to him jokingly, "That isn't going to get you anywhere." Weeks later, however, out of the blue his friend calls to describe a dream that he had. In it, there was a book. He opened the book, and there was a picture of Jesus. Below the picture were the words, "Do you really know me?" He then asks Fernando if he could help him to know Christ. Calling me for guidance, I tell him that he needs to go lead his friend to Jesus! He says, "I'm just a new believer. Wow, this is exciting!" After some instruction, I ended by saying, "You need to do this—because God has so many more! Once you have led him to Christ, let's connect him to church and engage in discipling him. Then we'll just have to see which of his friends God wants to reach next!"

The people can do mission. Ordinary Christians can fulfill the extraordinary feats fitting of a movement, if progressively trained. Due to the insufficient skill set of the telling paradigm, exhorting others from upfront to share the gospel is simply inadequate. In order to achieve results, the messaging part must get broken down. In *The Art of War*, Sun-tzu writes, "In general, commanding a large army is like commanding a few. It is a question of dividing up the numbers. Fighting with a large number is like fighting with a few. It is a question of configuration and designation."[5] If you divide or break down the skills to do battle then everyone, whether

5. Sun-tzu, *The Art of War*, 187.

individually or on teams, can. Does not every soldier learn to fight in our military?

Breaking down the equipping further is precisely what I want to do in this section. We have come upon a pivotal juncture in our journey together. So far, you have learned the drawing paradigm of *starting where they are, reading what they need, and knowing where to take them.* Also, you have observed Jesus's signature faith formation pattern, and the communication dynamics of the disclosure and description windows. You have contemplated specific drawing skills: Four ways to use disclosure, the gospel key, ministering holistically at each poverty level, and bridging your brokenness insights for influence. It is now time to add the skills of engagement. Herein, we look at the components of interaction from start to finish, A to Z. These skills position us to utilize all the others and will allow you to harness the power of process. They truly are a different skill type. Ancient craftsman utilized the right tool for each job: rasps, tongs, files, shears, augers, pliers, hammers, center punches, wrenches, angles, drills, lathes, and chisels—each having a specialized purpose. Similarly, certain techniques work directly for the engagement dynamics.

My hope in developing your engagement prowess is to give you that here's-how-to-make-this-happen confidence. The idea of conversing with a real live person may feel daunting at first. But when you see how the whole process unfolds it will greatly reduce anxiety—enabling you to get onto the adventure! I remind you that God has specific people lined up for you to meet. As Paul wrote, "For we are his workmanship created in Christ Jesus to do good works, which God prepared in advance for us to do" (Eph 2:10). Here you will be challenged to follow Jesus in being a "story creator" with someone outside the faith. God's assignments are very personalized. Think with me on just how specialized your calling is. You may not realize how much God has already equipped you for this task!

PERSONAL CALLING

"I will pay for you to fly anywhere in the world." These words from a career Delta Airline employee offering free round trip tickets were like a dream come true—the world was suddenly our oyster! For the next month we were plagued with the problem of figuring out which top world destination to choose. Having considered The Tropics, France, England, Italy, Germany, and Canada's Banff, we decided on Italy. The thought of touching its history, culture, and spirituality made it a great choice. Let me say without even an inkling of envy eliciting motive, it was an incredible trip!

The language barrier was never easy, but on the train from Rome to Florence we got the chance to sit down with a couple from English speaking Wales. Having only me to talk with for days, Robin was giddy to finally have an intriguing conversation. We both savored the moment with our new friends. After the usual introductions and small talk about travels, I decided to ask a spiritual question, "Do you attend church?" I will never forget their answer. The man said not only did they not attend, but did not know anyone who did—no family, relatives, neighbors or friends. Zippo! My heart pained as I contemplated the status of the church in parts of Europe, the biblical geography of our New Testament. Like many Christians traveling there, I had a sobering moment to reflect on what occurred. How did the great movement that transformed the Roman Empire lose its way?

Throughout the trip, I kept musing over the notion of spiritual influence. It is such a big topic, especially when we are considering whole cultures, the church institution, and how the two mix. It grew so big that I got discouraged, feeling powerless, like I couldn't make a difference; as we do, when we see huge forces shaping our world. But then something happened—a gift from God to bring me out of my malaise. On our second day in Florence, a European man walked over and asked for directions. I immediately thought to myself, "Did he think I grew up on pasta?" I am obviously not Italian. Why would he be asking *me* how to get somewhere in Italy? Yet it just so happened that the locale he sought was the plaza my wife and I visited the day before. With this little bit of acquired local knowledge, I proceeded to explain how precisely to get there. I laughed, "Who would of thought I'd be giving directions in Florence?"

In that interchange, it was as if God said, "Don't ever forget the simple realities of influence?" Though reaching people today is not easy we all possess some "local knowledge." Do you appreciate what you currently have? First, you have a deeply internalized story to share! As a believer reading this book, you may say as I did, "Who am I to be giving spiritual direction to others—I could never do that!" Perhaps you haven't been a Christian for long, or may have been a Christian for years, but feel intimidated talking with others. What is amazing about the Christian journey is how every Christian is embedded with vital data. Having responded in faith you know what it means to have your sins forgiven through the cross. You bear the story of God's love, and can provide understanding of what

Jesus does in a life. As you learn to engage, you will find opportunity to pull from your personal experience.

Second, you have a divinely appointed place in God's mission. It is not something reserved for pastors, missionaries and Bible college graduates. From the beginning of the church till today, God has entrusted his message to his people. We should pinch ourselves daily as a reminder that we are the ones who show others the way back to God and into eternal life. Is there anyone in the culture who has a greater calling? With all due respect to law enforcement, teachers, social workers, soldiers, and firefighting professions, we as followers and disciples of Christ are the ones who possess the message that has, as Paul said, the power to save (Rom 1:16). Very cool!

Within that calling each has a special sphere of influence. God has positioned every Christian to affect specific people. It is stunning to consider that there are people only *you* could reach. Let me say that again. There are people in your relational sphere that may not come into the faith, if someone does not help them who knows and loves them, *like you!* Many of these are outside the "joining circle" at this moment. Only you can touch them. Think about your kids, family, friends, work associates and community. The idea that only those with the gift of evangelism should lead people to Christ is entirely off base. The mission of the church belongs to everyone, partly because all have influence spheres. What was sad about our new friends we met from Wales was that no believers penetrated their relational world. We prayed for them.

ENGAGEMENT DETERMINATION

After moving to a new community, I had the intention of joining a softball team. One night, I get a call from Raul, the softball coach of an A-Level team (we are talking real deal ballers—the "used to play for the Yankees" kind of guys!). His PTA president wife told my better half that he coached a team, and she dropped a hint that I played a good game. After feeling out my ability, he proceeded to probe for my fit with his group. Hearing I was a pastor he says, "I want you to know the guys talk the talk—I mean they swear and talk trash to the other teams. Some of the other teams drink beers before the game, but we don't do that." He wanted to know if I would be okay with all this. He even mentioned the alternative: "You could get on a team in the church league?" He was right about one thing—I had a choice. The idea of hanging with my bros from church sounded so sweet!

The old hymn rose in my mind about "how blessed it is to dwell together in unity *on a baseball diamond*." Then coming to my mission senses, I told him, "I want to play." I didn't care how much they cussed and talked trash, drank, or if we would end up in fist o' cuffs with another team, I said, "I'm in." It is where I want to be.

Just like me, you have a choice to engage or not. Unrelenting is the mission principle: "Without contact there is no impact." It might be good to say that phrase repetitively when you encounter unsaved people. That year I began to connect with my teammate, Ty. As he got to know who I was, we eventually discussed faith. One day I said to myself, "I may be Ty's best shot at heaven." Fully realizing it is God who ultimately saves, we should appreciate the significance of our opportunities. An article on drowning caught my eye:

> Think drowning involves screaming, gasping, and flailing? Think it's easy to notice someone drowning? Well, you're wrong. Drowning is a silent killer. There's no waving or calling for help of any kind. It's not like what you see on TV. Many people would not even notice another person drowning at just 30 yards away. Even scarier is that in a small but significant percentage of kids' drownings, an adult will have watched the whole process, not having a clue what was happening.[6]

As I read this post I couldn't but think of how apathetic I can be toward non-believers. It is so easy to get disconnected from their reality, to live engrossed only in my concerns. Is it that way for you, too? We pass right on by not noticing where they are and what's at stake. They give no signs. Sometimes they do when they are desperate, but often we see nothing. We fail to appreciate they are drowning before us. The call to mission is serious.

During a church planter's assessment, a couple from Washington State had a vision of starting a network of church plants in a tightly compacted apartment section outside of Seattle. Working at Starbucks, he was in contact with many non-believing friends. He gave a message about his vision, and we assessed both his communication ability and the thoroughness of his plan. Within the assessment process we probed for potential issues that could undermine the dream. In this case, we picked up hesitancy to fully embrace this calling. We didn't know what hindered his heart. During the week, we prayed for God's resolution. In the final

6. "Drowning Looks Different Than You Think," modified March 11, 2012, http://shine.yahoo.com

interview, the lead assessor sensitively but directly asked, "Are you all in?" With emotion in his voice and moisture in his eyes, he replied, "I'm all in!" What a moment that was. God would take his full heart and do so much!

How does a person come to the place of saying, "God, when it comes to your mission— 'I'm all in.'" "I want to engage." "I want to fulfill my part of the great story." "I want to further the movement, and not have it stop with me." "I want to become your instrument to reach others for Jesus." I don't assume to know all the contributing aspects that lead people to become mission-focused, but it is my prayer that you come to your own "I'm all in!" moment. Maybe you are already there—and reading this book to increase your MQ. Perhaps you are on your way, and hoping to garner conviction. May God meet you now. Wherever you are at, I want to say it loud and clear: *You* have a pivotal role in the greatest story on earth!

DISCUSSION AND ENGAGEMENT

1. Discuss how fear has affected you related to sharing Christ or engaging in mission activity.

2. If you had better preparation to pursue a process with a non-believing friend, how would that help relieve fears?

3. Describe how it makes you feel to know that evangelistic engagement captures the attention of the angelic world?

4. Do you agree with the author who challenges you to jump in all the way with God's mission? In other words, do you think you can be effective in a halfway, half-hearted posture? Why or why not?

10

The Parable of the Glassblower

If you can't describe what you are doing as a process,
you don't know what you're doing.

—W. Edwards Deming

I could not help but feel mesmerized as she drew the pole from the burning hot flames. The Sawdust Festival in Laguna Beach, California was a browser's paradise, but nothing grabbed my interest more than the glassblowing exhibit. The woman "gaffer" stands before a furnace opening ironically named "the glory hole." This kiln portal provides access to the 2,300-degrees necessary to bring glass mixed with sand into a liquefied state. She dips and then retrieves the pole, spinning it to get a small ball at the end. When it is perfectly uniform she blows through the pole, which begins a bubble. She spins and shapes it on flat heat absorbing material called "the marver." Then it goes back into the furnace to repeat the process with even larger amounts of glass. She blows it much bigger this time, constantly spinning and shaping it toward her artistic vision. Again, it goes back in the glory hole and the process is repeated a third time. Then she pulls out new tools to cut into the glass for a vase-like contour, still working it with even more spinning and shaping, and periodic heating with a blowtorch. Finally, she adds strips of red color to the glass to obtain a new look. This is the intricate, timely process of turning liquid glass into an object of beauty.

* * *

It is worthy of contemplation that ever since I can remember, the church has envisioned gospel sharing in a non-process paradigm. The 1952 popularization of *The Four Spiritual Laws* tool[1] advanced the gospel and truncated it at the same time. Cementing the view of evangelism as presentation, this motif pervades current thought on spreading the faith. Although it has positively disseminated Christian content and become a vehicle for producing a significant amount of fruit, its moorings now deter a movement. If we view the gospel as something merely to be proffered, we fail to fathom the depths of gospel communication. This is what happens when we start with us, and not them. But many other issues surface within this longstanding paradigm.

Sometimes when I have more intimate discussions on evangelism, I spontaneously venture into dialogue on what personal evangelism is *not*. I reluctantly go there not wanting to come across negative or disparaging, but do so to define more clearly what it *is*. Contrast brings clarity, and clarity is what we need. In my view, even pastors do not always see the divide that exists between two very different modes of thought. Let me say up front, that whenever you say what evangelism is not, you create controversy. I expect that will be the case for some when they read the list below. I have watched the reactions through the years.

I confess my views have changed over time. In the planting of two churches, I did not see things with the eyes I have now. Old modes left me spinning my wheels and expending large amounts of energy that did not bring results. Just like you, I want to be fruitful. This list on what evangelism is *not* is really meant to help Christians focus on how to be effective. It's not intended to bash pastors, evangelists or churches. So, before you pelt me with vegetables, open your mind and let us reason together about what we are doing and why we're doing it. Is there any thinking that is hindering us from seeing greater impact for God's kingdom? Are you ready? Consider my "Not" list:

Evangelism is not:

1. . . . about sharing with strangers.

2. . . . a random word here or there.

1. Bright, *The Four Spiritual Laws*, 1952.

3. . . . a one-sided presentation.

4. . . . a sudden transition to get in a spiritual word (complete with the beep-beeps of the dump truck backing up to unload).

5. . . . a quick, clean activity.

✓ 6. . . . something we do and then leave the person behind.

From my observations, these points illustrate what is off with our thinking, and why the church is relatively impotent. Statistics tell us most Christians couldn't get another spiritually pregnant if they tried. Thom Rainer's research indicated that in the highest rated churches it took eighty-five Christians *per year* to reach one non-believer.[2] Maybe the reason is that we are not even doing evangelism. Could there be an imposter? Is it time to put that guy in the grave? If it feels like I am attempting to take several long galvanized nails and drive them deep into the lid of a coffin—it's because I am.

Let's just take the first statement about evangelizing strangers. People will undoubtedly argue for how God shows up in the miraculous divine appointments of the day to save people they run into on trains, buses, supermarkets and street corners. Certainly, God can "prompt" us to bring his word to someone at any time. I know this does happen—on occasion. I am not trying to put God and his gospel in a box. But are we to build our thinking from the rare exception or the rule? One of the biggest problems of the church is how it views its primary task of making disciples. From my observations, this clouded thinking goes all the way to the top.

In a 2010 interview with an outreach pastor of a four-figure sized church, I learned his favorite illustration. He loved to tell of the man who gave out tracts, but never saw any fruit through all the years of his efforts. At the end of his life, however, he heard that someone had read one and came to Christ. The pastor used this example to inspire his people. I saw how it could encourage those who never see responses (which itself creates a question), but I couldn't get past a more basic query: Is that what he wanted his people to do? Was this cold-call approach his view of evangelism? Why that illustration?

Unfortunately, this kind of thinking is no exception. Pastors routinely talk of the person they shared with who repaired their car, the waitress at the restaurant, or the person they sat next to on the plane. These are not people they know, but rather strangers they encountered, and then made a transition to get in a "spiritual word." Admittedly, these can make

2. Rainer, *Surprising Insights*, 23.

for great stories. It easily becomes glamorized; "I met this person today and God did this amazing thing, and before you knew it we were talking about Jesus!" This "stranger encounter" becomes the illustration they put before their people, or write about in their books. Thus, the congregation or readers see evangelism as having a spiritual discussion with someone they don't know.

Although there is a place for planting a seed with strangers, we have to ask, "Is this the picture we should have for what evangelism truly is?" A connected follow-up question is: "Does it work?" Is it that simple? All we have to do is strike up a conversation with a stranger, make a transition to spiritual things and presto: We have influence. Probing still deeper: "How much weight do we have with strangers, or acquaintances?" You might see this more clearly if you personalize it. How much influence do *you* give to someone who crosses your path? When someone of religious persuasion shows up at your door, pursues you outside a mall, or tries to talk to you at a party, how influential will they be with you? Be honest. Now granted, it is possible the non-believing stranger opens somewhat to the pastor's influence because they respect their role. This is positional influence derived from perceived authority. Yet the average Christian does not get that advantage. Sadly, in today's culture, many pastors don't get it either.

I recall during my college years when I tried to sell my car, a Ford Fiesta I affectionately called "The Red Rocket." This motorized tin can on wheels got good gas mileage, and being red was an attraction to my soon-to-be-wife, as well as police cars. Before its days were done, I posted an ad to sell it, hoping to turn a few bucks. I received a call from a guy who asked if I could come to his home and allow a test drive. Knocking on the door, I took notice when a nurse answered. She proceeded to call for Dan and he walked slowly out to meet me. I couldn't help but see how thin and pale he looked. As we test-drove the car, I noted "weak" could be added to that description; even using a stick shift seemed difficult. Obviously, he was ill. With it being the 80s and living in Long Beach, California with its large gay population, I couldn't help but wonder if he had AIDS, or another serious illness. I will never know, and in that brief moment there was so much I did not know about Dan. He chose to buy the car, and I was supposed to feel good about the sale, but instead a deep sadness hovered. I made an attempt to plant a spiritual seed, and left my ministry card, but at the gut level knew I lacked the one essential for influence—a relationship.

Literally hundreds of futile attempts with strangers have convinced me of a basic evangelistic truth. With all my spiritual knowledge and

honed ability to talk of spiritual things, without a relationship I am ineffectual. You cannot get away from this law of human nature. Some think
we just need to be better with our words. More forceful. More pointed.
More logical. More persuasive. We need to close the deal! If we just tell
them they need Jesus, then they'll invite him in as Savior. Again, I might
be a great apologist, but without a relationship my influence is nil. With
one, however, God works wonders!

Being introduced by a friend, I recently sat down with a young man
at Starbucks. He proceeded to disclose how he did not believe in the Bible
and heaven and hell, and a number of commonly held views. It turned into
a great initial conversation, and I decided to interact. As we discussed reasons for giving the Bible credence, I wrestled with how far to go in this first
meeting. Had I built enough rapport for him to receive it? The strength of
relationship is important not only for connection, but to uphold the message (I address this notion of "pace" with much more development in the
upcoming chapter, "The Art of Spiritual Dialogue"). Continuing with our
examination, does sharing with a stranger end up leading them to faith?

RESEARCH DOESN'T LIE

If stranger evangelism works then it would be clearly manifest in research.
So what does the data reveal? The *Vision New England Recent Convert
Study* of 354 congregations and 196 interviews with recent converts concluded: "For 71 percent, relationship with a caring Christian friend, neighbor, coworker, or family member is the single most important factor in
seeing a person come to a living faith in Christ."[3] It is perhaps no surprise
to hear that a secular study revealed 76 percent of the populace did not
believe advertisers told the truth.[4] But what we might not realize is how
much skeptical mistrust permeates almost every arena: media, politics,
business and religion. Fortunately, there is an exception. Helping church
planters interpret the culture, Director George Klippines, stated, "There is
still one trusted medium left in the world: my friends, their friends, and
everyone that we collectively respect!"[5]

Another strong support for this relational influence view comes
from a unique historical perspective. Rodney Stark, in his book *The Rise of
Christianity* builds a convincing case for the gospel spreading in the early

3. "The Vision New England Recent Convert Study," lines 18–20.
4. Yankelowich Spin Room, "You Don't Really Believe the Evening News Do You?"
5. Rowley, Lecture on June 7, 2010. *www.slidefinder.net/r/real_reason/32943400/p3*

church period through households and networks of relationships. Stark writes, "But the network assumption is not compatible with an image of proselytizers seeking out most converts along the streets and highways, or calling them forth from the crowds in the marketplaces."[6] We have a mental picture of cold-presentation evangelism as the primary means for how the message propagated; this sociologist believes that was not the way it occurred. Before Stark, there was noted missiologist Donald McGavran, in his groundbreaking work, *The Bridges of God*, where he observed the gospel's flow through natural familial relationships.[7]

If still not convinced, you might want to test what the research is suggesting by going down to your local Starbucks to strike up a spiritual conversation and see how far it goes. It's possible your targeted stranger may listen politely, and might even share a thought, but don't expect them to talk long, and don't assume it was impactful. Influence happens through people they trust, not strangers. With all the observational research, why are we using "stranger" illustrations? The answer is the presentation paradigm rules the mindscape of the church. In my view, this must change. People in our churches need to see evangelism through a new relational lens. If we think we are going to further the gospel we will have to enter someone else's world! If we just made this distinction, that in itself could reposition the church for a fruitful movement.

Another reason for the building-a-relationship angle is that most people need much more than a one-time chat. The *Vision New England Study* also revealed 86 percent come to faith through multiple conversations over months to years.[8] I found it fascinating to see Jesus practicing this truth. In John 5 he heals a man, but the man does not know what happened or who did it (12–14). The text describes how Jesus later "found him." That suggests Jesus circled back knowing the second encounter would be necessary (see also John 9:35). With the culture's deviance from Christian roots, most people need much more than a couple talks. It is not about making a presentation, but rather progressing into truth. This requires more than a conversational segue; it means framing an exploratory journey. Learning how to initiate these kinds of discussions will be the focus of the next chapter.

---

6. Stark, *The Rise of Christianity*, 56–57.

7. McGavran, *The Bridges of God*, 49.

8. "The Vision New England Study," lines 21–23.

LOVING THE STRANGER

Let's back up for a moment. Am I saying we cannot influence anyone outside our relational sphere? Not at all! We don't share with strangers; we love them. We are kind to them. We come alongside meeting needs and befriending in missional living. I cherish reaching out to people I don't know yet! We should all be warm and welcoming to our communities as Christian hospitality gets pointed in missional trajectories. It is amazing to see the walls come down after relationships form. If we love and befriend, we may even have the opportunity for influence.

This demarcation may seem like it is splitting hairs, but it's an important distinction. The adjustment could free the church to be far more focused and effective in all its outreach efforts. We love and befriend strangers; we evangelize those we are developing relationships with. When we engage in our missional groups and compassion ministries, we love and befriend first. Out of relationship, we read them and share relevantly. I am astounded by how many think evangelism is something we do with strangers; before any relationship forms Christians are trying to save people. This partially explains why church members are freaked by the "E-word." They think it's about putting a stranger on "the spiritual spot." Awkward and threatening, it's not surprising so many have ditched our most important call. As long as we think of evangelism in this dysfunctional way, the gospel movement lags.

In balance, there are contexts when stranger evangelism works. Because of campus community identity, colleges have a slight opening—one that will close as soon as they step into the real world! When internationals immigrate to America and a Christian belonging to their ethnic group shows at their door, they could have tremendous influence even though they just met. This is because the strong cultural bond already exists. Contrast that with the typical North American. What do you feel when someone knocks at your door unexpected? "What do you want?" "What are you selling?" "Why are you wasting my time?" This shows that we must read evangelistic influence within each cultural context. In this chapter, I am contextualizing evangelism for mainstream North America. The same contextual read will also apply even more intensely in Europe and other highly relational cultures. We must draw a line and acknowledge that messaging efforts belong inside a context; if pursued outside those parameters, they can be counterproductive.

Yet many in our churches predominantly think if we just make a transition and get in a quick spiritual word, then all it takes is enough people doing that and the person will eventually come to faith. This thinking is fundamentally flawed! Satan loves it. As long as we think in the presentation mode he knows we will reach few. As long as he can keep us from building trusting relationships where real influence resides, he has won. As long as he can keep us from developing ongoing dialogues that get to the heart, he has won. As long as he can keep us from being committed to the spiritual journey of another, he has won. Tragically, he is winning. Too many Christians are stuck in the past with the wrong view of our primary task.

It is not too late to alter course. While teaching at a church one morning on mission, a woman embraced me afterwards as if a light bulb had come on and all her past thinking had fallen down like a house of cards. She enthusiastically said, "It makes so much sense. We must go out to build relationships, get close and discern the gospel's appeal." When people finally see what it means to live missionally—it changes everything. Suddenly, evangelism becomes a holistic journey of coming alongside, entering their world, and excitedly figuring out what their unique path to faith is.

Pastors can inspire their people by modeling relationship building with unbelievers. Impact will multiply when they share not about the stranger, but the neighbors coming over for dinner each month, the ongoing conversations at the fitness club, or the new friend they are meeting weekly at the coffee stop. They should tell of the relational investment they are making, the inherent challenges, and the breakthroughs from God. People should see how they honor and dignify the non-believer, and what their pastor is learning from them! Their people can all be praying for God's drawing. When God does reach them, the whole congregation sees how their leader walked someone into the faith. This becomes a moment of joy for the congregation, and an experience they want for themselves. Then people will begin to learn what it means to be "on mission."

Let's hammer in one more nail. What happens when we view evangelism as a "hit-and-run" conversation with someone we don't know? If a person responded, we have no solid basis to discern if it was real and will "stick." Cold decisions do not make hot disciples! The calling of the church is to make full-on disciples, teaching them "all that I commanded you" (Matt 28:19–20). Bereft of relationship we cannot fulfill the discipling mandate. Who in ministry has not asked, "Where is 'what's his name' who came to Christ weeks ago?" Did we even know if he got saved, or was he faking it for his wife after last week's blunder? A top leader from a megachurch I interviewed admitted, "Results of people moving from a Sunday service decision into the new believer's class were abysmal."⁹ Whenever you see a gap between decisions and discipleship there is always lack of relationship. The angle is off. This is why some churches have shifted to doing evangelism in a relational community context. The group environment helps to produce a connected growing disciple, not merely a questionable decision. Allow me to note this: If your pastor is a gifted proclamational evangelist, then shore up the weak angle as best you can by connecting new believers right away to a key leader in charge of a discipling class.

JESUS HAD A "NOT" LIST

I am not the only one with a "not list." Take a moment to read the instructions of Jesus to his disciples on how to engage in mission, and pay keen attention to what he tells them to do, and *not* do.

> Go! I am sending you out like lambs among wolves. *Do not* take a purse or bag or sandals; and *do not* greet anyone on the road. When you enter a house, first say, 'Peace to this house.' If a man of peace is there, your peace will rest on him; if not, it will return to you. *Stay* in that house, eating and drinking whatever they give you, for the worker deserves his wages. *Do not* move around from house to house" (Luke 10:3–7, emphasis added).

Obviously, Jesus knew talking to a stranger on the road would not be effective. In another verse, he confirms this same idea by illustrating how sheep respond to their shepherd, "They will never follow a stranger; in fact, they will run away from him because they do not recognize a stranger's voice" (John 10:5). Reading his culture, Jesus also knew a quick stay at a home would not accomplish the mission. They were to remain at the home in the context of sharing community meals and hospitality over an extended period of time.

Despite his words, we could erect a modern argument with Jesus on why we should share with people on the streets, and only knock on the door and have a one-time conversation. We could make a strong case against his instructions saying, "This way we will be able to hit more homes, and you never know what God will do with those few minutes." We can defy his instructions with spiritual rationalizations, but why wouldn't we want to think in missionally wise ways? Just as the disciples listened intently before going out, should we not heed his words? Does he as the Son of

---

9. Comer, "Doctorate Study of 10 Mega-churches."

God not know the parameters of spiritual influence? Friends, don't you want to be effective and see real results? Do you really want to spin wheels or do you actually want to reach someone?

A NEW PARADIGM

If you care about being fruitful, let me shoot straight. Though there is a time to faithfully plant a seed, we need to stop thinking we are going to reach anyone by a random word here or there. Nor are we going to reach many by visual osmosis—people need more than just watching us. What we need is a process. My failed attempts at influence have distilled a conviction for an evangelism paradigm that truly works. In its simplest most skeletal form it looks like this—I call it the "Relational Evangelism Process." REP for short.

It can position you to draw others by putting you in the "sweet spot" for influence.

Being a task-driven personality, I tend to walk fast. Once out on a date with my wife, we started walking and minutes later finding myself ahead, I turned back to realize that I was twenty feet in front of her! If only it was the first time. I waited in deathly anticipation—when she finally caught up, she starred me down and fumed, "Walk with me!" That day, those words seared my soul. I would not run ahead ever again. I determined to make sure I'd be alongside. It has, perhaps, saved my marriage. It might just save your friend.

If I could wave a wand over the church to help us reach more, I'd sear souls with the same sentiment: *Walk with them!* Not way out in front expecting them to be up where you are. Not insensitively out of touch, but in-step, in tune with their journey. If we approach evangelistic relationships in this way it could change everything. It requires helping a friend process faith, and not abandoning, if they step backward. Evangelism is not a quick message thing, but a time of journeying with and loving someone. As indicated in the graphic, I am all for the presentation-decision part, but in a relational process there is the right time for that, usually later, when the subject of a decision becomes the natural dialogue.

People ask me if what I teach is "Friendship" or "Lifestyle" evangelism. I answer that obviously there are overlapping parallels, but there are major distinctions. Upfront, I do not like how *laissez-faire* they sound. Both seem to suggest that if we just have friendships and live our lives people will come to faith. I prefer to call it "Dynamic-Process," because it employs the soul whispering practice of Jesus in reading each unique person combined with the intentional progression of an evangelistic journey. Below I have listed how my model looks different than the modern paradigm that has existed, whether overtly taught, or covertly embedded in minds. Here are a number of contrasts that reveal a new set of thinking:

MODERN PRESENTATION	DYNAMIC-PROCESS
Share with a stranger	*Build deep relationships*
Divine appointments	*Divinely appointed relationships*
Make a conversational transition	*Frame an ongoing spiritual dialogue*
Give a presentation of truth	*Manage an exploring process*
Proclaim biblical truth	*Understand the person's starting point and discern relevant receptivity to truth*
Plant a seed	*Walk alongside all the way into faith*
The gospel outside relationship	*Incarnational relationship carries and embodies the gospel message*
Immediate response sought	*Well-processed decisions sought over time*
Emphasis on getting a decision	*Emphasis on making a disciple*

The distinctions are of critical importance. For example, if you do not create an ongoing dialogue, there is no chance for process. The conversation has no thread or path to progress. You made a transition to spiritual things and got in a few words. So what? What did that accomplish? Framing an ongoing conversation is entirely better. Thinking in process terms will take the pressure off with communication, and we would do well to communicate less content in the early period. In continuous dialogue, there's always room to circle back on interactions if you don't have a response or answer. One of my soul whispering laws relates to process: *What cannot happen today can happen tomorrow.* Don't feel like you have to achieve it all at once. Christians will benefit from studying the glassblower who understands stages.

As crass as it might appear to use a secular business parallel to evangelism, marketing guru Seth Godin's blog, "The Flipping Point" is spot-on. Referencing a misunderstanding of one of Malcolm Gladwell's popular books, he writes,

> When people say, "The tipping point," they often misunderstand the concept in Malcolm's book. They're actually talking about the flipping point . . . The tipping point is the sum total of many individuals buzzing about something. But for an individual to start buzzing, something has to change in that person's mind . . . The flipping point doesn't represent the sum of public conversations, it's the outcome of an activated internal conversation . . . It's easy to wish and hope for your project to tip, for it to magically become the hot thing. But that won't happen if you can't seduce and entrance an individual . . . Before the tipping point, someone has to flip . . . The flipping point (for an individual) is almost always achieved after a consistent series of almost invisible actions that create a brand new whole.[10]

We think of tipping; when what we need is flipping. Flipping requires more consistent activity from us that will accumulate toward actual influence. Perhaps closer to home, most believers have experienced growth dynamics in a small group. Would you see transformational impact if you got together only one time? Would spiritual formation occur if your group didn't consistently talk? This same principle applies in evangelism. You need to meet on an ongoing basis. This is when God draws faith. Dr. George Hunter, author and professor of evangelism, declares, "Conversation is the major operating power in worldview conversion—not usually one conversation, but multiple conversations over time."[11]

Another critical contrast of comparing the two approaches relates to how the message is received. If you share the gospel outside of having an authentic relationship you can easily be perceived as a peddler promoting something for his or her own benefit. The postmodern generation's radar is particularly in tune with this because they intrinsically value relationships and discern right away if you are really interested in them. Finally, as I have said before, without relationship we lack the angle for solid decisions and a discipling projection.

In the next few chapters, you will discover how to go about a redefined evangelistic process. You will learn to frame up, manage the dialogue, and

10. Godin, "The Flipping Point," lines 1–18.

11. Hunter, *Radical Outreach*, 179.

employ breakthrough techniques. Before we get there, look at my definition for evangelism. Definitions help us see something with its essential
parts. As you read it, see if you can identify the four vitals: *Partnering with
God in the process of shaping the mind and heart to believe and follow.* I am
sure you got it, but read it again in its broken form: Partnering with God
/ in the process / of shaping the mind and heart / to believe and follow.
Friends, that is evangelism!

Jesus told parables to disguise truth from some (those with hardened
hearts of ill-intentions), and to reveal it to others (Mark 4:11–12). In one
instance, after telling the parable of the seeds, he offered a rich interpretation about heart receptivity. Let us return to the glassblowing exhibit
at the Laguna Beach Sawdust Festival for my attempt with a parable-like
interpretation:

> The raw melted glass is the non-believer's mind and heart. The
> glassblower is the wise Christian who knows conversion, like
> a beautiful blown glass piece, happens inside a process. If the
> glassblower tried to do it all in one step, it would fail miserably.
> Although we are open about our faith, like the glassblower, we
> do not try to do too much at first. Often we wisely hold our
> tongues and focus on showing love. Substance can be added later
> when the relational bond is stronger and dialogue more natural.
> Even then, early conversations are not about the cross, but focus
> on faith's meaning. There is no expectation for response, since it
> is evident, that they are far from attaining the necessary forma-
> tion. Evangelism is a patient and progressive craft.

> As the glassblower uses a flat heat-absorbing surface to work
> the material over time, so the Christian frames an ongoing con-
> versation that allows for shaping. The pole goes back in the fur-
> nace to keep the substance pliable; likewise, the Christian shows
> love to soften the heart and truth to direct its form. This happens
> over and again. Within the dialogue, just as the glassblower uses
> tools, so the Christian applies special skills and techniques for
> effect. The constant use of the blowtorch signifies the intensity
> of prayer to draw the heart. The glassblower must make critical
> decisions before the glass hardens in an uncompleted state; in
> fact, once the process starts it cannot stop. So, too, the Christian
> maintains momentum with the journey.

> In the right time, the believer points to a faith response where
> the true power of Christ is realized. With ample preparation, the
> person contemplates following Jesus. Now the crimson is added
> as they gaze upon the red, bloodstained cross. Suddenly they
> appreciate color! When they choose faith, Jesus miraculously

saves with his forgiving love and seals with his Spirit. They, like a beautiful piece of blown glass, become a vessel to shine through. Afterwards, the Christian looks on in delight in what God and they have done.

Following my *Faith-Sharing* class, I periodically run into participants and if they can't avoid me by disappearing down the hall, I ask how they are doing. Though some are engaging, there are always those who are not. I sometimes think even after the training they still did not "get" the REP. There's the great recovery line: "It works, if you work it." I can teach people how to reach others, but I can't do it for them. They will have to connect with a friend, frame an ongoing dialogue, read the person's needs, and help them forward. This will be true of you also. C.S. Lewis so eloquently described this effort saying, the "burden of my neighbor's glory should be laid on my back."[12] Evangelism in its purest form is unselfish love. It is acting in the greatest way for the greatest good of another.

So no more spinning wheels. No more wasted energy. Now we can get about the business of being effective. The only question remaining is, Who? Which non-believer are you going to engage with? Is it a friend, work associate, recreational pal, or a neighbor? Think about that person and then hear the words of Jesus: "Go!"

DISCUSSION & ENGAGEMENT

1. In what ways have you seen the elements of process help you in reaching out to others?

2. Do you agree that spiritual influence happens primarily through relationships and not strangers?

3. What part of the parable of the glassblower is most instructive? Who has God put in your life that you could engage in the REP (Relational Evangelism Process)?

4. What do you need to do to begin building this relationship? If you do not have someone in mind, then what interests or connections could you pursue in your community to build relationships with people outside the church? This could be a sports team, hobby interest, community service, or just inviting a neighbor over for dinner. Talk about taking action!

12. Lewis, *The Weight of Glory*, 18–19.

11

The Lines of Spiritual Dialogue

We cannot hold a torch to light another's path without brightening our own.

—BEN SWEETLAND

Traversing through a darkened cave or jungle could be real scary. Who knows what lurks in the shadows? Can you picture being stranded in some wild exotic place without the means of light? You would surely restrict yourself from going anywhere in the dark. Facing this logistical limitation, the people of the past discovered that certain substances like tar, animal fat, whale oil, or pine pitch would burn for a long time. They dipped rags and tied them to flammable wood to create illumination. As retro as it sounds in our high tech world, the idea of making a torch is what we must go after in redemptive relationships. We don't want to merely have a one-time spiritual conversation, but instead, a dialogue that will burn long and create illumination for the whole trip. This chapter teaches the intricacies of how to light the torch, so to speak, so that an exploratory journey can begin. The next chapter focuses on managing the journey, and then the following chapter addresses how to breakthrough to the faith destination. Take a good look at the three essential stages of the REP (Relational Evangelism Process).

TORCH + **TRAIL** + **TRACTION**

These stages apply to individual and all types of group evangelism (community, missional, seeker, cell, discovery circles, "oikos," Alpha, evangelistic classes and church planting). This is because, even in a group context, you will need to execute each element. Both personal and group evangelism depend on the common denominator of spiritual influence between Christians and non-Christians. There's a critical beginning point of engagement, a processing journey, and the crossover to faith. Failure to reach people commonly occurs at each stage. But in many cases it doesn't have to be that way! Get ready to learn critical skills that will take you and your non-believing friends to some amazing new places.

* * *

"Greer called and they had their baby," I exclaimed. My wife excitedly asks, "Was it a boy or girl?" "A boy, I think." What did they name him?" "I don't remember, honey." She continues, "What was his weight and size?" Looking at me, her face drops. I don't have to answer this time. All I have is the sound-byte that a "subdivision" has occurred. My lame defense; "I am a man—we don't ask for directions, and never get details about babies!" In the big picture, that conversation revealed that my wife is exceedingly (she would say superiorly) more relational than I am. She naturally asks relationally oriented questions and seeks all the important relationship facts. It is instinctive to who she is and how she is wired.

Recognizing that influence is relationally rooted, you would think that this intrinsic strength would transfer over missionally. Yet one of the very interesting observations I have made about evangelism is that relational ability does not necessarily equate to influence. As much as my wife is a super-spiritual "Beth Moore" girl, with all her relational strength and likeability, relating conversationally with unbelievers is not natural.

Observing the same pattern in relationally astute Christians has confirmed this trend to me.

Interviewing a regional outreach director, she disclosed how uncomfortable it is to initiate spiritual conversations with her family, and if she did, how they would not receive it. With her being aware of my evangelistic passion, I shared how I would not pursue a discussion where it was not welcomed. She said, "You wouldn't?" "Never" I quickly shot back. But then added, "You need to learn how to create openness and safety to undergird spiritual conversations. I can teach you how do that." "Oh, that is what I want to learn," she replied. Seeing her story's pervasiveness, I began racking my brain on how to help the "relationally capable" into spiritual dialogues. God did not leave me wanting. Though you have to work at it, and find your own voice, there are ways to get conversations rolling. In this section, we look at how to "frame up" discussions, and also three examples of spiritual dialogues. In my view, your ability to create ongoing dialogue may be one of the most essential evangelistic skills. I say this because without the projection, the chances of reaching a person greatly diminish.

IT TAKES A RELATIONSHIP

In respect to human dynamics, a storied Pakistani book, *Three Cups of Tea*, teaches that friendship does not begin until one pours the third cup.[1] Friendship is a process of getting to know someone—unless, of course, you just hit it off! Because Christians can be neglectfully isolated from the very ones God wants to reach, we have to be intentional about building outer relationships. The whole process begins from there. Take a previewing peek at the important elements covered in this chapter:

Build Relationship > Frame Discussions > Create Safety > Utilize Lines

Whether it's a friend, neighbor, work associate, someone you meet on the ball field, or at the health club, personal evangelism requires loving a non-believer. You might have many outside-the-faith friends right now, but if not, evaluate your present circles. Consider your interests and ask, "What new circles can I draw by entering other groups?" Not church groups. Community groups such as: sports teams, clubs, community service, school, hobbies, support gatherings, recovery and neighborhood groups, etc. All it takes is getting out there alongside to breath the invigorating

1. Thomson, Mortenson and Relin, *Three Cups of Tea*.

air of mission. If you do not already know someone, typically Christians need to make friendship deposits before initiating spiritual dialogue. It helps when the person feels comfortable with you relationally. Building relationship requires you to:

- Be a genuine friend
- Listen intently
- Connect along interest areas
- Invest time
- Show how you care
- Share your life
- Use disclosure to deepen the bonds
- Sustain momentum

An ongoing committed relationship is essential for influence because when you talk to someone "once in a blue moon" you do not create necessary relational trust, dialogue, spiritual example, and prayer focus. Two wings make the evangelistic process fly:

Committed Relationship—Spiritual Dialogue

Real results will happen as you pursue both. When interacting, I recommend that you use the word "faith" in your conversations with unbelievers. It is less loaded than other terms, and the end goal, so it's a good choice! Let's now explore how to develop a dialogue.

FRAMING UP CONVERSATIONS

After investing relationally, where there is a comfortable level of friendship connection, you come to the place of desiring the spiritual dimension. This will deepen a friendship. It means you can talk about more than cooking, kids, or the Lakers! This simple goal, however, is challenging. How do you get the conversation to move along a spiritual projection? The best way to do this is to think in terms of conversational lines. The idea is to create expectation for an ongoing discussion. In essence, you need to first *have a conversation about having a conversation*. Does that sound strange? Yet this is precisely what you need to do. You need to talk about getting together to talk. This technique initiates the foundation for a meaningful spiritual dialogue to ensue. You are lighting a torch for a journey!

I do this all the time with people both inside and outside the church. Consider the following email exchange:

> Hi Gary! Unfortunately I am one of those people who don't have a full understanding of God and his existence. I try very hard to believe in him and the Bible but I question everything! I'm not sure how you feel about me continuing to take the classes and/ or if you recommend something else to help me start my faith. If you have any helpful advice or suggestions I'd be more then happy to hear it![2]

> My reply: Hi Jennifer, Thank you so much for this email! I appreciate your openness and honesty. Here are my thoughts. I think you should continue to come through the class, and allow it to clarify the questions you have. Then, I would like to get together with you outside the class for discussion. That way I could understand your thoughts more clearly and hopefully be of help. We could meet at the church and it might be a number of times. I can tell you are a sharp thinker. You and your questions are so important! Let me know how that sounds. I am praying for you and your journey!

Outside the church, I connect with non-believer Ryan, and eventually say, "How would you like to hook up each week at Starbucks? It would give us chance to get to know each other more, and we could discuss faith." Ongoing dialogue allows for shaping. Without it you will not see the fruit of faith formation. Again, think of it in terms of a small group. Would the transformational impact of a group experience occur if you did not meet regularly? If faith formation has a chance, then you must meet in a consistent manner. When that happens it is amazing to see what God will do! I am always looking for those divinely appointed relationships where I can connect and eventually frame up a continuing dialogue. Not that you will be only talking about spiritual things; often we are connecting broadly about life. Remember: You are making an investment in this other person because God has specially placed you in his or her life, and you value their personhood and company. Psychologists tell us that a child does not merely want to be loved; they want to be liked. They know the difference!

Here are some tips on how to frame the dialogue. *First, create a picture of what the time will be, and why it would benefit them.* In this way, you

---

2. Jennifer Perez, e-mail message to author, May 2, 2010.

are drawing their interest. Sometimes I'll say, "Learning about faith can do so much for your life." Focus the invitation on offering thoughts about what faith can mean and why it is an important subject matter. Tie the benefit to your desire for greater relationship: "It would be great to hang out and connect more."

Second, along with your invitation, communicate that the time together will be a safe, non-threatening experience. You can say something like, "It will be a time to learn together and interact on thoughts and questions." It should feel casual. We do not want them to feel like we are trying to convert them. The principle is: "We converse, God converts." Our role is to initiate conversations and allow God to draw. When you converse, however, it creates opportunity for the Spirit's miraculous work. We, then, begin partnering with God in the process of his divine activity. This becomes exciting! If you can establish an ongoing conversation, chances escalate that you will lead them to faith.

This safety feel is critically important because if they get even an inkling of a strong arm—they will not engage. A "safe" environment means you can have a conversation without any pressure to make changes, time limit, or threat to the existing relationship. It is their journey and you will honor their processing and perspectives. Unfortunately, many evangelistic conversations occurring today are anything but safe. When that scent is picked-up, non-believers know to find an exit.

Understanding the importance of safety, I sometimes illustrate the idea. On the *Steps to Faith* booklet's cover design, we purposely chose footprints on the beach running into the ocean's edge—to depict the journey to faith.[3] In every class, we use the photo to put them at ease by describing their processing steps, saying, "For some of you coming to faith is a few steps down the beach, for others, it may be far down the coast before you feel comfortable with that decision. We understand that this is your journey and whatever that needs to be is okay with us."

When I met with a gal struggling to accept the Trinity, she said at one point, "I am just needing more steps down the beach." She got it, and felt comfortable journeying at her pace. Others, even more analytic in mindset, would take a long time exploring every nook and cranny before crossing into faith. Regardless, we love and embrace these precious souls all the way into discipleship.

Another facet of creating this safe impression is to include the time element in the invitation. Notice how I did that in the email above when

3. Comer, *Steps to Faith*, 2009.

I said, "We will probably meet a number of times." This was telling her she would have room to look into it. In other words, I am not expecting her to make a quick decision. I am not going to pressure her in any way. Likewise, when we meet, I make sure not to overwhelm with too much too soon. This is the concept of "pace" that we will cover in the next chapter. We have talked about reading people, but the counter reality is that they are reading us. A big part of evangelistic success is putting them at ease, and creating a healthy environment for an exploratory time.

Third, put emphasis on learning their perspectives. This communicates that you care about where they are and what they think. Again, I did this in the email above. "I would like to understand more clearly your thoughts on this," and "You and your questions are so important." Again, the skills of framing a spiritual dialogue are critical. In real life you employ them from differing angles, but the principle remains the same. Let's now look at these engagement skills playing out in some scenarios utilizing added drawing techniques.

DEVELOPING DRAWING SKILLS

"We don't do the church thing in our family." This rather curt, walk-off response came from Liz to her friend Anne. How do you respond when a non-believing friend shuts down an attempt to discuss faith? Ever been there? Do we put our tail between our legs? Should we just let it go, and make a mental note to never bring it up again since we would not want to force anything? Most of us have had these moments. Here was my input to Anne.

First, you need to practice what Jesus modeled in his pattern of circling back and finding people (John 5:12). Liz's response is not an end, but can be a beginning to a rich, meaningful conversation. In faith sharing, establishing an ongoing dialogue is the goal. You must, like Jesus, circle back and then draw out. Your aim, as a caring friend, is to find out what is going on inside Liz. Evangelism always begins with their starting point. Typically, we don't know where that is until they express it. So, as you reconnect enjoying time together, when the moment is right, you circle back saying, "The other day, Liz, when you expressed that your family did not engage with church, I didn't understand what you meant. As your friend (who values knowing you), could you explain that to me?"

If asked in a loving sensitive tone, Liz will most likely open to share something. If she does not, that may indicate deep wounding. If Anne discerns a strong reaction, she will want to draw out the pain by encouraging Liz to talk so healing can begin. Sometimes we work through healing at the initial stage of the evangelistic process. It may require more circling back and drawing out. The structure looks like this: Ask a question. Listen. Then ask a follow-up question to get more clarity, or to draw out what is undergirding their response. "What do you mean?" "Why do you feel that way?" "Can you explain so I can understand you more?"

If Anne can draw out the true thoughts and feelings from Liz, then she would know where the conversation could develop in a meaningful projection. The only thing that is clear about Liz's initial statement is its ambiguity. Her family's "not attending" could mean a number of things such as: (1) I grew up in a non-Christian home and church was never part of our lives, (2) I had a bad experience when a Christian I didn't even know attacked my beliefs, so I made it a rule to not ever talk about religion with people again, (3) When my dad died of cancer, and I watched my mom suffer, it made me angry at God. Consider the disparity of sentiment behind these three very common responses. At this juncture, however, Anne truly does not know what is happening inside her friend.

Therefore, she must first draw her heart. This is the only way for Anne to see clearly what is needed for her friend's progression. When Liz shares her true thoughts, Anne will be able to process what an appropriate conversational path would be. Sometimes we respond right then—sometimes later. Each example noted above requires a distinct direction. Let's assume Liz's response is the simpler number one. Anne, now knowing what Liz's words meant, could respond saying something like this, "Liz, I know the faith subject is not always easy to discuss, but I believe it can be so meaningful with a friend. There was a time in my life when I didn't want to talk about spiritual topics either, but I was so glad when I did. I'd be honored to have that discussion with you. It can be so enriching. Rest assured, I want you to know that you don't need to do anything, and you don't ever have to come to my church. We could just meet to talk."

Let's review what just took place. The first sentence attempts to "frame up" an ongoing discussion. Again, that is the goal. When we do this, we always want to create positive anticipation of what that experience will be like. If Liz agrees to get together, the discussion often leads to dynamic results!" The qualifying phrases regarding expectations serve to create "safety." Anne would want to make sure that Liz knows that she can remain disengaged from church, and disagree about everything they talk on, and this in no way will change or jeopardize their friendship. Anne loves Liz as her cherished friend unconditionally. If you can establish "safety," then you can release an honest, incredibly impacting journey!

Consider another real example. Muslim Sallie calls her long-term friend Tania to talk about pressing issues. What Sallie wants is a relationship with a man. To appease her parents, he needs to be a Muslim, but she doesn't want him to be devout. In fact, in the conversation, Sallie says she hates Islam! She doesn't know what she believes. So she is trying to float under the radar making the faith issue nominal. Tania had never heard Sallie speak this way before. She reasons with her saying, "The best marriages usually have common beliefs that bind them together. Your beliefs matter, Sallie." Sallie responds by saying, "You just want me to go to your church. Tania, being fairly new in the faith, intuitively does exactly the right thing. She tells Sallie that she is not trying to get her to come to church. This creates safety. Two days later Sallie calls her back to talk more. Why? She knows Tania cares about her. She's a true friend. Tania is now attempting to establish an ongoing discourse with Sallie regarding beliefs. This would mean exploring the Christian faith to see if it is something for her. If a Muslim is open, a Christian will likely have a crucial part in their processing. Turning to Christ from another faith is a big transition. She will need support to do it!

Can you see why learning the drawing skills of "probing" and "framing" are crucial? Apart from drawing out and initiating an ongoing conversation, we do not get positioned to reach them. Referring back to the first example, Liz would remain in her place of distance. Stuck! Anne would stay on the sidelines of God's movement, being put off by a one-liner. Without reaching Liz, all the people she has influence with will potentially remain untouched by the gospel. Circling back. Probing. Framing up. Creating Safety. You are learning the skills of a soul whisperer!

You will have to discern with each person how much "framing" is necessary. For some, you might be able to move seamlessly into a regular connecting time. After teaching this in a class, Stephanie asked a neighbor if she wanted to walk and then discuss spiritual topics, which was comfortable for both of them. When the neighbor said yes, the exercise sessions became their weekly meeting. For others, you might need to spell it out, and make a case for getting together. You have to read your friends. Often, your probing questions will reveal where a meaningful conversation can begin.

To bolster your efforts, pursuing particular conversational lines is another method that can help. Hearing the names of the three lines will get your mind spinning and give you an immediate feel of where we are going: Story-line, Learning-line, and Question-line.

LEARNING THE LINES:

1) Story-Line: Get together to share stories.

This is when the conversation begins from sharing life stories, and eventually gets to how God can enter their story. It can start with the simplest of invitations: "How would you like to get together for a cup of coffee, and get a chance to know each other?" "Why don't we hook up, I would like to connect with you." Learning a person's story is a great relational angle because everyone loves to talk about themselves. As you invite them into sharing, make sure to listen intently, and take mental notes for later conversations—not immediately figuring out how to get them saved. Your initial primary role is to ask questions to draw out themes. Don't forget to inquire about their family, and beliefs. Do they have any church background? If not, you will know they have a secular viewpoint. If they mention a background or church, that does not necessarily mean they are Christian. It is possible they have only visited and are trying to make themselves appear more spiritual than they are (Christmas and Easter attendees = "Chreasters"). Do not assume anything. Listen carefully to discover their thoughts on spiritual things. If they had attended church previously, you might want to probe about their experience. Keep it open-ended, "What was it like?" Be interested and let them talk.

As a warning, do not counter beliefs in a first-time "get to know you" conversation. That would be the worst thing you could do! It would dishonor them, and may even shut down the dialogue entirely. In the same vein, be careful not to give as Gary Poole so poignantly phrased, "two-cent answers to million dollar issues."[4] Be relational and interact, but for the most part get to know them and enjoy their company. No one wants to feel like a project.

Then finish up by saying, "Let's get back together next week and I will tell you more of my story." When you do make sure you disclose your real life with its ups and downs. If you are willing to open "the disclosure window" some and let them see your journey, this could begin to deepen a friendship. They will sense how you trust them with real information that is shared amongst friends. Do not be surprised to find them reciprocating.

4. Poole, *Seeker Small Groups*, 106.

As you connect along this line, they will discover you are a person of faith, and you will get glimmers of where conversations might go in the future. God wants to be integral to their life, and you can help them see how meaningful that could be.

With this line, it helps to know key story-themes to listen for, that you will want to circle back with. This is how you uncover ways to bring God into their picture. Let me develop how this works. What makes a story interesting is something we had to overcome. You could ask, "Have you ever faced a barrier to your life dreams?" This is a great question with unlimited potential. What would you be willing to disclose? What will they be willing to share?

What may happen is they open up and tell you, "I am facing something right now!" "My kids are going through this" or "We are dealing with this situation." They could refer back to the big picture and say, "Years back this happened in my marriage." When they disclose look for the handprints of God in their pre-Christ story. Which lessons have stuck with them? Then importantly, what marks remain from their life journey? You will most likely need time in relationship to get to this place, but most have wounds. Those are powerful imprints that shape attitudes on life and God. This is why the "Story-Line" approach is a good one. If you can tap their deep drivers (motivations), you will be able to see their life compass. Of course, God has been there the whole way.

Watching *So You Think You Can Dance* is a family ritual. The show has as much talent as *American Idol* in our opinion. Aside from the dancing talent you get a chance to see the creativity of renowned choreographers. In the 2009 season, Choreographer Louis Van Amstel had taught a romantically themed waltz to African American dancer Vitolio and Asian dancer Osca, yet the chemistry between the two was not there. Osca confessed she was having difficultly because she was not attracted to her partner. Being a hunk, he responded emphatically, "How could she not be?" Observing this block, choreographer Van Amstel changed directions. He had learned that Vitolio had a tough upbringing, having grown up as an orphan. So instead of a romantic waltz, he made it a waltz about Vitolio's story of overcoming. This connected with both, and suddenly the waltz transformed into a piece of beauty. It moved my wife to tears—and I at least glistened!

Stories are powerful. Great stories come from barriers. There is a dream, but then a seemingly insurmountable obstacle comes into the picture, and the dream crashes to a halt. It is the barrier, problem, or conflict that makes a great story. We are drawn into wondering what will happen next.[5] How is the person going to respond? The best books or movies grab our hearts as we find ourselves rooting. We love to see the person who was knocked down but not out; who in the midst of darkness reaches for light; who stood up against adversity and prevailed; who digs down and fights for redemption, or goes after something they never thought they could achieve, or who just wouldn't quit. This is the stuff of story. It is also one of the ways that God transforms. Author Donald Miller insightfully blogs, "Conflict is the only way a character actually changes."[6] Sometimes it is good for us to look at our life in story.[7] You may be going through something hard, and yet that is the very place where God is forging you. He is drawing your character!

This perspective is something we can bring to non-believers. They look at their life and ask, "Where is God?" "Why do they have their problems?" We can help them to see how difficulties have purpose. They are actually part of God's grace working to shape them. They may also be how God is leading them to himself. Often, they do not see these things. When we speak into their story, their eyes open to God in a new way.

One night I viewed a documentary called *The Farm: Life Inside Angola Prison*, which chronicled the life of a woman, brutally assaulted by a man currently doing life. In an interview, she said, "I wouldn't have wanted it to happen, but in some way, I couldn't imagine my life if it didn't. Everything that happens to you makes you who you are. It forms the way you think." I sat marveling over this woman's deep level of perspective. This horrible thing happened to her, and yet somehow she saw it in a redeeming way. Convinced that the event had so formed her life, she struggled seeing any other path than hers. It created a profound motivational drive as she summoned the inspiration to write a book even though she had only a sixth grade education. Everyone was telling her she couldn't do it, and that it would take a real writer, but she didn't let that stop her saying, "Everyone with a story is a writer."[8] The book got published!

What she realized is that dark events take us to deeper places. God doesn't waste the events of our lives; not any of the hurts, losses, troubles and sins. Though he would have us avoid sin, he has a way of using and redeeming all things. This is hope for a non-believer. As Christians, we

---

5. Jensen, *Thinking In Story*, 21.

6. Miller, "How to Tell a Good Story with Your Life," lines 24–25.

7. Allender, *To Be Told*, 1–6.

8. Stack, Garbus and Rideau, "The Farm: Life Inside Angola Prison."

point them to the fingerprints of God. He is watching over them, and yet his full plan has not been realized. He wills to come into their lives in a dynamic personal way. He wants them to know how he can be trusted to fulfill his design for their lives. Author Stasi Eldredge believes, "A story is only as good as its ending."[9] Christian friend, do you realize that we have a message that will make anyone's story wonderfully good?! Jumping from her words, husband John expounds, "Without a happy ending that draws us on in eager anticipation, our journey becomes a nightmare of endless struggle. Is this all there is? Is this as good as it gets?"[10]

When stories are disclosed, we begin to see how God is already working. Our eyes get opened to their journey, and what God knows that we don't. Then the Lord can bring us alongside in partnering with him. God wants to infuse his life into their story, transforming it with the "living hope" of Christ (1 Pet 1:3).

2) LEARNING-LINE: INVITE THEM INTO A SPIRITUAL STUDY.

Again, we want to light a torch for an exploratory journey. Another way to do this is what I call the "Learning-Line." Inviting others to learn together is a simple way to create an ongoing spiritual dialogue. To work this line, you say, "I have found it good to keep sharpening myself through reading, how would you like to learn something together? We could pick out some interesting chapters and then meet to discuss them?" Granted, there are so many great authors and books to choose from. Pick your poison! Just taking John Ortberg's works as an example, you could read, *The Life You've Always Wanted*, or *If You Want to Walk on Water, You've Got to Get Out of the Boat*. Or if they leaned into the skeptical realm you could read *Faith and Doubt*.

If you are befriending another mom in your apartment complex, together you could read a book on parenting. Pick a meaningful topic for your friend from a Christian perspective, and allow the book to stimulate spiritual discussion. The simple approach works. Danielle ministers to foster kids as a mentor. In spending time with her teenage friend, they visit the Christian bookstore to jointly pick out a book for a learning-line discussion. Usually, you initiate this with a Christian book, or Bible study angle. This same idea can also be applied in a group way by connecting

9. Curtis and Eldredge, *The Sacred Romance*, 177.
10. Curtis and Eldredge, *The Sacred Romance*, 177.

with your neighbors to start a book club. Or just invite them over for coffee to talk on what the Bible says about family and faith. It is a great way to get the ball moving with your non-believing friends. Aaron, one of our church planters, gathers his non-believing friends to a fire pit every week. Several have journeyed into the faith over years of conversations. One of them, a former atheist named Curtis, who now attends church told him why he kept returning, "I loved that you never made me feel like I had to come to your church."

WORKING THEIR SIDE OF THE FENCE

Another way to work the learning-line, is to do what I call "working their side of the fence." This is when we meet to study their books or ideas, not ours. Should we do this? Yes! Sometimes we need to boldly venture into their world. To gain an audience we must start with learning their faith, views or interests, and perhaps look at their materials. This shows a huge level of personal interest. Because of your involvement, the relationship will grow and you will gain insights into what they believe and why. From their side of the fence, you will have opportunity to authentically share your faith. If you are able to speak without an air of superiority or arrogance, you create a conversation on equal ground. By showing them respect, God can use you to infiltrate their turf. Granted, I do not recommend this approach for a Christian who is not wellgrounded. But if you are strongly rooted in faith, this is a legitimate means for positioning yourself in someone's life.

I realize this idea stretches new mission muscles. In a community group, Tawny shared about her friend's encounter with a Muslim who gave her a Koran. Hearing this occurred, the husband reacted angrily, telling his wife to give it back! I know that many would think it a terrible thing to receive a Koran from a Muslim friend. It would appear as if they were winning and we were losing. But let's think a bit deeper. We are in the light of truth, receiving a Koran does not change that high position. It could actually go a long way toward reaching them for Jesus. I have the Koran bookmarked, and read it periodically. It won't hurt you!

Why not use it to create an ongoing conversation about beliefs. Paul quoted the Athenian poets to bridge his message (Acts 17:28). There is plenty of biblical precedent for starting a dialogue from another place other than our truth source. Sometimes, if we are going to reach another, we will have to venture to their side. Why do we as Christians think everyone has to come to us? Why do we think that every discussion must be based from our thinking? Does that not seem arrogant? We could instead enter their world seeking to understand them better first, and from that place, engage in meaningful discourse. Ponder how honoring this action would be. The Christian could say, "I would love to understand your faith more, and also share some of mine with you. Let's do some reading together and meet to talk each week." Tawny's Muslim friend would be so honored by that posture, and opened up to hear. Don't forget that the truth looked at by anyone long enough rises to the top. Let's position ourselves for such an opportunity!

Did not Jesus come from the most distant domain to enter our foreign world? Coming down from heaven he never flinched in the face of human misdirection or depravity. Heralded "The friend of sinners," he dove headfirst into lives, even at their darkest points. Why would we not be willing to cross over to do the same?

Sometimes, we do this along secular interests, not religious perspectives. By joining support groups, book clubs or community conversations, you learn what they are into, and examine their worldviews. Friends, venturing into another's world is the call of the missionary. In the study of missions, one scathing critique is how missionaries in foreign fields set up their own Christian compound, fenced off and secure. Although living in the land, the separation from the indigenous culture prevents true penetration. We can make the same mistake by remaining too far on our side, never entering their world. Thus, our influence doesn't have the chance to permeate. In North America, Christians have not yet learned to function in the new pluralistic climate. We are behind the curve assuming a home field advantage that no longer exists.

Another angle to this line occurs when you see a clear interest or need that God can meet. Usually, the non-believer has to share their lives first, unless it's obvious. But if they share a problem or issue, chances are there is a spiritual answer. Seeing their need you come alongside in love, and begin addressing the spiritual aspects. You simply create a learning-line discussion around helping them. What marriage problem is not ultimately a spiritual problem? There's the axiom, "Hand over your life to Jesus and nobody gets hurt!" Say, "Let's get together and learn something that will help you." It might be that the person has a hidden burden. As a relationship grows, we get the chance to bear it with them. Embarking on this line may take some probing. Ask how they are doing—really? Listen intently trying to understand how Christ could meet needs. Make sure that you participate practically as you are able—we are, after all, the hands and feet of Jesus. There will be times when your demonstration of love will be the thing that opens them to God. Sometimes, a community group at church takes on the care role for a non-believing family. This ushers that group into mission. As you meet direct needs, hearts open, and conversations naturally occur about faith. In time, a person or whole families come to Christ.

3) QUESTION-LINE: FRAME A TIME TO EXPLORE QUESTIONS OR FAITH.

Finally, the last conversational line is built directly from their questions. This question-line could be used with anyone who has even one hang up, but it is clearly the angle we pursue with those who are skeptical. In this relationship dialogue, a question or objection about God and the Christian faith will no doubt surface. All that does is show us where to begin an ongoing dialogue. They may have a completely different worldview, but are very open to discussion. It's not hard to frame the question-line: "I'd like to learn more about your view on that. How would you like to get together so you can explain more of your thoughts to me?" Or "That question you have is really important. Why don't we get together each week and discuss possible answers." Or "How would you like to hook up and discuss your questions about the Christian faith?"

We must realize that just because a person is an atheist, agnostic, coming from another faith or is filled with skeptical thoughts about Christianity does not mean they are unreceptive. We could mistakenly write them off when they have tremendous interest, and truly enjoy getting together and talking about their ideas. Some of the most amazing evangelistic journeys I have experienced were relationship dialogues that began from the question-line.

JUMPING TRACKS

What often happens is that you begin a line of spiritual dialogue and then jump tracks to another. This is inevitable. For example, your "Story-Line" angle of discussion raises a question, and you jump to "Question-Line." Or "Story-Line" jumps to a "Learning-Line" where you begin to study the Bible or a book together. You will need to jump tracks to keep the spiritual dialogue progressing. Whichever line you choose, the process requires a non-believer who is willing to discuss their religious viewpoint, ask spiritual questions, share objections to faith, or read and study with you. There has to be some interest for it to work. One thing we learn is that we can't make their decision for them, and we can't wave a wand and make them interested. Studies show people who come to Christ make efforts. We are looking for receptivity.

There are times when we need to cut through the trivial crud and get to heart issues. Some hide behind a charade of questions and viewpoints. If you sense this happening, you have to expose the underlying motives by asking second level questions that go below the surface. Also do not prejudge people based on reputation. Sinners are often attracted to the gospel. Neil Cole's church coined the catchy phrase, "Bad people make good soil."[11] Let us not ever think the gospel is about reaching the respectable folks. (By the way, I would never use the distinction between good and bad people when the difference is only degree, not kind. Biblically speaking, only God is good!) And who are we, then, to limit God's grace? In the parables of the lost sheep, coin and son, lostness does not alter value (Luke 15). In fact, if we study those stories, it seems like the more lost someone or something is—the more valuable it is!

Framing ongoing spiritual dialogues along specific lines is how we launch "discovery circles." At Sandals, we launch evangelistic circles by first reading what would work with the particular group of unbelievers. For example, the question-line group builds from questions they have expressed. The learning-line group builds from a book study angle. *Steps to Faith* is an attractional vehicle for those wanting to learn about the Christian faith. These small groups start with non-believers, and provide a gathering to discover spiritual truth. Special training for these groups is helpful for making them effectual, yet the principles of spiritual influence for reaching people are the same for an individual or group.

Initiating ongoing spiritual dialogues is one of the most significant evangelistic skills. It is the projection that matters. We are not merely pundits sneaking in an occasional spiritual word, but rather "journey creators." Grab your torch!

11. Cole, *Organic Church*, 175.

DISCUSSION & ENGAGEMENT

1. Do you consider yourself to be a highly relational person? On a scale of 1–10, share how comfortable you are with talking about spiritual things with non-Christians.

2. Have you ever framed up an ongoing spiritual conversation with someone outside the faith?

3. What insights did you glean on how to do that from this chapter?

4. Which of the three lines (story, learning, question) would be the easiest for you to pursue? Why?

5. As you begin building relationship with a non-believer, your assignment is to look for the right moment to "have a conversation about having a conversation."

12

The Art of Spiritual Dialogue

The conversation always comes back to God.

—*PHILO, 2ND CENTURY PHILOSOPHER.*

Why he wasn't on *One Night Stand* or headlining a major comedy club—I don't know. This undiscovered gem worked a massive crowd at San Francisco's Pier 39. The guy had the place rockin'! He was so good he didn't even have to arm-twist the crowd for an offering. Spontaneously at the end of his gig, people started hurling coins at the stage. How often have you seen that? Some in the crowd got a bit carried away, and instead of gently tossing, made him a target. I watched grimacing as he got beaned by an onslaught of quarters—some hitting his face.

At this moment when it seemed like only hunger for food money could have steadied his composure, he said something that would stick with me for life. It was simple but profound. He reached down, grabbed a coin, showed it to the crowd and said, "If you are going to throw one of these make sure you first take it and wrap it in a dollar bill." Berated by major league wannabes, he had us laughing once again; it was witty and applicable to the sympathies of his onlooking audience. Marveling, I thought, if only the church had such wisdom in handling the precious truth God has placed in our pockets. We often look more like reckless, thoughtless, loveless hurlers of spare change than people delivering a prized package in a way it can be received.

Years before DVDs and even cell phones, a bunch of high school buds sat in a theatre's sixth row to watch the King Arthur story retold. The 1981 release, *Excalibur*, had none of the usual big names, but we didn't care. We sat close, not just to watch, but to be in it. Filmed in luscious Ireland, the story unfolds with fog-infested battle scenes as the young Arthur, having pulled Excalibur from its stone, rises to his calling. Just when his kingdom gets established, Lancelot enters the story. Every boy and man's dream is to be like this handsome Jedi-like champion, brilliant in the art of swordsmanship. Searching for a king who is worthy of his sword, he guards a bridge, allowing none to cross until beaten in single combat. Arthur sends all his best knights one-by-one to challenge, until finally in frustration, the king himself goes to meet him face-to-face. Once again, Lancelot harnesses his superior skills to win, and yet, in a moment of desperation, the king calls on the mighty power of Excalibur to land a decisive blow, defeating him only through the breaking of Lancelot's sword.

The story creates a thoughtful comparison of styles. Skill versus power. When it comes to spiritual influence, which movie character do we emulate? Many today favor that power thing! They get all pumped up—"I got the truth and I am going to nail you with it!" They just love to put those non-believers in their place. Some in the church think all we really need is to brush up on our Bible verses, then, like King Arthur with Excalibur, we will overpower with truth. This attitude and spirit typically hinders the effectiveness of the gospel. The most essential thing is not the sword but rather the skills to properly wield its power. In this chapter, I want to show you why this idea makes a total difference; and why the finer skills of dialogue will win over power any day. Though, I do believe having both biblical and cultural knowledge is important and there's a place for passion, in this chapter I posit the proper use of knowledge is the indispensable skill many Christians lack. Informational knowledge can always be dug up, but the way we use it will "make or break" the evangelistic journey.

THE POWER OF YOUR PRESENCE

As we look at our model of developing close relationship and establishing ongoing dialogue with non-believers, we should recognize that influence flows from our personhood. With this being the case, I want to ask a rather pointed and personal question. What do people feel when they are with you? When someone enters your circle what do they pick up right away? This is a great question. Have the courage to ask it! You may want to seek out a trusted friend or two to give honest feedback on the vibe you're sending out intentionally or unwittingly.

They may say you are the most amazing wonderful person in the whole world! If so, thank them for the warm sentiment and ask for the truth. If they respond, "You can't handle the truth!" Tell them you can. Really. If they sense your earnestness in getting honest feedback, they may provide the useful mirror you seek. Honest responders may describe you as: loving, caring, interested, empathetic, genuinely friendly, and committed to relationships. Some of you need to realize how much non-believers would love to sit in your circle! Spending time with some in my faith-sharing class has prompted me to declare, "Being with you is like a slice of heaven. If you don't draw searchers into your circle, God will never fulfill the incredibly things he wants do through you!"

But it is also entirely possible that they could perceive you as: aloof, arrogant, uncaring, uppity, preoccupied, driven, selfish, indifferent, and bad-breathed. Is it a shock that Christians are readily described by these words? Do we need to ask why our message is brushed off? As Paul wrote to the believers in Corinth, if we do not have love we are no more than a noisy gong (1 Cor 13:1). Before we learn the essential art of dialogue, let us own the aura that is already there. Do we need to humble ourselves and ask for a personal presence makeover?

In a core beliefs class at Sandals, Marc brought his non-believing friend. Just before we started, the friend decided to leave. We shook hands and I said it was great to meet him. Later I asked Marc, "What happened?" He told me that his friend thought someone in the class was staring him down. I knew everyone in the group that night and none would do anything close, and for what reason? Marc acknowledged the issues in his friend who gets "spooked," but I also realized he picked up something. What occurred that night that I did not see but he saw? What do people pick up from us—as individuals, and from our group or church?

We need to be self-aware, and it often takes a loving person to reveal other's perceptions. Thank God for faithful, honest spouses. I have sometimes referred to my lovely bride as "my tenacious truth-telling wife!" She has been a mirror to me through the years. "Gary, you need to look people in the eyes." "Stop saying, 'you know' in every sentence." "Get that food off your face!" Because of her faithful, constructive feedback (without too much nagging), I have picked up all sorts of things that people pick up from me. I hate to say it, but I have my quirks.

In my years of pastoring, I have worked with apprentice teachers on what people are absorbing during their message. When I offer feedback, the presenter is often surprised. I tell them one of the key communication principles is likeability, and they must know what people perceive from the stage. Some give a message that fails to make them real, relatable, or show their heart for those they are addressing. They worked hard to bring the gift, but forgot the wrapping. As teachers and spiritual influencers we must care a whole lot about helping people receive our words. I am not suggesting we water anything down; to the contrary, a strong message may need extra loving care to make sure its punch is fully felt. Are you getting what I am talking about here? You need to. If you are going to be an influencer for Jesus you must know what others are absorbing from you. The good and the not-so-great.

ONGOING DIALOGUE

Having shaped the importance of your ambient character, I now want to examine the skills involved in managing a dialogue. By definition, a dialogue is a two-way conversation. Why don't we just make a presentation or proclamation of truth? Do we really need to interact?

Spiritual dialogue is often necessary to draw a person into exploration. Jesus did this beautifully with questions that piqued interest and created intrigue. Although dialogue can result in great conversation, let's admit that it is possible to engage counterproductively. We could easily and unintentionally shut down a conversation by dominating or responding discouragingly to the person on the other end. When properly utilized, however, dialogue works because it creates an interchange for learning. Educator and Socratic method advocate Robert Hutchins said, "Dialogue always assumes different viewpoints."[1] True dialogue means you can exchange ideas freely without immediate adherence.

Therefore, we do not approach conversations confrontationally. The exception is the rare person gifted in confrontational evangelism. They can do what 99 percent of us cannot get away with. If you have this gift then use it. Just make sure you have the gift—the Christian world has enough pompous jackasses with megaphones as it is! The fact is aggressive tellers

---

1. Hitchens quote, thinkexist.com/quotes/robert_m.hitchens/.

do real harm to the cause of Christ by recoiling people, and undermining the rest of the church who genuinely care to influence.

Continuing, the great majority must work within the relational paradigm. A common mistake for unseasoned messengers is to hear how the non-believer thinks un-Christianly and immediately tell them why they are wrong. This will only generate defensiveness, pushing them back. It's not wise. It is entirely better to say, "I hear what you are saying." If you can identify with their sentiments and thoughts in any way then do so. Often there is truth in their perspectives. They can be, as Tony Campolo captured in his philosophical examination of worldviews, partly right.[2] If so, we would do well to recognize it. "I get what you're concluding, however, I have an added perspective that I'd love for you to consider." At that point, share in a way that gives them an alternative. Guard your emotions and do not expect them to agree immediately. This open-minded tone of expressing thoughts will create a healthy exchange. Make sure you affirm them as a valued friend, amid the different views. One rule of thumb in relational evangelism is: *Never win the point and lose the person*. Trying to overpower resistance violates the heart. It would be better to back up and prepare them for receiving. "I know you have a different viewpoint, John, but have you ever thought there could be something behind this other idea?" You might just leave it there, until you pick up the conversation again. This is drawing at its best, not telling.

In addition, dialogue achieves an absolutely critical aspect to soul whispering: that is, getting a read on where they are. In the same way that Jesus purposefully interacted, we must learn the place where people are starting from and what their specific journey will need to be. As a practical rule, you never know their views until you hear them say it. Soul whisperers use questions to draw the thoughts and feelings from non-believers. Paul Weston determined Jesus asked 284 questions in the Gospels.[3] We ask and then listen. Listening before talking is critically important to the relationship. A sociologist interviewing the un-churched concluded, "Most people can't hear until they have been heard."[4] Studies indicate that people reached for Christ sensed someone loved them. In this soul whisperer role you listen well to exhibit love.

Sometimes a non-believer progresses by merely offering objections. As you draw this out into verbal expression, the mental stronghold

---

2. Campolo, *Partly Right*, 9–10.

3. Weston, *"Evangelicals and Evangelism,"* ed. Iain Taylor, 145.

4. Hale, *The Unchurched and Why They Stay Away*, 183.

suddenly loses its grip. Many times you will need to pursue follow-up questions, seeking to understand "why" they think or feel as they do. It is often the second question that gets to the heart. In sum, dialogue is the diagnostic tool to gain a read on where they are, and how they are progressing. It provides the essential information to lead them forward. We listen because we truly care about the person and their eternal destiny, not because we seek to appear spiritual or gain some type of ecclesiastical brownie points.

Referring back to the imagery of the previous chapter, once you have lit a torch by framing up a dialogue, you must prevent the torch from blowing out. The rest of this chapter will give you insight on managing the journey down the trail.

PREPARING THE ROAD

Growing up on an acre parcel in San Diego County, my family lived on the top of a hill. Though quite young, I still can picture the raw land my parents purchased, and all the work that went into planting trees, ice plant, and lawns. We prioritized the landscaping before addressing the dirt driveway, which worked fine, until the rainy season. This was when I learned about "sinkholes." The phenomenon occurs when water drains below the road eroding the earth until it eventually caves. I recall this happening numerous times in our 200-yard driveway, where eight-foot holes made us park and walk from the bottom. We usually went out and filled them in with rocks and dirt until the rains washed them out again!

One of the most significant people in the entire Bible is John the Baptist. As Jesus's forerunner, he came in the words of Isaiah, "to prepare the way for the Lord; make straight in the wilderness a highway for our God" (Isa 40:3). The imagery described the literal practice of the road crew preceding a travel procession to ensure the king's journey was passable, acceptable, and even enjoyable. That was a tall order for a time without paving companies. Yet these servants went before to fill in potholes and raise sections so the king's carriage did not sink or slide off the side. They removed boulders and debris, cut down tree branches, and straightened parts too windy for the carriage. After the work was done, the head of the road crew was accountable for his performance. What did they miss? Were there any hidden sinkholes?

This vivid imagery of preparation described John's amazing calling. His purpose was to prepare hearts spiritually for Jesus's coming. I hope you notice the parallel to the definition I use for evangelism: *Partnering with God in the process of preparing the mind and heart to believe and follow.* Yet sometimes we want results without preparing the way. Typically, this does not work well, just like it didn't work when a king had to journey over unprepared road. In redemptive relationships, we must do the work to prepare the mind and heart. Though the years of meeting with non-believers, I have discovered several serious sinkholes on the journey. In this section, I want to expose them so you can navigate the course. Each redemptive relationship is different, but chances are within the process you will deal with issues of: Pace, Honor, Friction, and Patience.

SINKHOLE #1: PACE

Talking of marriage on a first date is not only scary—it's weird and even a bit creepy! It's appropriate to keep things at lower intimacy levels with early conversations. Guys don't want to come on too strong; girls might even want to play a little "hard to get." The dating dance is a ritual with lots of nuance, and is very much part of our culture. Everyone must learn it to some degree. The dating analogy not only fits the biblical imagery of Christ, the bridegroom, pursuing his people, the bride; but it is a helpful comparison to evangelistic process. With non-believers we need to be sensitive to what is an acceptable pace for spiritual assimilation.

Sam begins to connect with Joe. He frames up a time to get together weekly to discuss spiritual questions. Sam had mapped out a plan to cover a number of topics—the first being creation. Afterward their first meeting, Sam reports that the time went extremely well; Joe even said that he now believed in a Creator. Home run! Sam calls to get together the next week, but Joe has something come up. Later, Sam tries again to reconnect but there's another engagement, or should we say, excuse offered. The journey forward comes to a rushing halt. Looking back, Sam thought perhaps he had gone forward too quickly and there was not enough relationship. Additionally, we could ask if Joe was ready to accept spiritual realities? Was he prepared to face truths that would challenge his life? If his mind and heart are not properly prepared, he could feel boxed in and threatened by the implications of it all. Joe thought he was interested in learning about God, but now it seems Sam made Joe feel uneasy. This dynamic varies depending on personalities, interest level, and openness. Can you see what we are up against? What can we do to manage this killer of forward progress?

Think with me here. If you are married, go back in recollection to your first date. Did you talk about marriage? Many would say absolutely not—inappropriate! Some married couples did talk about marriage on their first date, though they probably kept the conversation conceptual. My wife and I talked about marriage on our first dinner date, but not about marrying each other, only generally about the subject. We, and other couples, were not scared off because the "attraction element" was high so the conversation was okay. If someone you are not strongly attracted to talks of marriage then you will probably feel uncomfortable—especially on a first date! Most likely, that will be the last date you go on. It would be simply too much too soon.

Dating is a good illustration of how to assess pace in spiritual conversations. The question is: Does the non-believer have a strong "attraction" toward the spiritual life? In other words, does the non-believer see how the God thing could bless their life, benefit their picture, be the missing piece, or bring greater fulfillment? Is the spiritual life highly attractive? If the attraction element is not high be careful in going too fast. It can scare the seeker, who is not ready to deal with the reality of truth, the possibility of change, or the responsibility of believing. Sometimes we must build "attraction perspective" toward faith before the weightier spiritual conversations take place. This kind of read requires intuitive sensitivity. I say this because they are not going to come out and tell you: "I'm scared!" "I don't know if I want to change my life." "I'm not ready to accept this." You will have to discern this yourself.

Attraction-building helps them see what a relationship with God could mean. It fills out the picture of faith so the non-believer feels more comfortable with the conversation. To reach a person with the gospel, we need to help them see it as "good news." We must paint a picture of a preferred life; one that exceeds what they know, but does not unduly threaten their individual identity. If you do the preparatory roadwork you can help them forward in their journey, and not lose them down a sinkhole. With pace, sometimes the wise thing is to pull back to build relational trust, and emphasize the attraction elements. Granted, this tends to be a high-level read. Even, the top evangelists in the world can blow it on this one.

SINKHOLE #2: HONOR

When an expert in the law stands to test Jesus with a question about how to inherit eternal life, Jesus replies with two back-to-back questions to draw out the man's perspective (Luke 10:25–27). When he replies quoting the Scripture about loving God with your heart, mind and soul and adds, "Love your neighbor as yourself," Jesus states the man is "correct." I don't know about you, but I don't like it when someone tests me. If I were in this story things would have played out very differently. I would have shredded the chump! "Who are you 'so-called expert' to be testing me when I am the Lord of the universe?" In this case, Jesus has a full view of this man's under-minding motive, but still graciously confirms his answer. Though he will instruct him when he tries to justify himself, his first reaction is affirming. Jesus practiced this type of response throughout his ministry. In short, Christ honored people.

In another interaction, Jesus ignores the cries of a Canaanite woman (Matt 15:21–28) who wants him to help her demon-possessed daughter. When the woman won't go away, he exchanges uncomplimentary words equating her situation to that of a scavenging dog. The study of this passage is fascinating because at first glance it seems out of character. Yet as the dialogue develops, Jesus responds with tremendous honor exalting her faith! Similarly, one of the most staggering things about the Son of God is how he pulled up a chair with notorious sinners (Luke 5:27–32; 19:1–7). In doing so he honored them, not for their sinful lifestyles, but for their intrinsic, God-designed worth. As he sat at their table they knew they mattered to him and the God he represented incarnate. Honor is critically important in missional engagement, especially within conversations.

In a class session when we give people an opportunity to come into faith, three of the four non-believers did not even show up. Having invested myself, I was not giving up. I got on the phone, and providentially, got through to have incredible talks with each. It was like the Lord said to me, "You haven't done the work!" After the calls all three come to the next session ready to commit to Christ. In one conversation, nineteen-year-old Mike, told me how he was doing spiritually. His coming to church over the past year had been a big change. As I probed further, he told me that his standing with God was based on his pureness of heart. As I saw the red flag waving, I asked questions that verified his clouded misunderstanding of the gospel.

At that point, I am faced with what to say. Whereas in the past, I might have jumped immediately to correction and lost him down the sinkhole, this time I sensed it would be a mistake. I have corrected people before where it was not received well. I did not want to do that here. I slowed and felt the moment. As I prayed, it became clear that I needed to first honor his spiritual progress, even though he was way off in his thinking. Therefore, I stopped to enthusiastically celebrate his journey. I honored him for coming to church and the class—the great decisions he had made spiritually—and his heart for God. Then, without defensiveness blocking the message, I said, "Mike, there is further understanding of faith that you need to come into. I want to clarify that we do not have a standing with God based upon our devotion, purity or goodness. In fact, that is what the cross is all about. A right standing with God comes only through what Jesus has done for us." After some dialogue, he received my words and put his faith in Christ alone.

This "honoring" principle is critical in evangelism. We must learn to follow Jesus in the way of honor. You will see how sage this wisdom is when you are sitting across from a person you love and want to reach. Take a moment to contemplate several real-life scenarios where honor precedes influence:

- Honoring the atheist's intellect, yet challenging their conclusions.

- Honoring a person's intrinsic worth, yet encouraging him to seek needed repentance.

- Honoring one's Catholicism, yet addressing a misunderstanding of faith.

- Honoring them for being a good person with true qualities, yet teaching there is no such thing as a "good person" in God's eyes.

- Honoring their culture, and yet challenging the religious beliefs popular within it.

- Honoring their human dignity, yet deploring depraved human conditions.

- Honoring their parents, yet appealing for them to think for themselves.

Can you see the critical importance of this practice? The church has too often neglected giving honor in its messaging. How many times have we failed to have a "dignified exchange?" I hope you are able to glean this insight from the life of Jesus. Honor means you do not lose the person as you lead them forward spiritually.

SINKHOLE #3: FRICTION

Perhaps you are familiar with the proverb, "As iron sharpens iron so one person sharpens another" (Prov 27:17). You may not have ever asked the basic question of what is required for sharpening an iron blade. The answer is: friction. In a friendship, if there is not friction there is no sharpening. This rub dynamic happens in a relationship when one person envisions how another needs to change. At some level of risk, the subject gets out on the table and "friction" occurs. The receiving person has to wrestle with where they are, and the fact that a genuine friend does not believe it is the right place to be. In a context of love, the subject is discussed in the spirit of growing and changing. Friction must be present to sharpen another; it is a critical part of relational influence. This same concept applies within the context of evangelism. The Christian loves, accepts, respects, and honors a person for who and where they are, and yet, they do not want them to stay in disbelief. There is "friction." That does not mean an unloving tone, or confrontational posture, but rather, an intentionality to see a person embrace truth, and ultimately move toward seeking God.

People sometimes struggle with the idea of intentionality because they perceive it as being disingenuous. If you are interested in a person only for spiritual influence, you could be having a disingenuous friendship. But the desire to see them saved is not disingenuous. This is legitimate loving desire on the part of a Christian. We should not be apologizing for being intentional with the gospel. Although in practice, while we seek genuine friendships that are not dependent upon a favorable response, this does not mean we are passive. Let us realize that friction-intentionality is part of loving influence. Anyone who is a parent of teenagers lives with the tension of this reality everyday. Real love is highly intentional with degrees of friction because it seeks their best. If you truly believe in salvation, and the blessings of a relationship with Jesus, then you would want your friends to experience it. That is love! We want them to know Jesus. Let us be sincere and earnest about this. If that creates friction, then so be it!

When Paul faced King Agrippa, the apostle made a compelling appeal for this man in authority to become just like him, but without his chains (Acts 26:28–29). Part of our ability to reach people is the fact that we have something we believe in and want others to embrace. We can't be so *laissez-faire* casual that others think it is not urgent. This was part of why Paul said he was not ashamed of the gospel (Rom 1:16). He believed it! It radically altered his life and he was passionate about others knowing the Jesus he knew. In this account, Agrippa, was actually taken back by the fact that Paul tried to win him over in such a short period. I realize in the evangelism process we often relate along comfortable conversational lines, and yet, in the journey there will be moments when friction is necessary.

Here is an insight worth a billion bucks. You can have friction, if you have safety, pace and honor first. Can you envision why that is so? The non-believer can receive the challenge because it does not threaten the relationship (safety), its timely in the conversation (pace), and its done out of the highest respect for them (honor). When you have these relationally oriented factors working for you, friction becomes one of your tools. If you don't have safety, pace, and honor, friction could lead them down a sinkhole. Unfortunately, this happens way too often; Christians are notorious for confronting people about their beliefs before the right pieces are in place. Impatience is never a virtue, and is detrimental to spiritual influence and gospel reception.

With the other pieces firmly established, however, you can work at uprooting them from their complacency. Listening to a woman's testimony, she said that a friend once told her, "You can't sit on the fence forever." The splintering sentiment sunk, and she got up and chose to commit.

SINKHOLE #4: PATIENCE

Alluded to previously, because the REP (Relational Evangelism Process) develops progressively, we must learn to wait for the right moments. Great achievements rarely happen overnight, but through many strategic steps. Patience will help us succeed in building something solid and lasting. Some are ready sooner than later to come to Christ. They might come to a couple services, the pastor hits it out of the park, and moved by the Spirit they want salvation. If that happens, lead them to Christ. Often non-believers take awhile to understand and "feel right" about the major life decision of becoming a Christian.

Whenever I start pressing too hard with others, I have to step back and remind myself who is over the journey. It is good policy at those times to: *Press less and pray more.* By the way, quick decisions that are relationally cold do not produce hot quality disciples. When someone makes an un-weighed decision, it is not surprising when they drop out saying, "Christianity didn't work for me." Solid faith decisions typically take time. You might picture trying to turn an ocean liner. The course of life turns slowly, but eventually over weeks or months of conversations, exposure to Christians, prayer, and a few breakthrough moments, they come to faith.

The Art of Spiritual Dialogue

Be patient and allow the seeding to take root, and for God to accomplish his work. Most of all, keep the momentum ball moving. Relational neglect can easily become the sinkhole to kill the whole journey.

YOUR MISSION'S VOICE

Based on the true story of King George the 6th, the Academy Award-winning film *The King's Speech* centers on the crazy techniques of under-credentialed tutor Lionel Logue (played beautifully by Geoffrey Rush) to help a monarch with his speech impediment. It is hard for us non-stutterers to empathize with the harrowing experience of being a king without the ability to put together a sentence. This movie takes us deep into this agony. In the final scene, with the friendship support of Lionel, the king delivers a critical pre-world war II speech with the nation holding to his every word. The struggle to speak and find his voice as a king revealed how holistic communication can be. Having first learned to dig deeper to help shell-shocked soldiers of the Great War, Lionel insists on using the name "Bertie" (the name only used by the king's close family) as he dredges into his childhood story and psyche to peel back the insecurity engrained underneath. Raising stature and confidence is big for royalty and for God's royal kids, too!

Peter describes believers as a royal priesthood, God's special possession "that you may declare the praises of him who called you out of darkness into his wonderful light . . . once you had not received mercy, but now you have received mercy" (1 Pet 2:9–10). Captured within this eloquent phrasing is the concept of who we are in God's eyes. Our words most naturally flow from this authentic place. Being this, we declare this. Being in darkness, God has brought his light into our lives. Notice the emphasis on darkness, light and mercy. If you want to find your authentic voice, start with sharing your journey from darkness into light. Identify your growth areas first with God and then with others. It is always easiest to talk in real, honest ways. Utilize your "ongoing testimony" of who you are and how God is helping you. This requires vulnerability, but is a powerful way to backdrop the light of Christ naturally in conversation. Building from there, push yourself into discourse and trust God to guide you. Remember, you are his beloved representative! God will honor your faith and sharpen you through practice.

When planting our first church, the fifty-two consecutive sermon idea overwhelmed me. I tried to get ahead of the curve and work on multiple messages. It was hard enough to crank out one, much less dozens, so I began feeling crushed! God had to teach me to trust him one message at a time. I also leaned heavily into other pastor's messages for a while. One Sunday, I essentially gave another's talk. It wasn't me and the church knew it. One guy called me on it and it was embarrassing. I had to go home and think deeply about what I was doing. It took me time, but I eventually began to find my own "preaching voice." I studied the Word and paid attention to what resonated with me. I started to get a feel for the text. The shift led to increasing results as I grew in the confidence of using my voice, from my own thoughts, in my unique way.

When I teach missional living, I look into the eyes of church members of all ages, who are at various levels of spiritual growth, gifts and abilities. At my church, we have so many twenty- to thirty-year-olds. I search for how I can help them to discover their "missions voice." I tell them, "You are going to have to come to a place of feeling comfortable discussing spiritual things." Christian brother or sister, you have got to learn to speak in your own way, and appeal to non-believers from your mind and heart. The more you practice this, the more natural it will become. This is a needed step of growth for most. Find your voice!

DISCUSSION AND ENGAGEMENT

1. If in a group, take a moment and affirm something positive about each person's personal presence.

2. Can you recall a time when you tried to influence someone but looking back realize you were only working one wing of the plane? Please discuss what happened.

3. Have you ever had an evangelistic relationship hit a major sinkhole and come to a halt? Describe what happened.

4. Does the dating illustration make sense when it comes to courting someone spiritually? Talk about the issue of pace in new relationships.

5. Describe a time in your life where you either applied or failed to utilize the principle of "honor."

6. Which of the four spiritual dialogue sinkholes (pace, honor, friction, patience) will be most challenging for you?

13

Breakthrough Skills

*Laws are like spider's webs which, if anything small falls into them
they ensnare it, but large things break through and escape.*

—SOLON, ATHENIAN STATESMAN AND POET, 630–560 BC

I had fired every shot in my arsenal, but after eight months of weekly
meetings I still searched for the elusive silver bullet. Dave was a cool guy,
but proving tough to take down. We had established a solid foundation for
Christianity, but could not transcend his doubting apprehension. One day
he acknowledged, "I'm stuck." I felt depleted emotionally, not knowing what
else to say. The good thing about an impasse is that you open to new angles.
After a conversation where he expressed disbelief in the supernatural, with
a bit of angst, I touched on how God is actively working. It was Einstein
who said, "There are two ways to live your life: One is as though nothing is a
miracle; the other is as though everything is a miracle." Dave lived according
to the former. He could not see God's superseding hand. I appealed, "Things
in life don't just happen by accident."

Attempting to unveil divine fingerprints, I mentioned two examples
where he might possibly behold God's orchestration. One was meeting
his wife, with whom he is madly in love. This was pure opportunism on
my part. Did he think it was by accident that they were brought together?
Not that anything could ever compare with her, but the other example was

meeting me. I said, "It's no accident, Dave, that we have become friends. God wants you to process your beliefs and come to know him." This created a moment. He had to contemplate the notion of God reaching to him. Desperate for more traction, I sensed the need to be braver. Though I had not done this before, I felt that he should seek God directly. Therefore, I asked if he would be willing to pray a simple prayer, "Help me God to understand how you are working." To this my atheist-now-agnostic friend said, "I will do it."

From that moment on, Dave began trying to see God in daily events. The next week he went with several guys from church on a kayaking trip down the Black River, which is outside Las Vegas below the Hoover Dam. Dave described how he and one of the other guys mixed it up jokingly over which color kayak to take. Later, as they worked their way down the river, Dave noticed the three Christians had landed in yellow kayaks, and he, the non-believer, was in the red one. Since they had made such a fuss over the colors, he pondered if God had ordered this detail. On the way home, one of the men disclosed how he recognizes God's hand. He said, "You can't always see it going through, but it is amazing to see his hand when you look back." As Dave thought of this, his mind continued to open toward God's activity.

Three weeks later, when we met at the It's a Grind coffee place, Dave told me he had something to share. I could tell it was big and I was right—he was ready to become a Christian! I shook my head in disbelief. The intellectual foundation had been built for a while, but it was the experiential track that broke the stronghold. He had experienced God in a real way!

Before we go further, let me answer a common question. Are we being presumptuous? By taking this experience-focused line, are we overstepping in our expectation of God? I recall asking this once to a congregation and they did not in any way seem disturbed by the idea. The underlying question is, "Do we believe in the living and active God who is at work in the world and drawing people to himself?" Consider Jesus's words in John 5:17, "My Father is always at his work to this very day and I too am working." We are not presuming God to be something that he is not. To the contrary, we are helping people see the real God who is actively seeking them. God chooses to draw people in his mysterious ways, but promises if we seek him, he will be found (Matt 7:7–8). When it comes to reaching certain people, experiential seeking provides necessary leverage. This "going experiential" technique causes us to put our faith in the God who saves. *It makes Christians realize that evangelism is ultimately God's work, not ours. We cannot reach anyone unless he does it.* If you are sitting across the table from an atheist, you will have an overwhelming sense of this.

THE MISSING GOD LINK

Inspired in part by the writings of the Bible, Jeffrey Lieber, J.J. Abrahams and Damon Lindelof, created the smash hit, *Lost.* Thematic to all six seasons was the dilemma of destiny. One particular second season episode showcased its tension. The scene involves Jack, the lead character, who is skeptical to the notion that there is any overriding purpose for them being on the island. Despite seemingly connected events he continues to dismiss this idea. So just when Jack is determinably ditching destiny once and for all, while alone in the jungle terrain he stumbles into Desmond, a man he had previously met while running at an emptied stadium in a coincidental encounter. Looking into this face from his past he is shaken to the core. Watching this scene my son said, "The writers should get an award for that episode." Though that kind of happenstance can make a skeptic wobbly, the sense of a grand design is something we all desire.

Who isn't looking for a date with destiny? Deep within humanity is a longing for meaning that transcends our everyday existence. In my view, this is why so many TV shows showcase superhuman powers: *Heroes, Unforgettable, Alphas, Touch*—all tap innate desire for something outside us. Personally, I hunger to know what God wants with me. You likely feel the same pull. How amazing when we discover God's unmistakable intervention in our lives. It is exciting when he arranges an event in a way that has his fingerprints all over it! We love to experience those "God moments." This "larger than our lives" God is a resonating concept in postmodern evangelism. More than ever, people are looking for God to show up in real ways. Whether we like it or not, many will form their views of God from the daily things they experience.

GAINING TRACTION

I grew up in a four-wheel Jeep Club family. As a child, my dad took us on trips with his buds and their vehicles. I remember a trip into Mexico's Baja Peninsula where we slept under the stars at night, and had scorpions climb into our sleeping bags for warmth. Four wheels were meant for off-roading. When you are traveling through coastlands, deserts and hills you often need every wheel to make it. On the Baja coast we made a beeline through a long muddy section and many jeeps got stuck. Not only did they kick into 4-wheel drive, but we also would scavenge the landscape for wood branches to put under the tires. If necessary, several people would jump up on the bumper to give it weight and then bounce to get the tires connecting with the earth below. These traction techniques got us moving forward.

In the evangelistic journey, there's a time for traction! Certain techniques create forward impetus in REP relationships. People sometimes ask how many I use. The answer is—all of them! But I do it sensitively when the timing is right within the relational dialogue. Let us now look at five traction-gaining techniques.

ANTICIPATING THEIR COMING TO FAITH . . .

—Gets them to envision becoming a Christian.

Baseball is one sport utilizing visualization. Coaches teach players to picture the ball being thrown in their mind's eye and then envision the perfect swing. This prepares the mind for executing the swing through the middle of the ball. Many claim the practice has increased their batting average. Likewise in the church, effective pastors want the congregation to picture the action they will take following a message. This helps parishioners move into application. Recognizing the power of anticipation, popular speaker and author Tony Campolo says, "It's what you dream to become—that shapes you." Let's explore how this first tractiongaining concept can be applied in a missional direction.

Consider what happens when a non-believer begins to envision becoming a Christian. It's possible that they could be remotely distanced from that choice, but contemplating the idea is in itself a momentous step. In his book *Radical Outreach*, George Hunter studied how people have internal conversations on what they will do. This "self talk" is significant, since most non-believers talk themselves into decisions.[1] Thus, one of the things we can do is spur them toward the Christian vision. I like to say, "Be the first to believe they will believe!" Speak positively about the faith experience that awaits them. If they begin thinking seriously about it, they may be on their way! I recall saying to my friend, "What a day that will be when you become a Christian. Tricia is going to be in tears!" "I know," he responded. He was able to see himself becoming a Christian,

---

1. Hunter, *Radical Outreach*, 183.

and anticipated the meaning to his marriage, even though he wasn't very close at that time. You might say, "I believe you are going to become a Christian one day—I can see God doing great things through your life." Or "I am praying for you and your faith decision." The fact they know others are interceding for them shows concern and creates expectation.

Planting the seed of future change can also jab at their identity stronghold. Once I initiated this rather unusual line of dialogue: "Being an atheist has been part of your M.O. for a long time. Does the idea of changing that identity scare you?" It created an interesting conversation. I did not know its impact, but intuited that it was necessary. Perhaps it needed to be "put on the table" for him to begin letting it go! In my view, anticipation bolsters the emotional transition to faith.

According to the soul whispering paradigm, we should always read what is holding them up. Is it the rational side? Or is it something more emotional like the fear of change, fear of how people will view them, or fear of relationship loss? A change to the non-Christian identity they have lived in for so long is a big deal. Helping them process the choice enables them to relinquish their former life in exchange for following Jesus. People, typically, are not good at stepping out from where they are. Like boots stuck in the mud, you have to pull real hard to get to new ground.

CONFRONTING INTELLECTUAL INCONSISTENCY . . .

—Challenges them to align their beliefs with reason.

Pre-warning me that the car shakes at times, my future wife and I headed down the road when suddenly the steering wheel began jerking back and forth violently. It was so bad that I knew this alignment problem could not be overcome; so that day I determined to get her another car. Vehicles are not the only things that have horrific alignment issues; people do too. When you engage with a friend you will at times run into this phenomena. It happens when you try to establish a faith foundation, and they resist aligning with reason. This issue is particularly evident in the renegade thinking processes of skeptics. It is not uncommon to see the following equation occur:

> Skeptic . . .
> A + B = Illogical conclusion tied to doubt.

As we are engaging relationally and praying for God to draw them, we naturally become the one God uses to challenge their doubt-driven conclusions. In doing this, we are helping them align reason with faith instead of doubt. The alternative equation looks like this:

> Sound reasoning . . .
> A + B = Logical conclusion leading to faith.

Though all people face degrees of uncertainty, often doubt is nothing more than a bad idea. Like a cancerous cell, it does harm to one's life. Referring back to this chapter's opening, Dave found the prophecies to be convincing, was sold on the person of Jesus authenticating his divinity, and yet rejected anything miraculous. Though the rational evidence pointed one way, his disbelief trumped it all. Do you see what's happening? His doubt is winning. If I had hair I'd pull it out! This is what is difficult in reaching skeptics; they get tweaked in their thinking.

At these times, we need to challenge their conclusions by showing them what they are doing. I would say, "If solid evidentiary proofs point to faith, then why are you not adopting belief? Dave, what you are doing is not consistent? Can you see why this concerns me?" In my college ministry years we did a teaching series called, *How to Be a Christian Without Committing Intellectual Suicide*. When you see people holding to beliefs that are not consistent with rational thinking, you can rightly term it: "Intellectual suicide!" It is like they have a closed box for beliefs, and when logic and facts point to a different reality outside, they do not properly assimilate the new information. After investing enough time so they do not feel threatened, or think you do not care, you speak directly and objectively: "Your thinking is not consistent—it lacks intellectual soundness. Reason points one direction but your beliefs don't match it. That's a problem." At times, I come right out and say with conviction, "What you are concluding is not intellectually credible."

In a spirit of love, we do not let them settle with incongruity. It is not okay to have inconsistency between one's reason and beliefs. They can do it, but we are going to shine a spotlight, and make them wrestle with the misalignment. When you have laid down solid planks for belief, eventually they must gain new footing. We are challenging them to look hard at the platform beneath them and begin standing! In real life this might feel like an extended conversation going nowhere, but what you are doing is gathering branches to place under those stuck tires, and jumping up and down to get traction! Don't expect the alignment to reposition in the first conversation. Gently and patiently, you keep talking about the logic, proofs, rationale, and evidence. Eventually, God uses your persistence to break through! One skeptic who came to Christ was asked what helped him most. He said, "My friend kept challenging me." If the relationship is there, we can align their beliefs with reason.

CONTRASTING FAITH WITH DOUBT . . .

—Reveals how doubt is a closed door, while faith opens to new realities.

This is a helpful technique because it forces people to consider the bigger implications of their choices. A great insight comes from John Ortberg's book, *Faith & Doubt*, when he compares these two destinations. He first develops how all people live to some degree by faith and doubt.[2] Yet when it comes to the spiritual journey, faith and doubt are divergent paths with opposing outcomes. Stripping back his witty eloquence, the heart of the book exposes how the way of doubt is a door to nowhere. In contrast, faith opens a door to a new experience. Ortberg talks about the first time he attempted hang gliding. Winged up and ready, he inched his way out to the edge of the precipice, where the sight was so scary that he seriously considered aborting the whole endeavor. In the end, he chose to jump.

Later, he correlated his experience to the faith decision: "If I leap, if I trust, I do not know for sure what will happen. What I do know is this: if I don't leap, if I don't trust, if I don't hope, if I don't ask, I will never soar. I will never know. I will live and grow old and die standing on the side of that cliff."[3]

Faith is the step you must make if anything is going to happen. There comes a time, after you have laid the groundwork for believing rationally, when you lean into this logic. You can explain, "If you don't ever commit yourself, you will not know what it's like to experience what Christ offers. You will stay right where you are." Doubt is a closed door. In one of the most gripping invitations ever given, Jesus stood up amid a religious-water ritual in Jerusalem and cried out, "If anyone is thirsty, let him come to me and drink. Whoever believes in me, as the Scripture has said, streams of living water will flow from within him" (John 7:37–38). Like those who first heard this call, a non-believer will never know what he meant, if they don't come to him and drink. Faith opens a door to a whole new reality.

2. Ortberg, *Faith & Doubt*, 15–26.
3. Ortberg, *Faith & Doubt*, 74.

Additionally, explain that faith is the way God desires relationship. God has chosen that we would come to know him through faith. Because he has already intervened for us through Christ's sacrifice on the cross, we have a responsibility to respond. That is faith. In life, the best relationships are those of high trust; where we have full faith in another. This is the kind of relationship that God wants with them. By helping them see the dynamic potency of their faith, you are laying down another branch. At the right time for many, under the Holy Spirit's draw, it will be enough to garner response.

GOING EXPERIENTIAL . . .

—Has them "seeking God" to initiate a spiritual encounter.

In my doctorate studies, I came across the story of Christian minister and author Linda Bergquist. While an atheist in college, a man had the wisdom to "go experiential." He challenged her to pray that God would reveal himself if he exists, and to read the Bible everyday. Within days she felt something incredible happening. God began to draw her.[4] Our postmodern culture is open to experiential manifestations. A young Cambodian-American woman, Sakuna, asked a Christian workmate, "How can I learn about Christianity?" Sarah replied, "Have you ever prayed to him? Why don't you pray and ask him to reveal himself?" In earnest, she did. That week she recalls, "My eyes were different." A Bible verse on a license plate pops out in front of her. Never noticing before, suddenly, she realizes she lives by a church, and a Christian elementary school. She sees signs, "God loves you." "Jesus loves you." "It was all day," she said. "It was like he was all over the place." Consider the generalized distinction on how truth is assimilated with the two primary people groups.

> Modern: Truth is determined rationally.
> Postmodern: Truth is determined experientially.

Conventionally, we have thought of evangelism as an explanation waiting for the event, but in the postmodern time, it's often the event needing an explanation. I find myself explaining God to non-believers within their experiences, "God is clearly reaching to you." "He loves you so much and that's why that just happened." In essence, I am reinforcing the idea that God is real! They often experience him, before they come into

4. McRaney, *The Art of Evangelism*, 171.

faith. With most who are skeptical, "Going experiential" is not where we start. You must work the process, which begins with logic and reason. Yet reason alone may not get you home. So you have the experiential track as another branch, sometimes it's the lumber that leads to faith.

Although there are numerous ways to go experiential, allow me to highlight two of the biggies. The first is prayer. Coming from theologically conservative roots, I confess to having viewed prayer as the exclusive right of the Christian. After all, Christians alone are the ones with full favored access to God. Don't we pray in Jesus's name because he is our High Priest, enabling our prayers to proceed to the Father? Yet after my experience with my atheistic friend, I broadened my theological perspective. I had failed to consider the prime mission of Christ to draw all to himself. Why would God not answer the searching prayers of those on their journey to faith? The God of love who knows every thought of a pre-Christian, and who monitors carefully their heart, responds to those who seek him. Confirming this dynamic, Charles Finney's nineteenth-century research revealed that many had experienced answers to prayer before coming to Christ.[5]

Clearly, prayer is one of the ways people open to God. When helping a non-believer forward to Christ, encourage simple prayers . . .

> God, reveal yourself to me.
> God, help me to see you at work in the world.
> God, help me find a way out of my problem.

This third example listed is relevant and practical, but does have a risk element. If you encourage them to pray over their problem, you may need to walk alongside to make sure they see the answer. God might be doing something that they don't realize. Often our problems are self-induced and God must get our attention, or they may need to know that God doesn't rubber stamp everything we ask, because he has a better plan. The benefit of this seeking prayer, however, is that God shows up in some tangible way, and they are moved toward faith. This prospect is exciting!

A second "go experiential" angle relates to power. If you are not familiar with Alcoholics Anonymous writings, there is a section in "The Big Book" addressed to agnostics. AA has the challenge of getting people who do not believe in God, or don't know if they do, to follow a spiritual program where God is the answer. What they do is draw a wide "Higher

---

5. Finney, *Lectures on Revivals of Religion*, 108–11.

Power" net that leads people to seek.[6] In essence, they go experiential. For people all over the world the approach seemingly works. Albeit, some Christians may struggle with the wide definition, but we have to acknowledge that the experiential track opens minds to God.

We have power that people everywhere need! Let's not be shy in talking about what Christ offers. At times, we can challenge them to push out their hurtful enslaving practices and begin seeking Christ. This begins their discipleship journey. They must die to themselves, and seek God for his empowerment. Then, as they begin movement in a new direction, you can help them place full faith in Jesus's atoning work.

Many compulsive-addicted people are looking for a way out. They don't always know how to get there. Former front man to the Nu-metal band *Korn*, Brian Welch shows up at church loaded on meth and looking for hope. The pastor challenges the gathering to seek God. Desperate, Welch responds by coming forward. That day he goes home and snorts speed throughout the night. He recalls his experience: "I remember perfectly . . . I said, 'Lord, If you're real like that guy says, please take these drugs from me. I can't quit, I don't want to do them, but I can't stop. I want to be here for Jeanea. She lost her mom to drugs. I need your help. Just help me."[7] Within that week he had an encounter with God. We now know his transformation is legit!

When you consider the growing range of sin struggles and compulsion issues, this is not a negligible segment of the populace. Experientially focused evangelism is the right prescription, because God's power is what they need to break free. We should be forthright in telling others that God can change their lives, and when they have received Christ, the Holy Spirit will influence their inner desires. For some, they may need the practice of recovery principles also, which means connecting them with recovery meetings, Christ-centered *Celebrate Recovery*, or a fully open and honest healing group at your church.

Further, let me close this section by saying, everyone needs God's spiritual power. You don't have to have a compulsion to need God's transformational power everyday. When it came to the principle of abiding, Jesus said it so well, "Apart from me you can do nothing" (John 15:5).

---

6. Alcoholics Anonymous, "We Agnostics," 44–57.

7. Branson and Woodland, "Why Brian Welch Walked Away," lines 47–50.

ASKING WHAT'S HOLDING THEM BACK . . .

—Causes them to assess where they are with a decision.

There comes a time in the REP process when inquiring about the faith decision can be a leveraging move. Do not underestimate the impact of this simple probing. Many of us remember similar junctures in our journeys. Used at the right time, the question regarding where they are spurs non-believers into assessment. They have to think about "the decision" before them, or to reconcile why they have not yet responded. It might stimulate further discussion, which gives you the opportunity to speak into their processing. God works in these moments! Creating a time of assessment often creates traction. It can nudge them off the fence and forward with Jesus.

I personally experienced the power of this technique. A week before I came to Jesus, my girlfriend took me to Calvary Chapel. That evening I heard a strong gospel message by Chuck Smith Jr., and afterwards she led me over to talk with their counselors. The guy, probably sensing I was being strong-armed by my girlfriend, asked me if I was ready to commit. I told him straight up, "I am not." Though no decision happened that night, the thought of the commitment spurred me. It's like going down to the auto dealer and looking seriously at a car. You are not ready to lay down the cold hard cash, but it leads you into full contemplation. That is what happened with me. I wasn't ready, but it made me think deeply about the decision.

Then a week later, again with my girlfriend, God pulled me over the line through one of the most difficult interpretive passages of the New Testament. It happened in Seal Beach, California, in 1983, at a beach house, where we randomly studied chapter 6 of Hebrews. Look at it:

> It is impossible for those who have once been enlightened, who have tasted the heavenly gift, who have shared in the Holy Spirit, who have tasted the goodness of the word of God and the powers of the coming age, if they fall away, to be brought back to repentance, because to their loss they are crucifying the Son of God all over again and subjecting him to public disgrace (Heb 6:4–6).

Reading these words, I thought to myself, if I walk away now having come this far, I may never get back to this place again. That night I ventured out alone onto the beach sand and prayed my very first prayer. I asked the Lord to forgive me and told him I was ready to turn over a new leaf. God had drawn my heart to repentance. My girlfriend, Susan, had consistently kept the conversation going, earnestly wanting me to know Jesus. She had completed the REP with me!

The impelling need to gain traction naturally arises within the relationship. You will find yourself gathering branches in hopes that each addition might create forward momentum toward faith. As you place each one down below their tires, you will do your share of jumping up and down on the back end! Although we wisely employ breakthrough skills, we always do so in concert with prayer. The REP is a divine dance. Ultimately, the Lord must draw them over the line. The culminating moment is a gigantic step from the kingdom of darkness to the kingdom of light (Acts 26:18). We should never underestimate that invisible dimension.

THE BATTLE BEHIND THE VEIL

Sitting behind my "Christian Fellowship" table at Long Beach City College, out of the corner of my eye, I saw the man making a beeline over. My initial thoughts of him being a believer looking for connection changed as I stared into his raging bloodshot eyes. A barrage of attacking words against Christ and the Bible spewed from his mouth. Some have what is called the gift of discernment—radar to demonic influence. I had a person with this gift in my first church plant, and she would get an intuiting sense at times. In this case, no gift was necessary. I sat silent fully recognizing this guy was not himself. Eventually he tired of pouring his verbal venom and left.

Afterwards, I processed what I had witnessed. It was like someone pulled back a veil enabling reality to be seen. Early on in my Christian life, God allowed a glimpse of the battle that rages for human souls. In my twenty-eight years of ministry, he is the only man I have clearly categorized as "possessed." Satan seems to do a fair job of keeping his minions out of sight—a clear shift of strategy from the New Testament's overt activity. But we know they are there!

When teaching the evangelism process, I say, "I now want you to feel what the REP experience is like from a musical perspective." Playing the *Jurassic Park* soundtrack theme, we listen to music masterfully composed to capture the wonder of humans encountering dinosaurs. In this John Williams piece, it starts with a base drum and wind pipes, which sound like a giant step landing vicariously beside you. I narrate that at the front-end of a redemptive relationship both heaven and hell take notice.

The connecting occasion does not make the headlines of our world, but it stirs the interest of all players within the spiritual realm. This is the real story unfolding on earth—the hidden battle that rages for the soul. Satan's strategy with non-believers is to maintain the status quo. They don't like it when someone begins messing with their side. The music begins serenely with strings and then builds to higher and higher crescendos, ultimately climaxing in a sense of sheer wonderment.

I narrate the evangelistic story, which includes a deepening of relationship and spiritual dialogue. As the sweetness of relationship grows, there is also growing prayer intensity. The need for spiritual breakthroughs calls us, and others, to intercede on another's behalf. The battle is on! As the Apostle Paul wrote, "We fight not against flesh and blood, but against the rulers, against the authorities, against the powers of this dark world and against the spiritual forces of evil in the heavenly realms" (Eph 6:12). When the months of conversations move a person toward a faith decision the Christian feels the weight of the moment. This is also felt amongst the spiritual powers closely situated. They all know what's at stake and how a saving commitment will stoke the emotional state of heaven and rob the very corridors of hell!

DISCUSSION AND ENGAGEMENT

1. Have you ever experienced a moment when a non-believer got stuck in their spiritual journey? Describe what occurred.

2. Which of the five traction-gaining techniques seems most potent to you?

3. Have you ever made a journey with a non-believer all the way into faith? If so, describe what that was like from start to finish.

4. How important, in your opinion, is the prayer dimension? Share if you have sensed the spiritual warfare dynamic while reaching to a non-believing friend.

PART III

Paths:
Insights to Faith's Pathways

14

The Discovery Step

It is a dangerous business going out your door —you step on the road and if you don't keep your feet there's no knowing where you might be swept off to.

—Bilbo Baggins

As an avid snorkeler from Southern California, I have frequented the western trifecta of Laguna Beach, Catalina Island, and Hawaii. The coastline of Mexico is also in driving reach. On my honeymoon, my wife and I visited the Gulf's Cozumel Island, where the waters teamed with thousands of pellet-sized jellyfish. At this world-class snorkeling spot you can swim beside barracuda. In addition to the sea life, Cozumel offers a glorious sight that snorkelers miss. This is because you have to get distance from the shore, and then dive deep scuba style. But if you know the particular spot (Punta Sur), and dive ninety feet down, you can enter a passageway called 'The Devil's Throat' which takes you into a cavern nicknamed 'the Cathedral.' On the ceiling you will see a sponged cross formation, back lighted by sunlight streaming from the surface. For a Christian valuing the symbol, it is a sight to behold! One person said, "If I had another breath, it would have taken it away."

In life, there are things we will not see without a deeper look. Even with only a snorkel and mask, I am astonished at what comes into view at ear-popping levels. The next section focuses on diving deep into the non-believer's journey. Two different motifs provide insight on where to lead forward. The "Steps to Faith" offers a general picture of the processing steps all non-believers make. The "Paths to Faith" gives specific insight on eight redemptive pathways. What you will learn in these chapters will add layered dimensions of understanding. Take a good couple breaths and then one big one—let's go deep!

* * *

I like to say, "Do not ever take a job that is not over your head." At that moment, I knew I had, saying to myself, "Lord, this is crazy!" Along with my atheist friend, a second skeptic wanted to meet and discuss beliefs. I was not sure how to do this. Steadying my mind, I reasoned I would just have to take it one dialogue at a time. Evangelism is like every great endeavor, just one step before the other. Though I knew I did not have all the answers, something within me relished this challenge. We only go through life once, and who wants to sit on the sidelines? So with plenty of uncertainty, I committed myself to follow through with both. They may jump ship on me, but I wouldn't quit on them. I would walk beside each till they came to a decision on Christ one way or the other. That meant both David and Anita became friends—not relational projects, but real friends. I hope to keep in touch for the rest of my life.

What unfolded ended up changing everyone's lives. After journeying for nine months with my atheist friend, and then six months with my theistic skeptic friend, both came into the faith two weeks apart. It was an evangelistic odyssey unlike anything I had ever experienced. God used it to revolutionize my thinking. Without it, *Soul Whisperer* would not be a reality. Within these scenarios came numerous revelations. One of the biggest derived from my observation that each progressed through identifiable steps. If I had only met with one, I may not have seen it, but with God opening the door with these two simultaneously, these "steps" jumped out at me. Mulling afterwards, I found myself dissecting it like a scientific experiment. Fascinatingly, I noted how the man and woman each advanced through a series of mental progressions. Though I initially saw three; I later added what I call "The First Step." What I am going to reveal seems rudimentary, but it is, in my view, an extremely beneficial way to understand the non-believer's journey. In the most reduced form, the "Steps to

Faith" are: *Open to, Able to, Want to* and *Choose to*. In other words, each person must be "open to" believe before they are "able to" believe, and "able to" before they "want to" believe, and "want to" before they "choose to" believe. Like a stairway to heaven, every person moves through these steps on their way to faith, although they will not recognize it.

Open to believe > Able to believe > Want to believe > Choose to believe

At first glance you may not fathom the significance. But consider that if my two friends were not first "open to explore," neither would have become Christians. If God had not enabled both skeptics to be "able to believe" in God and the Christian faith, they would not have come to Christ. And if both had not moved from the head to the heart in "wanting to follow," they would still be unbelievers. If they had not crossed the line by actively "choosing faith" we would not have rejoiced.

You will observe these very steps when you interact with your unchurched friends. When you do, it will be dynamic! Alex attends our evangelistic class, and in the second session comes right out and says, "I don't believe in the resurrection." What do we now know about Alex? First, he is a non-believer who is open to explore evidenced by his showing up. Though open, he is not yet "able to" believe. Alex disagrees with one of Christianity's essential tenets—you can't be a believer if you don't buy the resurrection. So in the class, we address the logical rationale supporting belief in this historic event. Within just one session, God amazingly pulls him over that belief hump. Then two weeks later, he says, "I don't know if I want to follow Christ." What step is he on now? Clearly, he is at the "want to" level. That, too, is a barrier. Therefore, we begin digging into the motivational side. We take time in the class to interact about the alternatives of continuing to live his own life, or following Christ's footsteps. Quite a bit of dialogue and disclosure takes place on this issue of desire. Afterwards, it is difficult to discern where his heart has arrived. Probing, I talk directly with the non-believers in that class about where they are regarding faith. Alex says, "He is not at the place of becoming a Christian."

Reading the need for more time, I decide to extend the class a week just to keep the conversation going. Not wanting to ever cut short the process, I communicate that when the class ends, I would like to keep meeting with him. He agrees. Then, we gather for the final session and begin the teaching. At an early point, Alex shares his processing. He describes his visit to a local market. Angry and cussing, one man had words with the cashier. Two girls were discussing the previous night's sexual exploits. An older gentleman left loaded up with 24 ouncers. Then Alex embellished, "I used to be just like those unbelievers."

A team member, Ashley, who had watched his progression from the beginning, and recognizing what he was saying, gave out a scream! My co-teacher, Don, winked. Alex, unbeknownst to us had crossed into faith. He then told us outright that he's become a Christian, and was ready to be baptized. What a cool moment of watching God draw someone in five weeks through all the major steps. From his first step decision to attend, to not believing in the resurrection, to not knowing if he wanted to follow, to not being ready to become a Christian, Alex progressed through each step into belief. By the way, the progression concept inspired the design of my evangelistic course material, which is appropriately titled, "Steps to Faith." That course booklet addresses the non-believer's progressions, while teaching the core beliefs.

Let me be quick to add, we don't always see people progress through every step, like Alex. For example, suppose you are reaching to someone who has a belief foundation, but is not a believer. With that person, you'd begin where they are, which is the Desire Step. Yet every person in their journey will cover all four. There are no exceptions. By understanding this, you can see how the telling paradigm often misreads. This is, of course, why soul whispering works so well. The paradigm always starts by reading where they are, and then focuses on what they need next to progress.

Once you get the conceptual idea, your eyes will open to seeing the steps in the Scriptures. They are everywhere. Which ones do you think Jesus worked with Nicodemus and the woman at the well? They are not the same.

Simply listing the steps makes it sound easy: Four progressions and you're in the faith. But seeing people journey through them is an entirely different thing altogether, and something you must experience yourself! Specific movement can take days, months, years, or even a lifetime. With my atheist friend, the journey through all four took nine months of weekly meetings! As you can imagine, the majority of time focused on the "able to believe" step. Typically, in the REP it will be a month or more of ongoing conversations. You will find that each step can monumentally propel the non-believer toward Jesus. This is the breakdown's beauty from an evangelistic perspective. Keeping to our primary principle of beginning with where they are, when you understand their steps, you know what you are trying to accomplish in conversations, and when to give attention to the next level. Though that may sound mechanical, in real life it is an artful, thoughtful, and skillful process.

When you walk beside your friend you will discover they are somewhere in the range of these steps. In this chapter, I address the first critical "Open to" step. In the next three chapters, I will walk you through some of the fascinating intricacies of each. The following chart highlights the hang-ups and where you need to focus:

STEPS	"THE HANG UP"	HELP WITH...
1.Open to	Interest	Asking
2.Able to	Reason	Answers
3.Want to	Motivation	Appeal
4.Choose to	Response	Application

The "help with" column shows in a big picture way the kind of interaction required.

Using the grid as an evaluation tool, we can note that many churches today only minister to the "want to" and "choose to" people, and do little to reach the other sectors. The church is guilty of over-simplifying what is involved in faith formation. We need to be careful with our unspoken messages. Do people pick up, "If you already believe like us then we are the place for you." Or the same thing communicated negatively, "If you are not where we are, we have nothing for you." Take a look at the steps from a culture viewpoint.

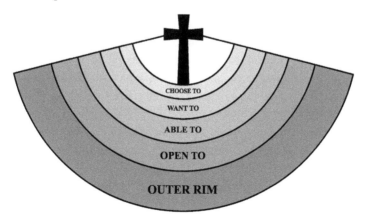

Here's a big take-away that you need to get. In the post-Christian era, the inner rings are shrinking and the outer rings growing. The church must adjust to draw those in the outer rings. Strategically speaking, we need Christians equipped to engage those "not open," and those open but "not able" to believe. Within the neo-pluralistic era, evangelism must broaden its conversation to draw in an increasingly distant populace. We are back to the prophetic words of the Samaritan woman who looked down a well and understood the challenge of distance. This is why learning "the steps" is both critical and timely. If we understand their journey, we can begin where they are, and help them progress at each juncture. Let us now focus in on how big and multi-dimensional each step can be. You must learn to read exactly where people are hung up. Your ability to zero on their particular needs will be key in spurring them onward.

In a big picture way, look at the steps through five links. Help them into discovery, help them to discern truth, help them to desire faith, help them to decide for Christ, help them forward as a new disciple. This is how we reach people like Justin, Anita and Alex.

Discovery > Discernment > Desire > Decision > Disciple

THE "OPEN TO" STEP.

The first step for the non-believer is having willingness to: examine, explore, learn, look into, or discuss the Christian faith. Usually, this happens with a Christian or inside a believing community. Incredibly for our day, research indicates a high percentage of non-believers would be open to spiritual conversations with some inside their relational circle. Ed Stetzer cites a study where 71 percent expressed openness to a conversation with a Christian friend.[1] The high regard for Jesus and openness to discussion is encouraging. We need to recognize and capitalize on this general attitude. The woeful thought is that open people have no Christian engaging them relationally; and the posture is wasted. Therefore, living missionally alongside people is a sound strategy. When you get to know someone, share your life, and probe for spiritual interest, you may very well uncover the openness that exists. Often, drawing people into interest and discussion can be done in a very soft relational way of framing up a time to get together or "having a conversation about having a conversation."

1. Stetzer, "The Fear, The Herd, The Witness," 108.

It is also notable that people go through seasons of spiritual responsiveness. Sometimes a significant setback or change creates a window of interest. These equilibrium busters have a way of turning the soil. When indications of movement occur, we must seize the moment. *Carpe diem!* I have witnessed these crisis times with friends. One had survived a horrific car accident and it so shook his world that he opened to God, and sought me out to talk. Another friend almost lost a leg and it created impassioned spiritual stirrings. When this happens, do not be low- key about faith. Step into their dramatic moment at the intensity level that God has birthed in them! I've made the low-balling mistake, but never again!

On the other side of rosy, however, is the reality of the closed posture. Have you encountered disinterest? People on the "outer rim" are everywhere, and remain closed for a great variety of reasons. My friend Britt described his non-believing friend as "a tightly wound onion" having layer after layer of protection, defensiveness, hurt, and false thinking. Yet if we look at common themes of closedness people generally fall into one of four groupings: Believing, Changing, Talking, or Borrowing. Let's unpack each.

BELIEVING: *THE BELIEVING-IMPOSSIBLE PEOPLE.*

If you have watched *The Princess Bride*, you have seen an all-time classic spoof. My favorite scene is the boat chase when Sicilian genius Vizzini fails to thwart Wesley and repeatedly yells, "Inconceivable!" After the third time his swordsman Inigo Montoya says, "You keep using that word. I don't think it means what you think it means." Unfortunately, that word represents the position some people have adopted towards Christianity. Yet our faith is not inconceivable—it may be incredible, but it is not inconceivable! When we encounter those with this view, it is necessary to counter their overly simplified conclusion.

To do this we simply spur a person's openness to our faith's believability. Nothing in the Christian faith is beyond reason. We need to engage in a discussion about faith, facts, and real possibilities. It might be they have written off Christianity because it is supernaturally based. But given the supernatural dimension of a Creator, the Christian faith makes consistent sense. Denying the Creator is the thing that causes believability problems. For that atheistic stance, I refer you to chapter 19 where I address skeptics. With this step let's just be clear that we must stand up big for our faith's believability. If someone has dissed it prematurely, our role is to demonstrate why it is reasonably possible.

I recall the time golfing when a conversation surfaced this smug skepticism. The guy thought Christianity was ludicrous. After hearing his thoughts, I essentially told him that his position lacked "intellectual integrity." He struggled to comprehend what I was saying, but I could not just let him remain loftily unchallenged. I had hoped to pull him into a discussion. In that case, I did not succeed. Yet with many others it has progressed into dialogue and further relationship. That is how you work the step. You meet and help them into being open to its possibility. Once that is achieved, you go to the next level, which zeroes in on the rationale for faith. Can you see how you work the sequence? It is vital at this stage to choose your words carefully and be aware of your nonverbal vibe, for you don't wish to belittle or ridicule someone.

CHANGING: *THE SCARED OF THE UNKNOWN PEOPLE*

With others, the closed position relates to faith's implications for change. The idea of changing terrifies lost people. It can be so scary, that they will not even entertain its reality. If we are to stimulate openness we will have to create a faith picture that lessens fear. I have addressed this issue in the "pace" section of the "The Art of Spiritual Dialogue" chapter, but it belongs here too, as one of the biggies in shutting down one's search. Recapping, we must help those fearing change by highlighting faith's "attraction elements." They will have to see benefits that exceed their fears. Often non-believers just want to call their own shots and will not let anything mess with that. Why have a conversation about faith? Yet self-seekers always have missing pieces—that's why they are lost! If we gain insight into them we may be able to draw them into the spiritual conversation. We must provide a window to faith that is compelling enough to garner their interest.

A youth worker mentioned his difficulty reaching out to a friend who appears fully content in his unbelief. My reply, "I would not be shy in telling him that what God offers is so much greater than anything he knows. God wants to bless him in ways that are beyond his imagination." Don't let them think they got it, when all they've done is settle for Satan's scraps. Jesus said, "The Devil comes to destroy, I came that they may have life in all its fullness" (John 10:10). They are being satisfied with something far below what Jesus offers. We must share this insight. Just make sure you cast a great vision, not a wimpy one!

TALKING: *THE MUTE-POSITIONED PEOPLE*

Still others remain closed based on a self-determined "talking" rule. It is not uncommon for non-believers to adopt a "no discussion policy." Have you experienced this? I have innumerably. You make an inference to spirituality, and they tell you straight up, "I don't want people shoving religion down my throat." That is code for: Spiritual conversations are off limits with me. They essentially shut you down before you begin. Though I do not pursue conversations that are not welcomed, I also will occasionally call out someone who makes such a rude reply. This response is not flattering, and we should let them know it if we have enough relationship with them. Why can't we talk about things of significance as friends? Getting shutdown by someone is hurtful and erodes the strength of a friendship. It is this closed positioning that we must seriously confront!

In American culture, we are taught not to talk about religion or politics. And what were our founders doing at their dinner tables? How sad to have lost the art of civil discourse in our country—so soon. We need to re-teach people how to talk openly about their views without it being a negative experience. I will say, "Why don't you share your thoughts, and I will share mine, and we can learn from each other. I want you to know I don't expect that we will see things the same. I am just glad you are open to share what you really think, and are willing to hear my thoughts, too."

Sadly, sometimes people have assumed the no-talk posture as a recoiling reaction to overaggressive Christians. The telling paradigm abuses have hurt the church here. Non-believers become fearful to begin a conversation not knowing what will happen, and wondering if they will have to fight off a person coming at them with the proverbial fire-hose! No one, neither children nor adults, want to experience another forcefully pushing their beliefs on them. Worse yet, how terrible to pronounce judgment. As a sensitive, loving Christian, you can provide a countering image by your calm demeanor and reassuring words, indicating that a conversation with you is safe. I will occasionally tell a person, "Hey man, I am not trying to convert you, we're just gonna talk. That's all." Granted, if the person feels safe to have a conversation that could end up down the road leading to a place of conversion, but they will never feel coerced, as they fear. Thus, my words are genuine. I am letting them know it is their decision before God, and I will honor that choice.

If you cannot respect wide-ranging viewpoints then you can jettison the journey with non-believing friends prematurely. In researching evangelistic groups, an overseer described how a leader jumped on people for expressing views outside his tight theological convictions. A director said, "What started as a large group shrunk because people didn't feel like their thoughts mattered." In contrast to this group leader, we aim to draw out what people really think and feel so we can see what is there. We need to be careful not to expect them to think or believe as we do. Often non-believers have good thinking for us to consider even if we disagree. We can learn much from them. I make concerted effort to praise non-believer's ideas when they have merit. This is the practice of "honor" we learn from Jesus.

When a person has determined not to discuss spirituality, our aim is unlocking the closed door. This is not easy, but we can pick the pins and move the tumblers subtly or directly. Being soft and gentle and not "in their face," but rather with genuine caring, you might seek permission to ask a question. "Is it okay if I ask a slightly personal question," "Does talking about faith feel awkward or threatening to you for some reason?" Another angle: "Do you feel hurt in some way by God?" Then sit back and listen. You are trying to sensitively draw them into an honest, positive discussion. With a closed friend, you want to open the subject matter a bit. Get it out there and listen to their initial thoughts. "I sense you are turned away by the faith topic." Being very soft and gentle, you might say: "Is there reason for that?" Here's a vulnerable one, "I sense your reluctance to talk freely—I hope I don't threaten you—I am not meaning to." That one is endearing, and it might draw them in.

You can be direct if you have this ability. "C'mon! Close-minded people suck!" Maybe that's too direct, but it's true! There are times to let them chew on their closed-mindedness. They might have a revelation when they realize how others see them. With some I actually want to leave them with my distinct negative impression of how closed-minded I perceive them to be. It is a very ugly trait! If you have relationship, these carefully placed words can work. Closed people suddenly realize their stance is not appreciated and this may even be ironic, because they have been critical of Christians for being closed or narrow in their views.

Tawny tells me about her conversation with her Armenian friend Dacia, who quickly shuts down her attempt to discuss faith. Armenians, by the way, are proudly Christian in the fact that they adopted Christianity even before Constantine. Yet Tawny senses her Christianity is merely cultural and not real. She asks me one night after our missional group, "How do you respond when she just laughs at me, and then says her faith is personal?" My counsel was to say something in this vein. Look her in the eyes and say, "Dacia, good relationships can talk about important things. If we cannot talk about something as significant as our faith, then our relationship is superficial. I don't want *you and me* to have that kind of relationship. Because of how much I value you, I want to have the deeper kind." Dacia will see her posture in a new light. She wants to avoid the faith subject, but now sees how it affects relationships. She may intuit that Tawny views her as inauthentic. This could make her reflect and change her mind. A door is opened.

The truth is Tawny does not want a shallow relationship. If Dacia avoids meaningful discussion, that relationship will not progress. As Christians, we know a relationship only goes as deep as its connection point. It's why we value fellowship, because we connect around something meaningful. Who cares about all the trivial crap of life? Don't you get tired about all the meaningless chatter? I want to talk about something big! God and faith are worthwhile subjects that should not be shelved by anyone. Dacia can remain a closed, shallow friend who doesn't share her real thoughts. Or Tawny could successfully draw her into talking openly about her life, beliefs and God.

Other times I reason: "Look at how many people in history rejected great ideas without giving them the time of day." Or how about this one: "Do you know what a sign of a dysfunctional family is? They don't talk openly." These conversational tactics require the right tone and tact. Yet used skillfully, you may move a friend into dialogue. That is where the journey begins! Obviously, there are times to just wait on the Lord. I do not always pursue closed people, but when God is leading, I will stir the pot to see if we can get anything simmering!

> Tact: *Enabling one to receive what you say, because your spirit does not encumber the message.*

One thing is for sure. Talking about God and who we are is one of the most important discussions of life. It is tragic to think that some will get gypped from participating in "The Great Conversation."

In the book, *Breaking the Missional Code*, co-author David Putman shares his conversational thread with a non-believer who believes in God but not that Jesus was God. Avoiding what could be a counter-productive conflict, Putman wisely says, "Bob, that's a great place to begin, but if you believe in God, then let me challenge you to pray the following prayer: "Dear God, I believe in you, and if Jesus is indeed your way for me and all people, then show me. I'm open." Notice how he did not close the man's search, but rather kept him moving in a posture of openness. Putman goes on to say that months down the road the man became a Christ-follower.[2] We have to promote, teach, and inspire openness.

Since you are a Christian with solid convictions, it is entirely possible that a non-believer might counter you by saying, "You are closed-minded in that you think Christianity is the only way." If this happens I would respond, "Christianity makes the most sense to me, but if you can convince me of another worldview that is more sound, I will follow it." I would listen intently if they sincerely believe they can. Of course, they will not be able to succeed, not because I am closed, but because other worldviews ignore the many pointers to the veracity of the Christian faith. I will detail the four rationale planks supporting the Christian faith in chapter 19—a must read! I often say, "If you look at anything long enough from enough angles the truth will rise to the top." That is why we are working for their openness. If they become open to examine beliefs, then, they will eventually see the Christian faith's truth and relevancy. This is how the "open to" step can eventually lead to their faith.

BORROWING: *THE PREPROGRAMMED PEOPLE*

A final form of resistance from closed people is "borrowed" belief. Obviously, many have borrowed beliefs from adopting what is taught inside a family or culture. When in a relationship with someone possessing borrowed beliefs, I will eventually appeal, "You need to learn to think for yourself." "Your views are based on assumptions others have made for you." That is not the right way to determine something as critical as one's view of God and reality. The best book demonstrating this error is, *Choosing Your Faith*, by Mark Mittelberg. He exposes the fallacies of the non-rational approaches.[3] We need to help people move from any unsubstantiated place. I appeal, "Why aren't you open to forming your own opinion based on reason, logic, evidence, facts and experience?" Can you see what I am doing? I want to draw them to engage intellectually with me about what is true? I want them to think for themselves!

2. Stetzer and Putman, *Breaking the Missional Code*, 130.

3. Mittelberg, *Choosing Your Faith*, 57–80.

If only our education systems tooled people to examine ideas critically. If only more Christians were trained to think, we'd all be in better place. Moreover, the issue of getting people to explore can be troubling for those with family-culture influences. I devote chapter 20 to reaching people of other faiths, and the "open to" step is often the whole enchilada! They either make this step or we will never reach them.

THE GREATEST MISSTEP

It had come down to the final *Jeopardy* question, and the pop-up category was "The Bible." I put my plate down saying, "This is going to be interesting." Three brains had battled it out over the last half hour, and now a Bible question will decide it. I hope they had gone to Sunday school. The pop up-says, "It comes between 'Ask and it will be given,' and 'Knock and the door will be opened to you.'" I knew it! My seminary training had paid off for something. I watched the first contestant draw a blank. Unfortunately he had bet it all and his earnings zeroed. The second guy had an answer, "Pray and it will be answered." Good guess but no cigar. Isn't it funny when people try to make up Scripture? He also had bet it all. Then it was the third contestants turn, certainly he must know the verse, but he too draws a blank. All three bet it all and lose everything. I sat amazed by what I just witnessed. Ponder the implication of the phrase none knew "Seek and you will find"—the irony of losing it all over Jesus's words on seeking and finding God. I wondered when they segued back to their regular lives if any grasped the significance of the line that sunk them?

Sometimes, I will appeal to people this way, "The claims of Christ are so great that you owe it to yourself to give them an honest look. He said he could give you eternal life. He claimed that he was God, and that through faith you could be totally forgiven, and brought into a blessing filled relationship. For your own sake you should look into it. If it's false you have lost nothing, if its true you could lose everything, and miss the greatest gift ever imagined." I realize that might sound strong, but there can be a right time to deliver that sentiment. In *Faith and Doubt*, John Ortberg coins the term "blind doubt"—the failure to examine faith.[4] As people sometimes accuse believers, usually falsely, of having blind faith, non-believers more often have blind doubt. We can help them see how that is no way to approach life, live, or choose. Again, "Open to" is the first critical step—without it we go nowhere. If we cannot get people to

4. Ortberg, *Faith and Doubt*, 31.

seek and explore, like the final *Jeopardy* question, they will lose it all! Most people think evangelism is merely talking about the cross, and might not realize how it reaches all the way out to drawing openness.

There is a scene in *The Fellowship of the Ring*, when Frodo must leave his home, and venture into a world he has never seen. How could he foresee the epic journey ahead and the significance of that first footfall from his doorway in the Shire? Every great passage taken on this earth began with a first step. We must entreat our friends to move toward exploration. They either become open—or they will miss life's greatest adventure.

DISCUSSION & ENGAGEMENT

1. Think about friends and family members you know who are outside the faith. Can you identify where they are within the four steps?

2. If you have a friend who seems not open to explore the Christian faith, which of the four closed categories best describes him or her?

3. Can you think of any other reasons why people are closed?

4. Why is this first step so critical?

5. What can you picture yourself doing to help a person become open to explore faith?

15

The Discernment Step

We discovered that apologetics was necessary.

—*Timothy Keller*

By the sheer unrestrained boundaries of dreams, Christopher Nolan's award- winning film, *Inception*, enabled digital artists to push the visual envelope. Fueling the dynamics, a dream maintained a state of flux as actions in the real world rippled across interconnected dreamspace.[1] According to producers, the most challenging visual effect was the "limbo" city at the end,[2] where Nolan charged his designers to create "something glacial, with clear modernist architecture, but with chunks breaking off into the sea like icebergs."[3] In this dreamscape, fifteen-story buildings line an oceanfront, and when forces threatened the dreamer's processing, whole walls cascade into the surf.

That particular scene offers one of those rare cases where a movie's images mirror the gravity of Scripture. In a striking parallel, Paul dramatically describes what must occur to reach the non-believer's captive mind: "The weapons we fight with are not the weapons of the world. On the

1. Paul, "Desiring-Machines in American Cinema," lines 24–31.
2. Russell, "How Inception's Astonishing Visuals Came to Life," lines 39–40.
3. Russell, "How Inception's Astonishing Visuals Came to Life," lines 45–46.

contrary, they have divine power to demolish strongholds. We demolish arguments and every pretension that sets itself up against the knowledge of God" (2 Cor 10:5). In a context of addressing false teachers, or should we say "false thinkers," Paul unveils a glimpse into a mindscape, where demonic entities have erected fortifications. Without the demolition of these false pretensions, and the creation of true ones, people will not make the journey to faith. Biblically speaking, both demolition and inception will be necessary in releasing the captive. This is the spiritual dimension of the "Able to" step.

Undeniably, drawing a person's soul involves a battle for the mind. Satan has his architects, too! They have worked long and hard to entangle the person's viewpoints, keeping them from truth. I will always recall a coincidental conversation with a man at a camp where I was speaking. Having the task of building a fire for a soon-arriving youth group, I asked if I could warm myself. With it being a Christian camp, I falsely assumed he was a believer. After my inference to the stars and God's wonders, he expressed a belief in other inhabited worlds. When I asked him to explain further, he disclosed his view of the universe, and smugly quipped on how misled religious people are. Like so many others, he had no clue that he was betting his eternity on bizarre, unfounded speculations. Blinded spiritually, he did not realize what Satan had erected and its devastating consequence. With the group arriving, the conversation got cut short, but I left marveling at how a single planted idea firmly rooted in a mind could rob one's search for God and destroy any chance for faith. If I had had the positioning to build an ongoing rapport, I would have loved the challenge of dismantling his false suppositions.

Our work is to demolish what is set up against God, and to rebuild new constructs for faith. The architectural concept for evangelism first came into view through my time with skeptics. After months of meetings it became clear that I was in the spiritual construction business. When I studied the "Big Book" of AA (a great education for anyone), Bill Wilson's use of architectural imagery captivated me. His teaching espoused the surrender to God as "the keystone of the new and triumphant arch through which we passed to freedom."[4] In some ways, evangelism is no different. We must learn to become builders of new mindscapes, with keystones solidifying the structures, enabling our friends to walk into new life.

When I teach the relational evangelism process (REP), I will inquire of the class if they believe non-believers are able to believe the gospel. This

4. *Alcoholics Anonymous 4th Edition*, 62.

question leads to contemplation. Consistently, the room of Christians will answer a definitive "Yes!" Asserting the gospel is for everyone, they will say, "Absolutely, all people are able to believe." But I am not asking if the gospel is offered to everyone, but rather, are people at the discernment level which enables belief? When I clarify this distinction, I suggest that the correct answer to this query is "No." Most non-believers are not able to believe. As an obvious example, my atheist friend was clearly not able to believe in Christ. He didn't even believe in God! How could he believe in Jesus?

What is surprising for many Christians is the realization that most are in the same general state as an atheist. They, too, are not able to believe, being either: confused, unclear, corrupted, skeptical, cold, entangled or questioning. Go have a conversation with your non-believing friends, and you will quickly see what I mean. In the class, making this point always creates a moment of disequilibrium. I pause to let them stew. Emotional disturbance is the right response! All true believers should feel churned up that people generally are not in a position, given their frame of comprehension, to respond to the gospel. How do you feel about this idea? Does it make you want to step up to close that gap?

I hope this realization evokes a Nehemiah-like response, when he kicked through the rubble of Jerusalem's broken-down wall, and found the resolve to do something about it (Neh 2:11–13). Let's kick some stones! When you discover what people are thinking, there are lots to kick. How do we go about building belief foundations? This is the heart of this critical step.

As you work through the progressions, if the person is initially open or if you successfully draw them into exploration, then we can begin a focused dialogue. The discernment step is all about helping them to be "able to believe." This can be the most time-oriented step of all. Sometimes, you will spend months of conversations on helping them to discern Christian truths. Of course, time will vary depending upon the person. Before we develop three distinct categories, let us examine this step biblically.

THE "ABLE TO" STEP

In Acts 8 and 9, we see the "Able to" step played out in back-to-back conversion stories, where an Ethiopian eunuch, and Saul of Tarsus become Christians. Whereas the eunuch is brought through this step by Philip's explanation, Paul is reached through God's supernatural intervention. These two interceptions reveal God's huge heart for Africa and the Gentiles of the world; the eunuch taking the gospel to Ethiopia; and Paul taking it to the Gentiles. This is the exciting thing about mission; we are furthering a movement! Each person coming to faith is God's extension to new places and peoples. This is also why the lack of evangelistic effectiveness can kill a church—the movement stops. In these accounts, God takes it forward swiftly through two key individuals. Unlike these stories, however, the "Able to" step is often the most difficult, time-consuming element of the evangelistic journey. The investment needed to bring someone through this step can be quite significant.

Both the eunuch and Paul were Judaistic, which provided a foundation for Christian belief. Many in our culture have little foundation. George Hunter coined the term "ignostics," for those having no Christian memory.[5] If you are starting with someone who has little knowledge, you will need to sufficiently fill in understanding. Notice, however, how contrasting the two conversions are. With the eunuch, God had already stirred his heart with questions from Isaiah 53 and then moved Philip into position to complete the picture. With Paul, God had to intervene in a dramatic supernatural interception. Then he affirms what has happened through his faithful servant Ananias (Acts 9:10–19). It shows us the scope of what happens with this step, some needing explanation, while others requiring a spiritual thumping!

Let's dissect the actual stories. In Acts 8, a Jewish or God-fearing eunuch is on his way back from a pilgrimage to Jerusalem. Sitting in his chariot, he is reading the words from Isaiah 53. Philip, being obedient to the Spirit, follows God's direction to get positioned beside the chariot, and seizing the opportunity inquires about his understanding. The eunuch simply responds, "How could I unless someone explains it to me?" (Acts 8:31). This is the most succinct biblical statement of the "Able to" step. The eunuch intuitively knows he needs help discerning the content. If no one explains it to him he will not be able to make sense of it. Filling out the missing data, Philip connects the dots between Isaiah 53 and Jesus. Once that occurred this Ethiopian was able to put his full faith in Christ. As they progressed on the journey he then wanted to respond, and when water presented itself, asks if he could be baptized.

Some, similarly, merely lack understanding of the essentials. I believe most people are farther back than this spiritually hungry pilgrim who God prepared to embrace the truth promptly. Take my two skeptic friends for

5. Hunter, *How to Reach Secular People*, 41.

example. They were open to meet and discuss things, but were they able to believe? Clearly "No." One would first have to believe in God to be able to consider Christ; the other believed in God but was far from believing the Christian faith was reasonably true. Neither of them were "able to" believe. The tricky thing is, there can be a wide range of reasons for this.

Expanding our perspective on how this step plays out in various ways is helpful. Unlike the Ethiopian eunuch's need for a simple explanation, some seekers have false thinking on what it means to be a Christian. Still others are not able to believe because they are hung up by questions or objections. Even farther away, others adhere to a different worldview altogether and do not accept any of the tenets of Christianity. Finally, some are not able to believe because of non-rational issues. Did it feel like we just opened Pandora's Box?

As soon as we get into the "able to" question, all sorts of things begin to emerge. This is because there are multiple reasons undermining preparation: lack of understanding, worldview assumptions, and assorted heart issues. When you realize your friend is not yet able to believe—you must zero in on what specifically is lacking or hindering. In your time of building and enjoying relationship—you intentionally probe with questions to discern how to successfully navigate this step. Browse the following diagram.

TYPE OF NON-BELIEVER	WILL COME TO CHRIST IF...
HEAR	*The gospel is explained with clarity.*
HURDLE	*They are helped over 1 or 2 of their question hang ups.*
HAMMER	*An entirely new Christian worldview is built for them (atheists, skeptics, other faiths).*
HURTING	*They find love being held, helped & healed in Christ & his church.*

HEAR.

In my second church plant, I discovered that some regular attendees were not believers, and yet they never answered my upfront calls. If you are a teacher, you may have experienced this puzzling lack of response. After an extended time, I decided to meet with one woman and find out why. Sitting down with her we had a pleasant and pointed conversation. Eventually, I uncovered her overly idealistic thinking. She told me she loved coming to church, especially for the worship (not my preaching!), but would never think that she could become a Christian. She said, "I would have to be perfect to be a Christian." As soon as her perspective became clear, it was not difficult to correct the warped outlook, and she and her husband both came to faith! Listen loudly to my point. There are people in our churches and neighborhoods who only need a clarified explanation of the gospel!

Did you miss the critical take-away from this experience? Oftentimes, explanation must occur in a sit-down dialogue. It's the interchange that helps you reach them. I wish I could claim this as an original insight, but others far greater than I have stumbled upon it also. Engaging extensively in tent meeting crusades, John Wesley once said, "We have accomplished more in one-to-one discourse than in ten months of preaching."[6] He observed the power of dialogue, where you listen, interact, and help people forward. If you want to reach more people, you need to create avenues for discussions that get to the heart of understanding. Churches that provide space for relational interaction within or after services are smart!

HURDLE.

Blessed by living close to a 3,000-acre parcel called Daley Ranch, I often went hiking there by myself where the usual companions were sagebrush, coyotes and rattlesnakes. But on this beautiful Southern California morning it was my non-Christian friend Bill. Heading out on a six-mile trek we engaged in conversation about his biking hobby, family, and eventually church. As Bill grew into his mid-life years, so did his spiritual thirst. Arriving at the rest stop, he initiated a conversation about faith and science. Bill acknowledged how the irreconcilable differences confused him. I tried to reframe his thinking, "It is possible to be a Christian and believe God created us through evolution," I said, "but there is good reason to believe in creation." I began to share some rationale, and after a twenty-minute talk his whole view of the faith-science divide changed. In the flow of the dialogue we discussed what it meant to place one's faith in Christ. I eventually asked if there was anything else he needed answers on. Surprisingly for me, he was suddenly at a place of conviction. Nothing else stood in the way of him becoming a Christian; so right there in the middle of our day hike, Bill accepted Christ as his Lord and Savior! Later I was at his fortieth

6. Wesley, "Minutes of Several Conversations," in Works 8:303.

birthday party when he shared his new faith with his friends—a powerful moment of going public!

Similar to this story, there is a category of people who are blocked by sizable question hurdles. Though this is not the case for everyone, in my experience, I have observed that many get hung up on one or two questions. That's it! When we help them over those hurdles they can quickly come to peace with a faith decision. Professor George Hunter commented on how the leaders at Willow Creek had made this same conclusion.[7] It reveals why apologetic skill enhances your reach ability. If you can offer solid answers to their questions and communicate new ideas in a tone that does not push them away, God will use you to reach "hurdle" people. Sometimes, all we have to do is get them over these obstacles.

HAMMER.

Some need explanation. Others need a question or two resolved. Yet for those who are more skeptical or coming from another worldview, they will need something far more substantial. These types need help to build an entire belief foundation. You might picture getting wood, hammer and nail and constructing a large platform to stand on. Let that illustration sink in! I spent seven months meeting with my atheist friend before he was "able to" believe. Because he was in this "hammer" category, we had to construct a whole worldview. It took deconstructing his atheism, and then building a reasoned foundation. On his own initiative, one day he put down on paper the rationale that undergirded his new founded stance. Although that apologetically driven effort was an enormous undertaking—it still was not enough. Frustrated, he said, "I basically believe as a Christian, but can't believe." This demonstrated profoundly the other steps. As I mentioned before, I noticed the same progression in Anita, too. They both had to "Want to" believe, and then also had to go through the decision process of "Choosing to" believe. No step was easy. God was schooling me!

When I wrote the *Steps to Faith* class materials for Sandals Church, I essentially aimed to achieve the four-fold progression through a four-week class. The reason it works in the shorter time relates to how God is already drawing them through church services. Though the class has reached scores, some leave still processing the "able to" and "want to" parts. We invite them to take the class again, or connect for individual interaction offsite. Although agnostics do attend, the materials are not designed for

7. Hunter, "Growing and Multiplying the Church Lecture," June 2009.

serious skeptics. If atheistic, or coming from a different religious world-view, the course materials typically will not be nearly enough, needing a longer more specialized process. This is why the upcoming chapters on the "Paths to Faith" are necessary. In those chapters, I show you in precise terms what must happen to reach different types. Depending on their starting point, there is a distinct path.

One thing I found fascinating about the hammer category was how reason alone will not do it. Being analytically oriented does not remove the spiritual dynamic. In Acts 9, knowing that a rational conversation with Saul would go nowhere, God does something extraordinary by encountering him in a way he could not deny! Boy, can God do this well: The words of Jesus, the light from above, the loss of sight—that gave Saul something to think about (1–6). It was exactly what he needed to snap out of it, and realize he had missed who Jesus was. At times, this is our situation. God must grab one's attention. In the postmodern era, people more than ever are looking for supernatural encounters with/from God. Although we may think Paul's story as out there, the intervening idea is relevant. There will be times when God must break through experientially. Reason and divine intervention are both big players in reaching the hammer types.

HURTING.

Each of the first three: Hear, Hurdle and Hammer all lean linearly left-brain. The "Able to" step is intrinsically given to reason. However, we know that many are not hung up on believing from that place. Illustrating the sound basis for the other steps, the primary barrier for these seekers exists in their heart, not the head. The church is errant in trying to win people rationally who actually need to be won affectionally. In his philosophic classic *Pensees*, Blaise Pascal says, "We know the truth, not only through reason, but through the heart."[8] With many people in this segment, they will have to be held, helped, or healed to come to Christ. Specialized church ministries can be the conduits for salvations when they are fully holistic.

Typically, evangelism books focus on communication send-receive mechanics, whereas I believe that we must be equally concerned about the heart texture for reception. Cognitive understanding may have little to do with receptivity. A striking illustration is Michael Green's somewhat controversial conclusion that the messaging spigot closed with the Jewish

---

8. Pascal, *Pensees*, 31.

people, when the tone shifted to a harder line in the second century.[9] Taking the gloves off, love found the door. With this change, according to Green, we lost this group. This heartbreaking history exposes the nemesis to rational apologetics. Winning people through reason alone can be one-dimensional nonsense.

When it comes to rational appeals, sometimes I'd rather lose a point if I can pry-open the non-believers posture. I often ask unconventional questions. Do I need take a hit? Be contrite? Make apology? Draw out their pain? Initiate healing? Back off? Fight through it with them? I am willing to read and adapt to get to the heart level. What words or actions will rake across the hardened surface to till up resistance? I am always searching for how to soothe or stimulate heart receptors, so the message can find a home. As soul whisperers, we are going deep within hearts to allow the work of the Spirit; that is often when God does his wonders! Of course, this is why the next desire step is indispensable. Without giving attention to the deeper motivations of people, our ultimate aim of seeding the good news may be thwarted.

DISCUSSION & ENGAGEMENT

1. How does it make you feel when you consider that most people are not "able to believe?"

2. From your interactions with non-believers can you see the different levels of what is needed to reach them? Share your thoughts.

3. Providing solid answers will be critical to reach those with questions, and those needing a new foundation. What have you learned that has helped in answering questions?

4. What questions have you heard that you would benefit by having answers?

9. Green, *Evangelism In The Early Church*, 105.

16

The Desire Step

Plant the seed of desire in your mind and it forms a nucleus with power to attract to itself everything needed for its fulfillment.

—ROBERT COLLIER

A married woman seeks help from her block to sexual intimacy. She had watched her father sexually abuse her sister, and though she did not recall much, this memory led her to shut down physically. The counselor, having exhausted his efforts, did not know what else to do, so he sought help from above, saying, "God, I invite you to minister to her." She sits bowed for a time, and then opens her eyes and says, "I was thinking about my father, and the thought came to me of how wounded of a person he must have been to do something like that." God had met her, and suddenly she was able to have compassion on him. Afterwards, she found herself able to re-engage sexually with her husband. The counselor followed up later by asking, "Would you like to know the person who healed you?" He went on to lead her to faith. According to Dr. Dave Ferreira, there is a particular order involved. He explained, "In the counseling realm, the heart is healed before the head."

When we engage with non-believers there will be times when we will find ourselves wondering where the block lies. Is it the head or the heart? Which will be the greater barrier to work through? I find it intriguing that

Jesus asks a blind man, "Do you *want to* be healed?" (John 5:6; see also Mark 10:51). Somewhere in the journey to faith is the heart's desire. In Christian witness we cannot reduce faith to mere intellectual belief. The gospel, which is the message of the love of God, penetrates to the deep recesses of the soul, to what David described as "the inmost being" (Ps 139:13). This soul dimension of life is where Jesus offers life's richest treasures. When you work the steps with people, you will realize how much the heart is at issue. Of course, Jesus knew this, and it is fascinating to observe how he appeals to the head with some, and the heart with others.

If we revisit the side-by-side encounters with Nicodemus and the woman at the well, we see both. With Nicodemus, Jesus explains the way of the kingdom. The illustration of the second birth is meant to introduce something new in concept. Notice the tension about "understanding" in the dialogue: "How can this be?" Nicodemus asked. Jesus replies, "You are Israel's teacher and do not *understand* these things?" (John 3:9–10). Nowhere in the conversation does Jesus say, "Nic, you got to get this bro, because it's gonna make your life a whole lot better. It's even going to impact your marriage—you and your sweetie-pie will thank me someday!" For Nic, the issue is the head. Jesus had just blown Nicodumus's mind, so to speak, in order to consider a new way to believe and live.

In contrast, Christ's conversation with Samantha appeals to the heart. "If you knew the gift of God and who it is who asks you for a drink, you would have asked him and he would have given you living water" (John 4:10). Jesus references spiritual birth again, but this time in a personally appealing way—this is something she would "want." Though she, too, like Nicodemus, did not understand all of what he was saying, the offer drew her at the desire level. If you follow the dialogue through Jesus continues along the same vein, until she, perhaps feeling uneasy with how real the conversation had become (five husbands and a live-in boyfriend) attempts to divert the dialogue from heart to head. She does this by bringing up the controversial topic of where people worship. At this juncture, Jesus provides her news that appeals to her understanding.

This back-and-forth pattern is typical in evangelistic dialogue. We go from the head to heart, and from heart to head. Both the "able to" and "want to" steps are critical, and must be interwoven in evangelistic conversations. Let's take another dialogue that is familiar to many Christians. When Jesus encounters the young rich ruler—is it the head or the heart that is at issue? If you study the passage, you will see how deeply off this man is in both arenas. Jesus's words challenge the understanding of goodness, while also exposing his heart idolatry. The purpose of this chapter is to zero in on the heart dimension. As you might imagine, this step will take you deep into people's lives.

THE "WANT TO" STEP

Introductions at the beginning of an evangelistic class can give you a glimpse of where people are at. Obviously in a dating relationship, Amber and Jarred describe themselves as agnostics. She proceeds to explain how difficult it is for two agnostics to encourage each other spiritually. This was hilarious! She drops a couple F-bombs in the conversation and my team all recognize we were in the right place with the right people. Well, it turns out that Amber has come off and on to Sandals for two years. Expressing that unlike other churches, she felt Sandals would be okay with her questioning, she proceeded to articulate her hang-ups with Christianity. First, how do we know the Bible wasn't written to further the author's agendas? Also, she struggles with believing in Jesus as her personal Savior. Knowing what I know now, these two questions represented both head and heart barriers. Contrary to what some might feel who want non-believers to behave like Christians and maintain some type of status quo protocol, I was delighted to have her share so openly. Mike, from the class leadership team, says, "It's cool you have come to the class—we hope within or outside the gathering that we can address those things."

I decide to alter the next session to deal directly with her question about the Bible. Gleaning heavily on Keller's insights from *The Reason for God*, I outline why we should not see the Bible as writer-fabrication. The New Testament writings are:

> *Too early*—Early accounts had to match eyewitness memories.
>
> *Too counter-productive*—Why would they purposely undermine their message by including questionable content, like the disciples' doubts and character flaws?
>
> *Too detailed*—Why include so many trivial details?[1]

I like to add *Too important* to his list. Though perhaps that sounds assuming, you just can't fabricate something about a public figure of his magnitude; nor could you later alter biblical content without serious scrutiny.

---

1. Keller, *The Reason for God*, 100–09.

By discussing these points frankly the members of the class come over the hurdle. The class builds into the third session where we cover personal faith. At the session's close, we invite them to remain seated if they want to have a commitment time with God. This created a moment with Jarred. When Amber arose quickly reflecting her ongoing heart issues, Jarred could have easily gone with her, but instead looked at me and stated with conviction, "I want to stay."

That meant Jarred became a Christian, while Amber continued processing. My team members dialogued with her afterwards highlighting God's reach saying, "It's no accident you have come to the class" and encouraged her to keep seeking. Excitement over Jarred's newfound faith is muted by Amber's resistance, and a genuine concern regarding her skeptical influence. I decide to call and see if I can further her progress. In the interchange, I begin to learn more of what is going on. Past abuse has created layers of hurt. This stuff is never easy. Compare it to being a soul surgeon where you get in there, uncover thinking and feelings, and try to diagnose a prescription for healing. In the phone conversation I say, "God desires for you to experience a gracious and loving relationship with him." In doing so I presented a vision for what could be, and expectation for that preferred place. I go on, "But right now there are things that seem to be blocking that from occurring. Amber, would you be open to getting together and talking about that?" She welcomed the meeting. Her story exposes the universal reality that humans are "affectual" beings. Life experiences leave indelible imprints that continue to influence thinking and behavior.

Impressioned feelings > Drives thinking > Drives responses

I gained insight on this through a family incident. On a beautiful Southern California evening, as twenty people socialized on a back patio, two dogs began barking voraciously on the bank. I wandered over guessing something must be behind the fence. Abraham, our Springer Spaniel suddenly became animated with protecting vigor, and then I saw it—a skunk! Abraham dove in, grabbed it in his mouth, and threw it to the side. The skunk recovered quickly and came down the bank toward the patio. Terror swept through the group, as they collectively screamed and scampered into the house to avoid what was surely going to come next.

For his heroics my dog took a direct double espresso shot in the face! He was trying to spit and kept wiping his face on the grass. Although we tried home remedies of vinegar water, and purchased stink remover (no we didn't try tomato juice), he proceeded to pollute the air everywhere he went for the next three months. Yet with his new pungently abhorrent smell, did it change our view of Abraham? Not one bit. We loved him. He was our dog. Somehow it didn't change the way Abraham felt either. The thought never entered his mind that he was now a stinker. He was as happy as ever, as long as he could act instinctually, and be our best friend and protector.

Observing this I meditated—if only us humans had the moving-on capability of a dog! In contrast, we feel the full affect of our volitional acts, and anything thrown at us leaves lasting impressions. In *God Attachment*, clinical experts Clinton and Straub declare, "Past experiences powerfully influence the way we think, feel, behave, relate, and perceive events today, but without any of our awareness of how the past is influencing the present. Not surprisingly, the perceptions a child develops about life at this early age strongly shape his or her view of God and every other relationship for the rest of his or her life."[2]

What occurs increasingly in evangelistic engagement is that we discover something in the past hampering them. Nathan tells me of his friend, Billy, whom he is trying to reach. What comes out in the initial conversation? Billy's distance from God roots back to his childhood where he saw his mother taken from him, and eventually die through drug addiction. Where was God? When people are imprinted by powerful experiences, we will have to lay bare the root drivers. What exactly is affecting them? Did a series of events instill that God had left them cold? This was Amber's story. But there are countless variations. Did they have a bad church experience? From research conducted by the Barna Group synthesized in *Unchristian*, three out of ten non-believers had some kind of bad episode with Christians or the church.[3] Ouch! What does that tell us? It might take a loving believer to befriend, be willing to hear them out, and say, "I am so sorry." We need to be quick to make confession and ask forgiveness for what our group has done. Christians commonly do unthoughtful things, or non-believers perceive actions that way. As believers, we are painfully human at times. Whatever it is that is troubling someone about a past negative experience with Christianity, I will personally own it in a snap—even if I'm just a representative of the real perpetrator—if it can help someone move forward with Christ.

2. Clinton and Straub, *God Attachment*, 55.

3. Kinnaman and Lyons, *Unchristian*, 32.

The next class session both Jarred and Amber came, and I pick up a different spirit from her. God is working! Though I didn't make much progress in the first conversation, I think she sensed my heart to help. One of the things I have found is that people who are stuck usually want to get unstuck—they just don't know how. Their heart issues, then, must become the focus of the evangelistic effort. This is something you can learn to do. It does help if you know what it's like to be stuck yourself. Many of us have these experiences if we are willing to look back introspectively.

SIZING UP STUCKNESS

When I first began dating my wife we took a day trip to Magic Mountain where I went on a ride called Z-Force. Have you been on it? It is similar to the Viking Ship that swings back and forth taking its passengers higher and higher, but this ride braces you in and completes two full circles. I knew the number because I deliberately counted the rotations—figuring I could handle it, and maintain my machismo in front of my very important "hot" date! I noticed after two rotations it slowed down and eventually ended. It still looked crazy and my girlfriend, usually adventurous, chose to sit this one out, as I got on.

As it swung back and forth everything seemed normal but when we completed the first rotation something happened—the hydraulics powering the ride clicked off. Suddenly we began to swing freely and much faster. As we picked up speed it went around the second time propelling us a third time around. This was a scary feeling, since I knew something was wrong! I feared with the increasing speed it was going to be unstoppable, but as we headed for the fourth cycle it began to slow having just enough inertia to get us vertical before it stopped—leaving us hanging upside down! I sensed panic running through the minds of the riders, and it didn't help that one of them said, "Oh no, we're stuck!" After a minute, they were able to get the hydraulics back on and got us moving again. Hanging there was a gnarly feeling. Getting stuck usually is. The truth was that Amber was stuck. She wanted to go forward in faith, but doesn't know how to move out from her current state. She now feels about as helpless as being on a ride you cannot control; it's a frightful place to be. You might be surprised to hear how many people are stuck spiritually. I listened to an interview with Paul Young, author of the massively best-selling book, *The Shack*, and he said he wrote it to help people who were stuck.

I remember reading the tale of the Alaskan bear attack on Johan Otter. He had a major life-threatening mauling from a grizzly as teenage daughter Jenna desperately tried to get the clip off her bear repellent spray can. The LA Times writer says the experience left her "haunted by guilt."[4] I conjectured it's not guilt but rather shame she's experiencing. Guilt is what you did wrong; shame is not only what you did; it's also the conclusion you make about yourself based on what you did. It becomes deeply personal as it attaches itself to your very soul. Can you hear the many voices going off in her head? "Why couldn't I release the can?" "Most people would have been able to do it, but not me." "How could I be so stupid?" This is the relentless inner voice of shame. "I must be a dumb, twisted, perverted, evil person." Can you see how it wants to invade your soul? The truth is she was not stupid. Getting the clip off a can in a moment like that is something many of us could have done, but the voice of shame would not let her go. So her father took her back to the place, trying to get her past it.

Although my calling is primarily helping others into their spiritual journey, I know what it's like to be stuck. For some reason, maybe because I was a pastor, I initially couldn't shake the shame from my now publicly exposed sin. I sometimes thought—only God could help me. Often in life we hope to say a prayer and it's resolved. But the reality is that God deals with many things through his servants. This became part of my story from an unpredictable source. In my doctorate program I met an African American megachurch pastor named Parnell Lovelace. No one had a church even close to the size of the one he planted in downtown Sacramento. He tells his 3,000-member church, "Say yes to God!" One day in class, Parnell came over and disclosed that God had led him to pray thirty minutes for me the previous night. I was stunned. At most I might pray thirty seconds for someone, and was touched to think he had prayed in this intercessory way. That night I told my wife on the phone, and it moved her too. As a side note, Parnell is something special. Most of us in class thought he was so unlike the prototypical "larger than life" megachurch pastor. In contrast he is beautifully humble, sweet in spirit, quiet in demeanor, and yet there's also something dynamic in his presence and none of us were fooled as to his bite as a big-time leader.

So we get together for lunch. He shares the amazing things God has done in his life. Having been raised solely by his mother he was the oldest of four kids. He experienced tough moments of loss, but also incredible leadings of God, blessings and success. In contrast, I didn't have a big

4. Curwen, "Haunted by a Bear Attack," 2, lines 36–37.

success story in ministry, and then I had this dark chapter in my midlife. I shared with him what happened and how I got in trouble, and then what God began to do afterwards. It was so painful to go through the humiliation of my sin, and the rejection from the church. It was confusing, and I told him it's changed me—I look at the church differently now. Parnell had noticed my internal fire.

I shifted to the positive, touching on the wonderful things God had done in the aftermath. My two skeptics friends came to faith. I started to write for the first time, and in the last minute God opened the door to a doctorate program. All this happened in April only two months after my departure. As I am sharing with him, he is looking at me in the eye, God's Spirit is there in a big way, and I feel all this emotion welling up. I am fighting it back; you know how when you really don't want someone to see your stark naked soul, but then he speaks with unusual insight into my journey—like he knew what God was doing. At a certain point I broke down and cried right there in the restaurant. My burger got soaked! As you might have picked up, I don't cry often. I remember when we left he prayed three times over me to experience God's "grace," then three times for me to know God's "healing." Then he told me that we are going to be friends. He feels God has intended for us to be in relationship, and that what God is doing in me must be guarded . . . that it's important . . . that there's a message for all the church. It was an incredible moment of healing. Have you ever been met by God in this way? Like Paul Young's Shack story—ever walk across the water with Jesus? God wanted to get me unstuck, and so he had Parnell, his agent of grace.

This is often what the experience with evangelism is like. You begin relationships and as you dig deeper you discover "stuckness." They want to go forward but for some reason they can't. So you find yourself trying to discern how God could use you to get them out from this place. Unstuck from years of hurt . . . from anger at God . . . from shame that is pushing away God's grace . . . from doubt that is blocking their response . . . from confusion about Christianity . . . from apathy in life. When we do the kind of evangelism that starts where they are, and reads their thoughts and heart-feelings, each of us becomes God's grace agent. Through you his grace finally washes over them and brings deep healing, power, forgiveness, direction, clarity, and hope. Then their heart is freed to respond to Christ and follow unencumbered by the past. That was what happened to me after my time with Parnell. What an amazing calling we have. Let us look at a few vital principles.

LEARNING LOTS FROM LOTSO

After my youngest said he didn't know if he wanted to figure out *Inception* we headed off to the movie theatre and watched *Toy Story 3* instead. Hoping for a cheerful, uplifting tale, we found ourselves face-to-face with a dark masterminding Teddy Bear named Lotso. The scenes before us were nightmarishly similar to Pinocchio on Pleasure Island, only this time it was toddlers doing the damage—smashing, beating and terrorizing toys. Eventually we learn Lotso's story. He was the prized possession of a young girl who took him everywhere. One day on an outing she gets injured and in the hustle of leaving, three toys are left behind. Abandoned, yet still determined, Lotso leads the long journey home only to find she has another bear just like him. This fills him with deep pain and anger affecting his entire outlook. But his is a case of misinterpretation. Lotso thought the girl left him, when she had only lost him. He thought her buying another bear meant rejection, when it really showed how much she loved him. He had made two terribly wrong conclusions. I exited the movie theater saying, "There are lots of 'Lotso's' in the world, and I am one of them!"

Though sometimes as a feeler I still lose myself in wrong thinking, usually when I am ministering I get it right. Good theology helps us to think rightly about God and ourselves. It is a powerful corrector of disparate thoughts that can be destructive. In mission with those distanced from God, we minister sensitively by offering the higher, hopeful perspectives.

Ryan and Jenny had lost their baby. We talked at the door as I farmed the community to start a new church. It took processing through a few delicate conversations, but he was finally able to get past it and become a believer. Lots of people are misinterpreting the stuff of life. What they do is confuse life with God. These two truths go side by side: Life is hard and God is good. These ideas are in no way contradictory, but because of how we feel—these concepts easily get confused. People commonly take life and equate it with God's character. A child dies: "God doesn't care." Something bad happens: "God is punishing me" or "God is angry with me." Who is going to help them reinterpret life's circumstances compassionately, and make an accurate assessment? The first principle to this kind of ministry is to sensitively reinterpret the difficulties of life by understanding the heartache, offering comfort, and extending the love and mercy of God to those who are hurting.

With Amber, I would compare these re-interpretations to the untying of a badly tangled knot. I listened carefully, and then as God granted insights, I began to speak into her life. Tangle by tangle, together we gradually untied her bound-up views. Sometimes that rope had to pass a long way for it to get unraveled. Finally, after weeks of extended conversations, the grace of God found an opening, and she follows Jesus to this day.

A second principle is prayer. A deeply spiritual dynamic exists in this process. Typically, with those who are stuck, God must intervene to break through. When our first *Steps to Faith* class began, one of the team emailed me about how he sensed God's "thick" presence. Let me say it again, we are partnering with God in his ministry of grace. In these heart moments you will sense his Spirit working. God loves hurting-twisted people! He chooses to use us as his agents to bring healing to their hearts. What a calling God has for us! What we need is to be sensitive to them and the Holy Spirit. There are times we seek God to minister in ways we cannot. Obviously, intercessory prayer becomes a necessary focus.

Third, we must plant seeds of desire. In traditional evangelism, people think predominantly of knowledge-based interactions. Yet if we honor the holistic nature of human beings, then we must address the affectual dimension.[5] We do so by learning to plant heart seeds too! Like Jesus with Samantha, we cast seeds of desire. To be effective we first wisely discern the key motivational drives of a person; then we can know what kind of seed to plant. This principle applies to people across the board, whether stuck or journeying.

When I reached out to my atheist friend, I remember having conversations about what it would mean to his wife for him to become a Christian. He began to anticipate that moment of bringing unity to his marriage—a precious gift to his family. Though his analytic mind held him back for a long time, the seeds of desire grew in his heart. He wanted to believe, he just didn't know how. When God broke through enabling him to believe rationally, the "want to" step was not difficult to achieve. He still had to process the commitment, which is the "choose to" part of the journey. With my friend Anita, she wanted to believe when she saw the benefit of having God over her future. Listening to her, I knew this was her pressing need. Her favorable response came directly from a desire seed. The practice of "the gospel key" is useful and often essential to reach people. Remember, with the key, we never promise a perfect life, but rather a preferred life where God is with us. After coming through the "want to" step, she too got hung up over misconceptions at the "choose to" level. That is why we need to explore in the next chapter, the final exciting step where people come to faith!

5. Hiebert, *Transforming Worldviews*, 85.

In summary, the Desire Step is deeply personal and dynamic. It will draw you into the life journeys of people in ways you cannot imagine, and often, bond you together profoundly. For most people it's a big deal to allow anyone to speak into their soul. So as you engage, appreciate the privilege of ministering and being used as God's agent. There's nothing better than that!

DISCUSSION & ENGAGEMENT

1. The "Want to" step reveals how the evangelistic journey goes beyond reason deep into the heart. In your opinion, which hinders more people today from coming to faith, the head or the heart? Why?

2. Have you ever gone through a time when you experienced a season of "stuckness?" Take a moment and share what that experience was like, and if possible, how you were able to move forward.

3. What heart issues can you identify in your non-believing friends? Do you think they might need some level of healing first before they can come to God? Or do you think healing will happen if they come to God?

4. How can you appeal to a non-Christian friend at their heart level?

17

The Decision Step

No sensible decision can be made any longer without taking into account not only the world as it is, but the world as it will be.

—ISAAC ASIMOV

He had completed every requirement but one. Don had given himself to the dream of becoming a firefighter. In the 1950s this was, like today, an esteemed profession. His preparation was meticulous. Maintaining top mental and physical condition, he had aced his pre- exams, but still faced a certain formidable obstacle. Don, you see, did not meet the height requirement for a fireman in 1958. He needed to be 5' 8" and was only 5' 7 ¾"—not tall enough to get in on the dream of his life.

Drastic moments require drastic measures. There was a solution. Back in Roman times they had a machine to stretch people. If images from the end of *Braveheart* are running through your mind you are not far off. As barbaric as this sounded, supportive friends located a mechanism similar to the Roman Rack. Just hours before the height examination, he laid down to have his body stretched—a whole quarter of an inch. Because 5' 7 ¾" was not enough. After they had pulled and stretched his sternum to the desired length, they rushed him over to be measured before his body settled back. He passed by 1/16 of an inch! Donald Betsworth became a firefighter, and a darn good one at that, finishing a thirty-one-year career as a fire captain.

Ever since the early age in which we began to compare ourselves to others we have faced the question of being "enough." At amusement parks kids measure their height against the line to see if they are tall enough to ride. Young athletes ask if they are skilled enough to make the team. Recruits of the armed forces ask, "Am I brave enough for battle?" Heading into school, students wonder, "Will I be smart enough to make the grades?" Young girls look in the mirror and ponder if they are pretty enough to attract a mate. Career seekers ask, "Am I experienced enough to get the job?" Whether it relates to physical abilities, looks, net worth, talent or virtue—we are always measuring our lives by this word "enough," and often we realize that we can rarely win the comparison game.

In the spiritual realm, this deep-seated question looms particularly large. Non-Christians wonder if they could ever be good enough, perfect enough, know enough or believe enough to follow God. Looming large before us is the question: *Who will help them make the transition from a Roman Rack to a Roman Cross?* This is precisely what we do in this final step. It is the culmination moment when non-believers enter the widely stretched arms of Jesus. It's when they learn that he is, and will always be—enough. Not only are we ushering them into this new positional standing with Christ, but this step involves a transition of heart captured by the biblical word: repentance.

My ever-reading son introduced me to a fictional book, *The Door Within*. It is the story about a sci-fi race of glimpses. They begin unified, but a rebellion occurs. A prince in the court named Paragor kills the High King, taking with him many followers. The evil act creates a transmissional affect by changing each glimpse in a physical way. From the event forward, the eye's glint would give away whom they serve. Those aligning with Paragor have a RED glint—for the innocent blood spilled. For the undecided, who are their own masters, the glint is GREEN. And for those loyal to the true King, the glint is BLUE—representing purity. Every time a glimpse changed allegiance you'd see it in the eyes.[1]

In the evangelistic process, people will come to the holy moment of heart alignment. This is when God draws hearts to his side. It is when we peer into the eyes of non-believers to see if they are willing to switch allegiances. Are they ready to take on the "BLUE" eyes? Because the "choose to" step is critical in helping people become disciples, over the years, I have

1. Batson, *The Door Within*, 159.

learned to approach it with great reverence. You are delving deep with people. I also have discovered that we have an important midwife role to play. Many in the church do not have a feel for doing it well. This chapter is written to help you manage the transition from the rack to the cross, and from the red and green to the blue!

PREPARING THE RESPONSE

How are you with obnoxious people? I don't like them. I can relate to the feelings of the disciples, who tell a boisterous blind man to shut up! Ironically, while Bartimaeus irritates the disciples, he impresses Jesus. So much so, in fact, that Jesus is not going to let his bold faith go unrewarded. He sends his disciples to get him, "On your feet! He's calling you." The text offers a rich detail, "Throwing his cloak aside, he jumps to his feet and came to Jesus" (Mark 10:50). Contemplate this action; If you are a blind person; you don't just throw your cloak aside. A cloak was his covering from the sun during the day and his blanket for warmth at night. This was crazy! What if he never got it back? Like his bold declaration of Jesus's "Son of David" messiahship, this act demonstrated his conviction about what Jesus could do. The story makes its way into the Bible precisely because of this man's abandon. How can we help people jump to their feet, cast their past securities aside, to respond full heartedly? It takes a preparation process that begins right from the start.

When teaching *Steps to Faith*, I introduce myself purposely by the three S's: secular, skeptic and sinner. I grew up in a secular family. I understand what it's like to be outside the church. I was a skeptic: Mine were the questions the humanities professor picked to illustrate the unfairness of Christianity. Finally, I am a sinner—of the capital "S" variety. I jokingly tell them I have most likely out-sinned them all. At my high school ten-year reunion, it shocked everyone that I had become a pastor. I'm clearly not bragging here—I have purpose.

From an evangelistic angle, I aim to create identification, level the playing field, and model humility. If we are to lead them to Christ they, too, must become sin "admitters." I am intentionally helping them see we are not Pharisaical moralists by accurately depicting the Christian life—following and relying upon Christ in our weakness. Anyone who is inherently sinful needs to be closely connected to life's source. Even in this introduction, we are beginning their discipleship.

With downward humility, non-believers need to come to the place of upward commitment. Though we create the environment for this turning point, the Holy Spirit authors all true repentance. At times this is abundantly evident. Once when we prepared a group for the decision, our team noticed a guy get up, leave to another room, cry, and then come back. The Holy Spirit was working him over in a major way. We just let God do his thing—it was totally beyond us, and he came to faith that night. There will be tears! If you've prepared them properly, they know this is a big moment.

In this step, like nurses attending to an expectant mom, we prepare them for the spiritual birth. In a new believer's class I suspected that a young gal was not yet saved, and began praying for the right time to talk. On the final night, God orchestrated it by bringing her thirty minutes early without her tagalong boyfriend. Probing, I quickly learned she had never made a faith commitment. As we discussed the salvation topic, it was obvious from her class progress and desire for baptism that she was ready. So I affirmed her faith by saying, "I truly believe you are ready to follow Christ—do you agree?" She said, "Yes!" I explained that in the session we were going to practice a salvation response out loud, but for her it would be real. She wrote this of her experience:

> This class taught me more about Christianity than I've ever known before. Coming into *Basic Training*, all I had was an open mind and things to learn. Coming out, I was completely changed. Not only did I learn SO much, I believed, and was ready & willing to commit my life to Christ. During those 8 weeks, I began to understand the life, responsibilities and joys of a Christian, and I can't wait to get baptized and really live the rest of my life through Christ.[2]

These stories are priceless—the whole team was pumped! Here's a helpful tip. When you work the "Choose to" step, more preparation is needed than you think. Do not be passive, or assume they know what to do without clear guidance. Regularly, just before the teaching on personal faith, key team members or myself will make calls to dialogue personally and create anticipation. Getting them thinking about a commitment beforehand will ready their response.

If you are doing community evangelism in a group or class, don't just tack on a response at the end. In the group or class context, I will read a prayer commitment early in the session, touch on its deep implications, and then circle back to it. Only after ample preparation, will we invite

2. Email from Chelsea Galvin to author, April 29, 2010.

them to remain afterwards for a meaningful moment before the Lord. Usually, that might be only another five to ten minutes. The concept is true for personal evangelism as well. It is wise within a REP relationship to talk about the decision to follow Christ many times before they actually respond. The principle is to prepare the heart before response.

DECISION POINT THEOLOGY

I fully recognize diverse views and traditions exist within the broad church family regarding salvation's point. Let's be gracious in this section, even where we disagree. I have chosen to express my positional thoughts in hopes of adding something to your current framework. It is obvious from biblical study and observation that a prayer does not always mark salvation. Faith and repentance are the biblical goal. How this is expressed may vary. I do utilize prayer because it is a good way to lead a response, but it's not always the means of a person accepting Christ.

The greater question relates to whether you formalize the decision point itself. There's actually quite a bit of rationale behind creating this moment. For what it's worth, here's why I favor doing so. First, I see faith as an active step. Thus, a decision moment provides a way to call people to an action, a marker to their spiritual commitment. Second, in my view, de-emphasizing a line of decision does not instill confidence in the new believer. We strengthen seeking people when they recall their faith response. If we don't rush through, but make it genuinely meaningful, it will be impacting. It was Jesus who stopped in the crowd and asked, "Who touched me?" (Mark 5:24–29). Calling the woman out affirmed the reality of her faith! In the same fashion, we call them to express their faith to affirm God's work in them. Third, a decision moment marks a transition to ongoing discipleship where they get firmly rooted in beliefs and practices. That transition is super-important for growth in kingdom life. Fourth, a specific faith response empowers people to reach others. In other words, a faith decision provides a reproducible example of evangelistic mission. As followers of Christ, new believers are called to spread his message to the world, and embedded in their own story is a picture of coming into the faith. Because of this, I believe a decision point furthers the gospel.

Granted, some churches use baptism to mark the decision. Regardless of theological distinctions, all will have some come to faith within that process. In my understanding, faith and repentance are the initial fruit of salvation. Although baptism can link closely to their conversion step, faith logically is antecedent. The book of Acts describes the order, "They believed and were baptized" (Acts 2:41). This order also fits the immersion symbolism, which pictures outwardly the possession of new life. Therefore, I prefer the clarity of having them express faith before, and if possible in the context of spiritual relationships. Utilizing a class is a great way to prepare respondents, with some expressing their faith before they demonstrate it publicly. But at other times, the baptism itself encapsulates the call to faith, being the new "altar call," so to speak. At Sandals, we have done it both ways coupled with clear biblical teaching.

MISCUES IN APPROACHING FAITH

As non-believers near a decision, let us be aware that Satan loves to snatch or entangle the seed! (Mark 4:4). His carefully placed detractors should not surprise us, since we are dealing a cunning Adversary and unregenerate minds. In a REP relationship, the blockage will become evident through dialogue. Typically, the non-believer will come out and express their errant viewpoint related to becoming a Christian. In an evangelistic group or class, however, I like to attack the faith miscues head on. You just say, "Let's look at some miscues in approaching faith." By exposing the lies to the light, I have seen scores released from Satan's snags! Take a moment to look at common miscues and how you can help them get untangled.

THEY MAKE TOO MUCH OF THEIR FAITH DECISION.

She said, "How can I now rely on God for everything in my life when my whole life I have trusted in myself?" What a great honest question! We need to answer it. Does she need perfect trust in God to become a Christian? I responded this way, "God will teach you how to trust him over the journey of your life, but right now God wants you to trust Christ to save you from your sins, and commit to him." She understood the distinction and became a Christian that day. Another type of this error, which is very common, is when they think they have to be perfect. As Christians we chuckle at this, knowing how flawed we are, but this notion remains a major snag for so many who are about to be born anew in Christ.

In a big picture way, this miscue category exposes the error of putting the cart before the horse. With faith-derailing consequences, non-believers can pick up that they must assimilate certain behaviors before entering the faith. They conceive adherence bereft of experiencing God's grace and power. Some have chosen not to become Christians because they are not yet ready to tithe or attend church regularly. I'm dead serious! This errant thinking takes crazy forms.

In an evangelistic class, a young college student from France attended. True to the demographics for his country, Vincent had never attended church and admitted he knew nothing of Christianity. Weeks into exploring with us, I wondered what he was thinking, and so I intentionally drew him and others out with questions. After one of the sessions focusing on the uniqueness of Christianity—its heavenly origins and grace orientation, my team pulled together to dissect the interaction. Heather astutely picked up that Vincent was equating becoming a Christian with having to convince others. As we covered Christianity's distinctiveness, he naturally linked mission as a pre-requisite to his believing. As right as the mission motive is, it was wrong for him. It could sink his search. We saw what was going on in his mind and made effort to clarify, though with other factors in play, we lost him.

When it comes to the gospel, Vincent needs to become a Christian for himself. When he experiences the grace of God, who knows what God might do with his influence. His story illustrates how we must restrain ourselves from unwittingly making behavioral characteristics the salvation measure. Otherwise, we create unbiblical barriers. Consider that the majority of Christians do not tithe, do not regularly engage in missional activity, do not live righteously all the time in every area, and do not trust God with everything. None of those things are salvation prerequisites. A person is a Christian by faith, not behavior. Anytime we see litmus-like expectations developing in unbelievers, we must make clear that salvation is based solely on faith, not works!

This is precisely the issue we face with some outside our moral boundaries. How does a gay person without Christ, become healed and whole? Don't they need Christ to help them make that journey? It was that way in Corinth with its great variety of sin expressions (1 Cor 6:9–11). We tell them they must change their behavior first, before they have the grace and power to do so (they will also need a support structure). Can I make a call out to other missional designers? Will several of you please step up with new books on reaching the gay culture? I have had some amazing gay friends—they are precious people that God loves. Give us a bridge!

Yet in balance, anyone coming into faith must come to repentance. For some they might identify specific behaviors they wish to rid themselves of beforehand and that's okay. Yet we should call them to faith in

Christ with an attitude of following, and allow Jesus to fulfill his work inside them. In reference to our examples, she didn't need to trust God for everything; she needed to trust in the cross. He didn't need to advocate for Jesus; he needed Jesus to be his advocate. She didn't need to become a giver; she needed to receive God's gift. He didn't need to correct all his behavioral issues; he needed Jesus for correctional power. In Acts 3:19 says, "Turn from your sins, *that times of refreshing may come from the Lord.*" It's the Lord who refreshes and empowers to live anew. A non-believer can never achieve this, nor understand it, without first coming to faith and repentance.

THEY MAKE TOO MUCH OF THEIR SIN.

"God could never forgive me for what I have done" they say. Here we need to help them see that Jesus's atonement is unlimited; his death is enough to cover all sins! He did not suffer the cross for the righteous but rather sinners. If they get hung up here, you might need to challenge their pride, which underlies the statement. Why can God forgive everyone else's sins, but not theirs? Some also assume they are such a mess that they need to clean themselves up first. This fundamentally flawed idea will never work. Jesus wants us to come as we are—mess and all. He will begin his restoration when we bring our full lives to him. If they are really stuck in unworthiness, then this is a time to dig down deep to disclose one of your darkest depravities, placing it on the altar of God's immeasurable grace, to release them from the hellish hook!

THEY MAKE TOO MUCH OF THEIR GOODNESS.

What I have found is that with this snag there are two different levels. One level is the person who says, "I don't need God's forgiveness, I haven't murdered anyone." This is a street- level assessment. Often, it doesn't take a whole lot to help them see that sin is much broader than "the murder measure!" As we expand their view of sin, they gain a truer view of themselves and begin to appreciate the cross. You could inquire on whether or not they have ever lied, cheated on a test, had lustful thoughts, or acted selfishly?" The goal is not to beat them down, but to open their eyes to what the Bible calls sin. You can say things like, "What if all your thoughts were put up on a video screen for everyone to see?" Also, sin is not just what we've done wrong, but what we haven't done right. Seriously now, how much have we helped others? Most people haven't done very much. Sin includes being prideful, and thinking more of ourselves than we should. In its essence, it is living self sufficiently apart from God, because God meant us to live dependently through him.

Yet distinct from this street-level moralism others take this viewpoint to more deadly degrees. These people are what I categorically term: "moralists." To them, human goodness is viewed at such a high level that they reject the basic tenet of sinfulness. In the next chapter, I have developed the path for reaching this more difficult type.

THEY MAKE TOO MUCH OF CHRISTIANS.

We've all heard it, "The church is full of hypocrites." At times non-believers get hung up because they see Christian failure. We can help them focus on Christ's perfection, and re-educate to a proper perspective of the church. As the adage says, "The church is a school or hospital, not a museum for saints." Christians have admitted their sinfulness and are on a journey toward wholeness and maturity. None have arrived. We all still have sin natures, and are in constant need of yielding to Christ (Rom 7:14–25). Hypocrisy has to do with pretending you are something you are not. We can say, "We're not pretending, we really are sinners!"

In balance, let's help them see Christ is the answer for people everywhere in that he provides the power to grow in a new direction. Although he enables transformational change, it's a life-long course. Universally, Christians will say they are better with Christ, than they were without him.

THEY MAKE TOO MUCH OF KNOWLEDGE.

Some people will get snagged here on the chain-link fence of knowledge, saying, "I don't know enough." There is a certain amount of knowledge necessary for a faith response related to the essentials. However, at some point they know sufficiently. We need to help them to not get stuck in "analysis paralysis." You do not need to know everything about faith, the Bible, and God before becoming a Christian. The message of Christianity is simple enough for a child to believe. We can also explain that deeper spiritual understanding will not develop until they have crossed faith's line, and God illumines their mind through experience (1 Cor 2:14–16). Faith is a step that opens new understandings through a spiritually renewed relationship with God.

THEY MAKE TOO LITTLE OF COMMITMENT.

Unbelievers commonly make "too much" of some things, but also err on the side of making "too little." According to the Bible there must be a heart attitude of turning which the Bible calls "repentance." One must turn from sin and the way of self, to live for Jesus. They must take on the blue eyes!

A person coming to faith is making a lifetime commitment of following Jesus. Similar to getting married, they have received a proposal, which Jesus has signed in blood! He loves them that much. This is the biblical imagery, Christ being the bridegroom and the church his bride. He wants nothing more than for her to accept his proposal, join and follow him. I once had a non-believer arrive at this metaphor by himself. He said, "The only thing I can compare my commitment to God is getting married." He got it! Another guy told me, "This is a level-five commitment." I had no idea what he was referring to, but knew from his inflection that level-five was at the top!

We don't need to spell out all the details, but they do need to be clear about going his way, alongside his people. Christ will take them forward one step at a time if their heart is prepared for following.

LEADING THEM TO FAITH

There are numerous ways to lead a faith response. Depending on the person, one might be more favorable, but all can be effective. Let us not take a simple message and make it overly complicated.

1. USE A METAPHOR:

Using a metaphor is a great method. I favor using Jesus's descriptive words, "I am the gate; he who enters through me will be saved" (John 10:9). It is such a rich analogy for evangelistic conversations, when we get to this final step. It includes all the simple elements of response: going through Christ, entrance to God's kingdom, expectation for what lies on the other side. Talk about the metaphor and lead them through the door!

2. USE ONE VERSE:

All you need is one verse to lead people to Christ. Although biblical knowledge helps, you do not need to know much. The early church spread primarily through conversations and a few oral sayings. When training new believers, we do an exercise of having someone open their Bible and blindly put their finger down on a verse. Whatever the verse, the class must then find a way to share the gospel. We've had some doozies! In our latest class it was a line from a parable in Luke 12:48: "But the one who does not know and does things deserving will be beaten with few blows." Can you see it? One neophyte said, "The beating was what we deserved, but Jesus took the beating for us so we didn't have too." That's powerful gospel truth! You can use almost any verse, but here are several direct ones: John 5:24; Rom 6:23; Eph 2:8–9; John 3:16; Rom 10:9–10.

3. USE YOUR STORY:

Leverage your personal story to guide their response. "I remember the day, I chose to follow Christ. It was the greatest decision of my life, and has brought enormous blessing. On that day, I committed my heart to God in prayer, and put my faith in Christ to forgive me of my sins. Are you ready to take that step? If you are, I can lead you in a moment before God."

4. USE BAPTISM IMAGERY:

The imagery of baptism pictures the whole Christian life. Dying to self, rising to live in the newness of Christ's power. You can ask, "Are you willing to follow Christ by dying to yourself, so you can live in his power?"

5. USE THE "BRIDGE" ILLUSTRATION:

The classic bridge illustration has visual appeal, and works well with the more analytical types who like to see ordered, logical sequence.

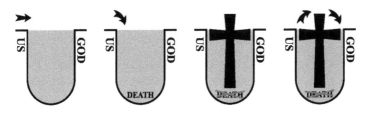

Simply explain the progression. People try to reach God on their own. The Bible teaches this will not work. We are sinful, and God is holy. Our sins have separated us from God and lead to spiritual death. Thankfully, God loved us in sending Jesus. His death on the cross pays for our sins, wiping away spiritual death. If we respond in faith believing Jesus to be our Savior and Lord, we cross over into a favored relationship with God.

At times, weigh in on the implicational meaning of the cross. In high school, I will always remember playing for the league championship against cross-town rivals Oceanside. When the announcer introduced the starters, their leader, a giant Junior Seau-like Samoan, pointed over to his friends who were positioned directly behind our bench. They began to scream threatening words in an obvious attempt to intimidate our team. I'll confess it was working! Seeing this, a former football player from our school headed over and demanded to sit down right smack between his six friends. When he sat down, they shut up! We went on to win!

With his work on the cross, Jesus sat down in heaven, squelching the voice of your accuser. You are declared righteous. He credits his righteousness to your account, as he takes all of your sin. The cross makes you 100 percent righteous in the Father's eyes even though you are not practically in this life. Teach them that their step of faith means they will be redeemed, saved, covered—forever! Because his death for them is entirely enough—they will win! As Jesus aptly spoke in his final breath: "It is finished."

LEADING A PRAYER RESPONSE:

Again, the Bible does not say we have to pray to receive Christ, but many people use that method to affirm a faith response. Pray short and simply . . .

> *"Lord Jesus, I believe you are the Son of God who died on the cross for my sins, and rose from the dead. I confess I am sinner who is in need or your forgiveness. I trust in you for the forgiveness of all of my sins, and thank you as a result for coming into my life. I commit to follow you from here forward alongside your people. Amen."*

Before leading this response, consider these preparatory steps. First, discern readiness for commitment. Second, focus them on praying to Jesus. Make it meaningful! You can say, "These words are for him. There are no magic words, it is the expression of faith, and a heart wanting to follow, that God welcomes." Third, have them pray out loud using their own words or lead them sentence-by-sentence, having them follow you verbally. Break it down into bite-size parts, "I believe you are the Son of God." Continue through the whole prayer.

DISCUSSION & ENGAGEMENT

1. Do you agree that we have an important part in preparing the heart for decision?

2. Have you ever led someone else to faith? If so, describe what happened.

3. Which of the miscues toward approaching faith have you heard voiced by others?

4. If you are in a small group, then pair off, and pick one of the gospel sharing angles (metaphor, verse, story, baptism, bridge) to role-play leading each other to faith. Go!

18

Perspective Shifts

The farther backward you can look, the farther forward you are likely to see.

—WINSTON CHURCHILL

I don't know if this reflects a masochistic desire for pain or sheer stupidity, but I have climbed Mount Whitney, three times. This day hike gets you up at three a.m. to make a twenty- two-mile trek from the base portal to the top and back, in one day. When you are done not only do you have a "body-buzz," but also the bragging rights to having conquered the tallest peak in the continental U.S.! Whitney tops out at 14,501 feet. It is a beautiful hike that takes you through distinctive sections: a gorgeous meadow, the famous ninety-seven switchbacks, and roped "cables" to cross the slippery ice of an underground spring.

The Trail Crest peak, with its vertical vistas, has always reminded me of a poignant phrase in the opening lines to *The Fellowship of the Ring*. Having described the gift of rings to the different races, the narrator adds, "But they were all of them deceived." Feeling triumphant over the switchbacks, you get a false sense of having made it when the next two miles are going to kick your butt! Your head begins to pound as it adjusts to the higher altitude where there's plenty of oxygen, but less air pressure to access it. The final rock-infested, moon-like section has a number of thousand-foot drops, and some who deliriously ventured off the path have fallen to their demise. In hiking, they say the person fell and bounced! When you finally crawl over the last rock at the summit, you are beat to the bones, and have a moment of bewilderment asking what could have possessed you to sign up for such torture.

Teaching at a men's retreat, I asked if anyone had hiked Whitney. A guy raised his hand, and then said he stopped a few hundred yards from the summit due to altitude sickness. His buddies, not willing to let that slide exhorted, "You quit!" They continued to rub it in throughout the retreat. A path marks a journey. Just because a path exists does not mean you will make it, but often a path is necessary to get there. This segment introduces the concept of evangelistic mapping. It fulfills the third principle of Jesus's drawing paradigm: *Know where to take them.* I aim to show what it will take to reach distinct categories of people. Knowing what it could take does not guarantee leading them to faith; yet having an understanding of their particular journey is extremely helpful. This kind of insight is becoming crucial in our increasingly pluralistic age.

The global community is spreading just about everywhere. When, as Christians, we begin to live missionally, increasingly we will encounter people of radically diverse starting points. I live in Southern California and am aware the rest of the country thinks we are a bunch of wackos. When I schooled at Denver Seminary, the lady apartment owner wanted to know where we were from. When I said California, she breathed a sigh of relief because she had a waterbed. I am not exaggerating; she actually believed all Californians had them. Some of you are saying—you mean you don't? She believed it like it was official state policy. Okay, we are a little weird and crazy—all of us. Something happens when you cross the state line—morphing everyone into the same kind of nut-jobs. Though there may be some truth here, what's most distinctive about California is diversity. Though not as cosmopolitan as world cities like London or New York, people from all walks of life are here.

A man at my church drives to work with four guys: a Jehovah Witness, an ex-Catholic, a Hindu, and a Muslim. No joke! I know it sounds like one: "A J.W., Catholic, Hindu, Muslim, and Christian walk into a bar . . ." Not only do we have all the secular and religious types, but we have subcultural groups like Wiccans (witches), vampire wannabes, Goths, and in California, God forbid—Raiders fans! (Please forgive me if you bleed silver and black). A gal from a class described her friend as highly intellectual with a PhD in Women's History, and is Wiccan. Long gone are the days of homogeneous Judeo-Christian backgrounds. In this way, the religious marketplace is more similar to the first century. For your encouragement, the gospel had amazing results amid the religious smorgasbord of that time. We, too, can see results if we aren't intimidated, but we must understand how to go about evangelism in specialized ways.

The mapping outlined in the next three chapters will enable you to see *where* you are attempting to take them. This, of course, is what Jesus knew, and navigated so well. If we can get them from where they are to the mapped designation we will have a chance to reach them. In this section we get specific, and to do so I have taken the liberty of categorizing people in illustrative ways. I have a deep respect for all these precious to God people (even the Raiders fans!) and would do everything to honor them, but have chosen to use graphic terms to increase clarity. Let's take a look at what the journey might be for: *The God Accusers, Cultural Christians, Self-Fulfillment Freaks, Goody Goodies, and Progressives.* In the next chapter we examine "worldview" building with theistic skeptics and atheists, and then in chapter 20, we'll look at those from other religions. In contrast to the worldview-building sections, the people in the first five categories are not necessarily far from Christian foundations. They are, however, blocked by particular viewpoints, or have hearts in the wrong place. Often it is a combination of both the mind and heart. This is why we see variations in Jesus's personal conversations. He knew what each uniquely needed. Again, soul whispering involves gaining insight of where to take the conversation.

THE GOD ACCUSERS

This accusing idea sounds terrible. Perhaps it is. But these are ordinary garden-variety people. They are not blowing up churches. They may not even be necessarily hostile to the church or Christians, but they are nursing a number of judgments about God, Christ, the gospel, or the church. I call them "God accusers." I have to acknowledge that I belonged in this category for many years. It was my God accuser questions that the college humanities professor selected to share with the whole class. Having each student write down objections to Christianity, he then perused the responses one-by-one, obviously looking for something, and when he got to mine he stopped and read both questions: (1) "What about the people who haven't heard the message?" (2) "How can you exclude people merely because they were raised to believe another faith—how unfair to punish them for being faithful to what they were taught." I recall the Christians squirming in defense as he threw his weight behind these sentiments. Thankfully, my skepticism did not stop God from reaching me! But how do we address these objections?

Let me introduce you to "God-accuser" Don. He is hung up on the unfairness of the Christian message. He can't get past the notion that some will miss heaven because they didn't have the same chance as others. Although this view could be a smokescreen-like excuse, it can also be an honest, legitimate block. That was true for Don. He wasn't blowin' smoke; this unfairness thing was hanging him up. Our role is to get them to see things from an entirely different view.

The way to do that is to help them move from "Judging accuser" to "Humble human." God needs to become bigger; they need to become smaller. Anything moving them in those directions will help. The best way to do this is to create a giant comparison between themselves and God. This technique is what happened in the book of Job, the oldest writing of the Bible. At the end of the book, when Job saw who God really was, his need for answers dissipated. Grasp if you can the words of God to Job, "Where were you when I laid the earth's foundation?" (Job 38:4). The question forced Job to compare himself with God. By the way, what is the answer to that question? How much can we offer God on laying global foundations? Zippo!

This line of reasoning can move people rather quickly from objections toward faith. I am not saying it would happen in one conversation, but it is staggering to see how influential it can be. This is because as human beings we are so far below the infinite power, wisdom, love, fairness, justice, and compassion of the true God. As evangelists, all we need to do is help others see this.

LIMITED GOD
Under Human Judgement

**GREAT GOD
Over Limited Humans**

This is how the conversation went:

> "It is easy to sit back and judge God and his ways. Yet are we suggesting that we know better? Is not God infinitely wiser? He created and designed the whole world. How can we say that we know better than him? Don, let me say it this way: How much do

we even know? Of all the knowledge that exists, what percentage do we possess? (Pause) Are we to think that with our "pea brain" understanding that we are better able to call the shots than the God who knows everything? God is not shortsighted. In his full wisdom he determined that people would come to know him through faith in his Son. He also determined the message would go to the world through people, and that each person would have to make a personal choice. God has reasons for it being that way—we need to trust his wisdom.

Don, the question about fairness suggests that we have more love and compassion than he does. How much compassion do we have? If the truth were known, most of us care only for our family, a few friends, and ourselves. How much have we really done for others? God has infinitely more compassion. Should we make this judgment, when he sent his Son to suffer the cross for everyone?"

In about a forty-minute conversation, Don put aside his objections, committed his life to Christ and eventually became one of the leaders in our church. I admit it does take a humble spirit, tact, and basic conversational skill.

There are various illustrations that can help, and you can use yourself as the comparison example to lighten the edge. "Compared to God, we're like an ant climbing onto a man's shoestring and then making the audacious claim that we know a better route to the Sports Arena." Another angle, "If you went down to *Barnes and Noble*, how many of the books have you read?" In my doctorate studies they introduced us to WorldCat. org, an online library, which contains the majority of books from most libraries of the world. Is that not mind-blowing? How many of the 15.5 million books registered on WorldCat have you read? (Nov 2009).[1] For average Joe, it is only a handful. Consider that all written material is only a drop in the bucket of all knowledge, and yet we possess a miniscule part of that drop. How then can we judge the God who knows it all? Not only does God have all the library knowledge, he knows everything undiscovered, and everything past and future. With his full view of all, he designed this world and the next one.

These are the kinds of conversations you have with people judging God. They are saying the world with all its sin and suffering is a big mental blunder on God's part. If he had only thought it through! They mistakenly think our world is Plan B, but it's not. Before the foundations of the world

---

1. Dempsey, "Counting," lines 10–11.

God had his plan of redemption (Gen 3:15; Eph 1:1–3). Our world is not plan B—it is plan A. The fact of God being all wise means his plan is working out just the way he intended and for the ultimate good.

They are saying the gospel message is unfair, indicting God as unloving and devoid of compassion. We are saying this is not true. He is infinitely more loving and compassionate than we are—look at the cross! Consider his words and deeds. In his love and wisdom he has chosen that we would live in this world before the next, and that we would choose if we wanted to follow him. God does not want followers who feel forced into relationship with him. For those dying young or who may not have heard, God will determine in justice where they will go. But for all of us in the know, God is absolutely clear that we must come to him through faith in his Son. Jesus did not suffer the cross for nothing! It is essential to one's salvation. There is no other way. A payment must be made for our sin to satisfy God's righteous character.

In all these matters, there is no divine oversight. Our role is to help them hear God's literal voice to Job, "Let him who accuses God answer him?" (Job 40:2). "Where were you when I laid the earth's foundation?"

THE CULTURAL CHRISTIANS

Many of us know people who are culturally Christian by their family affiliation with Catholic or Protestant backgrounds. The Armenian Church adopted Christianity in 303 AD, a decade before Constantine extended tolerance within the Roman Empire. If you are Armenian, then according to your culture, you are assumed to be Christian. This same kind of cultural association happens with people growing up in religious families. Whether Armenian, Catholic or Protestant, some adopt Christian identity by family heritage or association. Of course, this creates confusion. Salvation does not flow through bloodlines, infant baptism, religious practice or place of worship. As the old adage says, "Being in a garage does not make you a car."

If you have read this far, you know I am adverse to programmatic evangelism because it can be insensitive and out of touch with where people are and what they need. However, I recognize that certain questions asked at the right moment in the right tone can achieve a right result. It is in this scenario that I have used one of the Kennedy questions developed in what is called "Evangelism Explosion"—a classic programmatic evangelism training manual. This particular question is useful with a cultural Christian to discern where they are with Christ. It simply reveals what the person is trusting in. With this type we must expose the object of their faith. Are they trusting in . . . their religiosity . . . their goodness . . . their culture . . . their church affiliation? What is it?

TRUSTING WRONGLY **TRUSTING RIGHTLY**

Justin had come through the "Steps" class, and afterwards asked to discuss Catholicism and Christianity. Let me preface this section by saying I don't really care if someone is Catholic or Protestant, what I do care about is whether or not they are Christian. Both Catholic and Protestant churches have Christians in them and both have people who are not. Being part of a church does not make one a Christian. I happen to believe there are more non-Christians in the Catholic Church because they give mixed messages about salvation. I also know from first-hand contact that there are some evangelical Catholics out there who are on-fire Christians! However, Scripture, not tradition, typically guides Protestant churches, and the message of "justification by faith alone" is usually clear.

We decide to meet at Starbucks and after a bit of small talk and latte sips, we dive into discussion about branches of the Christian church. I give him a brief history lesson about the start of the Christian faith, Constantine's adoption of Christianity as the state religion in the fourth century, the split of Western and Eastern Orthodox in the eleventh century, and then the Protestant Movement. One of the things I like to do is point out the Protestant Reformation began with Catholics. It was a "protesting" attempt at reform that the church rejected. Thus, a new movement started based on the Scriptures as the sole authority for faith and practice.

After all the teaching he had heard in the core beliefs class, it was humbling to admit that it might not have gotten through. So I probed, "Justin, can I ask you a hypothetical question? I am trying to discern where you are with things. To do so, I want to ask you a question that might seem a little out there." He says, "Sure." In a humble tone and spirit, I ask, "Let's suppose you were to have an accident and die this week, and then found yourself at the gates of heaven, and Jesus (not Peter!) said, 'Why should I let you into my kingdom?' What would you say?"[2]

He replies, "I have gone to church and tried to be a good religious person." At this moment, I see how he has understood nothing. I look at him soberly and say, "That is not the right answer." He responds thoughtfully, "You mean all the rosaries and prayers aren't going to do it?" I looked at him brokenly and said, "Nope. Our religious devotion does not give us a right standing with God." As an explanatory note, what happens with people who are culturally Christian is that they become inoculated to the meaning of words; repetition without understanding and response numbs mental receptors, and the gospel's meaning gets lost in translation.

I go on, "There is only one right answer to Jesus's question. It is to say, 'I put my faith in your death on my behalf. Because you paid for my sins on the cross, you can let me in.' Only to that genuine response will Jesus open the door to his kingdom." I look at him, "Justin, brother—what we are talking about is so important. Friend, I want you to 'get it.'" This was the first time "the faith concept" registered. That day the light bulb came on, and he became a Christian Catholic. It unified his family spiritually, and they continued into our next class for new believers. Though I am not endorsing the EE approach in general, let's give credit for an effective diagnostic tool for this specific type of non-believer. We need to discern what they are trusting in, and then teach what biblical faith means.

THE SELF-FULFILLMENT FREAKS!

It is fascinating to consider that some of the most famous stories of the New Testament are about the self-fulfillment freak. The Prodigal Son may be the most renowned parable of all. Today the son would be labeled an addict, a user, an out-of-control reality show star. Yet many people can relate to the "voice" that prompts a person to go off the deep end and head out on a pleasure-seeking binge. The call of the wild, the "What happens in Vegas stays in Vegas" impulse appeals to a lot of people, not just a few. Can you relate to these whispers—calling you to grab the pleasures and gusto of life? I can.

The Prodigal Son story is about the compassionate love of a father toward a son who has wasted his inheritance money on the pursuit of personal pleasure. This journey out and home again can be relatively short or very long depending on the person. I know people who followed that

2. Kennedy, *Evangelism Explosion*, 18.

voice and came to their senses quickly. I once heard former NFL coach Marty Shottenheimer tell about the day he was sitting in a bar with a number of beautiful ladies, and in a moment steps out of himself and says, "What am I doing here?" He got up, walked out that door, went home, married his girlfriend, and began a family. He knew that voice was not for him. Others hear that voice and go down the path for a long time. All the bumps, bruises and bottoms along the way are not enough to get them to turn the corner.

Because this category encompasses the pleasure seekers of life, we have many here in the compulsion-addictive camp. When the turning point arrives, many will need significant structure to stay on course. Recovery groups can provide that. Churches providing recovery principled ministries are offering grace, understanding, and wisdom necessary to sustain life change. There are situations when churches must humbly recognize that what they are offering is simply not enough. Some hurting people don't just need a small group—they need an accountability call every day, to attend regular or even daily meetings, and be in a type of intensive rehab-like program. Of course we want them to know Jesus as their Higher Power. I relate well with all the recovery people because I have the "pleasure seeking" gene. I know that self-indulgent pull.

Self-fulfillment freaks are looking out for number one and believing excitement is theirs for the taking. All they need is the right guy or gal, or guys or gals, or a lucrative job and all the stuff, or the ability to do what they want to do, or the fix that leads to escape or ecstasy. What they really need, however, is a major perspective shift.

PATH OF SELF   **PATH OF CHRIST**

As human beings we have the ability to size up life's choices. The flashy lights of this world with all its glitz and glamour are alluring. Satan whispers that there's nothing wrong with trying something one time. However, his aim is to get us to repeat that one-time thing so that it eventually envelops our whole life. Give him an inch—he takes a mile! Yet as the great story unfolds, prodigal living leads to empty pockets and emptier people.

We have a gospel that offers something profoundly better. The topic of wise ambition and lasting pleasure belongs to Christians. We can help them see the real high comes in living for Jesus. He offers us the only thing that truly lives and lasts. This is why Jesus's appeal to the Samaritan woman is apropos. She is thirsty, and he offers her the only thing that can quench her soul.

Many have family or friends who are running down destructive dreams. Their pursuits are passing through distant lands, and we wonder what to do. Jesus encountered these exact people. Sometimes, all we can do is let them go. The father in the Prodigal Son story gives him the inheritance money early, and lets him do as he pleases. After his pleasure-seeking binge the son "comes to his senses" (Luke 15:16). Sometimes we only learn the hard way: the party lifestyle of sex, drugs and rock'n roll doesn't last forever. Some aren't going to turn back until they first hit bottom. It is a sad but real part of human nature that we all deal with at some level. Yet there are times when we can positively influence direction and lay the foundation for belief. Let us study how Jesus responded and snatch a page from his book.

POINTING TO THE END LINE

Has anyone ever challenged you to fathom the end result of your choices? This is what Jesus did so well. He used provocative lines like, "What does it profit a man to gain the whole world, but lose his soul?" (Mark 8:36). Embellishing, it is like he is saying, "Okay, so you get everything you wanted—so what?" "You gained the world, but lost your soul—what good is that?" Here we sit down with a friend or family member and ask them, "Where is this path you're taking going to end?" Or another angle is, "What are you going to become?" Then follow it up: "Is that what you want?" Bill Bright once had a chance to talk with a highly astute and successful lawyer friend of mine. In a brief exchange he said, "The danger is you could start working for money." Those were potent end-line words for my dear friend Marc. Did he want to be just another lawyer bought by the almighty dollar? He stepped back and took those words to heart. That was not who he wanted to be.

If you listen to Christian music, you have probably heard the haunting song by Switchfoot called *This is Your Life*. Can you hear the lyrics? "This is your life, are you who you want to be? This is your life, are you who you want to beeeeee? This is your life, is it everything you dreamed that it would be when the world was younger . . . " In the spirit of those lyrics we want the self-fulfillment freak to wrestle with the end result of their choices. We want them to feel the extending chorus of the song: "Don't close your eyes. Don't close your eyes . . ." The hope is that they see it, and arrive at their own conclusion. If they realize the direction is ultimately a "dead end" road, they might just make a U-turn.

Everyone who became a fan of the television series *Lost*, had their favorite character. In the first season's episodes mine was Locke. The amazing thing about the former paraplegic box company worker was how impactful he was with his words. He had the gift of sight—the ability to envision what people needed for their journey's next step.

- To Charley . . . helping him choose life outside of drugs: "I am going to hold onto your drugs and when you ask the third time I am going to give them to you."

- To Shannon . . . with her need to change her manipulating relationship patterns with men: "Everybody gets a new life on this island Shannon, maybe it's time to start yours."

- To Boone . . . over his codependent relationship with Shannon:
  Boone: "You drugged me."
  Locke: "I gave you an experience."
  Boone: "I saw her die."
  Locke: "How did you feel?"
  Boone: "I felt relieved."
  Locke: "Yes! Time to let go."

Each time, Locke, summons a perspective shift that produces real change. That is what we are trying to do with the end line. We are offering an important perspective in hopes that it registers.

Today, we have shows like *The Bachelor*, where the man has twenty knockout gorgeous women all vying for him. Young guys grow up with dreams of women—plural. Muslims describe paradise as being with one thousand virgins. There is the thought that you can jump in bed with whoever you want, indulge millions of porn images, be the ladies man, and then go on with your responsible monogamous life once all that runs its course. I challenged this notion one day with a college student, saying, "Guys can get to the place where it is virtually impossible to be faithful to one woman. There will always be another hot babe." The young guy suddenly thought of the end line. It caused him to realize what he was doing, and the fact his sexual pursuits may take his life to a place he did not want to be—to a point of no return. This conversation got through! He dreamed of being faithful to his future wife; it scared him to think he might condition himself so he could not achieve that. Is this what happened to Solomon in his older days? Why would the world's wisest man end up in such a dark place with all those foreign women? I think it shows how strong this temptation can be.

Jesus created the perspective shift often. It explains his chosen words in many encounters. Why did he make such an extreme request of the young rich ruler? This is the man who unflinchingly claimed he'd kept all the commandments since he was boy. In response, Jesus says the simple phrase, *"One thing you lack."* Thinking he was ready to chock up eternal life to go with his earthly wealth and status, he hears the words, *"Go, sell everything you have and give to the poor, and you will have treasure in heaven. Then come, follow me"* (Mark 10:21). Let's be honest here. What is your emotional reaction to the "one thing?" Does it seem to you, as it does to me, that Jesus is being rather hardcore? If you were this man what would you have done? The opportunity to give to the poor, have treasure in heaven, and become one of Christ's disciples was a huge offer. It was the chance of a lifetime, and yet, most of us wrestle with these outrageous words. It feels difficult since we are, after all, material boys and girls, with much esteem and identity tied to possessions. Most of us don't think material pursuits are wrong. Being a materialism byproduct myself, I wonder why Jesus didn't make it easier on him? Why didn't he say, "Keep most of your wealth, tithe ten percent, and follow me from a distance."

Apparently Jesus saw something far more insidious than we do. He saw a man with a deeply engrained false love. To Jesus, the one thing was everything! His words were a scalpel to the man's soul. Jesus knew as long as he remained bound by the material idolatry he would never be right. He had broken the first and greatest commandment to love God above all. Jesus sought his liberation. If only the man could have fathomed the amazing opportunity of walking alongside Jesus, but with his heart clouded, he couldn't make the step—at least not then. Church tradition speculates this man was the young Joseph of Arimathea. We don't know if the man came around, but I can only imagine the words of Jesus haunting him for the rest of his days if he didn't. Those were powerful words! If we are going to reach the "self-fulfillment freak" we must seek such words.

THE GOODY-GOODIES

Whereas "self-fulfillment freaks" often reject Jesus to pursue a path of immorality, "goody-goodies" reject Jesus because of their perceived high morality. It is interesting to note that moralism is the antithesis of Christianity. We might falsely think atheism is the antithesis, but rationalist thinking is consistent with Christian beliefs. Atheists need help to use their rational abilities to see the insufficiency of their position. Also, pleasure seekers are merely looking for satisfaction in the wrong places. On the contrary, moralists believe something entirely inconsistent and antithetical to Christian teaching. This is why Paul had such a reaction to the Galatians return to Judaistic moralism. The passion level is so high in the biblical language that Paul essentially cusses them out, although Bible translators have softened the language: "You foolish Galatians! Who has bewitched you?" (Gal 3:1). If any man is preaching to you a gospel contrary to that which you received, let him be accursed!" (Gal 1:9 NASB). The word "anathema" translated 'accursed' means eternal damnation. It's the equivalent of saying, "Let such a person go to hell!" The same righteous passion rises in Jesus with the premier moralists of his day, the Pharisees. He, too, has choice words calling them, "Whitewashed tombs!" (Matt 23:27). They look pretty on the outside, but are dead on the inside.

Every encounter Jesus has with a Pharisee could teach us something about moralists. Consider the contrast of the sinful woman and Simon, the Pharisee (Luke 7:36–50). She gets it. He doesn't. Simon fails to see even his own rude manners, forgetting the common courtesies of providing his guest a foot washing and kiss. To the end he seems to be incapable of comprehending the significance of Jesus's story. She understood her sin, his divinity, and what he did in forgiving her. He did not understand his sin, can't see who Jesus is, and is blind to his massive need for forgiveness. This is the moralist.

The young rich ruler was a moralist, too. He was the one telling Jesus he had kept all the commandments since his youth. In his mind, he had done them without even one slip! Obviously, he failed to understand the true meaning of the commandments. He interpreted them superficially, and failed to see the righteousness required by each, as expounded by Jesus in his sermon on the mount. Blinded, he could not see the evil idolatry possessing him. Jesus's call exposed the true nature of his heart. This is what we have to do with moralists. Somehow, we have to find the way to get through their thick, self-righteous skulls that they are really prideful, arrogant, and self-delusional! They, of all people, desperately need a

Savior. They are particularly ugly due to self-righteousness. Like the Pharisees, this category of person can be extremely hard on others, yet we see that Jesus had compassion on them. We should have that same heart to reach them too.

If you could win at golf with a high score—my shelves would be filled with trophies. I have never broken 100. My "hacker" ability level has created interesting moments like the time I played in front of Trevor Hoffman and Phil Nevin, two former stars of the San Diego Padres. Clearly one of baseball's greatest closers, Hoffman will certainly make the Hall of Fame, and there I was slowing them up for 18 holes. Because of their fame, when we pulled into the clubhouse, my partner Eric took our scorecard and had them autograph it—with my 121 score. It's now framed in his garage for all to see! What if in life we journeyed with scorecard in hand? Each time we blew it, had a misstep, lied, acted selfishly, lusted, exalted ourselves, tore ourselves down, neglected others needs, reacted unkindly, made evil choices, cussed under our breath—we marked it down. Instead, we conveniently forget what is uncomfortable to remember. We become deceived thinking we are golf gods when we are really stinkin' up the course! So the challenge with moralists is bringing them into awareness.

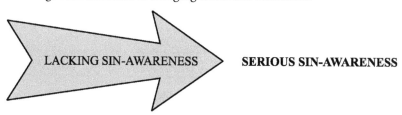

LACKING SIN-AWARENESS   **SERIOUS SIN-AWARENESS**

This is not usually an easy thing to do in a way that sticks. Sometimes we can talk about errant thoughts and motives reflecting sin. We can also touch on standards and how we fall short of God's, our own, and the ones we expect from others (Rom 2:1–3). Those are good biblical angles. Here are three other noteworthy awareness-raising ideas.

Expand the concept of sin.

Fascinatingly, Jesus declares to the moralistic Pharisees, "I know that you do not have the love of God in your hearts" (John 5:42). The vacuum of divine love evidences sin. The Pharisees had the external veneer of righteousness, but Jesus saw what was off at the deep core. We were meant to love. Only through God's power can we truly do it. Every moralist falls greatly short in how they relate with others in this world.

Explain sin in contrast to God.

In Romans 3:23, Paul develops his systematic case for how all, Jew and Gentile, are in trouble before God: "for all have sinned and fall short of the glory of God." I once watched a great sketch where the characters discussed their differing views on sinfulness. The dialogue asks each actor to indicate the degrees of their own sin by scoops of dirt: Are you a one, two, or three-scoop sinner? Each then scooped their self-determined number from a flowerpot, stirring the dirt into a clean glass of water. As you watched, you could see clearly Paul's point in Romans 3; it doesn't matter if you are a one-, two- or three-scoop sinner—we're dirty! Who would ever want to drink that disgusting liquid? God, by contrast, is pure righteousness. Comparing ourselves to others does not negate the dirtied state. Regardless of sin level, we fall massively short of his glory, and remain desperately in need of grace. Even moralists can learn to sing *Amazing Grace*. You don't have to be a former slave trader, like John Newton, to know that you qualify for his infinite covering.

Expose the sin of pride.

C. S. Lewis considered pride to be "The Great Sin." Pride took down the highest angel; it is the sin that took down man. He closes his essay with these words, "If anyone would like to acquire humility, the first step is to realize one is proud. If you think you are not conceited, it means you are very conceited indeed."[3] We can ask somewhat facetiously: Are you conceited? When they say "no," just look and chuckle! (Not too boisterously). It's like the question: Do you ever lie? If they say no, you point out that they are doing it right now! In doing this we are trying to help them. God is opposed to the proud but exalts the humble (1 Pet 4:2). The moralist champions the greatest sin of all. It has blinded and deceived them. We are trying to pull off blinders and give them a needed gaze of reality.

As to our sin condition, some of the most brilliant thinkers have weighed in on the human capacity for evil. Harvard professor and legal scholar James Wilson stated, "The veneer of civilization is very thin. Given

3. Lewis, *Mere Christianity*, 108–114.

the right set of circumstances anyone of us could commit unimaginable acts."[4] Similarly, Dallas Willard, USC professor and author, writes about a readiness to sin factor, "This ever-present readiness fills common humanity and lies about us like a highly flammable material ready to explode at the slightest provocation." He observes how quickly we enter the impulse to hurt or harm, to lie verbally out of self-protection, and to engage in wrongdoing.[5] What the Bible says is true. We have an internal propensity for sin. If anyone has the courage to introspect honestly, they can see something wrong. Asking for editorials on the question of "What's wrong with the world," one man wrote in to the newspaper, "I am."

In our first church planting experience, I got to know a moralist at an intimate level. I first met Avery when we started a church at a school in San Diego's North County. A retired lifer from Delta Airlines, Avery now worked for the school district as a custodian. He was such a warm and pleasant personality, always helpful. Over the months and years of growing the church, Avery often stood in the back and listened. We began to have a ministry to him. Then came the time of retirement from his custodial job. I distinctly remember the Sunday after, when Avery walked into the church and sat down as one of us. We had become his church family. I did the memorial service for his wife. It crushed him—they were a beautiful couple. My conversations at his apartment were at times difficult, only because he seemed to struggle with the gospel, and owning the sin concept. Even when we baptized him, I was not sure if he had come to faith. That doubt remained for years.

As his health deteriorated, I received a call from his sister that he was soon to die. I hustled down to the hospital to be with him. Arriving, I sensed a humility I had not seen before. He knew his time was at hand, his heart was penitent—he was finally ready to own his sin before God. I led him in the sinner's prayer, and he meant it. It was a divine moment. Then, something strange happened. When the Lord came into his life, he recovered. He went on to live another two years! His extended family then blamed his sister and me for affecting his turnaround. They said, "It all happened when you came to visit him." His retirement money eventually went dry, and they were resentful, and chose even not to have a memorial service in his honor.

Moralists are never easy to reach. We will not be fellowshipping with many Pharisees in heaven. Yet there are some. I look forward to seeing

---

4. James Wilson, Quotes.

5. Willard, *The Spirit of the Disciplines*, 225–27.

Avery in the next world, where his pride will be in Jesus, the Author and Perfecter of his faith!

THE PROGRESSIVES

The Christian church has image problems. According to The Barna Group's 2007 research in *Unchristian*, young non-believers ages 16 to 29 perceived Christians as hypocritical, judgmental, political, intolerant, out of touch, and homophobic.[6] In American media believers are routinely stereotyped as stiff, ultra-conservative clones that favor the rich and oppose sex. This is not an appealing picture for young people, who aspire toward image-values of service to the disadvantaged, tolerance and love to all. They view themselves as progressive, where Christianity is seen as old school "good ole boy" thinking that has led to all the deep problems. What is fascinating about these conclusions is that Jesus's contemporaries perceived him as a radical. If you take a close look at his life, Jesus was a revolutionary who was far too inclusive, tolerant, and compassionate for his own religious culture. How ironic is it that people today will reject Jesus over the very things Jesus rejected. The key to reaching progressives is reclaiming their perception of Christianity.

TURNED OFF TO
FALSE CHRISTIANITY

**TURNED ON TO TRUE
CHRISTIANITY**

In your dialogues, make sure you point out the *real Jesus* that they are being asked to follow:

- *Jesus identified with the poor, and championed justice.* His resounding message has given hope and inspired major worldwide compassion efforts. It is Jesus who taught us to humbly serve "the least of these."

- *Jesus is green and self-sustaining!* He may have cursed a fruit tree to illustrate his deep disappointment with Israel's readiness, but as its Creator, he is eco-friendly, and will one day bring about the total restoration of the creation that we all long for (Isa Chapters 54–66).

---

6. Kinnaman and Lyons, *Unchristian*, 28.

- *Jesus was a social revolution advocate.* In fact, he launched a movement that revolutionized how women are treated, how servants are esteemed; in essence, he conferred positional status to disenfranchised underprivileged groups.[7]

- *Jesus was gracious to sinners.* In the story of the woman caught red handed in adultery, Jesus's words disarm the self-righteous stone-throwers. He wasn't known for being intolerantly judgmental, but rather for extending amazing grace, a friend of sinners.

- *Jesus is pro-sex within its God-given marital design.* Our Bible even contains an erotically sexual book, the Song of Songs of Solomon (please don't tell me it's merely a metaphor for our relationship with God!). Sex is God's creation and gift to be celebrated within marriage covenant parameters, but not worshipped. Every good gift can be corrupted. And anything good that is made ultimate, other than God, becomes bad. Whenever God commands sexual boundaries, they are for our protection, not because he is a cosmic killjoy.

Despite all these culturally progressive aspects of Jesus, he was no people-pleaser. He spoke the truth about us, refusing to pander to or placate his culture, and nor does he do that with us either. We may not always agree with everything from Jesus, but in this we have to face truth, because he says it straight. If we are honest about what is best for our lives, we know how much we need to be unyieldingly challenged.

Progressives turned off by a wrong perception of Christianity will most likely have to be drawn by Christians they esteem. The rule with progressives is: "It takes one to reach one." Therefore, cultural progressives need to be influential parts of the church. Do you know any environmentally conscious, hip, fashionable, trend setting, compassionate activists and advocates for the disadvantaged? Some of you are saying: "That's me!" Thank God for any church creating a culture where they feel at home, and can find expression for their values. We need them to reach our expanding culture!

It's important to note from an evangelistic perspective that Jesus was apolitical. "Give back to Caesar what is Caesar's, and to God what is God's" (Matt 22:21). That doesn't mean we do not participate in the political arena, it does mean there is something higher to consider. Because my greatest call is to reach my neighbors, I am careful in expressing my political views, seeking not to put politics above God's greater aim. A fellow minister describes the time he placed a Protect Marriage initiative

7. Ortberg, *Who Is This Man*, 46–58.

sign in his yard only to learn later that his unbelieving neighbor whom he was reaching towards saw it and stepped back from their relationship. Mike said, "I will never do that again." He's concluded, "You cannot be political and an evangelist at the same time." In the church, we need to have wisdom so we can reach and not repel our culture.

* * *

A lone ship approaches the Spanish port of Seville. Eighteen barefooted men clothed in rags step to solid ground. The next day they proceed to the shrine of Santa Maria de la Victoria to fulfill their vows. How could witnesses at the port possibly conceive of what they had done?[8] They were the first to find a strait through the Southern Tip, a 338-mile, anything-but-straight, meandering maze. They were the first to cross the Pacific—one hundred days of endless ocean, leading starving men to eat sawdust to survive. They were the first to circumnavigate the globe revealing a world two-thirds larger than anyone had imagined. As human beings we have a propensity to miss the meaningful. The survivors of Magellan's crew had completed the greatest sea voyage ever. The implications—revolutionary![9]

When all history is finally written, the most revolutionizing and lasting journeys will not be the ones from antiquity's archives. Rather, they will be the journeys people made to faith. When you engage to help a person find their path to the cross, you are altering one's life course from here all the way into eternity. Your efforts have the potency to transform their lives and touch countless people through successive generations. May the gravity of the endeavor lift and sustain you!

DISCUSSION & ENGAGEMENT

1. Do you agree that different people have differing paths to faith? Why do you agree or disagree with this notion?

2. Describe any friends who would categorically fit one of the five paths: God accuser, cultural Christian, self-fulfillment freak, goody goodie, or progressive.

3. Which of the five paths was most insightful to you personally? Share what you got from that particular section.

8. Bergreen, *Over the Edge of the World*, 1–3.
9. Boorstin, *The Discoverers*, 259–66.

19

Platform Building

*Atheism turns out to be too simple. If the whole universe has no
meaning, we should never have found out that it has no meaning.*

—C.S. LEWIS

After I had referred to an atheist in a message, a national African pastor acknowledged, "That is coming here." The comment jostled my thinking as I realized that in Kenya virtually everyone believes in God. A similar moment occurred on a home building trip to Mexico, when a staff member from the Deep South mentioned how she had not ever met an atheist. Whereas unbelief is miniscule in certain regions, it thrives in others. Partly due to the disillusionment brought on by the devastation of two world wars, Europe is an atheistic bastion. When I met British author A. E. Wilder Smith, he said the question of God's existence in the light of suffering was the most critical topic for Europeans.

In North America, it is not uncommon to interact with those who do not believe in God. Skeptics, or as presidential speech writers term 'nonbelievers,' are part of the cultural fabric. With atheism's self-proclaimed empirical roots, materialistic philosophy dominates in secular colleges and universities across the globe. Faculty, who are analytically bent, personally vested and politically tethered to such a philosophy lead scores of young people to consider life from purely rationalistic frames. The sound of this voice from higher education is not lowering.

A quick Google search will reveal the rise of a reinvigorated atheistic shout. Richard Dawkin's book, *The God Delusion*, Sam Harris's *The End of Faith*, and Victor Stenger's *God and The Folly of Faith* are just three examples of the new aggressive face. As bold as these books sound, we should recognize that most skeptics are not of this stripe. Author Steve Prothero in *God is Not One* makes a distinction between 'angry' and 'friendly atheists.'[1] I agree with him that these categories are helpful. Those in the anger column champion atheism in a militant fashion. To them, religion is the core problem in the world. According to their rhetoric, September 11th is a prime example of how unchecked religion will eventually lead to terrible destruction, and puts everyone at risk.[2] This type of atheist is extremely difficult to reach since their life mission is to kick theistic butt. Militancy has a seed. Usually those deep festering roots are not easy to pull. Though I do think there are some big lessons the church should learn from this faction, it is a mistake to lump all skeptics into their camp.

What is occurring more pervasively is friendlier. Just as most postmodern people are not hardcore advocates seeking to destroy all truth, so most skeptics are not militant. They are typically educated people who've spent time in front of respected college professors who have convinced them of certain ideas. This has made them skeptics. Being exposed to evolutionary claims, and being analytical in nature, they categorically question the soundness of religion. They, too, can have emotional blocks regarding faith, but contrary to the entrenched atheist, these types are very reachable!

As you might already guess, it is never easy to save a person who does not even believe in God. In The Discernment Step chapter, I mentioned how analytical types need someone to help build an entire belief foundation. Illustrating, I compare it with getting wood, hammer and nail to construct a large platform to stand on. In addition to this platform-building interaction, skeptics often need to appropriate a new way of thinking that will free them from a doubter's prison and release their faith. This involves retraining the way they process and make decisions. Although this may sound intimidating, it is more doable than you think.

As stated previously, the challenge of reaching skeptics is that they have a long way to progress. Card-carrying agnostics and atheists have erected bigger barriers than most to the gospel. Because the barrier is

---

1. Prothero, *God Is Not One*, 319.
2. Dawkins, "Has the World Changed, Part 2," lines 1–9.

greater the effort to reach them must rise correspondingly. I want to ring the mission bell for skeptics! Just as we are called to love the "hard-to-love" people, so we also must stretch for "the hard to reach." For you, it might mean loving your neighbor—literally. You may have a loved one who is in this category. Or perhaps, you have a friend who comes to mind immediately. Every church can also begin ministries for questioning people. These Thomas-like, doubt-driven individuals exist in every congregation.

They are the tag-a-long spouses who come to church every once in a blue moon. Unable to reconcile their thoughts with the propagated truths of Christianity, they are not progressing simply because they do not have ample reason to believe. Not that they don't want to. Their mate has invested much prayer for them already. He or she is desperate for that key person committed enough to bring spiritual alignment to their family. Most skeptics have not taken the time to read the apologetic books available, and wouldn't know where to start. If they only had someone to guide them, a friend to help them dig deeper with the questions they have, and to question the conclusions they have made.

THE BENEFITS TO REACHING SKEPTICS

In this chapter, I will share my journey with an atheist friend who came to faith through a nine-month process. On learning that he became a Christian his wife broke down in tears! She could hardly believe that he now was a believer. She has thanked me profusely for what I did, which was a labor of love. I felt grateful to have the opportunity to meet with him. It helped me fathom his life condition without Christ, and to partner with God in his seeking love. You will grow to be more like Christ as you invest in the harder to reach.

Additionally, reaching to skeptics will sharpen you! One of my buddies used to joke about how he was not the sharpest tool in the woodshed. The aforementioned A. E. Wilder-Smith, prolific British author and contemporary of C.S. Lewis, used probing questions to check as he said, "the depth of the pond." He desired to engage his audience intellectually. Friends, let's be honest about preparation. Many of us are dull instruments for God's use. We haven't done our homework and haven't practiced intelligent discourse enough to compete in the ideological marketplace. My graphic design friend has a term: "Dumb Christians." It is his way of describing believers who cannot interact thoughtfully about their beliefs. Although unflattering, his use of the term derives from seeing the negative affect of believer's ignorance and idiocy. In an evangelistic class, we tell non-believers: "We want you to know, not just what you believe, but why." The same goes for Christians. To influence skeptics we must have a compelling rationale for our faith.

My graphic designer friend and his wife are currently engaging with an atheist neighbor. If you apply yourself to reaching a skeptical friend, it will produce something that you may not expect. Your influence ability will rise! In the relational process, you will get "street-equipped" for conversations. By interacting over rational queries, they have also uncovered a mountain of hurt in their friend from Christians who had told her she will go to hell. This, of course, has only pushed her farther back. They continue to pursue a loving relationship trying to learn how to bring healing and insight.

Finally, if you have the heart and willingness to reach skeptics, you will expand God's mission to a strategic segment. Converted skeptics become powerful apologists. Like an addict's unique ability to help another addict, skeptics understand what it's like to be caught in unbelief, and doubt. They have a story of getting out from that paralyzing place and finding faith. One of the dynamics birthing Lee Strobel's massive apologetic ministries was his story of being the card-carrying atheistic journalist at the Chicago Tribune. Fortunately, a church in Chicago had the heart for the skeptical questioners like him.[3] In terms of investment, consider that the day my atheist friend came to faith, the process had prepared him more than decade-old Christians. As we sharpen ourselves to reach them, God will multiply his movement!

ATHEISTS: THE JOURNEY OUTSIDE THE BOX.

The Great Tower rose high as the centerpiece of the city; it was magnificent! The city enjoyed the many good and abundant blessings of its existence. Often people would climb the tower staircase in a state of wonder and gratitude. It was so well built, and so benevolent that people knew it had to have come from another, whom they called, "the Great Architect." At one time everyone believed in the Great Architect. Not only had he built the Great Tower, he watched over all the city's inhabitants. Through centuries new ideas sprang forth, but nothing rivaled the belief in the Great One who made the Great Tower.

3. Strobel, *The Case for Christ*, 13–14.

One afternoon glancing at the tower, a man dared to wonder, "What if the great tower had really grown out of the earth?" The tower structure looked like parts of the earth, and it seemed to be interconnected. There were several observably apparent reasons behind the man's thoughts. He began to devote his life to study and writing on his new theory. One day this man and his favorite ten-year old daughter walked by the tower,[4] and a board fell from above killing the young girl. This event brought great pain into his life, which only tempered a waning faith in the Great Architect who watched over the inhabitants.

Soon a group began to form that felt enlightened by his idea that the tower had grown out of the earth. It was the only reasonable explanation according to their understanding. Now when they climbed the tower staircase it made them feel powerful. It was like the power that built the tower was somehow behind them. Many experienced a kind of liberating independence from the Great Architect. Some began calling themselves "the People of the Earth Tower." To them even the idea of the Great Architect seemed offensive. "There was no Great Architect, only the Earth Tower," they would say. This idea began to permeate community schools and even major institutions founded on the belief of the Great Architect. Others faithful to the Great Architect stood back in shock that such a thing could happen. But so it did.

GETTING INTO ATHEISTIC SHOES

Due to their refusal to practice their culture's civil religion, the Romans called early church Christians "atheists." Not every Roman citizen believed in their gods, but it bothered them how the early Christians would not worship in the civic sense.[5] "Atheist" was a derogatory term then, but not now. Many today are proud of their atheism considering it part of their identity and a badge of honor to their intellectualism. Atheists typically cannot see why anyone believes in God. Religion doesn't make rational sense. To us it seems obvious there is a God, and we can't see how they don't believe.

To bridge the chasm, let us try for a moment to understand their perspective. We could begin by agreeing that God has placed mystery in the universe. Just as he chose not to give us foreknowledge of the future,

---

4. Van Wyhe, *Darwin: The Story of the Man and His Theories of Evolution*, 41.

5. Aveling, "Atheism," lines 5–7.

requiring faith in him, so he did not make belief a given. We have to choose to believe in God. Additionally, some gravitate toward beliefs in definable categories. God is "out of the box," and anything but definable. He is not visible, measurable, or quantifiable in any way. Can you see why people with scientific, rationalistic thinking have a hard time with the un-test-tube-able God? Furthermore, it is said that believing in evolution is a bigger step of faith than theism. Though this may be true, atheistic faith is passive. It is where they already are, and does not require an active step of faith like Christianity does. That means it is easier for people to stay in the familiar comforts of their own reason. Finally, with a seemingly viable theory like evolution to explain the universe they can maintain their passivity. Mystery + Rational Bias + Alternative Explanation + Passivity = Atheism.

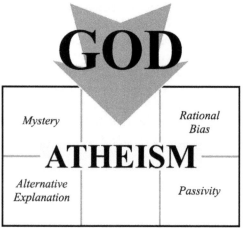

These factors shed light on why many bright, even brilliant people are atheists. Oddly, atheism attracts intellectuals. If you are a Christian, you should appreciate that C.S. Lewis, one of the best Christian minds of the last century was an atheist for much of his life, not coming into faith before his early thirties.[6] Though it is hard for us on the belief side to get into atheistic shoes, it is important that we try. A little empathy goes a long way. It might just help us stop judging them, and start figuring how to reach them. Our challenge is getting them to look outside their normal box of thinking. We want God to deliver them from that stifling, stuck place!

6. Downing, *The Most Reluctant Convert*, 12.

LET'S MEET AN ATHEIST

I love atheists. Let me introduce you to Dave. He is a thirty-eight-year-old website designer, with a beautiful wife and three munchkins at home. He is bright, loyal, and caring. It is not hard to see why his wife adores him, affirming his many qualities, saying, "He is a really good guy." However, not all is at peace with Tricia. Dave is not only a non-Christian, he doesn't even believe in God. She feels a deep responsibility and yearning for his salvation. Her attempts to talk with him go nowhere. She can't get through the wall of his bulwarked analytic thinking. Tricia begins coming to church and Dave follows supportively.

Being unfazed by my initial probing questions, I found that atheism had a lock on Dave. I left the first meeting feeling there was about as much chance of seeing him saved as me getting a call to play for the Chargers that year! This despairing emotion from first contact with an atheist is normal. All good things have to start somewhere, and in evangelism we start where people begin. Though it felt rather hopeless, there was one factor that was tremendously hopeful. I am referring to the fact that David was open to meet. He may have been an entrenched atheist, but his willingness to meet meant he was not a closed one. He was open to a search for truth, which is the first critical step. My role would be to frame a time of ongoing exploration, where an honest search for truth could take place. One advantage of engaging skeptics is that you know the conversation will be a "Question-Line" dialogue. They, typically, like to discuss their analytical viewpoints.

RELATIONAL KEYS WITH ATHEISTS

On the first meeting with Dave, I heard his view of science and evolution, and I shared a number of alternative scientific ideas. I did this, being mindful to be sensitive and respectful to his point of view. As long as we are merely presenting ideas of a differing position, it doesn't feel threatening. I chose my words carefully so as not to come across in a closed or condescending way, "Those favoring a scientific explanation for creation do that for a number of reasons . . ." What was most important in the initial talks was not the content or the points, but rather the tone. I needed him to see that he could disagree with me, and I was perfectly okay with that. In essence, he needed to feel comfortable with me. This meant we could have an open exchange of ideas without him feeling pressure or expectation to agree or convert. He also needed to know that I respected him, his intellect, and his views. This is the principle of honor. These relational intangibles are critical to establishing a basis for open discussion. Slow down. Rome wasn't built in a day. Nor do skeptics come to Christ in a day either.

Not only should we not "speak down" to people, we are wise to "speak up" to their rational abilities. Robert Schuller, who was, by the way, an evangelist, used to say to people, "Why does a good intelligent person like you not embrace the Christian faith?"[7] When I began with Dave, I knew intuitively I would have to appeal to his intellect and harness his analytical abilities to the right end, if he was ever going to come to Christ. Our aim is to show them how irrational atheism is when all perspectives are closely examined. But this will take time and is no easy task. The earth tower will not fall overnight. We must target our attacks upon its pillars and eventually it will come down. Let's pinpoint how to do this through a three-step progression.

ATTACKING THE PILLARS OF ATHEISM

(1) Expose the Arrogance.

Atheism has arrogance issues. The atheist believes they are right, and the majority of us are wrong. If we zoom out to a wider view of history, atheists hold to a position rejected by mankind. Did you see the movie *Contact*, with Jody Foster and heartthrob Matthew McConaughey? This sci-fi classic has Foster playing the atheistic scientist who first hears life from outer space, and McConaughey as the populist spiritual voice of the day. When a person is needed to represent the human race, she becomes a candidate, and he is invited onto the selection panel. Foster eventually becomes the top prospect, but then McConaughey blocks the motion, later articulating to her, "I couldn't come to bring myself in good conscience, to back someone who honestly thinks the other 95 percent of us suffer from some sort of mass delusion."

The fact is most people believe in God, and so did Einstein. Though we know from history the majority are not always right, the examples of believing in a flat earth, or the sun orbiting the globe are not proper comparisons. This majority believes in God because there are solid reasons to

7. Hunter, *How to Reach Secular People*, 89.

do so. Contrary to the politically correct scientific positions in universities, not everyone in the science community is convinced there is no God. Tim Keller, author of *The Reason for God*, notes how Richard Dawkins in his book *The God Delusion*, claims only 7 percent of the scientific community are open to belief. Yet Keller reveals the questions used in Dawkins survey do not properly reflect the scientific community's views. They were designed to "see" scientists with conservative, traditional belief, not general belief in God.[8]

Thus, Dawkins statistics offer a skewed perspective. Keller highlights that two research surveys in 1916 and 1997, showed roughly 40 percent of the scientific community believing in God or open to that possibility.[9] Counter to what Dawkins wants us to believe, there are scientific minded people looking to other factors to explain the vast world with all its complexity. Consider the words of atheist Thomas Nagel, who writes:

> It is natural to try to take any successful intellectual method as far as it will go. Yet the impulse to find an explanation of everything in physics has over the last 50 years gotten out of control. The concepts of physical science provide a very special, and partial, description of the world that experience reveals to us . . . it denies reality to what cannot be so reduced. I believe the project is doomed—that conscious experience, thought, value, and so forth are not illusions, even though they cannot be identified with physical facts.[10]

A second kind of arrogance is how atheists assert to "know" there is no God. Agnosticism is a more intellectually tenable position. It is one thing to say you don't know *if* there is a God, it is another to make the claim *you know* there isn't one. Can you see the audacity? We need to use that for leverage. You will have to pick your spots and deal your hand at the right time, yet there are times when we need to unveil its arrogance. We can ask, "How is it that you can say *for sure* that there is no God?"

(2) Entertain the "God" Possibility.

Just because God cannot be quantified does not mean he does not exist. Every atheist should acknowledge that there is a possibility that the world with all its beauty and complexity came from a Creator-Designer. When

8. Keller, *The Reason for God*, 84–92.

9. Keller, *The Reason for God*, 89.

10. Nagel, "The Fear of Religion," lines 147–56.

the time is right, usually a ways into the relationship take a moment to ask: "Can you at least admit there is a possibility that God exists?" This point may seem trivial, but when reaching to atheists, we must work to get them out of their closed thinking. Dave and I talked about the fact that so many people throughout history across the globe did believe in God. I humbly offered, "It is possible we are all be wrong." Then I turned and asked him to go where I was willing to go. I asked, "Is it possible that he could be wrong?" Dave had enough character to accept the possibility. That was a promising moment, because it portrayed a slight movement toward open-mindedness. An atheist needs to be challenged on this. Without creating defensiveness, we need to sensitively and wisely get the doubters to doubt! If we can create a crack in the box, then we have a chance for light to penetrate.

Resource-wise, we have many crowbars to dig in there for an opening. For all its trumped-up intellectualism, atheism fails to adequately explain our world. It assumes that everything, all its wonder and complexity, came from nothing. What we need to do is to frame up a long dialogical journey regarding the pointers to God.

(3) Examine the Multiple Pointers.

Notice how we are not building our case from the scientific argument alone. That could be foolish. Instead, we are taking everything into account, coming at it from multiple angles. If one pointer does not resonate, then move onto another. This approach can gradually build the case that theism makes more logical and rational sense than atheism. Take your time combing through each perspective and observe the progress. With Dave, I spent two full months of weekly meetings reading and interacting about C.S. Lewis's writings. Some meetings appeared to go nowhere, while others seemed to help. Without any definitive resolve, we transitioned to another pointer—then another—then to the next one. Over time, the cumulative affect of these conversations began to build. You are an architect who is using all the building materials available.

Let's take a look at the first line of discussion we pursued.

—Moral conscience points to God.

Engaging an atheist friend with the writings from C.S. Lewis is a great angle. You may want to tell part of Lewis's personal story. C.S. Lewis was an Oxford College professor, friend of J.R.R Tolkien (a Christian), and an atheist for many years of his life. He then became a prominent Christian voice when the British Broadcasting Company (BBC) asked him to give a series of addresses about his rationale for the Christian faith. These broadcasts became enormously popular and were put into a book called, "Mere Christianity."[11] In the first four chapters of the book Lewis argues for the existence of God. Below is my cliff notes like summary of Lewis's lengthy, detailed argument.

A paraphrase of C.S. Lewis' moral argument for God:

Unlike science that primarily looks to external observations for the existence of God, Lewis believes the most powerful argument comes from looking within. The truth about all of us is that we believe certain behaviors are right and wrong. This is evident because we all cry foul if someone wrongs us. If someone cuts us off on the road, lies, manipulates, or misleads, we all know a moral boundary has been crossed! Where does this moral code come from? Some respond: Society has determined these lines. People learn what is right and wrong from their upbringing tied directly to social values. Lewis, however disagrees with this popular notion, and refutes it by showing there is no "total difference" found in the societal values of world cultures. The story of civilization does reveal different beliefs, laws and practices, but people everywhere have generally held to the same moral standards. Throughout time people have intrinsically recognized what is good and right, and what is harmful and wrong. Lewis begs us to question: How could this be if each moral system came from its own independent place?

Additionally, if moral conscience is merely social, then we have no grounds to judge any other society's morality. Yet this is precisely what we do. We believe certain actions are right or wrong not because a society says they are, but because we judge them to be so. Tyrants who abuse their people are wrong, and so are terrorists. The Nazis were wrong in believing they were the superior race and so was exterminating the Jews. Slavery is inherently wrong. Lewis argues that when we say these things we are appealing to something higher than society. There exists a universal standard, or "law of nature" placed within humanity. Like our human shadow, we cannot get away from this internal compass. Even those who argue there is no such "law of nature," live and judge others as if there is. Everyone cries foul when they

11. Downing, *The Most Reluctant Convert*, 12.

are wronged, and routinely classifies it as injustice. Though it is clear that we do not live consistently by it, nevertheless, this law of nature is always in the mix of human interaction and decisions. The question then becomes, where did it come from? Lewis postulates the only logical explanation is that it came from the outside, placed within by someone who wanted us to behave in a certain way. Thus, moral conscience is a direct pointer to God.[12]

This is just one pointer of many. Consider the broad list:

Moral Conscience
Creation Design
Irreducible Complexity
Rational Thought
Beauty & Pleasure
Inherent Meaning
Human Nobility
Evolutions Failure
Spiritual Desire

You will find explanation for each in the Addendum section. If you work the process of examining these angles, God can use you to reach skeptics!

THE MOVE TO AGNOSTICISM

When the time is right, after you have effectively made a case for God's existence, you appeal to them, "You are really not an atheist, but an agnostic. It's not that you don't believe in God, you just don't know if there is or isn't one. When you are exploring both possibilities that makes you an agnostic." Once they become open to the possibility of a God, they are in a different place mentally. It's a beginning step toward faith. The next is to become a believer in God and Christ. The term "agnostic" comes from the Latin word, "ignoramus." There will be a time when you might want to gently point that out. They will not want to stay in the ignorant category forever, but in reaching atheists, the shift to agnosticism is significant.

ATHEIST   AGNOSTIC   APOLOGETICS   ACCEPTANCE
                         (4 Planks)   *(Believer)*

12. Lewis, *Mere Christianity*, 17–39.

Typically, covering Christian apologetics with someone coming out from atheism will take time since you are conversing with a highly analytic person. They will want to see all the evidence. As outlined in the next section below, you will need to work through the foundational planks for faith. If they are open to explore truth, they can be reached. Often, these former skeptics, like C.S. Lewis and Lee Strobel, turn out to be the next wave of Christian apologists.

It's easy to be intimidated by atheists and their arguments. If you are led by God to have interaction, be sure to prepare for each get-together. Pray. Have others pray for you. Educate yourself. Remember that it is ultimately God who opens hearts and minds. You are not alone in this process.

The day touring the great ship is one of my fondest early memories and a fascinating learning experience. For achieving the top grade in my sixth grade oceanography class (yeah!), I won a trip to the Queen Mary. The Queen launched in 1936, and served through four decades including a role in World War II before she was retired as a floating hotel and museum in Long Beach. Something surprising happened in the process of this transition that many people don't know. When restorers removed her three massive smokestacks to a dock for resurfacing, each stack crumbled before their eyes. Over the years, the ¾ inch steel had entirely worn away, but remained standing due to thirty-plus coats of paint.[13] The great argument for atheism will fall. It's just paint! We are going to have work hard at exposing its unsubstantiated assumptions through multiple viewpoints. We must be patient and persistent; like inspectors shining the light within these smoke stacks revealing them for what they really are.

THEISTIC SKEPTICS: A PLATFORM FOR FAITH.

It's time to build faith's platform. As you frame up a regular, weekly time to meet, each plank, 2 x 4, or joist becomes a topic of discussion, and may take weeks or months to construct. If you work through the content with your atheist friend, recognize that it will take time for him or her to embrace the concepts, the end result can be your friend coming into the Christian faith. Below I introduce you to what I call "the four platform planks." Further detail is provided in the Addendum of the book. When you engage in discussions with skeptics and those from other faiths, you are going to need to be tooled with knowledge to assist you in building

13. Holman, *New Testament Commentary*, Romans, 90–92.

a foundation. Thus, the Addendum section is critically important. Don't pass over it! You haven't really completed this book until you've soaked at least some of it in. Your ability to dialogue about the ideas, logic, facts, and rationale for the Christian faith is essential.

In this chapter, I want to expose you to the strength of each of the planks. Your skeptic friend may have other hang-ups, but I have found these four discussion areas are key to building a new Christian worldview.

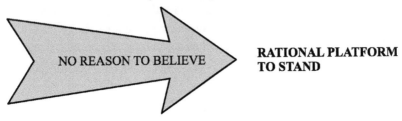

NO REASON TO BELIEVE

RATIONAL PLATFORM TO STAND

THE FOUR MAJOR PLANKS:

Plank #1: Fulfilled Prophecy

The concept of prophecy is pervasive in entertainment writing and exists in super-mega hits like *Star Wars* and *The Matrix* with its guiding oracles. The popular use demonstrates its universal appeal. Weather it is interpreted as fate or faith, prophecy is hot stuff, not only for the Psychic Network, but moviemakers, storytellers, religions, and cultures. When it comes to biblical prophecy we are not talking about fanciful imagination, myths, or conjecture, but rather the integration of foretelling with history. We now know the Mayans were wrong with their 2012 doomsday script, and so were many others; but God never is! With predictions becoming historical fact, this is a powerful proof and one we must use to garner the interest and intrigue of our friends.

This plank angle reaches all the way back to the ancient church, where a fiery debate raged within the Jewish culture over Jesus fulfilling the Scriptures. It resulted in many Jews becoming Christians in the early church phase. When we engage in discussions about Old Testament prophecies, we are feeling the evangelistic heartbeat of the neonate church. Let us think of whose company we have entered![14]

Although there will be countering challenges from today's Jewish community, and though Christians commonly exploit prophecies, making some appear to be more definitive than they actually are, we do have a powerful proof in the prophetic record. As we study the specific passages,

14. Green, *Evangelism In The Early Church*, 78–87.

prophecy can become a useful tool. One non-believer investigating the Christian faith acknowledged the most convincing argument of all for him was fulfilled prophecy. In the Addendum section you will find detailed listings and development of the big three: Psalm 22, Daniel 9, and Isaiah 53. Every Christian should be able to explain prophecy as being a significant rationale for our faith.

Clarify the Prophecy Concept.

As the biblical writer addresses his time and audience, there are places where the writing transcends the present to give a future picture. Sometimes it relates to what will happen to Israel or the surrounding nations. Interwoven within God's dealings, a picture emerges of a coming Redeemer who will accomplish God's plan. From many Old Testament passages we have data on the first and second comings of the Christ. When we talk to people about fulfilled prophecy we purposely focus attention on Christ's first coming. The accuracy of historical details fulfilled in the person of Jesus Christ gives evidence that biblical prophecy is indeed a snapshot of future history.

Fulfilled prophecy is one of the most compelling reasons to believe the Bible is the inspired Word of God. How could the Bible be a mere product of men when it contains future information? This stunning accuracy could only happen if the God who dwells outside of time and sees the future had inspired the writers. When we assemble these snapshots, it creates an amazing mosaic of the divine Savior-Messiah.

One day a friend questioned, "Couldn't it be that people who knew of the Old Testament prophecies directed Jesus to fulfill them?" As odd as this question may seem to us, it is just the kind of thought a skeptic will have. Let us not be afraid of their queries. By thinking with them we can help them over the hurdles they are facing. If we begin reasoning on our own it will sharpen us, too. There are two grounds why this suggestion could not be. First, several prophecies are beyond the possibility of orchestration. You cannot orchestrate the place and timing of a man's birth (Mal 5:2). Second, and equally convincing, is how we could never orchestrate the divine personhood of Jesus. Much prophecy is about who Jesus is, not merely what he will do.

See the Addendum for these related sections:

• The Big Three Prophecies
• Prophetic Detail Regarding Jesus

Plank #2: Historical Authenticity.

Is it possible that people today could flat out deny "the Holocaust?" Did you know this is why Steven Spielberg made the movie *Schindler's List?* As lame as it sounds to us, people actually began to suggest the Holocaust never occurred. If you watched him the night of the Academy Awards receive his Oscars for best picture and best director, you heard him make an earnest plea to teachers in schools: "Teach this stuff!" To hammer home his point on the reality of history, he ends the movie by transitioning from black and white to color, bringing us from the past to present day, and then parades before us the living descendents of Schindler's Jews to place flowers at his grave. It profoundly came through as a film record for all time—this happened, people! Here are the living descendents—the witnesses can not be denied!

Mark Mittelberg, writes of his visit inside a mosque. He is told by the Imam (prayer leader) to believe in Allah and his true prophet Mohammed, and how God is not divided, and does not have a son. During a time for discussion, Mittelberg feels led to ask the Imam to answer how he can ignore the historical witnesses about Christ's death, which Islam claims did not occur. Unwilling to engage in dialogue, the Imam tells him to believe in Mohammed.[15] If Mittelberg had the chance, he would have kindly pointed out that Mohammed lived and wrote six hundred years after Christ. He was not a contemporary of the crucifixion, and denies the witnesses who were. Islam takes the historical record from hundreds of eyewitnesses, including four painstakingly detailed accounts of Jesus's life, and tosses it in the trash. It is the equivalent of saying the Holocaust never occurred.

When it comes to the events of the life of Christ, there is a historical record from witnesses that should not be denied. Yet we live in a culture prone to write off history, and see it as man's creation for his own ends. Our role is to help people see just how authentic and reliable the New Testament record is. We want to give them clear reasons to believe the testimony of the witnesses. Although we cannot parade the actual descendants before their eyes, we do have convincing points to build our case. Paul appeals to King Agrippa, "This did not happen in a corner" (Acts 26:26). Jesus was a well-known figure, crucified in the public arena. That means we have an accessible record to examine. To dig through significant historical proofs, see the Addendum for:

15. Mittelberg, *Choosing Your Faith*, 57–59.

- Extra Biblical Sources
- Reasons to Believe the New Testament's Reliability

Plank #3: The Resurrection and the Case of the Missing Body.

Have you ever played the board game *Clue*? "Mrs. Peacock with the candlestick in the library." The story of the Resurrection is like a grand court case where you put together all the clues to make a truly grand conclusion. The scene: A notable public person is dead. A tomb is prepared. The body is placed in the tomb, and then days later the body is indisputably missing. From simple logic, if we had the body we would not have Christianity. With these basic facts, we have to figure out who did it, and how? Where is the body? Was it lost? Stolen? Moved? Risen? Like a prosecuting attorney we scrutinize all possible suspects for motive and examine all material evidence to solve the mystery of the missing corpse.

Let's examine suspect motives. Here we ask: Did any of the suspects have motive to do anything with the body? The answer is clearly yes. The Jewish leaders had motive to secure the body in the tomb. By doing this they could effectually diffuse the Jesus movement, which threatened their authority and traditions. This motive leads them to take a number of precautionary measures to protect the tomb. They petitioned the Romans to post a guard. In addition to the customary large stone closing the tomb entrance, they also strapped the Roman Seal over the stone, which told others to stay away; breaking the Roman Seal was punishable by death. The Nazarene had talked about rising from the dead in three days. All the Jewish authorities had to do to squelch his words was to secure the tomb with body inside. Here's the body; here are the bones. He's dead—its over! They could once and for all crush the Jesus cult; this they desperately wanted. They had motive.

The disciples could have had motive too, perhaps wanting to take the body and create the notion of the Resurrection. Though this idea is conjecture and not substantiated, it is possible based on the events. Yet, when entertaining this idea we cannot overcome the fact the disciples lacked sufficient means to pull this off. The idea of these common men, mostly fisherman, gaining both the courage and skill to overpower the Roman guard is not credible. Military history assesses the Roman guard as a legitimate fighting unit in the Roman military typically comprised of four to sixteen men.[16] These trained soldiers were equipped with three weapons, a dagger, sword, and spear. They slept in rotations to not be surprised and faced the death penalty if they ever left a post (see Acts 16:27).[17] These Marines of the ancient world were no pushovers. The suggestion that the disciples overpowered them is just not believable.

In summary, the Jewish leaders had motive, and all the means necessary through the Roman authorities to secure the tomb. The disciples, on the other hand, could have had motive to steal the body, but had no means. How then do we explain the empty tomb and missing body? The only reasonable answer remaining is the Resurrection. If this supernatural possibility is contemplated, can we observe any other supporting details?

Let's examine suspect behaviors. Here we ask: What do the behaviors of the suspects tell us? Interestingly, the parties' behaviors show two opposite reactions pointing to the same conclusion; the Jews are silent, and the disciples will not shut up! (Acts 4:18–20). If the Jews had the body then they would be speaking out refuting false ideas from spreading. They would be saying, "It's a fraud. We have the body right here. See!" Legal scholar and apologist John Warrick Montgomery said, "The silence of the Jews shouts of the Resurrection."[18] On the other hand, the disciples are suddenly so filled with courage and conviction about his resurrection that the Jesus movement takes off. The spread of the early church is itself a strong indicator of its credibility. The teaching of the risen Christ was believed, and believable on the streets.

From a purely logical standpoint, it is unlikely that a group of men would stand together unto death over a falsehood. Their resurgence, passion and martyrdom points to the authenticity. The gospel accounts reveal how significant this event was to them personally. Peter, for example, having heard the initial news from the women, runs to the tomb (Luke 24:12). Why would he run? Because his resurrection would mean everything to him, the recovery of his failure, the renewal of his hope, the beginning of his mission. People needing hope run!

Additionally, we see an entire movement of people who believe in the Resurrection. N.T. Wright describes how a new worldview perspective sprung up immediately following the death of Jesus. Virtually overnight, people's view of the cross transforms. It morphed from an electric chair like object of torture into the beautiful symbol of redemption. Can

16. McDowell, *A Ready Defense*, 228.

17. McDowell, *A Ready Defense*, 228–29.

18. Montgomery, *History and Christianity*, 78.

you imagine wearing an electric chair on your neck? That is exactly what we do today—because of the Resurrection! Wright demonstrates that a worldview shift of that magnitude would typically only occur from debating and discussing over long periods of time. Instead, we see something unprecedented in history, a new belief breaking forth from the witnesses.[19]

Let's examine the witnesses. The Gospels record nine separate resurrected appearances by Jesus over a period of forty days. Paul writes in 1 Corinthians 15:6 that the risen Christ had appeared to more than five hundred believers at one time, most who were still living at the time of his penmanship.

Let's examine its feasibility. J.I Packer notes in his classic book, *Knowing God*, if we believe in Christmas, that Jesus is God incarnate, then it is only natural to believe in his rising from the dead.[20] The Resurrection is entirely consistent with the teaching of Christianity, that Jesus Christ is the God-man with power over the world, its laws, and even death. Jesus is the author of life. For our supernatural God, resurrection is no problem!

Case Summary: The motives, behaviors, witnesses, and feasibility all point to a real resurrection. From the examination of the possibilities, there is no other viable explanation for the missing body. The Resurrection remains a signpost to the human race. See the Addendum for further content.

Plank #4: Jesus Himself.

Living in San Diego, I was accustomed to viewing military ships docked in the harbor, but nothing prepared me for what I would see one beautiful day at the Coronado Peninsula. Meandering along the rocky shoreline, we found a place to sit down, as our kids climbed on the rocks looking for crabs. We had taken our eyes away from the ocean when suddenly a thousand-foot-long Navy aircraft carrier streamed past making its way into the bay. It was an amazing sight! The height and size of the great ship dwarfed everything around it.

I once heard Bill Hybels describe a similar scene during a sailing regatta where the arrival of a carrier created a navigational spectacle. In his message, Hybels revealed an unspoken boating law: *Aircraft carriers have the right of way—by virtue of what they are!* The great ship forced every watercraft to move. As you might of guessed, nobody played chicken with

19. Wright, *The Resurrection of the Son of God*, 578–83.
20. Packer, *Knowing God*, 46.

the carrier that afternoon. None tried to bluff the great ship to make it alter course. Everybody in the bay divided right down the middle going to one side or the other.[21]

The comparison of Jesus Christ to an aircraft carrier entering a crowded bay is a properly sized illustration. When God entered the human race, the sheer magnitude of who Jesus is should cause all people to make a choice. By his claims, personhood, heritage, words, and works, all people must ultimately move toward belief or denial. No one can just stay in the middle; everyone has a decision to make. Of course, Jesus knew this saying, "You who are not for me are against me" (Luke 11:23).

In evangelism, we want to help people see the magnitude of Jesus's life, so they can choose wisely. When they see Jesus for who he is, many will be drawn to believe! We can achieve this ultimate awareness through a number of highly effective ways. One story I like to discuss with non-Christians is Mark 2. While Jesus is staying at a home in the small town of Galilee, friends bring a crippled man before him. When Jesus makes the controversial statement, "Your sins are forgiven," the religious leaders in the crowd cry out: "Objection! Master, you can't say that! Don't you know that only God can forgive sins?" (5–6). Jesus responds, "Which is easier to say your sins are forgiven or rise up and walk home?" Can you picture them looking on dumbfounded pondering the incomprehensibility of what he just asked? Which one was easier? Neither! Both were virtually impossible in their minds. Only God can forgive sins, and telling the crippled man to rise and walk would mean having divine capital "D" powers at your disposal.

Grasp, for a moment, the implication of forgiving another's sins. We can forgive someone who has wronged us, but that is not what we're talking about here. Jesus is forgiving all the man's sins. The ones he has committed against God and others throughout his life. No mere human being can do that. It would require being in a position as the Creator and Judge, where one's sins must find their accountability.

So what does Jesus do? To demonstrate that the Son of Man has the authority to forgive sins, "I tell you, get up, take your mat and walk!" (10–11). They are thinking neither is easier—Jesus says I will do both! I will show you who I am. Stunned witnesses see the man gradually move, as feeling and strength coarse correctively into his lame limbs. Having not walked for his entire life he slowly gets to his knees and then stands wobbly

---

21. Hybels, "Reasons For Believing in Jesus Christ," 1994.

for the first time. People watching hold their hands over their mouths, their hearts bursting with amazement. The man begins to walk around!

What kind of person miraculously heals and forgives sins? Is he a normal human being? Christian brothers and sisters, hear me now. We have incredible material to work with when it comes to the personhood of Jesus Christ. He is no Messiah poser-wannabe. Jesus is the real deal in every way, and the star of our defense! We should help others to see him for who he was, and is!

Addendum: C.S. Lewis's Famous Appeal.

DISCUSSION & ENGAGEMENT

1. What kinds of questions did you have in your spiritual journey to faith?

2. Do you have any friends who fit the skeptic category? How prepared would you be to help them out from where they are and into faith?

3. The author talked about moving them in a progression from atheism into agnosticism, and from agnosticism into apologetics. Does this make sense to you?

4. Why is it wise to approach atheists from multiple points of view?

5. Which of the four platform planks is most convincing to you of the Christian faith?

20

Pinhole Light

Where there is an open mind there will always be a frontier.
—CHARLES F. KETTERING

When two people mentioned having Hindu neighbors, the teacher replied, "You don't have to learn their religion, you only need to share what Jesus has done for you." Though his simple sounding sentiment soothed the class, I simply had to disagree. This commonly held view reflects something wrong in the church today. We think we don't have to do the work of the missionary. Believers in less Christianized countries know how to respond to pluralism, but for too long, our home field advantage meant we didn't have to.[1] Like spoiled kids, we grew up not needing to venture to the other side of the tracks; if others want to play, they'll just have to come to our neighborhood.

Compounding the errant thinking is the fact that we all are commercially affected by a quick-fix, instant-solution society. As we unveil the topic of reaching religious people, let's be clear on one thing—reaching anyone from another faith is anything but quick or instant. Reaching someone from a religion is right up there next to atheists in the degree of difficulty factors. In my opinion, it is often easier to reach an atheist than

1. Nida, *Message And Mission*, 112.

it is a religious person. He should have said, "If you truly want to redeem a person from another faith, you are going to have to learn something about their beliefs." If you do not, you will not know where their starting point is. Evangelism always starts where they begin. No shortcut around this. If they come from another faith, you will not know what they truly believe until you hear it expressed.

Allow me to illustrate the importance of this from Christianity. As believers, we know some merely identify themselves as Christians and may not even be saved. Others genuinely believe, but do not follow Christ in transformative ways. Still others believe and live with full-hearted zeal. The same distinguishing levels exist with other faiths. Therefore, if you are connecting with a religious person, you have to do two things:

1. Understand the basics of their particular beliefs.
2. Discern their ownership level.

Let us take a look at each. Understanding the basis of their faith requires doing your homework. Allow me to qualify that you do not need to know everything about their religion. What you need to learn is what they think and feel. This makes the discovery challenge more reasonable. Vast content exists with most faiths, but you can have influential conversations if you merely discover what they have gotten from it. As an example, three major divisions exist in Islam. You do not have to know all the differences, but you will need to know their particular viewpoint.

Discovering their starting point will do something critical for us. It will build love and empathy. Missiological theologian Leslie Newbigin describes the starting point of a devout Hindu in this way:

> heir to four thousand years of profound religious and philosophical experience, there is something truly scandalous in the suggestion that, to put it crudely, he or she must import the necessities for salvation from abroad. Is it really credible, the Hindu will ask, "that the Supreme Being whom I am my ancestors have loved and worshipped for forty centuries is incapable of meeting my soul's need, and that I must await the coming of an agent of another tradition from Europe or North America if I am to receive salvation? What kind of god are you asking me to believe in? Is he not simply the projection of your own culture-bound prejudices? Come! Let us be reasonable! Let us open our treasures and put them side by side, and we shall see

that your symbols and mine are but the differing forms of one
reality shaped according to our different histories and cultures."[2]

Realizing where they begin can be unsettling. Let it shave down your arrogance. May you vicariously feel another faith's tempting pull. A Hindu's faith incorporates expressions through every place and time, where ours is particularized. All encompassing is better, isn't it? Maybe you should be a Hindu? I am playing with you, because I want you to feel where they are. In their minds, Hinduism is far superior to Christianity (in contrast to theism where God is personal and transcendently distinct from the creation; pantheism believes that God impersonally encompasses or is identical with the cosmic universe. Thus, their vast array of culturally conceived gods is representative of the One).

Likewise, the Muslim has received direct divine words through God's latest prophet. It's a newer faith, with a book far more revered than the Bible we toss around so flippantly. Allah, being so exalted, would never stoop to human levels, or be divided. Islam is clearly superior to Christianity in that it makes logical sense. Newer and more rational is better, isn't it? Understanding them may be just what is needed to break our hearts, and shore up resolve for the mission. Champions rise to big challenges. Welcome to an adventure of the most difficult kind!

In his book, *God is Not One*, Stephen Prothero uses classifications to get a handle on pre-suppositional distinctions. Take a look at how Christianity and Buddhism vary:

> Christianity:
> The problem: Sin
> The solution: Salvation
> The technique: Faith
> Buddhism:
> The problem: Suffering
> The solution: Nirvana (a way to escape suffering)
> The technique: Noble Eightfold Path.[3]

The comparison highlights why understanding is crucial. A Buddhist perceives the problem of life differently. If we do not comprehend this we could be talking of things not even on their radar. We must get to the pre-suppositional level and examine the question of Buddhism. Is the problem of life really suffering? This might be what you explore in depth with your

2. Newbigin, *The Open Secret*, 66.
3. Prothero, *God Is Not One*, 14.

Buddhist friend. If you think Gautama (Buddha) has this locked—is it not true that suffering produces tremendous good? As taught in the book of James and elsewhere, does not some of the greatest growth in a person's life happen through trials? Making a statement about the character-forming aspect of suffering, church leader John Wimber quipped, "Don't trust anyone who doesn't walk with a limp." Suffering shapes us in profound ways. In sharing Christ not only are we teaching about God, but also introducing ideas that might not be familiar or valued. If the concept is not valued it will not reach them. We have to discover their belief lens in discussions and build from there.

Second, we must expose their adherence level. Admittedly, discerning this can be tricky. Sometimes, they themselves, do not realize how aligned they are with their religion. Consider the example of Stephen, a non-practicing Jew. Being the owner of a sign company, Stephen became the sign man for our church. I began building a relationship in hopes of pointing him to Jesus. I learned of his Jewish roots but also that he was not practicing. He made it abundantly clear that he was not religious in any way and did not identify with a synagogue. One day we were talking about faith, and I decided to bring up the topic of Old Testament prophecies and Christ. He fired back, "There are no prophecies fulfilled by Jesus!" He went on to spin out a number of Jewish rebuttals to specific prophecies, showing that he knew his stuff. My initial attempt of starting a discussion went nowhere. What I learned that day was that although Stephen did not practice the Jewish faith, he had a territorial tenacity about it. In this way, he did not realize how inconsistent his life was—something he downplayed—was actually super important to him.

That day I chose not to pursue the conversation because it was not on good footing. I purposed to talk with him again after reframing the discussion. What I needed to do was disarm the emotion so we could interact constructively. I surmised it would require talking directly about his passion for Judaism, even though he downplays it, and highlighting how emotionally charged he is. I would want him to see how zealously Jewish I perceive him to be—that would likely lead to his dialing down to hear another's perspective.

People who are not practicing a religion can be extremely tied to its beliefs due to family tradition or even guilt or shame. On the other hand, highly religious people who are practicing can be unconvinced and uncommitted. When you are building relationship with someone of a religious background, a Muslim, Hindu, Buddhist, or Jewish person, you have to find out where they are. This means asking questions and having them explain their beliefs, and observing conviction levels. Do they believe it, and if so, why? Do they regularly attend a place of worship? Finding their true starting point will help you see what you are up against, provide clues to their degree of openness, and insights for conversational angles. With this category of person, the first "Open to" step is paramount and foundational to getting anywhere.

America is a pluralistic society. Long gone are the days of neighborhoods filled with people uniformly aligned to the Judeo-Christian worldview. Today's neighborhoods, including mine (we have a mosque just a stones throw from my house), are populated with varied faiths from all over the world: Jews, Muslims, Buddhists, Hindu's and Animists (the dominant worldview of the tribal societies believing in a spirit-animated world). I recall a day surveying our community, when I met a Hindu woman decked out in cultural dress with the red stone pasted on her forehead (the "bindhi" or "kumkum" placed between the eyes is said to retain energy in the human body). She was stunning! It gave me all sorts of missiological thoughts on reaching religious people from an ecclesiastical view: Crazy ideas like starting the neighborhood Hindu-Christian church—culturally Hindu, yet theologically Christian.

Stealing the phrase from the television series *Lost*, the church sees foreign faiths like "the others." They come from a different place and look through a lens we do not understand. When it comes to changing religions, cultural groups are not easily turned. This is because beliefs typically anchor to family affiliation and tradition, not always personal choice or rational investigation. Please understand I am not suggesting there is no rationality with other faiths; some have developed extensive apologetics. What I am saying is your attempts to share the Christian message can go nowhere if you do not understand their sociological loyalty. This same phenomenon is evidenced with secularists. College student Melanie decides not to follow Christ because doing so would mean her secularist, unbelieving parents would be damned. She denies her intellectual conclusions, and remains apart from Christ out of loyalty to her mother and father. Likewise, a nominal Jew I know named David expresses it is important for him to keep solidarity with the Jewish people of the past and present. This historical connection stymies his openness. Can you see what we are up against?

This is why the first apologetic needs to focus on their "openness to investigation." The real issue is a closed-minded rejection of exploration.

They must become open to look honestly and follow what sound rationality points towards. This is what some will not do, and tragically why they will remain in their religion or secular state. Thus, the initial goal is to spur them into thinking for themselves. Without the "first step," there will be no salvation.

CLOSED TO INVESTIGATION   OPENED TO TRUTH

An excellent resource on how people adopt religion is a book I mentioned previously— *Choosing Your Faith,* by Mark Mittelberg. He exposes the fallacies in choosing faith through anything other than rational inquiry.[4] When I refer to "rational investigation" it does not mean there is not an experiential aspect to the discovering process, but rather, that if one is choosing faith from family tradition or cultural expectation, it is inherently vulnerable to error.

At a baptism class I asked everyone to introduce themselves by briefly sharing their spiritual story. When Sakuna spoke, she mentioned growing up Buddhist. Tempted to ask hundreds of questions, I instead scheduled a time to get to know her. One thing that can help us reach other faiths is to learn from those who've made the journey. Listening to Sakuna revealed insights to her starting point, and the common barriers for those in Buddhist and Eastern faiths. In *The Tangible Kingdom,* the authors Halter and Smay make a nice contribution with a breakdown on Western, Eastern, and Post-mod tendencies. When it comes to Eastern culture, a profound connection to the past exists, leaning all the way back into their ancestry.[5] In fact, though she did not understand why, Sakuna prayed to her ancestors. It is hard for Westerners to appreciate this value. True to form, it created enormous conflict as she questioned her belief system but felt guilty doing so. She did not want to be unfaithful to her lineage. Yet her questioning heart and the encouragement of Christian friends created a countering inertia. Eventually, they encouraged her to "go experiential." After almost two years of searching, God broke through and drew her into the faith!

4. Mittelberg, *Choosing Your Faith,* 57–80.
5. Halter and Smay, *The Tangible Kingdom,* 59–81.

If we are to reach people from distant starting points we will need to show tremendous love, interest, patience, and commitment to their journey. Kris and Jaime took time out of their busy schedules to meet with a Muslim woman named Nasra. Because of cultural taboos related to being in the company of a male, Kris got dropped off, as Jamie picked her up from her Los Angeles home. They did this drop off-pick up dance routine over many months. With the opportunity to talk about Christianity, Kris gently challenged her belief system, which caused her to dig into the Koran and the Bible simultaneously. Having not actually read the Koran much, she found herself shocked by its contents. According to Kris, Nasra absorbed the Bible at an incredible pace. Numerous months later with lots of Christians offering input, she eventually made the step to faith, and is now doing apologetic ministry for Jesus! All of that would not have happened outside of relationship building and love. We will not ever get away from those foundational dynamics of needing to create the context for truth to stick.

As we engage in dialogue, what can we do practically to help them progress?

MIRROR BACK WHAT THEY ARE DOING

The idea of mirroring may initially feel confrontational, but can be done in a relationally honoring way. Here you are attempting to help them see what they are doing by committing to a closed system. When the moment is right, talk directly, "You seem to be 'closed-minded' and not open to all the information. In a court of law, the jury must look at everything with an open mind." At times I might press the issue in a framing manner, "What would be the purpose of our discussion if you are already biased? If you have predetermined what is true based upon your religious affiliation then you are not open to anything outside your pre-set views. In scientific terms, we'd call that 'tainted research' or 'corrupted investigation.' In logic it's called a fallacy—that is, when you make a conclusion in a false way. Just because a group of people believes something does not make it true. Many people thought the earth was flat, because that was what they were told, but it wasn't true. You have to look at all the facts to discern truth."

OR: "Before we begin a discussion, you must commit to think for yourself in a non-biased way. As much as you can, you must rid your mind of all preprogrammed ideas, and pursue an honest search for truth. Wherever the search leads, pray that God gives you the courage to follow it. Can you do that?"

Again, trying to mirror back to them what they are doing, there are times when you might want to use a graphic metaphor, "It's like you are putting your head in the sand, or are, in a sense, brainwashed, because you won't look openly at the alternatives to see which stands up to scrutiny." Like the dialogue between Jesus and Nicodemus, this kind of conversation may not bring the desired result immediately, but could leave them spiritually disturbed (John 3:8–9). If done in a relationally safe and loving way you might find it to be exactly the right medicine. They need to get upturned.

OFFER TO EXPLORE THEIR RELIGION

The primary question is, Why should I believe your religion over other alternatives? What reason is there to believe in Judaism over Christianity? Or why should I believe in Islam instead of Christianity? This question engages them in a conversation about why they believe. You can even offer to commit your life to their faith, if it convinces you through reason, logic, facts, historical evidence and spiritual experience. I am not afraid to do this, because my faith is grounded through a multiplicity of evidence. For instance, I would never be won to Judaism, because the evidence is overwhelming that Christ is God—the Jewish Messiah. They would have to show me that the prophecies really weren't about Jesus, and Jesus's words came from a common man, and the Resurrection never occurred, and the courage and conviction of the Christian movement was all based on a lie. This they will not be able to do because the evidence points in another direction. With careful investigation the truth always rises to the top. That is exactly why we are trying to initiate an honest and thorough investigation.

Rodney Stark's masterful work, *Discovering God: The Origins of the Great Religions and the Evolution of Belief*, is significant because he creates criteria to evaluate whether a religious writing is divine revelation. To pass the test, revelation must reveal God. It also must be progressive in that it provides additional revelation to humankind. He designed a fascinating way to look at religious sources, and he comes to pointed conclusions: Judaism is revelation, Christianity is definitely further revelation, Islam is neither. He argues that Islam does not offer revelation of God. Though splattered with poetically beautiful writings, the bulk of the Koran is law stemming from a sixth-century world. Stark observes, it does not offer further revelation of who God is. In fact, it teaches that we cannot know God; he is in essence unknowable. Though the Koran uses many descriptive words for God, unlike the Old and New Testaments, it does not offer revelation of God's personhood.[6] Additionally, it does not provide revelation that is progressive. In fact, it is contrary to the revelation with Judaism and Christianity. Please note: Using this type of apologetic would need to be set up in the right way conversationally to avoid or minimize offense. Doing a learning-line discussion where you read Stark directly with an open mind and then converse about it, could work well!

Sometimes we need to jump in on their side of the fence. This is one of the learning-line options. I have read the Koran, partly because I wanted to see its core teachings, but also to have a place of reference when God opens up opportunity to befriend Muslims. I am always ready to jump in and learn from them. They are amazing people!

I am currently conversing with a Hindu friend, Aadit. As a second-generation Hindu American, he is fully assimilated into California culture and holds to his family's faith. At his mother's passing, he went back to India to perform the many ritualistic practices consistent with the Hindu religion. I asked him a series of questions trying to understand what they did, and also his level of connection. The whole conversation focused on his faith. Right now I am listening and learning. God will provide the time of interactive discussion later when our relationship is stronger and my understanding of his starting point is clearer.

HIGHLIGHT THEIR VITAL INFLUENCE

With the love of family being such a strong mooring for people of other religions, we must attempt to turn that on its head. A way to do this is to explore the "What if it's true?" scenario. "What if Christianity is true?" I might say, and follow up with some conjecture, "You are perhaps the only one in your family who's open to even have a conversation. If the Christian faith is true, then God must be choosing you to open that all-important dialogue. If it is actually true, denying the truth about Christ will hurt you and your family!" This would need to be a timely conversation, but we must open their eyes to this possibility. Just like with other non-believers, we paint a picture of what they could become. We can say things like: "You will become the 'light' to your family and friends;" "You could be the one who helps them see the truth;" "Instead of betraying them, you would actually become a bridge to their salvation;" "By investigating what is true, you are not hurting, but rather helping them." Here we are reinterpreting that they are not un-loyal betrayers, but rather courageous liberators!

6. Stark, *Discovering God*, 390–95.

DEFEND THE TRINITY

Judaism and Islam stumble over the triune God. One religion came before Christ, the other six hundred years after, but both trip up on the Trinity. Although the Trinitarian idea is not irrational, the human mind falters in comprehending it.[7] No illustration we have does it full justice. Nevertheless, we believe in the Trinity because the one God has revealed himself to be three distinctly equal persons. One thing we can all agree on is: Christianity is not what we would have created. Since the Trinity defies conventional human thought, it presents a view of God that is clearly not man-made. It is not culturally conceived, but rather heavenly received. As Jesus said, "You are from below; I am from above" (John 8:23). This is a powerful apologetic itself, separating Christianity from all other faiths.

Generally speaking, most theists embrace the logical notion that God is different than us; that God, by his very name and essence, is distinct and infinitely greater. "My ways are higher than your ways" (Isa 55:8–9). The Trinity fits that notion. Further, the Trinity does not defy reason; it just offers a more sophisticated picture of the Creator, where a unity of community exists between three persons. This is incredible to ponder! From the theistic premise of man being created in his image, our experience as communal beings needing relationship matches the triune character. As to relationship quality, the Trinity presents a harmony where each person honors the other: The Father honors the Son; The Son the Father; The Spirit the Son; The Spirit the Father, etc. In this way, the Trinity demonstrates love in perfection.[8]

Of course, the greatest proof of the triune God is Jesus himself. This is where the rubber meets the road in discussions. Jews and Muslims must be willing to take an honest look at the person of Jesus Christ—the second person of the Godhead. If they are willing to look openly at his words and life, they could be won to Christianity. There is no one like Jesus! Not only would we not have come up with the Trinity, we could not have come up with Jesus's authority and wisdom. This is a powerful apologetic—Jesus is out of this world! No human being ever spoke with such words. No respectable religious teacher made his claim to be God, offered to forgive sins,[9] or rose from the dead. If only people would be open to examine Jesus, their eyes could discover the lover and Savior of their souls. As C.S. Lewis pointed out, he's either a liar, a lunatic or Lord!

7. Keller, *The Reason for God*, 215.
8. Keller, *The Reason for God*, 214–15.
9. Lewis, *Mere Christianity*, 55.

Three college-age Muslims came to faith through a learning-line discussion over the book, *Jesus and Mohammed*. Seeing Christ in a new way, when one came to Christ, the other two fell like dominos. Of course, their decisions created family upheaval, but they got through it. When I interviewed Christians from Iran, and asked about how they dealt with the concept of the Trinity, they said they embrace following Jesus first. A leader replied, "The Trinity is too much for them to understand before becoming a Christian." Afterwards, they will learn more of the theological concepts. That means we need to teach about Jesus. We can be flexible and adaptable just like God is. They do not have to pass a theology test to come into faith. Just like us, there is much we will not understand until we cross faith's line.

THE PATH OF HEROES

I received an email from a pastor asking for input on reaching his Muslim friend. I wrote, "She must be won to openness, truth, and then courage. That's the way I see it. The evangelist must give attention to all." Take a look at what a path could be for a religious person.

OPENNESS   TRUTH   COURAGE   FAITH   **INFLUENCE**

When engaging a friend of another faith we must be appreciative of their cost in following Christ. Undeniably, it may be the most courageous decision we'll ever witness. They are today's heroes of faith!

During my second church-planting venture, I spent time "farming" the community. That is church planters' jargon for walking and knocking on doors, dropping a whole lot of seeds in neighborhoods and seeing what comes up. Because I was in a new suburban area with many new residents, this approach worked. I spent three to four hours a day knocking on doors, taking a survey, and just talking with people. After a while, you get good at reading the community. One day I knocked and a Middle Eastern-looking gal opened and kindly obliged. I guessed right that she was Muslim, and after the survey conversation, I asked, "How are you doing with the five pillars?" (Muslims are required to live out five specific actions).

When she heard my words, her face fell. Like the young rich ruler's face when he heard "the one thing" lacking was to give up everything. She looked at me and said, "I am not doing very good. Many Muslims here do not always practice our faith." I looked at her with compassion and responded, "That sounds like you are in trouble." With Islam, an unsubmitted life equates to probable damnation. I could tell she felt both the guilt and fear of being under a law she had not lived. I never delight in being the heavy, and hated to highlight her perceived predicament, but did so because I wanted to create a contrast with Christianity. I proceeded to share with her about grace. I watched her eyes light up from my story, and the way of Christ. Grace! I wish I could say she bowed a knee to Jesus right there, but it was never my expectation.

She has to face Jesus's words when he challenges people to love him above even their family. "If anyone comes to me and does not hate father and mother, wife and children, brothers and sisters—yes, even life itself—such a person cannot be my disciple" (Luke 14:26). She will have to break from her family's faith. I believe she wanted to. Someone will have to come alongside and help her see more of the truth, and inspire her courage to rise above the cultural backlash and ostracism. When the opportunity is there, we need to make significant investment for their souls. The chances of reaching them in North America are higher than in Muslim countries. A 2011 survey indicated that over the last decade mosques in the U.S. have proliferated 74 percent with 2,106 mosques popping up in urban and suburban locals.[10] When it comes to penetrating the veil of Islam, this is awesome news!

Jewish or Muslim people who become Christians will have strategic influence. The investment is worth it. Interviewing the director of an Iranian church planting mission, she told me those reached in Iran immediately share Christ. The description of the underground movement sounded similar to the early church, as a liberating truth percolates beneath religious oppression. The Iranian Christians carried "before and after" photos to show people. This is how I was "before" I became a Christian—this is what I'm like "after." The difference from oppression to joy was so real that it radiated into their countenances! Yet there is tremendous fear in spreading the faith. Fellow Christians, we need to stand with these heroes of our time. The Jews, Muslims, and those of Eastern faiths too, who give up all to embrace Jesus should be celebrated and supported!

PLANT SEEDS AND PRAY

In the raging spiritual battle, we know that God must open hearts for an honest search. If the people we reach out to become earnest investigators,

10. O'Brien, "U.S. Mosques grow 74 percent in Decade," lines 1–7.

they can then discover strong evidence for the Christian faith. If they do not open their hearts and minds, they will probably not be reached. This is disturbing! We need to befriend, love them, plant seeds and pray. In a conversation with a Muslim Christian, I asked about how he went about evangelizing other Muslims. It impressed me on how he appealed with simple logic. He asked me, "Who wrote the New Testament?" I wasn't sure what he was getting at—but he jumped in pointing out that they were fishermen. He then asked, "What is the biggest selling book in the world?" "Obviously, it's the Bible." He then said, "How do we explain that fishermen wrote the best-selling book if God was not behind it?" He also stated he will talk to his Muslim friends about Mohammed's life and the people he killed. He then asks, "Would God have to do it that way?"

I remember in college talking to a Muslim who expressed, "You know what intrigues me about Christianity—you have all those stories of lives changing. In Islam, we don't have any of those." What a reflection! I seized on it, and tried to connect the dots even stronger by saying the changed lives revealed God's authentic move in Christianity. He was early in his questioning, but what an observation he had made!

We need to listen and learn. I have included a number of book resources in the Addendum about reaching specific types. Don't be afraid to dive in. There are some amazing Jewish, Muslim, Hindu, Buddhist and Animist people out there for us to befriend. Jesus loves them! We need to love them too, and do all we can to bring them and their friends into eternal life. Each person reached from another faith is punching a hole in a veil of darkness. May we help fulfill Jesus's words when he declared, "I am the light of the world."

DISCUSSION & ENGAGEMENT

1. Please share what you know about people from other religions.

2. The author talks about understanding their basic beliefs, and their adherence level. Why does that make sense?

3. Why do you think it might be easier to reach someone from another religion if they live in North America?

4. What is the most courageous decision you have made? How does it compare with the person coming out of another religion?

21

Our Time

*Don't wait for extraordinary opportunities. Seize common occasions
and make them great. Weak men wait for opportunities; strong men
make them.*

—ORISON SWETT MARDEN

As a sport enthusiast, I have my rack of memories of where I was when
something awesome went down. Of all those imprints, none stands
out as prominently as the 1980 Winter Olympics in Lake Placid, New York.
The "Do you believe in miracles?" hockey story. Disney Pictures created an
inspirational movie about an unforgettable moment for many. One of the
things I liked about the flick was how it was not so much about the team,
but rather, the coach. Someone first had to dream bigger than what anyone
expected. Herb Brooks took on the challenge of designing a program to
beat the Soviet Union's heralded hockey machine. None of it would have
happened without him. Before the big game, the movie depicts his speech
to the players. It reflected a culmination of vision reaching for realization:
"You were born to be hockey players. If we played them ten times, they
might beat us nine—but not tonight. This is your time!"

Christian friend, do you realize what time it is? How fitting that Peter
used Joel's prophecy to bookend what he titles "the last days." Beginning

with the outpouring of God's Spirit at Pentecost, it ends with dramatic Tribulation imagery—from fiery tongues to fiery skies. In between these markers is the age of grace—a time when "everyone who calls on the name of the Lord will be saved" (Acts 2:17–21). Pastor Wayne Cordeiro writes, "When we get to heaven, we will see wonderful things: golden streets, mansions, angels, cherubim and seraphim . . . but let me tell you one thing we will never see again. We will never see another non-Christian."[1]

The time to reach people is now! It is our time. Allow me to get personal. How much does this idea grip your life? What level would you rate your missional conviction? Does the Lord approve? Or would he raise it higher to meet the challenge of our moment?

Seeing the gospel spreading through the apostles, the Jewish authorities tried to invoke a gag order, "It's fine for you guys to be out here doing this, we just have one little rule for you to follow. You know that long-haired fellow—what was his name again?—you know that guy you hung out with. As you go around just don't say anything about—him." Look at their response. "But Peter and John replied, 'We cannot help speaking about what we have seen and heard'" (Acts 4:20). I love the word: "cannot!" Might as well tell us not to breathe, eat or sleep. It's seared into our souls—we must share.

Their "cannot" expression reminded me of a visit to the catacombs outside Rome. These underground burial chambers in Europe are significant to Christians because the early church used them to congregate. How exciting to see drawings depicting first-century belief in Christ and the afterlife! How ironic that just outside the Catholic capital, the people at the catacombs refer only to "the Christians."

As much as the history stirred our spirits, after the tour we pulled aside to discuss our favorite part. The woman showing us boxes with bones still in them also described the message Christians believed. As she expounded on the resurrection, we knew this was no mere job or repeated history lesson—our hearts burned listening to her! We told others afterwards, "The best part of the catacombs was the guide. God's Spirit was testifying—it was powerful!"

It made me think of the woman at the well, who left her water jar, because she just had a crazy encounter with a Messiah-claiming man who could actually back it up! Something so deeply authentic resonated in her inflection that this irreputable woman convinced a whole town to look for themselves.

---

1. Cordeiro, *Doing Church as a Team*, 27.

These stories convict me. I know at times my soul-reaching fire has burned low. I have been a distracted, joyless, indifferent, loveless Christian for too many days. Yet when I see the apostles "can't gag me" resolve, the conviction of the guide at the grave, and the excitement of the woman at the well, I want to be passionate for Jesus. I want faith and mission to be something others catch from me—something that is so real that it resonates at my core. Something I don't have to think about—it just oozes from my pores, as natural as the blinking of my eyes. How about you? Is God fanning your heart's flame? I pray so. It is hard to imagine a time more critically needed than now.

FAITH AND MISSION

Building homes in Mexico, we encountered an unexpected problem. Due to space constraints we had framed the roof on the road and then realized we could not get it past the entrance gate. Oops! Racking our brains, the only possible solution was to carry the roof over the roof. I'm not kidding! It was one of the crazier ideas I have bought into. It took all of us, lifting and careening it over a metal gate and under a wire, fighting off neighbor dogs, jumping to the roof, carrying it across, and then scooting it into position at its final resting place. Succeeding, we all sat around exulting saying we will never forget "the roof over the roof."

Even greater joy must have filled four men after lugging a stretcher through a crowd, lifting it onto a roof, and then busting unabashedly through it. The fantastic four's effort succeeded to position a friend before Jesus in a crowded room. Defying our theological constructs, Jesus sees "their faith" and says, "Son, your sins are forgiven" (Mark 2:5). The principle of this text is absolutely clear: *Our faith is directly related to their salvation!* That is a challenging idea: Without your faith in what Jesus can do, your friend may never get saved!

Maybe it's Jesus's out-of-box pattern that keeps us open to the possibilities of an infinite God, who refuses to be defined by our finite human conceptions. As we move toward this book's close, let us remind ourselves of exactly whom we represent. Do you need a miracle to reach your loved one? The supernatural is deity's norm. God is Spirit. He does the miraculous.

I will always recall the time that I made a gargantuan effort with a skeptic. Seeing his locked-up analytical bent, I pulled out my big hammer and took him through some major plank building, only to have him stare at me unfazed. Afterwards, I went into a spiel with my team, telling them how this is going to be a long course of many months journeying alongside Stephen. Everyone needs to be ready to pitch in. Within the next two weeks, unbeknownst to me, my team corralled him, answered his many queries, and led him to Christ. Crossing paths at church, he tells me he is now a Christian! My jaw dropped in humble surprise, saying to myself, "What do I know?" Only that God can turn a heart on a dime! I have learned to never count people out when it comes to God.

Let me catch you up with Michael. He is still journeying, friends. I had hoped when I wrote "The Signature" chapter that we would see the breakthrough. When he faced financial need we coughed up some cash in a faith formation gesture. I still believe it will happen, but not yet. Chris continues the relationship and is increasingly bold regarding his faith. God has his perfect timing for such moments. Michael needs to seek. That is what we keep praying for. When those germinating seeds take root something supernatural will follow. I am envisioning the day when "Pure Evil" turns into potent light!

What was so fantastic about those four guys? They believed their paralyzed friend could be healed. Let me say it again: Faith undergirds mission. We have to believe that God is working. We have to believe that he can turn a heart on a dime, and that he shows up to reach atheists, those from other faiths, and even Satanists! We have to believe that he can use us. He can take sinful human beings and create supernatural stories. We have to believe that his grace reaches farther than any of us can imagine— that the Samanthas of our world are loved beyond measure—and are to be reached, not judged. We have to believe that he is faithful to his own and will never allow the Adversary to get the final word. We have to believe that God goes before us—that he wills fruitfulness, and when we step up to engage with a non-believing friend, the journey will not be in vain. Faith is a huge part of the missional picture. We look forward to a day of celebrating another friend's salvation.

I cannot amply express the lingering, hindering doubt I experienced with this book project. I feared a publisher would not print something from a "recovering sinner" like me. I doubted the writing would be up to snuff. I resisted wrapping my heart tightly around the dream, always qualifying it for myself and others saying, "It may never happen." Yet amid all this doubting haze, I also told people that I sensed God's wind behind it. In my heart, I believed that God had orchestrated all the pieces and given insights to accomplish his perfect will—that my life, marred and imperfect as it was, would be used in his perfect plan. He was simply greater. This faith kept me prodding forward. Kept me hoping. Kept me writing. That is what faith does. It leads us to go after the things of God.

When I neared completion, I could only think of how it was not meant to stay only on my computer. Looking at my stack of rejection letters from publishers, I thought to myself, "Well, that was like throwing a really good incomplete pass." I knew it achieved nothing unless it reached you. As I wrote, I kept thinking of all the awesome grace-oriented Christians who God is positioning for the greatest movement in history. You! All anyone has to do is study the nation-to-globe demographics to realize I am not blowing smoke. We have an opportunity like no other generation. The world has arrived at our doorstep or lies accessibly within reach. Let's start dreaming big!

It's amazing to see what occurs when God stirs our dreams. It happened with me one day holed up at a coastal inn that offers discounts to pastors. I was out of work, and unhireable by most churches in the land. I had walked on at Sandals, just like my college football days, when I was not good enough to get a scholarship. Sitting together with my wife on the rooftop deck we had a deep, once-in-a-lifetime conversation. Having read Mark Batterson's dream-chasing book, *In a Pit with a Lion on a Snowy Day*, we wondered: "What precisely were the lions roaring at us?" And: "What should I go after now?"

In that sobering moment, I redefined the dream saying, "Hundreds of salvations, hundreds of churches helped." That was it. Years later, those words are still written on the top of my office whiteboard. My prototypically security-driven wife stopped me to add her own color commentary. This godly girl wanted to point out that the lions had nothing to do with a job! Instead of that being perceived negatively, we sat basking in a sense of liberation. The financial need staring us down wasn't the greatest thing. Nor was my honor or status at a church. Through the loss and brokenness, God had stripped us to have a moment of pure clarity. We had, spun our own *Inception* totem, so to speak, grasping what is, and what truly matters. As that totem spun its way out, and fell solidly, immovably on the table, it became clear what God wanted to achieve. It was like the Lord said, "Step down from your past pastoral dreams, and start chasing my new one. Let go of all other concerns—pursue your new assignment—and I will be with you."

The occasion solidified the redirection that God had spoken earlier at a conference. I would no longer be the generalist pastor I had been for sixteen years. My life would now align to a single purpose: The evangelistic-missional development of the church. As we served voluntarily in the local context, the conversions began to grow, and with it, a sense of movement. God blessed as we reached to outsiders and multiplied missional disciples. He began to expand my role in consulting with churches to do the same. Lacking financial means, we backed into launching *Soul Whisperer Ministries*. Yet everything I reluctantly backed into, later proved to be God's forward leading. A pastoral colleague, Guy Pfanz, uses a line he learned from his own journey, "God wants it more than we do." He will get you where he wants you to be—no problem. My story is testimony to that truth. So is yours.

GOD GOES BEFORE YOU

God has a plan that is so massive for your life! As we sit at the edge of neo-globalized culture like the world has never before seen, God is positioning *you* for influence. He has chosen you for such a time as this, when a whole world is coming together—a time when we need to meet people of diverse backgrounds precisely where they begin—a time when honest disclosure equates to big-time influence—a time when Christians need to become skilled influencers not merely simplistic tellers. By making the investment to develop the drawing skills throughout this book, God's sovereign call could not be more evident. He wants you to emulate his soul whispering ways. He wants you to become much more like him.

Who are you going to reach? It is incredible to think of the exciting redemptive relationships God has prepared beforehand! (Eph 2:10). Because specifics make something dynamic, consider my 10–100-1,000 rule. May I quickly say these numbers represent names! Every Christian, within their life span, has ten people they can reach directly. No exceptions. Some are family members including children, others friends, and some an outer mission field. If you have the gift of evangelism, God wants you to reach in the hundreds. You need to become highly adept and use your gifting to train others. If you are a proclamation evangelist pastor, the numbers move into the thousands. Granted, most Christians cannot point to many they have led to Christ. I am stunned that Christian leaders do not make relational investment with unsaved people either. Are we so busy doing church work that we forgot the work of the church? Last time I checked my Bible, Jesus did not give "Get out of mission free" cards to anyone. If Jesus didn't relinquish himself from the Father's mission—why would we?

All this really means is that we have work to do. He desires to use *you* as both a messenger and movement catalyst. In the upcoming era, the church must fulfill its equipping mandate. For you who are in leadership, here are a few pertinent questions: What new gospel vehicles will you launch to outer pockets of unreached people? What training must get scheduled to prepare others for engagement? What kinds of experiences need to occur for your people to rise up missionally? What structural projections have to get in place? It is our time to push through barriers that exist in every church. Go break down some doors!

For all my other beloved readers, let's stop for a moment to assess where you have come. You've read another book. Congratulations! Let's be clear, though, on one thing. It will be what you do with it that matters! If you integrate the mission concepts into your life, you will find that these skills hold unusual promise. They should change the way you see and interact with family members, friends, and all those you cross paths with outside church walls. If you put these skills into practice, you will become an influencer for Jesus. Before closing the final pages, please receive five practical affirmations:

First, your commitment to building relationship with unbelievers should now be off the charts. God has some wonderful new friends waiting in the wings. Get out there and get to it! Second, your view of reaching others will now take a process shape. You know that faith formation will require consistent effort and time, and that if you give the gospel seed a chance to grow, God will do miraculous things! Remember to work the process and it will work for you. Third, utilize this book as an ongoing resource. As you engage with your non-believing friends, reread specific sections. In that preparatory vein, you have an assignment to peruse the Addendum at the book's end. This apologetic material will majorly sharpen you! Although you can always dig up answers as you go, increasing your knowledge will build confidence in conversations. Fourth, you now represent the powerful multidimensional gospel. When you interact, you will seek to use its symphonic keys to draw the interest of others. Practice the drawing paradigm: *Start where they are, Read what they need, Know where to take them.* Fifth, following the footsteps of Jesus, you are forever committed to God's mission and the gospel's movement. In this, you are Christ-like. Never forget that with every person you newly disciple that the gospel can then flow to expanding numbers. Do not think of reaching one, when God wants his gospel to penetrate whole relational networks!

I am humbled that God has chosen us fallen vessels to be his ambassadors. Why not the angels? God certainly could enlarge his glory without us. Yet in his design, he determined we would be inextricable players. We're like a bunch of hockey-loving-college-kids called on to take down the evil empire! When I think of Jesus as the soul whisperer, I am moved to make him known. It burns me how others do not give him praise. Yet each time we help someone to faith another worshipper populates our planet.

I saw this profoundly one Sunday when two came to faith. Going into the service they sat in the very first row of the auditorium. If a concert, those would be seats only the wealthy could afford, in spitting distance from the stage. I sat marveling at the sight: new believers having the best seats in the house! It depicted precisely what had occurred—every person reached magnifies exponentially the glory of God. Picture the earth in your minds-eye and then imagine a new light popping up to heaven with every soul. Can you see the light spreading? You love to bring God worship—then why don't you expand his worship through mission?

Jesus's name will be lifted up! The Lord is with us to complete his mission all the way until the end of the age. He promises his words will not return void.

> The voice of the LORD is powerful
> The voice of the LORD is majestic
> The voice of the LORD breaks the cedars
> The LORD breaks in pieces the cedars of Lebanon (Ps 29:4–5).

Your words. God's powerful voice. Amazing! Let the soul whispering begin!

Addendum
Apologetic Support

This is your soul whispering toolbox! Although the content and resources listed are not meant to be comprehensive, they will provide you numerous conversation angles with your questioning friends.

CHAPTER 19: MULTIPLE POINTERS TO GOD:

Creation Design

It was Aristotle who first said, "A design calls for a designer." What we see in the created order theologians call "General Revelation." Romans 1:20 teaches that God has revealed himself to all through what was made. This is the most obvious argument for God that we should not ignore in conversation. We live in a world of wonder! These sensory observations should mirror what David proclaimed in the Psalms when he said, "I am fearfully and wonderful made" (Ps 139:14). How do we best explain the beautiful multi-dimensional design in the created order? Let's help our skeptical friends to open their eyes to this ever-present reality.

In the apologetic resource guide, *The God Questions*, the authors note the banana's intricate design. Here is my simplified adaption of their illustration. You could bring a banana as a discussion prop!

> Hold the banana in your hand. Notice how it fits perfectly. It comes in a non-slip surface so it is easy to hold. Its container is also time sensitive, telling you by color if its contents is ready to eat: Green means too early; brown means too late; yellow means just right. Notice how like a Coke can it has a pop tab at the top. It even makes a sound when you pull it. As you do this, the container opens precisely according to pre-made perforations in its

four sides, which fall gracefully around your hand. Then look how the banana bends toward you and is the size and shape of your mouth. Bite it! It tastes delicious. If you have a yellow one! It also is filled with nutritious, bodybuilding calories, great for muscle movement, and easy for the stomach to digest. Finally, its wrapper is made of biodegradable substances that enrich the soil. If left uneaten it is preprogrammed to reproduce itself into a whole new fruit-bearing plant providing a virtually inexhaustible food source (Seed and Grider, *The God Questions*, 9).

Let's move out from the banana tree to the jungle. What about the worlds "eco-systems" that we keep messing up? Notice how the world is integrated with delicate balance. Our world is not randomly thrown together. Design, by its nature, defies random occurrence. This point can be easily illustrated with a mechanized (non-digital) watch. What is the likelihood of that type of design coalescing by mere accident? What if we dismantled a watch, put all the parts in a bag, and shook it? How long would it take before it became a watch? From basic observation, something with the sophisticated design of a watch cries out for a watchmaker!

Irreducible Complexity

Intelligent design (ID) takes the creation design argument a step further in showing how parts of creation are so complex in function that they could not possibly have evolved. As the knowledge to the creation's complexity escalates, the argument of "Intelligent Design" has become the front line of debate between the proponents of creation and evolution. Intelligent design argues that the creation is too complex to be reduced to an evolutionary process. We see this level of complexity in many life functions such as blood clotting in the human body or the way Celia operate with many animal and lower plant cells (Dembski and Kushiner, *Signs of Intelligence*, 93–96). Another example is the eye with its camera-like abilities.

The mechanics of the eye are "irreducibly complex" because the human eye will only function when multiple interdependent mechanisms work together. Eliminate one part of the eye's mechanics, and it will not perform. Therefore, you cannot reduce the eye's development to evolutionary steps or gradations. In other words, gradual evolutionary change does not logically or sufficiently explain the functionality of the eye.

Sizing Up the "Simple Cell"

Complexity exists in all reproducing life. The movie *Expelled* with Ben Stein uses computer imagery to picture the complexity of the cell. In a poignant moment, Stein asks a scientist about the knowledge we currently possess in comparison to the early assumptions made about the "simple cell." In other words, if the early evolutionists knew what we know now, would they say the cell is simple? The movies answer: "The biological cell with its DNA spiral containing information code is more complex than the universe and anything we could have imagined!" Bill Gates said this, "DNA is like a computer program, but far more advanced than any software we've ever created." The computer imagery in this movie gives a mind-blowing picture to make the point! You might be able to use it for discussion.

Rational Thought

C.S. Lewis, in his essay *Miracles*, asks how the first brain insight or inference evolved. It is amazing how many unexplained assumptions are made by evolutionary theory. (One of the giant leaps of faith of evolutionary theory is that life came into being without an agent or designer). Lewis argues that the step from life to objective thought is a "light year" jump, not possible through an evolutionary process. Reading Lewis can make your head swim. But try to think with him here:

> If there is nothing but Nature, therefore, reason must have come into existence by a historical process. And of course, for the Naturalist, this process was not designed to produce a mental behavior that can find truth. There was no Designer; and indeed, until there were thinkers, there was not truth or falsehood. The type of mental behavior we now call rational thinking or inference must therefore have been 'evolved' by natural selection, by the gradual weeding out of types less fitted to survive. Now natural selection could operate only by eliminating responses that were biologically hurtful and multiplying those which tended toward survival. But it is not conceivable that any improvement of responses could ever turn into acts of insight, or even remotely tend to do so. The relation between response and stimulus is utterly different from that between knowledge and the truth known. (*The Complete C.S. Lewis Signature Classics*, 220).

Addendum

Beauty and Pleasure

How does evolution explain the immerse scope of beauty and pleasure in the world? G. K. Chesterton observed that Christianity is the only worldview that has an explanation for their existence. It could only be a God of goodness who creates a world where its creation finds enjoyment and pleasure (Chesterton, *Orthodoxy*, 57–72; Yancey, *Soul Survivor*, 53–60).

Inherent Meaning

This philosophic argument is powerful because we don't feel like mere evolutionary accidents. On the contrary, we feel like our lives have purpose, meaning and intention. One of the ways to discern if something is true relates to livability. Truth shows itself in real life. If we make a claim that is not consistent to life experience, we should question it. The fact is nobody lives as if they are an accident, or as if their life doesn't matter in a meaningful transcending way. This suggests we are more than what evolution postulates.

Human Nobility

Francis Schaeffer, like Lewis, argues for God's existence from a non-scientific philosophic basis. One example is what he calls, "the nobility of man." Although he fully recognizes man's sin nature, he asks us to wrestle with man's upward capacity. He writes, "There is something great about man." How do we explain that without God? (Schaeffer, *He Is There and He Is Not Silent*, 3–35).

Evolution's Failure

Be aware that people can get "huffy" about the subject of science. Hearts get wrapped around beliefs. You don't want to win the battle and lose the war. You don't have to win, its okay to disagree. If you share a creation science viewpoint, it is possible this will be the first time your skeptic friend hears an alternative view. Many people have bought into evolution "hook, line and sinker." With some you will need to move carefully; you might even ask them for permission to discuss an alternative scientific perspective: "Is it okay for me to share with you why some believe science points toward creation?"

You also have to accept that it will take time for anyone to move from the evolutionary stronghold. With higher education teaching only one viewpoint, people are not trained to think critically, nor are they equipped to interact about conflicting ideas. The first step could be mentioning that there are different interpretations of the scientific data. Here are some worthy discussion points:

- Through our most powerful telescopes, like Hubble, it is scientifically verified that the universe is expanding. This implies a beginning. Although evolutionary scientists have no answer for the creation of this beginning, they deduce from the universe data that a Big Bang occurred. Yet the Big Bang idea does not do full justice to the observable universe that looks nothing of the chaos inherent to a random explosion. To the contrary, we have a universe of sophisticated order; the initial burst brought fine-tuned balance. These balances are so intricate that if we messed with them even slightly, the earth would not sustain life, and the universe could not have become what we have today. Listen to scientist Francis Collins:

> There are 15 constants—the gravitational constant, various constants about the strong and weak nuclear force, etc.—that have precise values. If any one of those constants was off by even one part in a million, or in some cases, by one part in a million million, the universe could not have actually come to the point where we see it. Matter would not have been able to coalesce, there would have been no galaxy, stars, planets or people (Collins, Interview on Salon.com http://www.salon.com/books/int/2006/08/07/collins/index2.html).

In simpler terms, make slight changes to the tilt or rotation of the earth, or distance from the sun and we are in trouble. The same intricate order exists with the fine-tuned molecular balance of matter.

- Although we commonly observe micro-evolution (adaptation of a species), macro-evolution is not observable today. Why don't we see species of animals in transition to other species? Everything we observe is what the Bible describes: "Species reproducing according to their kinds" (Gen 1:24–25).

- The fossil record does not support macro-evolution. The problem with the missing links is that they are still missing! Darwin himself recognized this issue in his observations when he wrote, "Innumerable transition forms must have existed. But why don't we find them embedded in countless numbers in the crust of the earth? Geology assuredly does not reveal such finely graduated organic change and this is perhaps the most obvious and serious objection that can be argued against my theory of evolution." (Darwin, *The Origin of Species*, 503).

Consider how Harvard Professor Steven Gould tries to adapt evolutionary theory to account for the missing links in the fossil record. Gould concludes,

> 120 years of fossil research after Darwin, it has become increasingly clear that the fossil record will not affirm this part of Darwin's predictions—a species does not arise gradually by the gradual transformation of its ancestors. It appears all at once, fully formed.

Gould, a non-Christian scientist, attempts to explain the lack of transitional forms in the fossil record by suggesting one species changes quickly into another species. With this "sudden change" theory he essentially trashes the basic tenets of evolution; no gradual adaptations; no natural selection and survival of the fittest; just sudden change. His radical reach demonstrates how creative people can be to support their own materialistic philosophy. Yet his view of the fossil record is honest! (Gould, "Evolution's Erratic Pace," May 1977).

By its failure to support its own doctrines, and explain the big questions about who we are, evolution itself points to an alternative worldview.

Spiritual Desire.

This is a biblical based philosophic argument that C.S. Lewis developed. In Ecclesiastes 3:9, it says that God placed eternity in the human heart. Most people recognize spiritually related desires. We hunger for something to worship, for righteousness, for an eternal existence, and for ultimate paradise. Lewis argues from logic that hunger and longing give indication to the object's reality. How strange it would be to long for sex, or to hunger for food, if no such thing as sexual relations existed, or if there was no such activity as eating (C.S. Lewis, *The Weight of Glory*, 8–9). Thus, desire for the spiritual is a pointer to the existence of spiritual realities, and ultimately God.

THE FOUR MAJOR PLANKS:

Plank #1: Fulfilled Prophecy

Facts on Fulfilled Prophecy:

- Jesus taught his disciples, "Everything must be fulfilled that is written about me in the Law of Moses, the Prophets, and the Psalms" (Luke 24:44–46).
- Paul presented Jesus in the synagogues using Old Testament Scripture, "As it is written" (Acts 13:33).
- The gospel creed which mentions the resurrection was "according to the Scriptures" (1 Corinthians 15:3–4).
- Matthew's Gospel is written specifically to the Jewish people, showing how Christ's life fulfilled what the Old Testament foretold.

The Jewish Apologetic Defense.

Let's examine how the Jewish people explain away Christological interpretations. One example is from Isaiah 7, where Jewish apologists challenge the translation "virgin" by saying the word means "maid" or "young girl." Though they are right in showing the various uses of the Hebrew word, we should not ignore the additional information within the immediate and wider contexts. Isaiah 7:14 says the child born will be called "Immanuel," which means "God is with us." Also, Isaiah 9 gives further detail as to "who" is being born in Isaiah 7. "For to us a child is born, to us a son is given, and the government will be on his shoulders. And he will be called Wonderful Counselor, Mighty God, Everlasting Father, Prince of Peace. Of the increase of his government and peace there will be no end. He will reign on David's throne and over his kingdom, establishing and upholding it with justice and righteousness from that time on and forever" (Isa 9:6–7). Although these contextual verses do not solve the translation debate over "virgin" they do support a divine birth.

We do have a powerful proof in the prophetic record. As we study the actual passages, prophecy can become a useful tool. One skeptic acknowledged that the detailed scope of fulfilled prophecy was the most convincing proof for the Christian faith.

Addendum

The Old Testament's Savior-Messiah:

- He would be born of a woman (Gen 3:15).
- He would come through the family line of Judah (Gen 49:10; Matt 1:2).
- He would be born of a virgin, and be called Immanuel "God is with us" (Isa 7:14).
- He would be born in the town of Bethlehem (Mic 5:2).
- He would be eternal, from everlasting (Isa 9:6, Mic 5:2).
- He would be a teller of parables (Ps 78:2).
- He would be a light to Gentiles and stumbling block to Jews (Isa 60:3, Ps 118:22).
- He would enter Jerusalem on a young donkey (Zech 9:9).
- He would be a king (Ps 2:6, Zech 9:9).
- He would be betrayed for thirty pieces of silver (Zech 11:12).
- He would be crucified, but no bones would be broken (Ps 22:17).
- He would suffer and be whipped (Isa 53:6).
- He would make atonement for people's sins (Dan 9, Isa 53:4–5).
- He would live on after his death (Ps 16:10, Isa 53:10).

The "Big Three" Prophecies.

Which prophecies are most compelling? Do you know? Here are three that all Christians should have in their back pocket.

#1 PSALM 22.

This "Psalm of the Cross" speaks specifically about crucifixion hundreds of years before it was practiced as a form of capital punishment. History reveals crucifixion was used among the Persians, Seleucids, Carthaginians, and Romans beginning in the sixth century BC (Encyclopedia Britannica, http://www.britannica.com/FBchecked/topic/144583/crucifixion). In the year 337 AD, Emperor Constantine I abolished the practice, out of veneration for Jesus Christ. This Psalm, which makes reference to hands and feet being pierced, is written by David a thousand years before the birth of Christ and four hundred years before crucifixion became a killing method. Additionally, it describes in vivid detail what happened at the crucifixion of Jesus as recorded in the Gospels.

> Specific spoken words of being "forsaken of God." (v 1)
> He is mocked, insulted (v 7)
> He is poured out, bones out of joint, heart has melted within (v 14)
> Encircled by evil men (v 16)
> Pierced hands and feet (v 16)
> No broken bones (v 17)
> Gambling over his garments (v 18)

#2 DANIEL 9.

In this passage the prophet Daniel reveals the timing of Christ's entrance to Jerusalem, his sudden death, and the impact of it. Here is what you need to know to demonstrate the precision of this prophecy.

Date: Sixth century BC.
Daniel lived during the exile of the Jews to Babylon.

Key Verses: "Seventy sevens are decreed for your people and your holy city to finish transgression, to put an end to sin, to atone for wickedness, to bring in everlasting righteousness, to seal up vision and prophecy and to anoint the most holy. Know and understand this: From the issuing of the decree to restore and rebuild Jerusalem until the Anointed One, the ruler, comes, there will be seven and sixty-two sevens" (Dan 9:24–25).

Facts:

- We know precisely when the issuing of the decree happens. Nehemiah 2:1, tells us the specific date: "In the month of Nisan (March) in the twentieth year of King Artaxerxes." Based on the history of the kings that is March, 444 BC.

- Daniel says from the date of this decree it will be 7 and 62 sevens before the Anointed One comes to Jerusalem. This is a way the ancients used to describe years. 69 X 7 = 483 years. Adjusting for the 360-day calendar used in their time period, Daniel says, the Anointed One, the ruler, will come to Jerusalem in March 33 AD. (Hoehner,

Chronological Aspects of the Life of Christ, 115–139). Stop for a moment to appreciate this. Jesus died in his early thirties. The West revised its calendar according to the time of his birth. Look at how precise this prediction is!

In confirmation to Daniel's specific time reference, history has Jesus entering Jerusalem on what we now call Palm Sunday, riding on a foal, which fulfills another prophecy, and being hailed as the Messiah King of the Jews (Zech 9:9). In addition to the timing of his entrance to Jerusalem, Daniel tells us the Anointed One's coming will make atonement for sins, and bring a new covenant of righteousness, and that this will happen by him being "cut off." History tells us he was crucified; theology tells us it was to atone for sins and to establish a new covenant with man.

Interestingly, on the day Jesus enters Jerusalem, he prophecies the coming destruction of Jerusalem including the detail of the city being leveled to the ground. This "raising" happens through Roman General Titus in 70 AD (Luke 19:39–44).

#3 ISAIAH 53.

This text gives us a deeply personal, highly descriptive view of Christ's sacrifice. Take a moment to read it. Isaiah prophesied in the reigns of Uzziah, Jotham, Ahaz, and Hezekiah—dating his writings from 739 to 681 BC. Many have never considered that such a vivid picture of Jesus's life, suffering, crucifixion, atoning death, and resurrection is contained in the Old Testament.

In response to this passage being used to support Christianity, the Jews came up with an alternative explanation, saying the "suffering servant" is the people of Israel not an individual. What looks to us like a slam-dunk is explained away with metaphor that does gymnastics with sound interpretation (hermeneutics), going far beyond its straightforward meaning. For your own sharpening, read the argument by Origen to his Jewish friends in the second century:

> I remember that once in a discussion with some whom the Jews regard as learned I used these prophecies. At this the Jew said that these prophecies referred to the whole people as though of a single individual, since there were scattered into the dispersion and smitten, that as a result of the scattering of the Jews amongst the other nations many might become proselytes. In this way he

explained the text: 'Thy form shall be glorious among men" and 'being a man in calamity.'

I then adduced many arguments in the disputation, which proved that there is no good reason for referring these prophecies about one individual to the whole people. And I asked which person could be referred to in the text: 'This man bears our sins and suffers pain for us' and 'but he was wounded for our transgressions and he was made sick for our iniquities'; and I asked which person fitted the words 'by his stripe we were healed.' Obviously, those who say this were once in their sins, and were healed by the passion of the Savior, whether they foresaw this, and put these words into their mouths by the inspiration of the Holy Spirit. But we seemed to put him in the greatest difficulty with the words, 'because of the iniquities of my people he was led to death.' If according to them the people are the subject of the prophecy, why is this man said to have been led to death because of the iniquities of the people of God? Who is this if not Jesus Christ, by whose stripe we who believe in him were healed, when he put off the principalities and powers among us, and made a show of them openly on the cross? (Origen, *Contra Celsum*, I:55).

Plank #2: Historical Authenticity

Extra Biblical Sources

Although the four detailed historical New Testament accounts of Jesus's life could be sufficient evidence alone, we should not ignore the fact that other historians affirm many details in Scripture. These "outside the Bible" histories provide corroborating evidence to the witnesses. Below are just two examples of many such records:

> Josephus, Jewish Historian: The Arabic text is as follows: "At this time there was a wise man who was called Jesus. And His conduct was good, and [He] was known to be virtuous. And many people from among the Jews and the other nations became His disciples. Pilate condemned Him to be crucified and to die. And those who had become His disciples did not abandon His discipleship. They reported that He had appeared to them three days after His crucifixion and that He was alive; accordingly, He was perhaps the Messiah concerning whom the prophets have recounted wonders." (Josephus, *Antiquities*, XVIII. 33)

Addendum

Plinius Secundus, Pliny the Younger:

As governor of Bithynia in Asia Minor (A.D. 112), Pliny was writing the Emperor Trajan seeking counsel as to how to treat the Christians. He explained that he had been killing both men and women, boys and girls. There were so many being put to death that he wondered if he should continue killing anyone who was discovered to be a Christian, or if he should kill only certain ones. He explained that he had made the Christians bow down to the statues of Trajan. He goes on to say that he also "made them curse Christ, which a genuine Christian cannot be induced to do."

In the same letter he says of the people who were being tried:

> They affirmed, however, that the whole of their guilt, or their error, was that they were in the habit of meeting on a certain fixed day before it was light, when they sang in alternate verse a hymn to Christ as to a god, and bound themselves to a solemn oath, not to any wicked deeds, but never to commit any fraud, theft, adultery, never to falsify their word, not to deny a trust when they should be called upon to deliver it up (Secundus, *Epistles*, X. 96).

Reasons To Believe the New Testament's Reliability:

Multiple Eye Witnesses.

The four Gospel writers were either Christ's actual disciples or closely related to the eyewitnesses. The account of Jesus's life was not made up by one person off in a cave somewhere. Nor was it a dictation from God unconnected to history and verifiable events. Each account was a testimony of what happened, having been observed by multiple eyewitnesses. No one possessed the exclusivity to just make things up about an eminent public figure like Jesus. All four accounts are consistent with each other as to the main events while providing different views and details. The multiplicity of accounts substantiates that this is indeed history.

Early Writings

Many scholars concede the book of Acts must have been written before 60 AD, because its author, Luke, did not reference major historical events occurring afterwards. If Luke had been writing during the 60s, he would certainly have contained information about the deaths of his three main characters—Peter, James and Paul—who all died between 61–65 AD. Instead, the book of Acts ends with Paul alive awaiting trial. Additionally, a war between the Romans and Jews occurred in 66 AD, as well as Emperor Nero's infamous persecution of Christians in the mid-60s. None of these big events are mentioned, nor the destruction of the Jewish temple in 70 AD by the Roman General Titus. These omissions in Luke, who characteristically used time markers, have lead scholars to back the pre-60 AD dating. Since the book of Acts is the second part of a two-part work, the first part, which is the biography of Jesus, Luke's Gospel, must have come even earlier. Luke writes each work to the same addressee "Theophilus" (Luke 1:1–4; Acts 1:1–4).

Corroborating, most scholars believe Paul's letters date before the Gospel writers, which puts the New Testament's origination extremely close to the actual events. The significance is that an early record counters the notion of fabricated, legend-like information evolving. In essence, early writings had to match eyewitness testimony. For instance, Paul wrote of hundreds who had witnessed the resurrection who were still living (1 Cor 15:1–3). If people witness a significant public event and a writer spins something contrary, that account would be subject to serious scrutiny and rejection. In sum, with so many witnessing the events of Jesus's life, the New Testament writers had to be accurate to be credible for their own time.

Can you see how the combination of multiple authors, the public nature of Jesus's life, and early writings support an accurate history?

ACCURATE DETAILS

New Testament historical details align with modernized knowledge. In *The Case for Christ*, Lee Strobel tells of the Apostle John's observation of blood and water coming forth from Jesus's body when speared by the Roman soldier (John 19:34). This remote detail fits with modern medical knowledge of how water fills the heart of a person dying from asphyxiation, the cause of death during crucifixion. According to medical journals, when asphyxiation takes place the heart fills with a water based "periodic fluid." John, in the first century, could not have been aware of this medical insight. Yet the Bible contains a description that is perfectly consistent with a CSI-like explanation. How is that so? The answer is simple. He didn't know human anatomy, he just recorded what he saw. These kinds of details affirm the New Testament's authenticity (Strobel, *The Case of Christ*, 198–200).

EMBARRASSING DETAILS

The New Testament also demonstrates authenticity in how it reflects the failures of the early disciples. If these writers fabricated the facts, why would they make themselves look bad? Instead, we see their lives displayed with embarrassing flaws. The leader of the movement, Peter, makes major missteps. Richard Bauckham reasons that Peter himself must have provided the detailed information of his denials (Baukham, *Jesus and the Eyewitnesses*, 170–78). Why would he do that if the New Testament writings were a fabrication for his personal agenda? (Thank God for this real life picture! It helps us to see the Christian faith as the message of grace to fallen sinners, like you and me).

Contrary to the notion of the disciples conjuring a record for wide acceptance, the New Testament includes details unpopular to first-century biases. For example, why in a male dominated culture, were the lowly regarded women the first to see Jesus resurrected? (Luke 20:11–18). Certainly this part of the story would have been edited out, if the writers wanted to make the strongest case. And why include the disciples' doubting? These types of details are counterproductive to their message. Why during the crucifixion do they have Jesus declaring that God had abandoned him? Clearly this would have offended the highly religious people in the first century. Yet the New Testament authentically provides a detailed story that is not always easy to accept. This, in itself, is a powerful reason to believe in the record's reliability (Keller, *The Reason for God*, 105).

CONFIRMING ARCHEOLOGY

Archeology, like science, is open to interpretation. At times these ground explorers have questioned the veracity of biblical statements. What is fascinating to observe, however, is how new digs so often affirm the Bible. Some secular archeologists have made statements against scriptural claims only to be refuted by later discoveries. We should first note that the basic picture of the world presented in the Bible is supported from history and archeology. That ought to say something to any questioner. The Christian faith is rooted to history. The big picture of empires, people groups, issues and conflicts are all fairly represented in Scripture. Also, one of the

Gospel writers, a doctor named Luke, turns out to be a first rate historian. Although each Gospel is history, Luke pays significant attention to the historic time period in which he writes. The many details about those in authority, and what was occurring at the time, give him high marks for accuracy with notable historians.

After his own investigation of Luke's record, one of the greatest archeologists who ever lived, Sir William Ramsey said, "Luke is a historian of the first rank; not merely are his statements of fact trustworthy . . . this author should be placed along with the very greatest of historians." Yet because of Luke's detail, critical secular archeologists question his claims. Take a look at few definitive examples as listed by Josh McDowell in *Ready Defense*:

- Critics argued Luke got it entirely wrong with all the events around Jesus's birth (Luke 2:1–3). They said there was no census, Quirinius was not governor of Syria, and everyone did not return to his ancestrial home. Discoveries then revealed the Romans did indeed keep taxpayer records and had censuses every fourteen years. Then, an inscription was found in Antioch ascribing Quirinius to be the governor. It turns out this man was governor twice —once in 7 BC, and then in 6 AD. Finally, a papyrus found in Egypt contained directions for a census, which included the return to the place of their family of origin. The same kind of substantiation occurs with other critical disputes.

- Luke refers to Lysanias the Tetrarch of Abilene (Luke 3:1). Again, critics see this as a fabrication, until an inscription dated between 14 and 29 AD was found near Damascus: "Freedman of Lysanias the Tetrarch." Other regional designations are questioned, and then a new find shows Luke, again, was right.

- Luke is also accurate on cultural details. In Acts 21 he mentions the Jews accusing Paul of bringing Greeks into the temple. One discovery in Jerusalem that now resides in Istanbul, is a Greek inscription which reads:

  NO FOREIGNER MAY ENTER WITHIN THE BARRICADE
  WHICH SURROUNDS THE TEMPLE AND ENCLOSURE.
  ANYONE WHO IS CAUGHT DOING SO WILL HAVE HIM
  TO THANK FOR HIS ENSUING DEATH. (McDowell, *Ready Defense*, 108–11).

Addendum

The Dead Sea Scrolls Significance

In 2007, the Dead Sea Scrolls came to San Diego. The 1947 discovery by an Arab boy has been heralded as the greatest archeological discovery of the modern period. The scrolls date before the time of Christ. The main takeaway from the Dead Sea Scrolls from a Christian viewpoint is that the writings of Scripture have not been changed through the centuries. As one example, the entire 66 chapters of Isaiah found at the Dead Sea revealed a virtual match with what we have in today's Bible (Pfeiffer, *The Dead Sea Scrolls and the Bible*, 103–9).

Notable New Testament Facts:

- The high number of early New Testament copies (24,000) secures its translation integrity (McDowell, *A Ready Defense*, 44–47).

- The entire New Testament can be recreated by pulling verse references from the writings of the second-century Apostolic Fathers.

Plank #3: The Resurrection

A recent documentary produced by James Cameron (The Titanic producer) called *the Lost Tomb of Jesus* suggests that Jesus's body was never raised. The basis for Cameron's thesis was that a tomb with several ossuaries in it had been found in Jerusalem. Death in the ancient world was a two-stage process. When someone died, the body was placed in a tomb or a cave. Then, after a period of time, the bones would be collected and put in a box called an ossuary.

One of the ossuaries in this particular tomb had the name "Joseph" inscribed on it; one of them had the name "Mary"; and one of them may have had the name "Jesus," but the name was a little hard to decrypt. The documentary claims that these ossuaries indicate that Jesus was never resurrected. Interestingly, scholars have actually known about the tomb since its discovery in 1980. None of the scholars involved, Christian or not, thought there was even a remote chance that it was the tomb of the family of Jesus of Nazareth, partly because the names were so common in first-century Jerusalem. Tom Wright, a New Testament scholar, says that they are so common that finding a tomb with those names on the ossuaries would be much like finding a New York phone directory with the names John and Sally Smith in it. Nine hundred tombs have been found around Jerusalem over the last century or so, and numbers of them contain ossuaries that are labeled "Jesus, son of Joseph." (Ortberg, *Faith & Doubt*, 94–95).

Ortberg shares other reasons why Cameron's thesis should not have aired: Joseph in the Bible lived in Nazareth, not Jerusalem. For a comparison of eyewitness testimony bias between that of the Titanic and the resurrection, see my blog: "A Titanic Mistake" (http://soulwhispererministry.com/misc/a-titanic-mistake).

RESURRECTION FACTS:

- The Resurrection is foundational to Christian beliefs. Paul declared that if Jesus did not rise from the dead our faith is futile (1 Cor 15:14).

- Jesus himself predicted he would rise from the dead saying it plainly many times over (Mark 10:32–34). He talked about the sign of Jonah referencing the number of days in the earth. The Jews misunderstood when he said, "Tear down this temple and I will raise it in three days," thinking he was referring to the temple in Jerusalem, not his body.

- People have become Christians through researching the resurrection. Frank Morison set out to disprove the Resurrection and ended up following Christ. He wrote the book, *Who Moved the Stone?* Professor Thomas Arnold, who authored the famous 3 Volume *History of Rome,* was appointed the head of Modern History at Oxford said this:

   Thousands and tens of thousands of persons have gone through it (the evidence) piece by piece, as carefully as every judge summing up on a most important cause. I have myself done it many times over, not to persuade others but to satisfy myself. I have been used for many years to study the histories of other times, and to examine and weigh the evidence of those who have written about them, and I know of no one fact in the history of mankind which is proved by better and fuller evidence of every sort, to the understand of a fair inquirer) than the great sign which God hath given us that Christ died and rose again from the dead.

- The disciples renewed courage came from their story that Christ rose from the dead. Most of the disciples were killed as a result of this belief. On the theory that the disciples propagated a lie:

Who would says to themselves and to each other, "We know this resurrection didn't really happen; we know we're going to have to lie about it for the rest of our lives, acting in complete disobedience to all Jesus taught us about telling the truth; we know we're going to be persecuted and probably die for this lie; we know we've got nothing to gain and everything to lose; we know we'll never be able to respect ourselves or look each other in the eye again; we know that the religion we're inventing will be a complete sham; we know we'll be judged eventually by God for all this; and we know we don't have to do this. But we're going to get our stories together and tell them to the ends of the earth anyway. We're all going to give the same false report—all the way to prison or until we die as we stand united for this myth. Is everybody in?" Can you imagine it? I can't. What would have been the upside? The real truth is this: *Nobody dies for what they know to be a lie.* (Mittelberg, *Choosing Your Faith*, 211–12).

- "Why would the disciples of Jesus have come to the conclusion that his crucifixion had not been a defeat but a triumph—unless they had seen him risen from the dead?" (Keller, *The Reason for God*, 208).

Plank #4: Jesus

When C.S. Lewis became wearied of hearing people say Jesus was merely a good teacher, he clarified that Jesus's claims make him a radical far beyond the "good" title:

I am trying here to prevent anyone saying the really foolish thing that people often say about Him. "I'm ready to accept Jesus as a great moral teacher, but I don't accept His claim to be God." That is the one thing we must not say. A man who was merely a man and said the sort of things Jesus said would not be a great moral teacher. He would either be a lunatic—on a level with the man who says he is a poached egg—or else he would be the Devil of Hell. You must make a choice. Either this man was, and is, the Son of God: or else a madman or something worse. You can shut him up for a fool, you can spit at Him, and kill Him as a demon; or you can fall at His feet and call Him Lord and God. But let us not come with any patronizing nonsense about His being a great human teacher. He has not left that open to us. He did not intend to. (Lewis, *Mere Christianity*, 55–56).

EXPERIENCE THE WORDS OF JESUS

A college minister had an effective approach for reaching people. He would give non-believing students a Bible with the words of Jesus in red, and make the challenge to read them all. Have you ever done this? You should not underestimate its impact. He saw scores of college students drawn by this evangelistic technique.

Some people say that there was never a man with Jesus's integrity; he was sinless therefore we should believe in him. Though this is true, what is most compelling about Jesus is not as much his integrity, as it is his authority. In fact, that is what we see stated repeatedly in the Gospels (Matt 7:28–29; Mark 2:8–12). When he spoke the people were amazed because his words had the authoritative ring! If Jesus was indeed the God-man, we would only expect this to be so.

Have your non-believing friend read through the red letters of Luke chapters 12–15 and then ask them, "Who speaks like this? Is this a normal human being? What kind of person speaks with authoritative conviction on spiritual and heavenly matters? What sort of human being has such insight?" With earnest examination, many will be induced into reckoning that his words derive not from this world, but from above. In sum, there is no other religious teacher who claimed to be God, and had the wisdom, authority, and life to back it up. In fact, if we were going to attempt to make up a fictional person like Jesus, and gathered all the smartest creative people on the planet, we would not be able to produce the stories, truth, and wisdom that we find in his words. Does not this fact alone scream out who he is!

The great British apologist Donald Soper,

> I can't argue you to belief in Jesus Christ; what I have tried to do is to offer you reasonable grounds for taking him seriously. The next step is with you. I can't prove that He is the Master—He alone can do that, and He will. If you will really get to know this Jesus of History, you will find that He is the explanation of all that He taught and the vindication of every claim He made (Soper, *Tower Hill*, 70).

CHAPTER 20: RESOURCES

Below are a number of book resources for reaching people from other religions:

Addendum

General Apologetics

Keller, Timothy J. *The Reason for God : Belief in an Age of Skepticism*. New York: Dutton, 2008.

McDowell, Josh, and Bill Wilson. *The Best of Josh McDowell: A Ready Defense*. Nashville: T. Nelson, 1993.

Prothero, Stephen. *God is Not One: The Eight Rival Religions That Run the World—and Why Their Differences Matter*. New York: HarperOne, 2010.

Lewis, C. S. *Mere Christianity*. Macmillan paperback ed. New York: Macmillan, 1960.

Mittelberg, Mark. *Choosing Your Faith : In a World of Spiritual Options*. [s.l.]Carol Stream: Willow Creek Resources;Tyndale House Publishers, 2008.

Stark, Rodney. *The Rise of Christianity: A Sociologist Reconsiders History*. Princeton: Princeton University Press, 1996.

Stark, Rodney. *Discovering God: The Origins of the Great Religions and the Evolution of Belief*. 1st ed. New York: HarperOne, 2007.

Strobel, Lee. *The Case for Christ : A Journalist's Personal Investigation of the Evidence for Jesus*. Grand Rapids: Zondervan, 1998.

Wilder Smith, A. E. *Let Us Reason*. Pro Universitate e.V., Roggern, CH-3646 Eigigen, Switzerland and T.W.F.T. Publishers, 1987.

Wright, N. T. *The Resurrection of the Son of God* Christian Origins and the Question of God. London: SPCK, 2003.

Wright, N. T. *Evil and the Justice of God*. Downers Grove: IVP Books, 2006.

Wright, N. T. *Simply Christian: Why Christianity Makes Sense*. 1st ed. [San Francisco, Calif.]: HarperSanFrancisco, 2006.

Jewish

Brown, Michael L. *Answering Jewish Objections to Jesus*. Grand Rapids: Baker Books, 2000.

Fruchtenbaum, Arnold G. *Jesus Was a Jew*. Nashville: Broadman Press, 1974.

Rubin, Barry. *You Bring the Bagels, I'll Bring the Gospel*. Old Tappan, N.J.: Chosen Books, 1989.

Islam

Coplestone, F. S. *Jesus Christ or Mohammed: A Guide to Islam and Christianity that Helps Explain the Differences*. Christian Focus Publications, 2006.

Gabriel, Mark A. *Jesus and Mohammed: Profound Differences and Surprising Similarities*. Charisma House Publishers, 2004.

Stark, Rodney. *Discovering God: The Origins of the Great Religions and the Evolution of Belief*. 1st ed. New York: HarperOne, 2007.

Hinduism

Gidoomal, Ram, and Margaret Wardell. *Chapatis For Tea: Reaching Your Hindu Neighbour: A Practical Guide*. Guildford: Highland, 1994.

Corduan, Winfried. *Neighboring Faiths: A Christian Introduction to World Religions*. Downers Grove: InterVarsity Press, 1998.

Mangalwadi, Vishal. *The World of Gurus: A Critical Look at the Philosophies of India's Influential Gurus and Mystics*. Rev. ed. Mumbai: GLS, 1999.

Buddhism

Chanthavongsouk, Inta. *Buddha's Prophecy of the Messiah*. La Mirada: Lao Conference of Churches, 1999.

Lim, David, and Paul H. Neui. *Communicating Christ in the Buddhist World*. Pasadena: William Carey Library, 2006.

Thirumalai, M. S. *Sharing Your Faith with a Buddhist*. Minneapolis: Bethany House Publishers, 2003.

Atheism

Dawkins, Richard. *The God Delusion*. Boston: Houghton Mifflin, 2006.

Dembski, William A., and James M. Kushiner. *Signs of Intelligence: Understanding Intelligent Design*. Grand Rapids: Brazos Press, 2001.

Dembski, William A., and Jonathan Wells. *The Design of Life: Discovering Signs of Intelligence in Biological Systems*. Dallas: Foundation for Thought and Ethics, 2008.

Hitchens, Christopher. *God Is Not Great: How Religion Poisons Everything*. 1st ed. New York: Twelve, 2007.

Ortberg, John. *Faith & Doubt*. Grand Rapids: Zondervan, 2008.

Schaeffer, Francis A. *He Is There and He Is Not Silent*. Wheaton: Tyndale House Publishers, 1972.

Wilder-Smith, A. E. *The Natural Sciences Know Nothing of Evolution*. Pro Universitatee.V., Roggern, CH-3646 Eigigen, Switzerland and T.W.F.T. Publishers, 1981.

Bibliography

Alcoholics Anonymous: The Story of How Many Thousands of Men and Women Have Recovered from Alcoholism. 4th ed. New York City: Alcoholics Anonymous World Services, 2001.

Allender, Dan B. *To Be Told.* Farnham: CWR, 2006.

Arnold, Thomas. *The History of Rome.* Reprinted entire, from the last London ed. New York: D. Appleton & Co., 1846.

Attwood, Tony. *Asperger's Syndrome: A Guide for Parents and Professionals.* London and Philadelphia: Jessica Kingsley, 1998.

Aveling, F. "Atheism." NEW ADVENT: Home. http://newadvent.org/cathen/02040a. htm (accessed May 29, 2012).

Awe & Reverence. Film. Highway Media, "Item #: Awean-0003–016-01076.

Barrs, Jerram. *Learning Evangelism From Jesus.* Wheaton: Crossway Books, 2009.

Batson, Wayne Thomas. *The Door Within.* Nashville: Transit, 2005.

Batterson, Mark. *In a Pit With a Lion on a Snowy Day.* Sisters: Multnomah, 2006.

Bauckham, Richard. *Jesus and the Eyewitnesses: The Gospels as Eyewitness Testimony.* Grand Rapids: William B. Eerdmans, 2006.

Bergreen, Laurence. *Over the Edge of the World: Magellan's Terrifying Circumnavigation of the Globe.* New York: Morrow, 2003.

Bloom, Allan David. *The Closing of the American Mind: How Higher Education Has Failed Democracy and Impoverished the Souls of Today's Students.* New York: Simon and Schuster, 1987.

Boorstin, Daniel J. *The Discoverers.* New York: Vintage Books, 1985.

Booth, William. "Reality is Only an Illusion, Writers Say." Washington Post (Washington DC), August 10, 2004, sec. C.

Braveheart. Film. Directed by Mel Gibson . Hollywood: Paramount Pictures, 1995.

Brown, Brene. "Listening to Shame." Keynote speech, TED Conference from TED, Hazeldon, March 16, 2012.

Brown, Brene. "The Power of Vulnerability." Keynote speech, TED Conference from TED, Houston, June 1, 2010.

Brown, Matt. "Gospel of John" Message, Sandals Church, February 10, 2010.

Calvin, Jean. *Commentary on a Harmony of the Evangelists, Matthew, Mark, and Luke.* Grand Rapids: William B. Eerdmans, 1949.

Campolo, Anthony. *We Have Met the Enemy, and They Are Partly Right.* Waco: Jarrell, 1985.

Chesterton, G. K. *Orthodoxy.* 2007 ed. New York: Barnes & Noble, 2007.

Bibliography

Clinton, Timothy E., and Joshua Straub. *God Attachment: Why You Believe, Act, and Feel the Way You Do About God.* New York: Howard Books, 2010.

Cole, Neil. *Organic Church: Growing Faith Where Life Happens.* San Francisco: Jossey-Bass, 2005.

Collins, Francis. Interview on Salon.com, http://wwwsalon.com/books/int/2006/08/07/collins/index2.html. Last accessed March 22, 2012.

Comer, Gary S. "A Titanic Mistake," Soul Whisperer Ministries. http://soulwhispererministry.com/misc/a-titanic-mistake

Contact. Film. Directed by Robert Zemeckis. Burbank: Warner Bros., 1997.

Coplestone, F. S. *Jesus Christ or Mohammed: The Bible or the Koran?* Fearn: Christian Focus, 2000.

Corbett, Steve, and Brian Fikkert. *When Helping Hurts: How to Alleviate Poverty Without Hurting the Poor— and Yourself.* Chicago: Moody Publishers, 2009.

Cordeiro, Wayne. *Doing Church as a Team.* Rev. and expanded ed. Ventura: Regal Books, 2001.

Crouch, Andy. *Culture Making: Recovering Our Creative Calling.* Downers Grove: IVP Books, 2008.

Curtis, Brent, and John Eldredge. *The Sacred Romance: Drawing Closer to the Heart of God.* Nashville: Thomas Nelson, 1997.

Curwen, Thomas. "Haunted By a Bear Attack." *L.A. Times (Los Angeles)*, November 21, 2008, sec. U.S.

Darwin, Charles. *The Origin of Species by Means of Natural Selection: Or thePreservation of Favored Races in the Struggle for Life[,] and The Descent of Man and Selection in Relation to Sex.* New York: Modern library, 1936.

Dawkins , Richard. "Has the World Changed?— Part 2." Latest US news, world news, sport and comment from the Guardian | guardiannews.com | The Guardian . http://guardian.co.uk (accessed May 18, 2012).

Dawkins, Richard. *The God Delusion.* Boston: Houghton Mifflin, 2006.

Dembski, William A., and James M. Kushiner. *Signs of Intelligence: Understanding Intelligent Design.* Grand Rapids: Brazos Press, 2001.

Downing, David C. *The Most Reluctant Convert: C.S. Lewis's Journey to Faith.* Downers Grove: InterVarsity Press, 2002.

Encyclopedia Britannica, Online ed., "Crucifixion." http://www.britannica.com/FBchecked/topic/144583/crucifixion (accessed June 10, 2010).

Engen, Charles Edward van. *God's Missionary People: Rethinking the Purpose of the Local Church.* Grand Rapids: Baker Book House, 1991.

Expelled. Film. Directed by Nathan Frankowski. Salt Lake City: Rocky Mountain Pictures, 2008.

Ford, Leighton. "Be Agents of Reconciliation." Reformation: The Global Conversation, 2010.

Finney, Charles Grandison. *Lectures on Revivals of Religion.* Cambridge: Belknap Press of Harvard University Press, 1960.

Finochio, Ross. "Nineteenth-Century French Realism." Heilbrunn Timeline of Art History. http://metmuseum.org (accessed November 18, 2011).

Fruchtenbaum, Arnold G. *Jesus Was a Jew.* Nashville: Broadman Press, 1974.

Gladwell, Malcolm. *Outliers: The Story of Success.* New York: Little, Brown and Co., 2008.

Godin, Seth. "The Flipping Point." Seth Godin. http://sethgodin.com (accessed May 17, 2012).

Gould, Stephen J. "Evolutions Erratic Pace," in *Natural History*, 86:12–16, May 1977.

Green, Michael. *Evangelism in the Early Church*. Grand Rapids: William B. Eerdmans, 1970.

Green, Michael. *Thirty Years That Changed the World: The Book of Acts for Today*. Grand Rapids: William B. Eerdmans, 2004.

Guenther, Margaret. *Holy Listening: The Art of Spiritual Direction*. Cambridge: Cowley Publications, 1992.

Hale, J. Russell. *The Unchurched: Who They Are and Why They Stay Away*. San Francisco: Harper & Row, 1980.

Halter, Hugh, and Matt Smay. *The Tangible Kingdom: Creating Incarnational Community*. San Francisco: Jossey-Bass, 2008.

Hamilton, G. H. *Manet and His Critics*. Norton: [s.n.], 1969.

Harris, Sam. *The End of Faith: Religion, Terror, and the Future of Reason*. New York: W.W. Norton & Co., 2004.

Hesselgrave, David J.. *Paradigms in Conflict: 10 Key Questions in Christian Missions Today*. Grand Rapids: Kregel Publications, 2005.

Hiebert, Paul G. *Transforming Worldviews: An Anthropological Understanding of How People Change*. Grand Rapids: Baker Academic, 2008.

Hirsch, Alan. *The Forgotten Ways: Reactivating the Missional Church*. Grand Rapids: Brazos Press, 2006.

Hirsch, Alan, and Lance Ford. *Right Here, Right Now: Everyday Mission for Everyday People*. Grand Rapids: Baker Books, 2011.

Hoehner, Harold W. *Chronological Aspects of the Life of Christ*. Grand Rapids: Zondervan, 1977.

Hunter, George G. *How to Reach Secular People*. Nashville: Abingdon Press, 1992.

Hunter, George G. *Radical Outreach: The Recovery of Apostolic Ministry and Evangelism*. Nashville: Abingdon Press, 2003.

Hybels, Bill. "Reasons for Believing in Jesus Christ" message, 1994.

Hybels, Bill. *Just Walk Across the Room: Simple Steps Pointing People to Faith*. Grand Rapids: Zondervan, 2006.

Inception. Film. Directed by Christopher Nolan. Burbank: Warner Bros., 2010.

Janson, H. W. *History of Art; A Survey of the Major Visual Arts from the Dawn of History to the Present Day*. New York: Abrams, 1962.

Jensen, Richard A. *Thinking in Story: Preaching in a Post-Literate Age*. Lima: C.S.S. Pub., 1993.

Johnson, Paul. *Modern Times: The World from the Twenties to the Eighties*. New York: Harper & Row, 1983.

Josephus, Flavius, William Whiston, and Charles F. Pfeiffer. *The Works of Flavius Josephus*. Grand Rapids: Baker Book House, 1974.

Keller, Timothy J. *The Reason for God: Belief in an Age of Skepticism*. New York: Dutton, 2008.

Kennedy, D. James. *Evangelism Explosion*. 3d ed. Wheaton: Tyndale House Publishers, 1970.

Kimball, Dan. "Why Justice Requires Evangelism." Outreach, September 2010.

Kinnaman, David, and Gabe Lyons. *Unchristian: What a New Generation Really Thinks About Christianity— and Why It Matters*. Grand Rapids: Baker Books, 2007.

Bibliography

Kinnaman, David, and Aly Hawkins. *You Lost Me: Why Young Christians are Leaving Church— and Rethinking Faith.* Grand Rapids: Baker Books, 2011.

Kruidenier, William M., Max Anders, and Kenneth Boa. *Holman New Testament Commentary - Romans.* Nashville: B & H Group, 2000.

Lady in the Water. Film. Directed by M. Night Shyamalan. Burbank: Warner Bros., 2006.

Lewis, C. S.. *Mere Christianity.* New York: Collier/Macmillan, 1943.

Lewis, C. S.. *The Complete C.S. Lewis Signature Classics.* San Francisco: HarperSan Francisco, 2002.

Lewis, C. S. *The Weight of Glory and Other Addresses.* New York: Macmillan, 1949.

Lewis, C. S. *The Four Loves.* New York: Harcourt, Brace, 1960.

Lost. Film. Directed by J.J. Abrams. Burbank: Buena Vista Home Entertainment, 2004.

Lupton, Robert D. *Compassion, Justice, and the Christian Life: Rethinking Ministry to the Poor.* Ventura: Regal Books, 2007.

MacDonald, Gordon. *Rebuilding Your Broken World.* Nashville: Oliver-Nelson Books, 1988.

Miracle. Film. Directed by Gavin O'Connor. Burbank: Walt Disney Pictures, 2004.

McDowell, Josh, and Bill Wilson. *The Best of Josh McDowell: A Ready Defense.* Nashville: T. Nelson, 1993.

McGavran, Donald A. *The Bridges of God: A Study in the Strategy of Missions.* New York: Friendship Press, 1955.

McRaney, Will. *The Art of Personal Evangelism: Sharing Jesus in a Changing Culture.* Nashville: Broadman & Holman, 2003.

Miller, Donald. *Blue Like Lazz: Nonreligious Thoughts on Christian Spirituality.* Nashville: T. Nelson, 2003.

Miller, Donald. "How to Tell a Good Story with Your Life." Donald Miller. http://donaldmiller.com (accessed March 21, 2012).

Mittelberg, Mark. *Choosing Your Faith: In a World of Spiritual Options.* Carol Stream: Tyndale House, 2008.

Montgomery, John Warwick. *History & Christianity.* Downers Grove: InterVarsity Press, 1971.

Morison, Frank. *Who Moved the Stone?: A Skeptic Looks at the Death and Resurrection of Christ.* Grand Rapids: Zondervan, 2002.

Mowat, Farley. *The Snow Walker.* Boston: Little, Brown, 1975.

Murphree, Jon Tal. *A Loving God & a Suffering World: A New Look at an Old Problem.* Downers Grove: InterVarsity Press, 1981.

Myers, Bryant L. *Walking with the Poor: Principles and Practices of Transformational Development.* Maryknoll: Orbis Books, 1999.

Nagel, Thomas. "The Fear of Religion." The New Republic. http://tnr.com (accessed November 14, 2011).

Newbigin, Lesslie. *The Open Secret: An Introduction to the Theology of Mission.* Rev. ed. Grand Rapids: William B. Eerdmans, 1995.

New World Encyclopedia, Online ed., s.v. "Realism ." St. Paul: Paragon House, 2008.

Nida, Eugene A. *Message and Mission: The Communication of the Christian Faith.* Rev. ed. Pasadena: William Carey Library, 1990.

O'Brien, Matt. "Survey: U.S. Mosques Grow 74 Percent in Decade." The Press Enterprise (Corona), March 1, 2012, Inland Southern California edition, sec. Nation.

Oden, Thomas C. "The Death of Modernity and Postmodern Evangelical Spirituality." In and *The Challenge of Postmodernism: An Evangelical Engagement*, edited by David D. Dockery. Sun et al., 19–34. Grand Rapids: Baker, 1995.

Olson, David T. *The American Church in Crisis: Groundbreaking Research Based on a National Database of Over 200,000 Churches*. Grand Rapids: Zondervan, 2008.

Origen: *Contra Celsum*. Cambridge: Cambridge University Press, 1980. Secundus, Caius, and Wynne Williams. Correspondence with Trajan from Bithynia: (Epistles X). Warminster: Aris & Phillips, 1990.

Ortberg, John. *Faith & Doubt*. Grand Rapids: Zondervan, 2008.

Ortberg, John. *Who Is This Man? The Unpredictable Impact of the Inescapable Jesus*. Grand Rapids: Zondervan, 2012.

Packer, J. I. *Knowing God*. Downers Grove: InterVarsity Press, 1973.

Parish, Fawn. *Honor: What Love Looks Like*. Ventura: Renew, 1999.

Pascal, Blaise, and Louis Allard. *Pensees*. Translated by Roger Ariew. Indianapolis, IN: Hackett, 2004.

Patterson, Kerry. *Crucial Conversations: Tools for Talking When Stakes are High*. New York: McGraw-Hill, 2002.

Paul, Ian Alan. "Desiring-Machines in American Cinema: What Inception Tells Us About Our Experience of Reality and Film." Senses of Cinema. http://sensesofcinema.com (accessed January 17, 2012).

Pfeiffer, Charles F. *The Dead Sea Scrolls and the Bible*. [Enl. ed. Grand Rapids: Baker Book House, 1969.

Piper, John. *Desiring God: Meditations of a Christian Hedonist*. Sisters: Multnomah Books, 1996.

Poole, Garry. *Seeker Small Groups: Engaging Spiritual Seekers in Life-changing Discussions*. Grand Rapids: Zondervan, 2003.

Prothero, Stephen. *God is Not One: The Eight Rival Religions That Run the World—and Why Their Differences Matter*. New York: Harper One, 2010.

Rainer, Thom. *Surprising Insights From the Unchurched and Proven Ways to Reach Them*. Grand Rapids: Zondervan, 2001.

Reinicke, Melinda. *Parables for Personal Growth: Tales for Your Healing Journey*. San Diego: Recovery Publications, 1993.

Richardson, Rick. *Evangelism Outside the Box: New Ways to Help People Experience the Good News*. Downers Grove: InterVarsity Press, 2000.

Root, Jerry, and Stan Guthrie. *The Sacrament of Evangelism*. Chicago: Moody Publishers, 2011.

Rubin, Barry. *You Bring the Bagels, I'll Bring the Gospel*. Old Tappan: Chosen Books, 1989.

Russell, Terrence. "How Inceptions Astonishing Visuals Came to Life." Wired.com . http://wired.com (accessed January 8, 2012).

Sun-tzu. *The Art of War*. Translated by Ralph D. Sawyer, New York: NY: Fall River Press, 1994.

Schaeffer, Francis A. *He is There and He is Not Silent*. Wheaton: Tyndale House, 1972.

Seed, Hal, and Dan Grider, *The God Questions: Exploring Life's Great Questions About God*. Vista: Outreach, 2007.

Searcy, Nelson, and Jennifer Dykes Henson. *Ignite: How to Spark Immediate Growth in Your Church*. Grand Rapids: Baker Books, 2009.

Shoemaker, Samuel M. *How to Become a Christian*. [1st ed. New York: Harper, 1953.

Bibliography

Snyder, Howard A. *Radical Renewal: The Problem of Wineskins Today*. Houston: Touch Publications, 1996.

Soper, Donald. *Tower Hill, 12. 30*, London: Epworth Press, 1963.

Stanley, Andy and Ed Young. *Can We Do That?* New York: Howard Books, 2002.

Stark, Rodney. *The Rise of Christianity: A Sociologist Reconsiders History*. Princeton: Princeton University Press, 1996.

Stark, Rodney. *Discovering God: The Origins of the Great Religions and the Evolution of Belief*. New York: HarperOne, 2007.

Stearns, Richard. *The Hole in Our Gospel*. Nashville: Thomas Nelson, 2009.

Stenger, Victor J. *God and the Folly of Faith: The Incompatibility of Science and Religion*. Amherst: Prometheus Books, 2012.

Stetzer, Ed.. *Planting New Churches in a Postmodern Age*. Nashville, Tenn.: Broadman & Holman, 2003.

Stetzer, Ed. "The Fear, The Herd, The Witness." Outreach, March 2008.

Stetzer, Ed., and David Putman. *Breaking the Missional Code: Your Church Can Become a Missionary in Your Community*. Nashville: Broadman & Holman, 2006.

Stevenson, Doug. *Doug Stevenson's Story Theatre Method*. Colorado Springs: Cornelia Press, 2003.

Strobel, Lee. *The Case for Christ*. Grand Rapids: Zondervan, 1998.

The Barna Group. "New Marriage and Divorce Statistics Released." The Barna Group - Barna Update. http://barna.org (accessed February 17, 2010).

The Farm: Life Inside Angola Prison. Film. Directed by Jonathan Stack, Liz Garbus and Wilbert Rideau. New York: A & E Home Video, 1998.

The King's Speech. Film. Directed by Tom Hooper. Beverly Hills: Anchor Bay Entertainment, 2011.

The Lord of the Rings: The Fellowship of the Ring. Film. Directed by Peter Jackson. Burbank: New Line Productions, 2001. From Author J.R.R Tolkein.

The Making of Steven Spielberg's Jaws. Film. Directed by Laurent Bouzereau. Grand Rapids: Universal Home Video, 1995.

The Metropolitan Museum of Art. "Nineteenth-Century French Realism." Heilbrunn Timeline of a. http://metmuseum.org (accessed May 16, 2011).

The Princess Bride. Film. Directed by Rob Reiner. Beverly Hills: Twentieth Century Fox Film Corp., 1987.

Thomson, Sarah L., Greg Mortenson, and David Oliver Relin. *Three Cups of Tea*. Young readers ed. New York: Dial Books for Young Readers, 2009.

Walsch, Neale Donald. *Conversations With God: An Uncommon Dialogue*. New York: G.P. Putnam's Sons, 1996.

Wesley, John. "Minutes of Several Conversations," in Samuel Jackson, ed., *The Works of John Wesley*, Grand Rapids: Baker Book House, 1978, 8:303.

Weston, Paul. "Evangelicals and Evangelism" in *Not Evangelical Enough*, ed., Iain Taylor, Carlisle: Paternoster, 2003.

Wilder Smith, A. E. *The Natural Sciences Know Nothing of Evolution*. San Diego: Master Books, 1981.

Willard, Dallas. *The Spirit of the Disciplines: Understanding How God Changes Lives*. San Francisco: Harper & Row, 1988.

Wong, Desmond. "Comparative Analysis: Manet's The Dead Christ With Angels and Basien-Lepage's Joan of Arc." scibd.com. http://scibd.com (accessed April 18, 2011).

Wyhe, John. *Darwin: The Story of the Man and His Theories of Evolution.* London: Andre Deutsch, 2008.

United States Center for Disease Control & Prevention: *Prevalence of Autism Spectrum Disorders: Autism and Development Disabilities Monitoring Network,* Washington: GPO, 2012.

"Vision New England Recent Convert Study." Vision New England. http://visionnewengland.com (accessed October 6, 2011).

Vittone, Mario. "Drowning Looks Different Than You Think." shine.yahoo.com/parenting. http://shine.yahoo.com (accessed May 17, 2012).

Yancey, Philip. *Soul Survivor: How My Faith Survived the Church.* New York: Doubleday, 2001.

Young, Wm. Paul. *The Shack.* Los Angeles: Windblown Media, 2007.

Also by Gary S. Comer

MISSIONAL ENGAGEMENT SERIES:

Empower the People for Mission!

STEPS TO FAITH:

Where Seeking Friends Become Solid Followers

This course leads people through key progressions to come into the faith. It guides nonbelievers to openly explore, resolve head and heart issues, and eventually place their whole trust in the Lord Jesus! *Steps to Faith* can be utilized as a class (4 extendable sessions), or also as a one-to-one guide for church member evangelistic efforts.

BASIC TRAINING:

Turning New Believers into Missional Disciples

New Christians are uniquely positioned for influence due to the high ratio of unchurched friends. As Jesus modeled in his post-resurrection appearances, the church must establish new believers in faith, and also empower them for mission! This 9-week course develops four disciplines (Bible devotional pattern, prayer, abiding, church involvement), and two directives (showing love and sharing Christ). Want to create a gospel movement? Just watch what God does when you strategically equip them from the get-go!

Also by Gary S. Comer

COMMUNITY GROUP MISSION GUIDE:

Moving Small Groups into Mission

This mission guide charts the course for groups to engage in community outreach activity. The 8-week adventure teaches Christians the skills of biblically based, relational evangelism (soul whispering style). Groups will invest time with non-believers, touch their community through acts of love, and walk alongside others right into the waters of baptism!

* Separate *Leaders Guides* provide clear instruction for teachers or facilitators to maximize course impact!

Wipf and Stock Publishers: Resource Publications

CPSIA information can be obtained
at www.ICGtesting.com
Printed in the USA
BVHW041323090322
630949BV00004B/9